I0118689

JAMES HILLMAN UNIFORM EDITION

7

Uniform Edition of the Writings of James Hillman
Volume 7: *Inhuman Relations*

Series Editor: Klaus Ottmann

Copyright © 2021 by Margot McLean
Introduction copyright © by Scott Becker
All rights reserved

Published by Spring Publications

www.springpublications.com

First edition (2.1)

Cover illustration:
James Lee Byars, *Untitled,* 1960. Black ink on Japanese paper.
Estate of James Lee Byars, courtesy Michael Werner Gallery,
New York, London, and Berlin

Library of Congress Control Number: 2021905235

ISBN: 978-0-88214-942-4

JAMES HILLMAN

INHUMAN RELATIONS

Edited and with an Introduction
by SCOTT BECKER

SPRING PUBLICATIONS
THOMPSON, CONN.

The Uniform Edition of the Writings of James Hillman
is published in conjunction with

Dallas Institute Publications, Joanne H. Stroud, Director

The Dallas Institute of Humanities and Culture
Dallas, Texas

as an integral part of its publications program concerned with
the imaginative, mythic, and symbolic sources of culture

⚬══╫══⚬

Additional support for this publication has been provided by

Elisabeth and Willem Peppler

The Fertel Foundation, New Orleans, Louisiana

Pacifica Graduate Institute, and
Joseph Campbell Archives and Library,
Carpinteria, California

Contents

ABBREVIATIONS

CW = *Collected Works of C.G. Jung,* edited and translated by Gerhard Adler and R. F. C. Hull, 20 vols. (Princeton, N.J.: Princeton University Press, 1953–79), cited by paragraph number

UE = *Uniform Edition of the Writings of James Hillman,* edited by Klaus Ottmann, 12 vols. (Putnam and Thompson, Conn.: Spring Publications, 2004–)

SE = *The Standard Edition of the Complete Psychological Works of Sigmund Freud,* edited by James Strachey, 24 vols. (London: The Hogarth Press and The Institute of Psycho-Analysis, 1953–1973)

CP = Sigmund Freud, *Collected Papers,* translated by Joan Riviere et. al., 5 vols. (London: The Hogarth Press and The Institute of Psycho-Analysis, 1924–50)

in memoriam

Joanne H. Stroud

(1927–2021)

Introduction

AEGIS—
IN DEFENSE OF ARCHETYPAL PSYCHOLOGY

Simmering Slowly: The Alchemy of *Inhuman Relations*

J ames Hillman first conceived of this collection of essays over a decade ago, and he identified each of the essays that he intended to be included in this volume of the *Uniform Edition*. When he contacted me in the fall of 2008 to ask if I would contribute to this volume, he mentioned that it contains what could be described as more "clinical" content, and he was aware of my background in clinical psychology. Hillman chose the title, *Inhuman Relations*, to emphasize the archetypal forces that shape our human interactions—the myths behind our messes, as he says in this volume ("How do we stay Psychological?"). Or as he sometimes quoted Auden, "We are lived by powers we pretend to understand." Hillman made it clear that he did not want the essays to be arranged chronologically, and he initially suggested a thematic structure that included sections such as "Jungiania," "Psychotherapy," "Mothers and Children," "Marriage," and others.

In order to augment this thematic format, we agreed on a novel approach: the material could be presented in terms of its rhetorical and psychological process, focusing on the ways in which Hillman's writing subtly functions as a form of alchemy, as the usual boundaries between writer, text, and reader are dissolved in a unifying imaginal space, engaging the reader not only through instruction and insight, but also facilitating psychological transformation. Returning to Hillman's chapter headings in *Re-Visioning Psychology*, we opted to arrange a number of the essays under the headings of "Personifying or Imagining Things," "Pathologizing or Falling Apart," "Psychologizing or Seeing Through," and "Dehumanizing or Soul-making," with essays in each section that illustrate these operations and allow the reader not only to appreciate the wide-ranging content of the essays, but also to become aware of their experiential influence.

As Hillman's health declined, he placed this volume on a back burner ("Our project must simmer, slowly..."), and we were unable to return to the final editing prior to his death in the fall of 2011. Over the next several years, volumes 4 and 8 in the *Uniform Edition* were published (*From Types to Images* and *Philosophical Intimations*) as well as Hillman's final book, *The Lament of the Dead*, with Sonu Shamdasani, and the first volume of Hillman's biography, *The Life and Ideas of James Hillman* by Dick Russell, to which Hillman had asked that I contribute the psychological commentary. Then, in the fall of 2019, Klaus Ottmann, the series editor for the *Uniform Edition*, contacted me and indicated that we were ready to move forward with this project, with the goal of publishing in 2020. At that point, no one could have predicted what 2020 would bring. While this project was slowly simmering, the world was quickly being brought to a boil.

During the past year, the world has become increasingly aware of the destructive impact of an interlocking oligarchic power structure. The economic, social, political, and ecological injustices inherent to this system have risen to the level of an acute crisis, including the rise of authoritarian governments, poverty and food and water insecurity, police violence, gender inequality and rape culture, racism and xenophobia, climate change and the threat of a sixth global extinction, and perhaps most dramatically, the Coronavirus outbreak. In short, life on this planet is profoundly threatened, and it is still unclear whether the global crisis constitutes a death or a rebirth, or perhaps both.

As a result of this overwhelming situation, this volume of the *Uniform Edition* is being published in an historical moment vastly different from the one in which it was written—and by extension from the time in which archetypal psychology itself was conceived and developed by Hillman and others. Given this radically different context, the consensus at Spring Publications is that this introduction, in addition to presenting the content of Hillman's essays, should attempt to respond to the seismic shift, the literal and figurative sea change that the world is undergoing, and to illustrate the utility of an archetypal approach to understanding and responding to a world in chaos. In doing so, we are acknowledging that we are all in a planet-sized crucible, and we are reaffirming the vital relevance of Hillman's perspective in tempering that fire and forging a new vision for our collective future.

This introduction therefore has a dual focus: This first section aims to draw out the alchemical method of Hillman's writing by focusing on the underlying unity of psychological and philosophical ideas (*eidos*), fantasy images, and soul (*psyche*), and by applying this unity to the imaginal experience of the reader. As we entertain Hillman's ideas, so we imagine, and as we imagine, so our psyche undergoes a structural transformation. (*Caveat lector,* reader beware, for you may become the subject matter of the essays, and therefore you may also be re-visioned along with the material.)

In the second section, we will apply this method to the current state of the world, addressing the global crisis in which we find ourselves by using Hillman's mythopoetic, alchemical approach, finding imaginal depth and archetypal coherence in the seemingly disparate symptoms of our time: misogyny, racism, oligarchy, and environmental destruction.

These goals are not considered to be two separate processes: the first subjective and internal, and the second objective and external. Rather, Hillman's nondualistic approach allows both domains to be part of a unified imaginal process, drawing on a Neoplatonic, alchemical, and astrological understanding that the distinction between inner and outer, subject and object, self and other, mind and world, is false and unnecessary. As the astrological maxim goes, "as above, so below; as within, so without." Our understanding of the world deepens as we enter its images, as the form of the world and the form of our minds begin to cohere. As Plotinus said, "No eye ever saw the sun without first becoming sun-like; nor can a soul see beauty without becoming beautiful." Hillman's work actively facilitates this process, by simultaneously revealing the image and using that image as the lens through which we see. Outer object and inner subject, or what we see and how we see, meet, and form a single, unified whole in the image. Understood this way, working on ourselves is working on the world, and vice versa, not because of a naive heroic fantasy, but because we are in the *metaxy,* the middle realm that underlies the mental and the material, the quantum entanglement of the soul.

Given that both our mental and material worlds are currently in tur-moil, our inner world panicked and the outer world a swirling chaos, find-ing the right image may prove difficult. As Margaret Atwood put it,

> When you're in the middle of a story it isn't a story at all, but only a confusion; a dark roaring, a blindness, a wreckage of shattered glass and splintered wood; like a house in a whirlwind, or else a boat crushed by the icebergs or swept over the rapids, and all aboard powerless to stop it. It's only afterwards that it becomes anything like a story at all. When you are telling it, to yourself or to someone else.[1]

Nevertheless, finding our collective story is the task of the second sec-tion of this introduction. This search may require some courage on our part—a willingness to lose our bearings and to face the terrifying ugliness of the world we have created. To paraphrase Paracelsus, no eye ever saw chaos without first becoming chaotic. But if we look behind and beneath the facts for a series of images, we may find a myth within the chaos. We may be able to find the eye of the storm, to see through that eye, and to discover its source.

Here we are also highlighting a relatively neglected aspect of Hillman's work: his intent to see through the problems of the world, not primar-ily to build an integrated theory, but to actively and critically respond to crucial issues that require a deeper understanding or re-visioning. Hillman was not orderly so much as opportunistic, responsive, timely, and goal-oriented:

> There is not a systematic metatheory behind my thought. I come from New Jersey where we have sea gulls who fly right down and get what they want from the oceanside. I am like them, dropping down into the depths of our culture and seizing what I need to understand things and make a point![2]

To expand on this idea, we can say that Hillman was not only trying to make a point, he was trying to be useful. Because of Hillman's frequently martial style and his plutonic deconstruction of his subject matter, some

---

1. Margaret Atwood, *Alias Grace* (New York: Anchor Books, 1997), 298.
2. Quoted in David J. Dalrymple, *Restoring Soul: The Contributions of James Hillman's Archetypal Psychology to the Study of Religion* (diss., Chicago Theological Seminary, 2007).

critics have understandably tended to overlook the fact that he was, by training and temperament, a psychotherapist, and that his therapeutic intent continued long after he left the world of psychoanalysis proper. His passion was in the service of compassion. That he accomplished this by holding up a mirror to our follies does not detract from his therapeutic intent. Quite the contrary, our disillusionment and discomfort were the required first steps to letting go of our destructive ideas, a necessary *nigredo* phase as we descended, fell apart, went bugs. We had to lose our minds to find them.[3]

And so, in the second section of this introduction we will be following Hillman's lead by attempting to offer something useful to the reader and to the world. We write as a concerned clinician, attempting to identify the world's symptoms, to reach an accurate diagnosis, and to formulate a treatment plan. In the process, we need to consider Antonio Gramsci's apocalyptic vision, written in 1930 from his prison cell in Mussolini's Italy: "The crisis consists precisely in the fact that the old is dying and the new cannot be born: in this interregnum, morbid phenomena of the most varied kind come to pass."[4] Notably, Gramsci is often mistranslated as: "The old world is dying and the new world struggles to be born. Now is the time of monsters." In the second section of this introduction, we may discover that our tendency to see monsters, to see our problems as enemies to be slain, is one of our "morbid symptoms."

Our approach will also follow Hillman's method and style by using images and language that are mimetic to our subject. This is another underappreciated aspect of his work, as he used his literary and rhetorical skill to evoke his subject matter in both form and content, style and substance. In his book *Inter Views*, Hillman offers this vivid description of his fantasies while writing several of his well-known essays:

---

3. In considering the impact of Hillman's personality on this aspect of his work, I recently contacted his son, Laurence Hillman, a well-known astrologer, about his father's birth chart. Laurence confirmed my sense that Hillman had the sign of Cancer on his ascendant, with Pluto in the 12th house. For those unfamiliar with the field of astrology, this placement reflects Hillman's emotional and intuitive traits, sometimes hidden behind his hard-shell persona. Pluto in the 12th also reveals what Laurence described "hidden power," and Hillman's profound insight into the underworld of imagination.

4. Antonio Gramsci, *Prison Notebooks*, vol. 3, ed. and trans. Joseph A. Buttigieg (New York: Columbia University Press, 1996), 32–33.

When I was trying to finish [Re-Visioning Psychology], I was drawing battle maps. I played the game of trying to fortify and seal whatever pages were still weak.[5]

Then later in the same section, he writes,

I remember writing "Abandoning the Child" in 1971 for an Eranos lecture. My image of it was a collection of very simple water colors. And I just wanted to do a little one here, one there, a little one on the "dead child," a little one on the "tree and child"... like you go through a gallery, and it didn't matter which picture came first.[6]

A third description follows:

When I worked on Dionysus and Hysteria [Myth of Analysis, part 3 (1969)], I remember saying I feel like I'm inside one of those great big sculptures, a Henry Moore, or one of those huge things of steel girders, and I'm doing all I can to weld huge chunks of steel together. It was like a great physical, exhausting, sculptural work. So those images of what I'm doing when I'm writing have nothing to do with what I'm writing, but they become necessary for my imagination to do it. It's like it prevents and it forms.[7]

In these accounts of Hillman's creative process, we notice a critical element of his work: the confluence of his subject matter, his writing process, and his rhetorical style.

Seeming to refute this confluence, Hillman claims that "those images of what I'm doing *when* I'm writing have nothing to do with *what* I'm writing,"[8] and yet it seems clear that there was a deep resonance between the process and the content. For example, in creating his seminal work, *Re-Visioning Psychology*, originally delivered as the Terry lectures at Yale, he was laying out a radical, new direction for the field of depth psychology, and in defending it from his prospective audience of skeptical academics, he imagined a battle front that needed shoring-up, an intellectual bulwark.

In a similar process, but with markedly different content, while carefully exploring the image of the archetypal child, he imagined a series of

5. James Hillman, *Inter Views: Conversations with Laura Pozzo on Psychotherapy, Biography, Love, Soul, Dreams, Work, Imagination, and the State of the Culture* (Woodstock, Conn.: Spring Publications, 1991), 158.

6. Ibid.

7. Ibid., 158–59.

8. Ibid., 159.

simple, light paintings that he also confessed felt like "an utter failure...
I felt the mode—the rhetorical style didn't work. It seemed too soft. Or
my thinking was weak."[9] And yet, how remarkably appropriate this style
was in expressing the vulnerability and insecurity of the child! And how
consistently mimetic in his rhetorical process. His thinking informed his
imagination, which informed his approach—and which allows the reader
to enter the same imaginal space, and to adopt the same ideational, psychic structures.

In the third example from *Inter Views*, as Hillman was attempting to
enter the dysregulated emotional field of Dionysus and hysteria, he imagined himself inside a huge, steel sculpture, as if he was building a solid
container around himself and the wild, primal energy that he was evoking. In each of these three cases, Hillman's method is to deeply enter the
archetypal/imaginal/mythic structure of his subject matter, and in effect
to become his subject matter, to let it speak through his writing. (This
method is even more explicitly evident in some later essays, for example,
in "Pink Madness" when he adopts the first-person voice of Aphrodite, or
in the essay in this volume, "Marriage, Intimacy, Freedom," in which he
begs to be free of Hera and the Olympians, choosing Freya instead.) This
alchemical process is found throughout Hillman's work, and it has direct
implications for our reading of Hillman.

Too often, the intellectual rigor and density of Hillman's work is cited
as the sole obstacle to the reader's initial understanding. Instead, we
might shift our focus from his conceptual complexity to the evocative
power of his imagery and the novelty of his vision. Perhaps our initial lack
of understanding is also a function of our psychological resistance, and a
symptom of our imaginal structures being challenged to transform.

To illustrate Hillman's method and its effect on the reader's imagination, we can touch on a few examples from this volume, each illustrating
one of the process-oriented themes from *Re-Visioning Psychology* mentioned
above. In using these examples, and more broadly in assigning each essay
to a thematic heading, we are in no way suggesting that each essay exclusively uses one of the four processes. Rather, we acknowledge that each
essay, in fact all of Hillman's work, uses all four approaches—personifying, psychologizing, pathologizing, and dehumanizing—but that each can

---

9. Ibid., 158.

be used to highlight a particular approach. Our goal is not to categorize Hillman's writing but to encourage a reflective style of reading, a more conscious, participatory understanding of his method.

First, in "Your Emotions Are Not Yours," Hillman engages in personifying by moving from a subjective, physiological model of emotion to a fully autochthonous, imaginal one. He does not accomplish this with abstract, theoretical language (a style that tends to emotionally distance the reader). He does begin with a concise summary of the mainstream models: "Certainly, [emotion] is inside the skin, deep inside the hippocampus, the normal system, the personal animal body." But in the very next sentence, Hillman offers one of his classic reversals:

> My contention, however, shall be, that though they be felt there, and we suffer emotions physically, this fact does not make them "mine." Rather, I believe emotions are there to make us theirs. They want to possess us, rule us, win us over completely to their vision.

This move is not merely rhetorical, conceptual or logical; it is a visceral, parabolic attack on our complacent, reductive attitude that confines emotions to subjective experience or a mere function of the body. The verb "possess" evokes a daimonic world that invades us; "rule" grants emotions royal authority over us; and "winning us over completely" implies being swept off of our feet, falling in love, and succumbing to "their vision," thereby seeing the world through the eyes of emotion. Hillman's method here is subtle but powerful, and it works on the reader's mind on several levels simultaneously, using conceptual logic to describe the autonomy of emotions, but also using the pronoun "They" as a subtle form of personification, making emotions the subject of the sentence, and the reader, "us," the object, linked by intensely active, infinitive verbs, "to possess," "to rule," and "to win over." Hillman's writing has already placed us, the reader, in a vulnerable, subservient, and rapturous position, even before we consider the objective validity of his assertion. This style is not merely a form of poetic license, it is a true *poiesis*, a "making," or a making over of the reader's perspective, an invitation to enter the very experience he is describing. Even as we read the words, we are read by them, as the language itself possesses us, rules us, wins us over completely.

Second, the contrast between what Hillman refers to as "pathologizing or falling apart," and "psychologizing or seeing through," is subtly illustrated in another text in this volume, "A Psychology of Transgression

Drawn from an Incest Dream." The content of the essay, a clinical study of an incest dream, would initially suggest that Hillman is engaging solely in pathologizing. (What could be more pathological than incest?) And yet, the process of the essay can also be characterized as psychologizing, seeing through the manifest content to its underlying archetypal structure. Hillman intentionally adopts a markedly clinical tone at the beginning of the essay, using the traditional analytical, or even psychoanalytical structure of identifying a patient, laying out the background and relevant biographical context of the case, and approaching the patient's dream as the core issue to be analyzed. Certainly, the patient's own attitude is presented as framing the dream as profoundly pathological: an assumed but unremembered incident of incest that was neither depicted in the dream itself nor available to the patient's memory, leading to a guilt-ridden, obsessive focus on the question of whether, when, or how an actual incident may have occurred. Taken literally, the pathological material is the incest itself, the "fact" of its occurrence, and this would seem to suggest that Hillman's narrative will follow a clinical course, exploring the source of the incident, identifying the defenses involved in its repression, and describing a course of treatment (and presumably of atonement or accountability). Instead, Hillman's approach is to take the dream's content metaphorically, and to see through its central image of "incest" to the actual pathology, which is the ruminative guilt and self-recrimination, the felt sense of transgression that "must have" occurred. Even more importantly, Hillman then uses this perspective to explore a metapsychology of "transgression" by critiquing the usual philosophical divide between fact and fantasy. He uses the tension in the case (i.e., did it happen, or did it not happen?) as a way of seeing through a faulty assumption embedded within our conventional theories that divide material reality from immaterial psyche, or the literal from the archetypal. Here is a sample passage in which this seeing-through, this metaphorical deconstruction, takes place:

> Suppose we make a different move. Suppose we maintain the dream's paradox just as it is, true to the manifest content, sticking to the image. There is no sexual incident, yet there is conviction that incest has occurred. If we hold to both sides of the dilemma, then there is an occurrence without a happening, an incest with no event. Something happened that did not happen. So, what did happen? Not incest as event, but incest as conviction, as belief.

The dreamer's certainty lies not in facts from the past but in faith from the dream. Incest did not happen in memory (no memory of it, he said, neither in dream nor in history), but it surely happened—in psyche. Memory and psyche have been rendered by the paradox into a contentiously troubling opposition. The dream seems to draw a dividing line between them; and the dreamer tries to resolve the tension by forcing one side to concur with the other: he supposes repression and forgetting in order to realign memory, and he imagines literal evidence from a literal daughter to support the tenets of his faith.

Hillman's "different move" is to take the interpretive dilemma (real or unreal?) as the true pathology of the "patient" and the clinician. Our need to keep the mythic world separate and interior leads to the inevitable encroachment of our fantasies on what we otherwise imagine to be our factual, material, objective lives. The dream therefore draws the patient, the clinician, the writer (Hillman), and the reader into the central tension of psychological existence, namely that "reality" is constantly being invaded by fantasy, and the waking, rational ego is nightly invited to "transgress" into the pathological, distorted, daimonic world of myth, fantasy, and dream. Hillman's essay subverts the reader's desire to "know the truth" about the incest by making "incest" the metaphorical, imaginal "truth."

A third example of Hillman's method, in this instance adopting a style of dehumanizing or soul-making, is found in "How Do We Stay Psychological?" In this essay, originally delivered as a public address to an audience of therapists in 1997, Hillman asks how the field of psychotherapy can remain psychological in the face of multiple challenges to its depth and complexity, embodied in the essay as the Four Horsemen of the Apocalypse: "In competitive economics, in genetic reductionism, in white transcendent spiritualism, and in the practical adaptations that wear the pallor of niceness." A better example of Hillman's capacity for personifying could not be found, but this is not ultimately the goal of the essay, which is to dehumanize psychotherapy by moving deeper than the mainstream attitude of humanistic values. Hillman expands the idea of "deep" beyond the usual, romanticist realm of human emotions and into the depths of "thought, insights, ideals, visions, memories, and acts of courage and generosity." He then offers his (dehumanized) definition of depth, and provides the source for the title of this volume:

Depth evokes and makes present those inevitable eternalities that nourish and destroy every one of our lives. They bring the inhuman dimension to human lives. These are the eternalities that compose the substance of Greek tragedies, of Bible stories, of myths and classic unvarnished fairy tales. Deep refers to the archetypal necessities and inhuman persons that form the imagination of great art and music and writings.

In this passage, Hillman is addressing a room full of therapists who have been, for the most part, trained to think in terms of personal feeling, identity, and relationships, of humanistic values such as empathy, compassion, and kindness. Without overtly dismissing these ideals, Hillman broadens and deepens them, moving his audience into an otherwise invisible realm of gods and monsters, of ancestors and mythic creatures, and of tragedy that lies beyond the best intentions of the helping professions. He concludes the essay with this appeal to civic duty, to a sense of calling and destiny, and to awareness of the tragic dimension of life essential to soul-making:

That "civil calling" is the world as civilization into which we must throw ourselves fully aware of the horsemen. "Immerse yourself in the destructive element," said Joseph Conrad. "We can only begin to live when we can conceive life as Tragedy," said Yeats. "Call the world the vale of soul-making," said John Keats. And Unamuno adds, "…become your uniqueness by acting in such as way as to make our annihilation, our death an injustice—to make others feel that we ought not to have died." This is destiny lived; this is being your image and standing in depth. Of course you are not thereby saved, or creative, integrated, or wise, nor even good. But at least you are you.

With these reminders of Hillman's dynamic intent, alchemical method, mimetic style, and therapeutic goals, we introduce this collection of his essays as living reminders of how he worked: he did not attempt to spiritually soar over the psychological landscape, or to "explain" and level it by making empirical or abstract observations. Rather, he descended, embraced the pink madness, dissolved the ego, entered the fray, and joined the maenads in their dance rather than spying on them, helping us to "under-stand" by standing below, in the underworld of imagination. He was always closer to Pan and Dionysus than Pentheus or Apollo. There was indeed madness in his method.

Said differently, the ideas and metaphors in Hillman's work are not conceptual or Platonic forms; they are not disembodied archetypes *per se* but living images that draw the reader closer, farther in, deeper into an experiential and imaginal space, while at the same time offering perspective, insight, resonance, and clarity. In this way, his work was truly poetic and visceral, not only awakening the reader's mind but touching the heart, moving the soul, and kindling the spirit.

It is in this alchemical manner that we will, in section two of this introduction, face the problems of our twenty-first-century, apocalyptic world, not only seeing its monsters, but seeing through them. We may even learn to see ourselves through their eyes.

Facing Chaos: An Archetypal Response to 2020

At the time of this writing, much of the world is reacting to multiple, escalating crises and acute threats that reflect a global system on the brink of collapse. The list is daunting and seemingly random, but as we will argue below, with an underlying coherence and a common source. Beginning with political and social issues, we are witnessing in the United States the deliberate mishandling of the Corona pandemic as a political weapon, resulting in thousands of needless deaths. We are also facing the related threat of economic collapse as millions of people are being forced into poverty due to the lack of governmental support. For the past several years, we have been lifting the veil on Western culture's entrenched misogyny and homophobia, with an increased awareness of the pervasive issues of sexual harassment, discrimination, and violence against sexual and gender minorities, the ongoing attempt to control women's reproductive sovereignty, and the endemic nature of rape culture. In the United States, these injustices are being challenged by the #MeToo movement and the resurgence of feminist and LGBTQ activism. All these trends are occurring against the backdrop of increasing domestic and international terrorism, as well as the relentless presence of war and the threat of nuclear weapons. We are confronted by the malignant growth of White Supremacy movements and the growing awareness of institutionalized racism, forcefully exposed by the disparity in the mortality rates among people of color during the pandemic as well as the pervasive issue of police violence against citizens of color, and the recent evidence that White supremacy groups have been infiltrating police departments across the US, as well as the brutality of ICE detention camps that have been deliberately separating immigrant children from their families and forc-ibly sterilizing women in custody. These racist and xenophobic practices have resulted in a wave of largely peaceful protests and violent coun-ter-protests, including the recent plot to kidnap a state Governor. Last but not least, recent research, news reports, and documentaries have confirmed that digital technology and social media have been disrupt-ing social relationships, eroding cognitive functioning, increasing the prevalence of cancers and other health issues, disseminating propaganda and using algorithms aimed at creating political polarization. Whistle-blowers and investigators have also exposed the presence of a pervasive surveillance culture in which citizens are being monitored and manipu-lated by corporations and their governments.

Behind this overwhelming list of "morbid symptoms" is the overarch-ing scourge of globalization and the exposure of what has been variously called neoliberalism, oligarchy, plutocracy, or perhaps the most common political term in the U.S.: patriarchy—rulership by a very small group of wealthy, mostly White men, impacting all aspects of world culture, including politics, economics, education, religion, social structures, gen-der norms, race relations, sexuality and reproductive rights, and our rela-tionship to the environment. In short, all the social and political issues we are currently facing have come to a head, and they seem to have a common source in the hidden rulers of the world.

At the same time, the planet itself seems to be attacking us, unleashing famine, drought, continent-wide fires, extinction of plants and wildlife, the steady destruction of the Amazon rainforest, the accelerating melt-ing of the polar ice caps, the resulting release of viruses and bacteria, the plight of climate refugees, rising CO_2 levels, and the steady increase in the intensity and frequency of storms and flooding, culminating in mod-els that predict a sixth planetary extinction. The COVID-19 pandemic itself appears to be a plague unleashed by the planet, evidently resulting from the encroachment of urban centers on surrounding habitats, eras-ing the ecosystem that formerly acted as a buffer that prevented count-less viruses from making the jump from animals to humans. We are, in effect, confronted by a world, a Great Goddess, whose wrath against our patriarchal system we may not survive. We are caught in the middle of an inhuman battle. Or as the African proverb says, "When elephants fight, it is the grass that suffers."

Trapped between our monstrous leaders and equally monstrous natural threats, our collective anxiety is escalating into what might accurately be called a global panic, manifesting in multiple forms, including anger, fear, and dissociative numbing or apathy. Our goal in this essay is to reveal the ways in which Hillman's work can respond theoretically and therapeutically to this panic, by offering a form of imaginal reflection and mindfulness that allows the reader to more deeply and accurately imagine the threats that we face, and ultimately to face them differently.[10]

Before we attempt to place our symptoms in an appropriate mythic context, we will begin by examining them through a strictly contemporary, clinical lens. If we consider our collective response to the current state of the world as a form of traumatic stress, we can say that people around the globe are in varying degrees of the fight-flight-or-freeze response: the alarm function of our limbic system is being "kindled," and our frontal cortex is being overridden. Put more broadly, our animal survival instincts—fueled by conflicting information and overt propaganda[11]—have begun to overshadow our reason. Here, in the United States, our national response to the outbreak has been anything but united, as we continue to witness the chaotic results of this fear-mongering process. Instead of a calm, coordinated response, we witness the "fight" reaction in the form armed protestors, rioting, and a social-media

---

10. In using the metaphor of "facing," we follow David L. Miller's language in his essay on imagining and confronting nuclear apocalypse: "But facing also means 'putting a face on something,' giving it form and figure, image and shape, so that we know what it is we are 'facing,' what we are up against: naming it, imagining it, like Adam with the animals. This two-fold meaning seems to say that unless you imagine something, giving it a face, you cannot participate in it realistically, and therefore will not be facing it. It seems to imply that, in order to be literal, one has also to be poetic. And at the same time." David L. Miller, "Chiliasm: Apocalyptic with a Thousand Faces," in *Facing Apocalypse*, ed. Valerie Andrews, Robert Bosnak, and Karen Walter Goodwin (Thompson, Conn.: Spring Publications, 2021), 5–26.

11. The BBC documentary, *The Century of the Self,* provides an excellent overview of the history of modern propaganda based on Freud's theories, first developed by Freud's nephew, Edward Bernays, a talent agent who was contacted by President Wilson to generate a slogan that would convince an isolationist American population to endorse entering W W I. Bernays's slogan, designed to tap into the Id's primitive fears: "Make the world safe for democracy." For the past one hundred years, propaganda has become a science and a pervasive but largely invisible element of Western, globalized culture.

frenzy; the "flight" reaction in the form of frantic denial and manic refusal of the quarantine, and the "freeze" reaction of dissociative fear, as many citizens experience a sense of paralyzing dread, or what Robert Lifton called "psychic numbing," and Hillman has described as "anesthesia." This internal paralysis mirrors what is happening externally, as governments lock down, citizens slow down or shut down, and the economy threatens to break down. Our individual and collective paralysis masks an underlying agitation, an increasing pressure that threatens to explode. At its extremes, fight-flight-or-freeze can become quite primitive, separating the reasonable mind from the enraged, terrified, or numbed body, thereby evoking primal, violent clichés as our panic causes us to "lose our heads," our social media posts hiss with venomous rage, and in our petrified state of dissociation we begin to resemble deer caught in the headlights.

Hidden in these clichés of fight-flight-or-freeze and in the literalisms of neurophysiology are images—metaphorical threads that can be woven into a narrative and, ultimately, into a myth that speaks to our troubled times. The myth we have in mind manages to bridge the long arc of Hillman's work with our current crisis, and it allows us to simultaneously accomplish three tasks: first, to reaffirm the value and continuing relevance of archetypal psychology in a chaotic world; second, to use Hillman's work as a way to fully imagine and respond to the current chaos; and third, to locate the origins of this crisis in the mythic past and a forgotten chapter of human history. In doing so, we are consciously defending Hillman's work from any latent criticism (for example, that it is outdated or of little use in our current crisis), and we are also using his work as a defense: our shield as we attempt to face a world and a set of world leaders that seem to be trying to destroy us.

In framing this introduction as a defensive maneuver, we are ironically enlisting one of the great foes of Hillman and his archetypal approach: the hero and his foolish fantasy of slaying monsters and saving the world. In naming our heroic fantasy of Hillman, we are evoking a specific mythic figure and immediately subverting it, laying down our weapons even as we take them up, refusing the salvific mission and realizing that the giant may be a windmill, the monster a goddess. We may also realize that it was our heroic vision that created the monster in the first place.

Those familiar with Greek mythology will have already recognized the images and the story in which we find ourselves: Perseus beheading Medusa with the aid of Athena, with its images of venemous anger, petrifying fear, a reflecting shield, and a crescent-blade sword. The image of beheading is, of course, the most violent and literal depiction of dissociation, severing mind from body. Significantly, this myth has taken many forms over the centuries, suggesting that the way we approach Medusa may constellate the form that she takes.

An early version of the tale from Hesiod's *Theogony* depicts Medusa as one of three monstrous sisters—the Gorgons. Hesiod views them as primordial monsters, the daughters of Phorcys and Ceto: sea gods who also produced the sea monster Scylla and the snake-tailed Echidna, known as the Mother of all Monsters. As such, the Gorgons, the "terrifying ones," are envisioned as emerging from the fearsome depths of the sea, the primordial source of terror that turned sailors into the rock formations that later caused shipwrecks. (Fear begets fear.)

Hesiod, therefore, imagines Medusa as fear itself—and specifically as the terror that petrifies. There are many valid ways to imagine our current global crisis, but Medusa certainly embodies our intense fear reaction. She is the deadly threat that petrifies; we are unable to face her multi-headed tangle of venomous snakes. Her image accounts for our paralysis in the face of the reptilian gaze of psychopathic leaders, the propaganda that activates our deepest fears, the virus that steals our breath away, and the monstrous hurricanes and typhoons created by global warming. We are overwhelmed, unable to act, turned to stone.

Viewed in this way, Medusa becomes a symbol of our fear of Nature itself, its unknown depths, its volatility, and its toxicity—Mother Nature in her most destructive form: Kali with her necklace of skulls.

In order to confront this horrifying creature, Perseus obtains a number of weapons that amplify his heroic power: Athena's shield, Hades's helm of invisibility, Hermes's winged sandals, and Hephaestus's oddly curved sword, as if Medusa's head is to be harvested by a sickle. The heroic ego requires warlike weapons, which the Olympians gladly provide. Most importantly, Perseus cannot face the monster directly, and he must instead gaze at Medusa's reflection in the polished brass of the shield. Athena provides the wise protection of the reflected gaze, the gift of warlike imagination. And as we know, Medusa, whose name means "guardian" and "protection," becomes the face of Athena's shield, which is renamed the Aegis and carried by the war goddess into battle to terrify her enemies.

And so, in Hesiod's tale, the disciplined hero conquers the wild, animalistic monster and reclaims it in the service of the city, of logos, and of civilization. The monster is both defeated and subsumed, the primordial threat absorbed and sublimated as a defender of civic order. If we accept this version of Medusa's myth as the backdrop to our current problems, what better protection could we ask than Hillman's martial energy (son of Ares that he was), allowing us to use the power of imaginative reflection to face our fear, cut off its head, and use it in the service of life, law, and order? And yet, this aggressive solution is not the only way to approach the Gorgon. Perhaps we need to engage in further reflection, to imagine her differently.

If our globalized problems have emerged from our attempts to dominate Nature, to control her and steal her resources, and to build our city walls to keep her out, then attacking her may not be the wisest approach. Further, if the viral threat we now face is re-imagined as Gaia's immune system, her reminder that we cannot live separately, that we cannot shut her out, and that we need to live in some form of harmony that honors her power, then our best approach may be to recognize that her anger may result from an earlier injury.

In looking for a different version of the myth, we do not need to engage in postmodern deconstruction. We need only turn to Ovid's retelling of the story in his *Metamorphoses,* in which he offers a more complex origin story of Medusa, portrayed not as a monster but as a beautiful woman with golden hair, a priestess in Athena's temple. In this version, Medusa becomes the object of Poseidon's lust, and he "ravishes" (rapes) her in Athena's temple, inviting Athena's wrath, which she inflicts not on Poseidon but on her mortal priestess: "...for fitting punishment [Athena] transformed / The Gorgon's lovely hair to loathsome snakes."[12]

It must be noted that modern feminist interpretations of this version of the myth reject the idea that Athena's cursing of Medusa was fair and just, and these authors generally portray Medusa as the survivor of Poseidon's sexual aggression as well as Athena's misdirected outrage, pointing out

---

12. Ovid, *Metamorphoses* 4.800–801 (trans. A.D. Melville).

that both the assault and the curse are inherently misogynistic and victim-blaming. In these interpretations, Medusa's innocence and humanity are emphasized, and her monstrous, terrifying transformation is seen solely as the result of Poseidon's (patriarchal) transgression. In viewing our current ecological and health crises against the backdrop of this myth, a feminist perspective begins to make room for understanding that the terror caused by global warming and the Coronavirus may be the result of a patriarchal injury: the symbolic rape of the planet and its vengeful response.

However, to fully understand the implications of Poseidon's rape of Medusa, we must go further and question the veracity of the Greek and Roman versions of the myth, traveling back in time to discover an older and therefore more authentic image of Medusa. In this move, we are extending Hillman's suggestion in *Re-Visioning Psychology* that we travel "south," leading psychology out of northern Europe and returning to southern Europe, but going even farther south in order to discover Medusa in her original context, and thereby in her true, sovereign, powerful, and divine form.

In this older, deeper search for Medusa, we find that the Hellenistic and Roman versions of the myth are a form of revisionist history, specifically an effort to justify, or forget, the archaic encounter between the patriarchal Hellenes and the matriarchal cultures of northern Africa. Annis Pratt, in her illuminating study of the early origins of Medusa, references Joseph Campbell's account:

> Perseus was an Olympian by birth, and, like so many Greek heroes, was born of rape [that of Danae by Zeus]. Such rapes, Joseph Campbell tells us, were narrative accounts of the takeover of pre-olympian goddess figures by the conquering Hellenes: "The particular problem faced by Zeus in that period was simply that wherever the Greeks came, in every valley, every isle, and every cove, there was a local manifestation of the goddess-mother of the world whom he, as the great god of the patriarchal order, had to master in a patriarchal way...everyone has heard of his mad turning of himself into bulls, serpents, swans, and showers of gold. Every Mediterranean nymph he saw set him crazy.[13]

13. Quoted in Annis Pratt, "Aunt Jennifer's Tigers: Notes toward a Preliterary History of Women's Archetypes," *Feminist Studies* 4, no. 1 (1978): 163–94.

Pratt alludes to but does not directly comment on the thinly veiled misogyny of Campbell's comments, and the whitewashing of the actual rapes that presumably occurred during the subjugation of the matriarchy. She also refers to Jane Ellen Harrison's earlier work on "rites of riddance," which were Hellenistic stories intended to "repress prepatriarchal figures that had dominated the minds of the inhabitants." Pratt goes on to elaborate this idea:

> Myths in which heroes conquer dragons and gorgons and snakes and other monstrous figures are essentially stories of "riddance" in which the beautiful and powerful women of the pre-Hellenic religions are made to seem horrific and then raped, decapitated, or destroyed. In some strange manner, however, a memory of the beauty of the goddesses remained encapsulated in the captured spirit, particularly of women.

Pratt's work makes it clear that Medusa's story is one of many in this tradition, and that these myths form the basis of a historical trauma and collective amnesia regarding our Western cultural origins. This amnesia forms the mythic foundation for the patriarchal, dualistic world view with which we are currently struggling, including the hierarchy of masculine over feminine, reason over emotion, mind over body, and humanity pitted against the natural world—a world imagined from Hellenistic times onward as wild, base, and primitive. (The attribution of this split to Greek or Enlightenment sources—for example, Aristotle and Descartes—tends to overlook its origins in the ancient suppression of the goddess.)

Archeological and mythographic evidence has further identified a world-wide, archaic motif in myth and iconography that reflects the ubiquity of this historic split and the ensuing battle between the (masculine) culture hero and the (feminine) animal/monster. In German, the term for this motif is *Chaoskampf,* the battle against chaos, and its most common, almost universal, symbol is that of an eagle defeating a serpent of dragon, an image found in Mesopotamia, the Mediterranean, Asia, Europe, and the Americas, and found in the Eagle symbolism of warring nations for thousands of years, including the Roman empire, the Nazi movement, and the United States.

Returning to Medusa's origins, other mythographers have found that she was one aspect of a great goddess, or the Great Goddess, variously named Neith, Anatha, Metis, and Medusa, depending on the region in

North Africa or the Mediterranean. (Notably, Anatha, following the Hellenic invasion, was co-opted in the Olympian myths and renamed Athena.) Neith was a powerful goddess who, like Kali in India, embodied both sides of the opposites and was known as "the goddess of the beginning and the end, of life and death."[14] She was associated with the west, the setting sun, and the realms of the dead, but she was also depicted as offering water in her hands, and she was associated with the astrological sign of Aquarius, the Water Bringer. Neith/Medusa was often depicted as having scales, either reptilian or those of a fish, and these scales were very consistently depicted in the "meander" pattern of parallel lines that are the traditional symbol for Aquarius, so that astrologically, we are currently entering the Age of Medusa.

Demetra George, an astrologer known for her work on the mythic sources behind asteroid goddesses, informs us that Neith was known to have risen from a primordial flood, and that her name means "I have come from myself." An inscription on one of her temples reads, "I am all that has been, that will be, and no mortal has yet been able to lift the veil that covers me." These assertions of Neith's originating power and nonduality seem clearly present in the self-description of Elohim in the Hebrew tradition, "Ehyeh Asher Ehyeh" (I am who am I am), as well as "The Thunder: Perfect Mind" from the Nag Hammadi scrolls:

> I am the first and the last
> I am she who is honored and she who is mocked
> I am the whore and the holy woman
> I am the wife and the virgin.
> I am the mother and the daughter ...[15]

What we find in these ancient texts is an emerging form of the pre-Olympian image of Neith (Medusa) as a Water and Earth goddess, prior to her subjugation by the Hellenes and their sky gods. We also can hear an echo of this subjugation in the Nag Hammadi:

> I am she whom they call life,
> and you all called death.

---

14. Willem H. Zitman, *Egypt: "Image of Heaven"–The Planisphere and the Lost Cradle* (Amsterdam: Frontier Publishing, 2006), 194.

15. *The Thunder: Perfect Mind,* translated by Hal Taussig, Jared Calaway, Maia Kotrosits, Celene Lillie, Justin Lasser (New York: Palgrave Macmillan, 2010), 1.

I am she whom they call law,
and you all called lawlessness.[16]

To further elaborate this watery, life-giving image of Neith, we find
that in Libya she was known to have arisen from Lake Tritonis, the Lake
of the Triple Queens. George offers this vivid summary:

> She displayed her triple nature as Athena [Anatha], Metis and
> Medusa, who corresponded to the new, full, and dark phases
> of the moon. Athena was the new moon warrior maiden who
> inspired the Amazon tribes of women to courage, strength, and
> valor. The Sea Goddess Metis, whose name means "wise coun-
> sel," was the full moon mother aspect of this trinity who, in later
> [Olympian] mythical tales, conceived Athena from Zeus. Medusa
> embodied the third, dark aspect as destroyer/crone, and she was
> revered as the Queen of the Libyan Amazons, the Serpent God-
> dess of female wisdom.[17]

In her dark aspect, Medusa was often considered the ferocious face
of Neith that guarded their temples, with masks of her terrifying image
intended to warn away evil (hence Medusa, "protector").

As George points out, the Triple Goddess was further subsumed in
the Olympian myths that presented Metis not as the Mother aspect of
the goddess but as the mother of Athena and the "wife" of Zeus. However, Zeus, threatened by Metis's pregnancy, swallowed Metis and their
unborn child, and Athena then erupted from his head. This is yet another
"rite of riddance," as Anatha is coopted as Athena, Medusa is turned from
a crone into a monster, then raped and beheaded, and Metis is literally
swallowed by the patriarchy. The goddess is defeated through a strategy
of divide-and-conquer, and the Olympian account becomes the corner-
stone of our traumatic amnesia, the mythic cover story and the ultimate
victim-blaming.

What we forget in the process includes a much more nuanced and
powerful figure, as described by C. Osborne: Medusa was the four-
winged goddess of bees in her underworld aspect, as beeswax and honey
were used in embalming; the "Mountain Mother"; the goddess of contra-
ception and menstruation (since blood was imagined as turning men to

---

16. Ibid., 3.

17. Demetra George, "The Serpent-Haired Queen Medusa (Sovereign Female
Wisdom)" (online at *https://www.tapatalk.com/groups/solitarywitch/medusa-t1306.html*).

stone); the goddess of graveyards, hence the places where the dead were turned to stone; and the sun (as she rode a golden chariot across the sky long before Apollo). We also learn of other aspects of Medusa in this remarkable passage from Osborne:

> Medusa travelled across the sky, watching over children and guiding schools of fish, symbolic of unborn souls. At night she sailed in a stone boat across the ocean, from where it covered the upper Earth to the Underworld. There Medusa heated thermal springs and imbued them with healing power, according to Goodrich her keen gaze went on twinkling in the sky as the star now known to be an eclipsing binary and called by the Arabic name Algol "serpent's eye." Only the very fortunate saw Medusa's sacred island, home of mermaids, enclosed in willows, representing her genital centre.[18]

We also learn from Osborne that, "Medusa's priestesses...wore their hair long, in dreadlocks or just matted into rough strings. It was imperative never to cut or interfere with the growth of this hair, because it symbolized their shamanic power, which the priestesses demonstrated by walking across burning coals in bare feet without injury." This passage brings forward a theme the reader may have already recognized: the implicit element of racism in the Hellenes' invasion of North Africa, their domination of the Great Goddess and the murder of her priestesses, with their dark skin and dreadlocks that symbolized the snakes on their goddess's head, as well as their ferocity and their willingness to walk through fire for her. In fact, the tribes of North Africa were variously called the Amazons and the Gorgons, which in modern Greek means mermaid: γοργόνα (gorgóna). Their grey-haired warriors later became the basis for the Olympian myths of the Graiai, the sisters of the Gorgons who reluctantly helped Perseus to find Medusa after he stole the one eye they shared as a group. What in contemporary terms would be called the intersectionality of racism, ageism, and misogyny, or the war on elderly women of color, we find embedded in the myth of three gray-haired, one-eyed, one-toothed crones who are forced to betray their sisters.

As we move closer to seeing Medusa in her true form, she regains her chthonic, underworld power, and her fearful aspects are still on full

---

18. Carla Osborne, "The Amazon Nation: A Sourcebook" (online at *https://www. moonspeaker.ca/Amazons/PartOne/chaptertwo.html*).

display, but we also come to recognize that she is not monstrous or cursed, but rather represents the primordial nonduality of life, death, and rebirth, the poison that can kill or heal, the face that can petrify or protect the souls of unborn children, suggesting she may also lie behind some of the functions of Artemis, who presided over the life-and-death aspects of pregnancy and childbirth. [19]

So, with all of this in mind, beginning to see the outlines of Medusa's original, authentic, sovereign face, we pause to remind ourselves that we are seeing this image in Perseus's shield, that protective reflection that we have ascribed to Hillman and his archetypal method, the hermeneutic circle and the alchemical mirror that allows us to face our fears and approach the terrifying creature we sought to kill. But what we see in our polished shield is not the face of a monster, nor a traumatized maiden, but a goddess of the threshold between life and death, a generative, destructive power who can only be approached with humility and reverence. What, then, do we do with our shield, received from Athena, who supported our quest to murder the Gorgon, whom we now recognize is actually the navel of the world, the Queen Bee, the Dark Side of the Moon who watches over our beginnings and endings? What is this shield? From what does it shield us? Medusa's ugliness? Her beauty? Knowledge of our own heroic, ignorant violence?

One final detail from the North African stories of Medusa, a final reflection: as we pass the fearsome, snake-haired masks that guard the doors to her temple, as we enter her sacred space, we glance at the wall and see our own reflection in a round, burning mirror, and we realize that our shield—like the images, signs, and symbols of Medusa herself—was also stolen. Her mirror has become the warlike symbol of the patriarchal system that destroyed her, the very weapon used to find and murder her. As Osborne puts it, "Even the sacred burning mirrors of the Goddess were turned against her, recast as Perseus's shield."[20] We see ourselves in her mirror, and we realize that in a mythic sense, like Perseus, we are all children of rape, and like Athena, children of matricide,

---

19. Cf. Ginette Paris, *The Psychology of Abortion* (Putnam, Conn.: Spring Publications, 2007).

20. Osborne, "The Amazon Nation: A Sourcebook," loc. cit.

our culture the result of Zeus devouring Metis and claiming Athena as his daughter and shield maiden, rendering the city that she protects, and every Western city, a forgotten mausoleum to the Great Goddess. Perhaps when George Floyd cried out for his mother, he was calling for all mothers, or for our Great Mother.[21]

Before we place our shield—her mirror—back on the temple wall, we might use it in a different manner, with a different intent. In it we see the reflected images of our troubled times: the burning forests, the rising oceans and monstrous hurricanes, the dying bees, the women fighting for their civil and reproductive rights in pussycat hats, Black Lives Matter activists and their allies around the globe protesting systemic racism and the grim history of police violence, and the virus that forced a manic, globalized planet to its knees. If we look with a mythic eye, we can see Medusa's face behind each event, and in her reflected gaze an indictment and a call. As Rilke said, "... For there's no place from which you can't be seen / Begin now: You must change the life you are."[22]

As it dawns on us that our destruction of the natural world, our racial prejudice, our fear and hatred of women, and our relentless, manic greed are the result of thousands of years of patriarchal exploitation and destruction, we recognize that our "morbid symptoms" are of our own making, that in a sense the planet is ill and we are the virus, suggesting that the Coronavirus and global warming may be Gaia's immune system—her feverish attempt to rid herself of our invasive infection.

Here we must make an important distinction between our cautious approach to Medusa and the popularized version of Gaia as Mother Earth or Mother Nature. In the environmental literature, particularly in the field of ecopsychology, there has been a fairly sanguine attitude about the mythic consequences of our offense to Gaia and our destruction of the planet. In this narrative, we have injured our Mother, and to repair the relationship we need to become more mindful, considerate, and loving in order to reverse the effects of climate change and restore ecological (and mythic) balance. The implicit assumption here is that Gaia is an endlessly

---

21. Rachel Steinman, "George Floyd Summoned All Mothers When He Called for His Mama" (online at https://psiloveyou.xyz/george-floyd-summoned-all-mothers-when-he-called-for-his-mama-f916c0393151).

22. "Archaic Torso of Apollo," in Rainer Maria Rilke, New Poems, translated by Len Krisak (Rochester, N.Y.: Camden House, 2015), 173.

compassionate and forgiving mother who has been patiently waiting for us to see the error in our ways—humanity is imagined as a willful child or unruly adolescent. As a result, we assume that Gaia will instantly welcome us home as the prodigal son. Infinite grace.

This fantasy is well-articulated by Richard Tarnas in his exceptional book, *The Passion of the Western Mind*, which offers the image of a profound reconciliation between patriarchal Western culture and the sacred feminine, a *hieros gamos*. Tarnas acknowledges that this marriage must be preceded by "a sacrifice, an ego death":

> The Western mind must be willing to open itself to a reality the nature of which could shatter its most established beliefs about itself and about the world. *This* is where the real act of heroism is going to be.[23]

This divine marriage would be the culmination of the long arc of Western history, which Tarnas imagines as a heroic journey, a necessary developmental separation from Nature and the divine womb that permits self-awareness and the clarity and precision of abstract thought, an escape from the (presumably primitive, undifferentiated, and unconscious) mode of the *participation mystique*. The result is that the Western mind is now able to know itself fully and to return to its feminine source in a conscious union that would create a divine "child" that unites masculine and feminine energy:

> We seem to be witnessing, suffering, the birth labor of a new reality, a new form of human existence, a "child" that would be the fruit of this great archetypal marriage, and that would bear within itself all its antecedents in a new form.[24]

As inspiring and optimistic as this metanarrative clearly is, it does not directly account for an ancient, cross-cultural myth, in both Greek and earlier traditions, of Gaia, or the Great Mother, becoming enraged, even annihilatory, in response to missteps or offenses by humanity or by other gods. With this divine wrath in mind, we need to consider the possibility that the Great Mother may not be as forgiving as we would like to believe her to be, and that we may need to face her rage, here imagined as the

---

23. Richard Tarnas, *The Passion of the Western Mind: Understanding the Ideas That Have Shaped Our World View* (New York: Random House, 1991), 444.

24. Ibid.

face of Medusa, even as we attempt to correct several millennia of patriarchal offenses to our sacred Mother.

And so, as we enter Medusa's temple, as we lay down our weapons in
contrition and remorse, we realize why humanity has been brought to
our knees (by this viral outbreak, by activism, by climate change, and by
the planet herself), and we remain there, kneeling before her, asking for
forgiveness, submitting to her ferociously beautiful, terrifying gaze with
fear and trembling. As we await Medusa's judgment, we realize that we
may be facing our own death for the crimes against her over thousands
of years. True submission must include the possibility that our contrition
is too late, that in a literal sense we have damaged the planet beyond its
capacity to rebalance itself without a sixth extinction-level event, caused
by our own hubris, destruction, and theft, our offenses against her. But if
it is not too late, we might find that she removes her burning mirror from
the wall and returns it, asking us to bear the Aegis in her name, protecting
her sovereignty as her servants, her mirror our shield.

Medusan Psychology

In the confines of this essay we cannot draw out all of the implications
of this re-visioned myth, but we can begin to see the mythical coherence
that lies beneath the chaos of our current political, economic, social, and
ecological crisis. A deepened understanding of Medusa in her original
form, along with a mythologized account of the Hellenes' invasion of
her culture, allows us to draw together the major problems of our times:
misogyny, racism, xenophobia, White supremacy, globalization, and climate change. We can also begin to consider the ways in which an archetypal psychology informed by Medusa allows us to navigate our global
crisis and to imagine a form of global re-vision, a rediscovery and reconciliation with a "matriarchal" world view that may help us to mend our
relationship with the natural world and to repair the various philosophical, psychological, and political "splits" that have resulted from patriarchy,
capitalism, and globalization.

Here we are not using the term "matriarchy" in a literal, historical
sense. We are not offering nostalgia for a pseudo-historical political system run exclusively by women, nor are we envisioning such a system as
a romanticized, utopian future. Instead, we are suggesting that Western
culture has been fundamentally shaped by Olympian mythology (and

Judeo-Christian monotheism), resulting in a hierarchical system of power and control that reifies and enacts a wide range of dualisms, such that "masculinity" and "femininity" serve as the overarching metaphors for the split between spirit and matter, mind and body, reason and emotion, humanity and nature, self and other, White and Black, and perhaps most pointedly, life and death. Our goal in evoking Medusa, Neith, and the ancient, African culture they represent, is to provide a mythological fantasy of return, an imaginal form of remembering framed in an elaborate historical, geographic, and gendered metaphor.

Medusa and Neith—as aspects of a nondualistic goddess who embodies and holds the tension between the "opposites"—allow us to experience a primordial unity between subjective consciousness and the "objects" of its perceptions, thereby deepening our empathy and identification with the Other and our unity with the Source, echoing the Hindu idea of Tat Tvam Asi, thou art that. White, straight, cisgender-masculine, Cartesian (or better, Olympian) consciousness is both narcissistic and paranoid, perceiving a world of lesser beings, in women, children, Blacks, gays, foreigners, and the natural world (reduced to stock-at-hand resources). These objects must serve masculine consciousness, else they constitute a threat that must be dominated or destroyed. This extreme, dualistic form of masculinity is indeed "toxic," in that its megalomania and paranoia can never be satisfied or annulled, resulting in a world view that is at its heart homicidal (and by extension ecocidal and omnicidal). Any form of consciousness that cannot imagine past its own death, that refuses to die and that seeks control and immortality, attempts to become Death itself. The goddess, however, cannot be killed, and will eventually reclaim death as her domain. Masculine consciousness cannot commit matricide, which ultimately renders its destructive impulse suicidal.

In evoking a matriarchal myth and a nondualistic, androgynous form of consciousness, we are honoring and extending Hillman's vision of Dionysian consciousness presented in Psychological Femininity, seeking a form of contrition and reconciliation that restores our primordial relationship to the natural world and to each other, and ultimately to our own mortality, repairing the split between life and death, seeing them as a circular, soulful process of death-and-rebirth, rather than a literalized, ultimate ending of ego-consciousness. For if we cannot imagine some form of letting go, of dying before we die, of connecting with eternalities that lie outside ourselves and beyond our personal lives, there is little chance that we can make the sacrifices necessary to deconstruct our current power structures, institutions, privileges, and beliefs, thereby creating a more just and sustainable world-culture. Medusan consciousness knows that "I" am the "Other," that life and death are aspects of the soul (Avicenna), and that in order for Life to go on, my own life must end, returning to the ground from which it came.

We hope to accomplish this transformation through a new set of symbols that are in one sense familiar and in another sense novel, "foreign," or "alien,"[25] thereby jarring our collective imagination into a radically different collective vision of reality and the seemingly intractable, literalized problems we currently face on a global scale. Medusa's gaze, reimagined and reflected in her own mirror, may shock us out of our habitual world view and our usual, "masculine" methods of problem-solving, thereby awakening us to our peril and the opportunities that may lie beyond it, if she is willing.

Medusa, as the apotropaic, protective crone or "death" aspect of Neith–the Great Goddess who personifies our mythic Source and the planet itself – might now be imagined as the ferocious Protector of the divine "feminine" energies that have been oppressed, co-opted, persecuted, or destroyed by our patriarchal, capitalist system. Drawing on an archetypal understanding of this subjugation of the goddess allows us to see her presence in multiple domains, from the natural world, to history and culture, and to the inner world of subjective experience. We find the pain and rage of the goddess in women's marches, protests against

---

25. Neith is described in ancient mythology as a member of the Nummo—amphibious, androgynous beings who were said to have emerged from the waters after a great flood to teach and guide humanity. We might also note that there is a contemporary theory—most notably presented by Shannon Dorey, author of *The Nummo*, and *The Master (Mistress) of Speech*—which tracks this mythology, including images of amphibious, hermaphroditic beings throughout the ancient world, and which proposes that the Nummo were in fact alien life-forms who literally traveled to Earth from another planet, and who may have engaged in genetic engineering to create the human species. As such, the "alien" nature of this mythology has taken the form of an empirical hypothesis of ancient alien contact. We are not taking a position here on the objective validity of this idea; rather, from the perspective of archetypal psychology, the theory reflects our deep need during the current crisis for an alternative mythology and an alternative origin story for humankind.

institutionalized racism and police violence, and environmental activism, and we find her persecution in domestic violence, sexual harassment and assault, discrimination and hate crimes, and in our own internalized misogyny, racism, and disregard for the natural world. If we view Medusa's reflection solely in the polished metal of a patriarchal shield, we fail to recognize her sovereignty and sacred power, and we perpetuate Perseus's violence.

A revised account of the Hellenic invasion reveals that Western culture did not emerge as a gradual, organic shift from a matriarchal to a patriarchal world view; instead, Western culture can be understood as the result of violent, traumatic battles whose lasting impact has been obscured by the veneer of a revisionist mythology told by the victors—as feminist scholars have pointed out, history is "his story." This mythology depicts the victims of the invasion as monsters who deserved to be killed, or as lesser goddesses who served and submitted to the Olympian gods.

The Great Goddess, Neith, had her primordial power diluted and dismembered, as Athena was recast as Zeus's daughter, Metis his devoured wife, and Medusa a horrifying monster or a mere maiden. The Hellenic myth of Perseus perpetuates the historical and mythological trauma of this invasion even as it obscures and justifies it, creating a Western culture that views masculine violence as heroic and feminine power as demonic. As such, "rape culture" as a sociological term can be broadened to encompass all forms of economic and ecological exploitation, including the rape of the planet entailed by late-stage capitalism. Our Olympian mythology enshrines the traumatic loss of the sacred feminine as a form of cultural and economic progress, and it casts the symptoms of that loss, including the catastrophic results of patriarchy, capitalism, White supremacy, and globalization, as chaos to be further dominated and defeated, as if life could be sustainable under a totalitarian system that seeks to eliminate justice, beauty, truth, and life itself.

And so, we return to Hillman's work, which has long recognized these issues and their mounting implications, articulated especially in his essays on Titanism, anima and anima mundi, psychological femininity, and the history of psychotherapy, as well as his essays on the archetypal Mother and paranoia contained in this volume. As Hillman put it so succinctly,

"...the World's Getting Worse."[26] What we suggest here is that Hillman's recognition of the fundamental splits in Western culture provides a theoretical and methodological foundation for addressing a world in which these splits are becoming wider and more dangerous, verging on apocalyptic in the mythic sense and world-ending in the literal sense. Now is the time to return to Hillman's understanding that messes are contained within myths, and that if we are to address the mess in which we find ourselves, we must first recognize the mythologizing process that allows us to see through it.

Saucius Lector (the Wounded Reader)

Whether this introduction will succeed is ultimately up to you, the reader. As you enter the essays in this collection, including this one, consider the ways in which Hillman has always invited us to enter the crucible of self-reflection, the alchemical process of finding ourselves in each image, each story, each metaphor and myth, not only learning new information, or thinking differently, or even perceiving the world differently, but imagining differently, transforming the images that make up our own psyche, becoming what Hillman described in *The Dream and the Underworld* as the imaginal ego at home in the dark, and re-entering a world that is personified, pathologized, psychologized, and dehumanized.

Our human relations have always been inhuman, our lives infused with the gods, including their pathologies, their suffering, their culpability, and their *infirmitas.* Our world is indeed wounded, broken, and chaotic, perhaps now more than ever before, and yet this is a primordial, eternal condition. Hillman suggests that by embracing that woundedness, by seeing that brokenness within ourselves, we can engage the world differently, tending to its images, mending what we can, and accepting the wounds that cannot heal but that allow us to participate in the world with deeper understanding and compassion. Archetypal psychology allows us to remember Hillman's insight that the wound and the eye are one and the same.

SCOTT BECKER

26. James Hillman and Michael Ventura, *We've Had a Hundred Years of Psychotherapy—And the World's Getting Worse* (New York: HarperCollins, 1993).

Anamnesis

1

TRAINING AND THE C.G. JUNG INSTITUTE, ZURICH

It is the aim of this paper to describe and discuss the training program at the C.G. Jung Institute, Zurich.[1] I shall set about this from "within," as it were, by describing what the programme consists in, some of its virtues and difficulties, its justifications and criticisms. To compare from "without" the problems and methods of training in Zurich with other programmes, one might begin with Szasz (1958) and his excellent bibliography, and Ekstein and Wallerstein (1958).

Training is a process that leads to qualification. At the C.G. Jung Institute, qualification is signified by the award of the diploma. The training process goes on in three areas, and the candidate must prove competence in all to qualify. They are: *personal analysis, study, practical case-work.* Proficiency in the personal analysis is attested to in writing by the training analysts; in study, it is tested by examinations and a diploma thesis; in case work, by case reports and by written recommendations of the supervising analysts who perform the controls. It is curious that these three areas are not necessarily interdependent. Individuals appear in whom learning and knowledge may lag far behind practical ability as evidenced in therapeutic success. Or there may be a long history of personal analysis with extraordinary psychological gifts, wisdom even, coupled with deep learning, and yet little practical ability or a practical sense limited to only certain patients. Therefore, it is probably best to discuss proficiency in these three areas separately, even if in the "ideal analyst" there will be that happy union of maturity, culture, and ability. Whereas the three areas are covered in the training facilities, the interweaving of

---

1. The contents of this paper have been agreed to by the members of the curatorium of the C.G. Jung Institute in Zurich.

the three, their integration, is a gift. This gift is, to use a distant analogy from Brahmanism, *satchitananda* (pure being, consciousness, bliss). Interpreted for our purposes it becomes *sat* (fullness of being), *chit* (knowledge of truths and values), *ananda* (bliss bestowing ability), which can be only a teleological impetus to a training program.

Analogies of this sort may perhaps be the only way in which we can get at the archetypal pattern for training an analyst. Sixty years is a short time to fix what analysis is and what an analyst does and what he must be to accord with an archetypal pattern. There is no tradition in our field, as in training for medicine, or for religious orders, East and West, or even as for the arts. Works of Jung (1944, 1946), Eliade (1951), Meier (1949), Maeder (1960), Kerényi (1956), as well as studies in Socratic dialectic, the mysteries, primitive medicine, and initiation ritual would together provide at least a beginning for working out a pattern upon which training might be based. Until we have found this basic pattern and become conscious of a tradition, what we do is highly experimental. It is in this sense of the experimental that what follows must be taken.

Selection of Candidates

Requirements for admission to training can be minimally described. Candidates must have attained the age of 25 by the time they take the propaedeutical examination (28 for the diploma); they must submit a rather full curriculum vitae and two letters of recommendation from analysts, former teachers, employers, or professional associates; they must have completed the Swiss *Maturat*, or the American B.A., or a European equivalent. They must have done at least one semester's study at the C.G. Jung Institute, Zurich, and present a letter of recommendation from their training analyst. It is up to the training analyst to decide at which point they are prepared to give this letter.

There is no fixed number of hours or years of analysis required before someone may be recommended for training. There are no limitations concerning the academic or professional field from which the candidate may come. Nor is it necessary to have completed a graduate academic degree in order to begin training. The graduate degree is desired before the propaedeutical examination and is required before the diploma may be awarded. All questions of academic qualifications are evaluated individually by the curatorium. The following are the usual minimum graduate degrees acceptable for the diploma: Ph.D., M.D. (Swiss, U.S.), M.B., B.Ch. (British), M.A. (British, and in some cases American).

This lack of restrictions is due to the simple fact that people usually do not ask to begin a Jungian training "cold"—and those who do take more than three years. Candidates generally arrive after some years of analysis and having some familiarity with Jung's works. It was to accommodate foreigners, by making their stay in Zurich the minimum period necessary, that it was decided to require only one semester of study before the status of training candidate could be granted. It is the rare person who begins training after only a few months; and with very few exceptions all graduates were in analysis for at least five years before gaining the diploma.

The selection process goes on continuously. A candidate may be dropped at any point upon the decision of the curatorium. For instance, a breach of the Code of Professional Ethics, which everyone enrolled (candidate and auditor) must sign, would give cause. These are the main occasions when the candidate comes up for review:

1. application to enroll for courses;
2. application for the status of training candidate;
3. admission to the propaedeutical examination;
4. evaluation of results at the examiners' conference;
5. permission to begin control case work;
6. admission to the diploma examination when the candidate's complete dossier is again evaluated;
7. evaluation of results of the diploma examinations.

The record shows that trainees have been excluded at nearly every one of these stages; nevertheless, once candidates have passed step two, endurance may see them through to the end. Similar comments can be found in the literature about other training programs. If this be so, *training analysts must be very circumspect with their first recommendation.*

Candidates may be divided into four sorts:

1. *Part-time candidates,* usually Swiss, working as physicians, teachers, etc., while they train. They have the advantages of being somewhat older, of a "real life" around them, and of a relatively slower transition from their former profession to that of analyst. On the other hand, they have less time and energy for study, usually only at evening courses.

2. *Full-time candidates,* usually not Swiss, helped by a grant or with private means. They either have just finished their graduate work, or have some years of professional experience behind them. For them at first, even though to be at the Institute has been a long-desired goal, the transition is difficult, from authority and responsibility to the learner's bench and the analysand's chair, coupled with the indignities (seductive as they might seem) of living abroad without work. Inflation, personal problems, then a sense of lostness and humiliation, followed by a dread of returning home, tend to appear in turn. The outcome depends on quality: whether they will be able to integrate the *bouleversement* of Zurich into their lives on return, and not merely to add another diploma to their accomplishments.

3. *Student-cum-candidates,* preparing for their doctor's degree. Unless individuals have behind them a good piece of analysis and a roughly neurotic life, the transition from the *provisorium* of student to the real life of professional can be a shock. No amount of seminar papers, reading, or lectures can help this transition, the first stage of which is control case work. Most must postpone this until they have finished their academic work; others seek, on their own, experience in nearby clinics. Ego development through practical experience is a main consideration in their training.

4. *Professional auditors,* who are not candidates, but who work with them in some seminars. They are usually highly qualified people (physicians, psychiatrists, psychologists, pastors and priests, educators, etc.), many of whom come from abroad and are able to spend only three months to a year in Zurich for learning and not full training. (Not included are the other auditors, because their activities are extraneous to training, except where they apply after some time for a change of status.)

It is the quality of the candidates that makes them more or less favorable for selection, and not whether they are young or old, male or female, married or single, working or studying, rich or on a grant, Swiss or foreign. "Quality" I take to mean those traits that lead the training analyst to recommend a candidate in the first place, among which moral integrity, psychological gifts, cultural level, and a sense of vocation are probably the most important.

Ideally, selection follows vocation, and the Institute's job would be to choose from among the called. The Institute provides a process (the program) to test the calling, a process in which selection takes place automatically, according to the steps mentioned above. It trains those who ask to be trained, and bases its choosing mainly upon calling as attested to by the training analysts. When the curatorium keeps its eye on the gift, the inner necessity mandatory for this "holy profession," which so often, paradoxically, makes a candidate a failure in all their former attempts to establish themselves, its training program is put to proper use: *to add professional competence to an individual calling.* If instead it should try to select and produce analysts through training, it could then happen that many were chosen but few are called.

Personal Analysis

Before 1918–1920, that period, which Balint (1948) refers to as the "prehistoric period" in the development of modern psychotherapy, the blessing of an analysis with Freud or one of his original co-workers was a sufficient qualification. Jung seems to have been the first to recognize the importance of the personal analysis. He wrote (Jung 1951, 115): "Freud himself accepted my suggestion that every doctor should submit to a training analysis before interesting himself in the unconscious of his patients for therapeutic purposes." In Zurich, this method of qualification, that is, an analysis with Jung or one of his original co-workers, was enough until 1948 when the Institute was founded. Now that the Institute exists, any bypassing of formalized training by setting, for some persons, lower standards than the standards of the diploma ought to be a cause for some unease.

This is not to deny the right of anyone to recommend their pupil for qualification, but it would be best to reserve this method for instances when the person is hindered by the academic requirements of professionalism. It is useful for making socially valuable those people too often excluded for "good" reasons. These living "fossils," to continue our metaphor, are to be welcomed, even if they present taxonomic problems to the International Society.

With the founding of the Institute in 1948, rules for training were described that also governed the personal analysis. Habits already long in practice became institutionalized, namely: working with an analyst of each sex; an analysis of three hundred hours or about three years, *minimum;* a list of approved training analysts to choose from; and the submission of written recommendation to practice from the training analyst—not directly to the candidate, but to the curatorium who in exchange issues the diploma.

What effect has institutionalization had on the personal analysis? For one thing. it has burdened the analysis, as we shall show further on. I imagine—because I cannot answer from my own experience—that the analysis could run the risk of becoming less central and more programmatic than it is ideal.

That qualification depends less on the analysis than it once did is more or less in keeping with the drift described in the literature. According to Fordham, "it is the function of the supervisor, and not the analyst, to exert control over the trainee's application for membership to the Society" (1961). He suggests that the analyst and the supervisor should keep their separate areas of work demarcated as clearly as possible. Thus the personal analysis is removed one step at least from being *the* criterion, as it was prehistorically.

At the Chicago Institute for Psychoanalysis, the "question 'Who analyzed him?' is heard less frequently...," because "the importance of the person analyst for the student's subsequent training and future career has been considerably lessened" (Piers 1960, 7). Thus, there is a shift of responsibility for the analyst-to-be from the training analyst who knows him best to an institutionalized group. The separation of the personal analysis from professional training goes so far that Clara Thompson (1958) finds that the sanctity of the personal analysis is violated if the training analyst gives any information about the candidate to the training supervisors. Training is in the hands of an institute (e.g., William Alanson White Institute, New York) and the personal analysis is an adjunct to it—private, secret, perhaps even peripheral. Ekstein and Wallerstein (1958) of the Menninger Foundation bear this out recommending personal analysis for all therapists, *but not insisting on it*.[2]

Shifting analysis toward the periphery of training aims at reducing not the role of personal analysis but that of the personal *analyst*. In fact, the shift is supposed to increase the importance and benefits of analysis

---

2. [The institutional dilemmas that Hillman is describing take place in an inherently unpsychological, or one could say modern and postindigenous culture. Training analysis and graduate training are arguably poor approximations of shamanic initiation. Also, the expectation of Apollonic reason and detachment within the context of Dionysian or Eleusinian madness and dissolution of consciousness is arguably impossible. Ironically, Hillman's later work can be seen, retroactively, as a commentary on all of these issues.—Ed.]

(Piers 1960; Thompson 1958). The concern is with the power of the personal analyst over the professional future of the candidate and how this power problem can work destructively upon the analysis. If the authority of the training analyst is limited by separating personal analysis from professional training, the personal analysis has a better prognosis, they suggest. It would remain uncomplicated by these power problems.

Szasz (1958), too, worries over power partly from another angle. Issues of training (technology and power) have replaced issues of doctrine. There is a shift away from *what* should be taught in favour of *how* it should be taught and to *whom*. This trend also can be understood, I believe, in terms of the weakening of the position of the personal analyst. It is their beliefs, attitudes, mind, and spirit that lead pupils toward a doctrinal system. Of course, it is just this doctrinal compliance which the new institutions want to avoid. This produces, then, the poor substitute of eclectic professionalism, a fear of orthodoxy, and a dwelling upon technical and anamnestic details, which no increase in the numbers of seminars or years of apprenticeship can improve.

The question "Who analyzed him?" echoes back to the master-pupil relation of traditional teaching. It is a natural hierarchy, an archetypal pattern if you will, maligned when reduced to the parent-child power pattern. Diminishing the power of the personal analysts diminishes their effectiveness. This, in turn, diminishes their capacity to constellate personality development.

The decay of interest elsewhere in personality development is the one ground, I believe, for all these negative phenomena: power problems, loss of concern with doctrine, and the gradual shift of importance away from personal analysis in favor of institutionalized training. Elsewhere, analysis would seem to have become but *a useful prophylaxis, a hygienic precaution* to clean out the unconscious of candidates so that they can use more effectively the tools given them in training.

At the Institute in Zurich, this clear separation of training and analysis does not exist. Training analysts, seminar leaders, supervisors, examiners, and curatorium have been and still are, more or less, the same people. This reflects the attitude that training is analysis and so cannot be separated from it. In Zurich, personal analysis is today no less central than it ever was. It is still the *Kernstück*, the *pièce de résistance* of the work. Professional secrecy is maintained, information belonging to the analysis is not transmitted to the curatorium. But the analysts give in writing to their colleagues their opinion as to the suitability of a candidate. This opinion remains crucial. If an analyst is opposed to an candidate's further candidacy, the curatorium will not override their judgement. They retain this power. The Institute, with all its regulations, examinations, etc., remains the adjunct to the personal analysis rather than vice versa. To put it another way, the Institute is a learning center, not a training center. In so far as the practice of analytical psychology requires learning, the Institute trains. But the primary training takes place in the dialectic between candidate and analyst.

Since so much depends upon the personality of the analysts in Jungian therapy, the personal analysis can but remain central. This personality is ideally supposed to develop in a way reflected by the training program, the steps of which are mentioned above under the heading *Selection of Candidates*. A programmatic sort of analysis could result, especially in the case of the candidates who, owing to financial or family circumstances, have only a short time in Zurich. And this works most positively because the problems of training come straight to the foreground. Each step of the program is bound up with the analysis, as, for instance, the transition from auditor to candidate corresponding to the change from mere interest to an attempt of commitment; or the transition to control case work with the attendant's anxiety and inflation. Again, there is often a crisis, usually connected with the thesis, just before completion of the training and departure from Zurich. In this moment, the good or bad parent aspect of the Institute looms large.

The personal analysis, then, is played out against the reality background of training to become an analyst. This burdens the analysis, because the goals are continuously subject to revision in the light of unconscious material. The aims there revealed must in some measure accord with the training goals in order for the analysts to make their recommendations. And these recommendations will, at best, refer to vocations revealed through the analysis of unconscious material. A further burden on the analysis of the candidate is the *Auseinandersetzung* with the persona and the collective conscious attitude toward the profession of analyst. Individuality and collective responsibilities may present conflicting interests. Thus, a personal analysis that is also a training analysis is more complex, heavier to carry, and more thorough because it is driven to deal with issues that are not necessary in a personal analysis alone. It must take up the issue of analysis itself and, without any Archimedean point, question itself.

Because of this institutional and training background, the personal analysis is not perhaps what it once might have been—a journey into self, free of all ideas about the goal, and out of which might one day come an analyst. No doubt the older generation had the advantage here because they were *not merely trained but transformed* into their profession, involved with Jung in great new discovery, *enthused, burning.* Programs and training seminars are not the same thing; but one cannot go back to the past. The separation of personal analysis and the training program could mean at best a separation between training and transformation. At this stage, when the general consensus is so much with organization and training, it might be well to press this point. There was a time when some Jungians might have been looked upon as transformed but untrained. A sound, difficult program leading to a diploma aims to solve this disparity. But if we stick too much to the rules, we may deliver well-trained people who are untransformed. Training and the content of training, which are emphasized in an article of this kind, are not the main factors at all. They are secondary, even if necessary, only additions and compensations, *the church that stands where the flame failed.* The conclusion is *that training is a tension, a conflict even, between an institutional program and the personal analysis.*

The unique value of Jungian psychotherapy is just this emphasis upon the personal individuality of the analyst, and personality has never been a product of a program. It depends much more upon the natures of the analyst and the candidate and the spirit in which they work. The training analyst thus has a superhuman burden, but if this profession is a "holy" one, superhuman elements belong, and the work will always be marked with the sin of failures and betrayals. The training analyst's job is to be those individuals who can maintain the opposite pole to the increasing power, social prestige, and professionalism of the training institute. If they remain aware of this, they will not slip the burden to a board of examiners, a curatorium, or an international society. The responsibility for allowing someone you have taught to go out and analyze belongs only to you who recommended them for the profession. Thus, and we come at the end to the personalities of the training analysts and their dedication to their own individualities. This is surely the chief influence upon the transformation of the trainee.

Teaching and Study

Let us be quite clear from the start. At the C.G. Jung Institute, therapy is not directly taught, and I do not believe that Jungian therapy can be taught. If we take therapy to be more than the effect of the analyst as agent upon the patient, more even than the product of their personal interaction; if we take it to be a *by-product of their interaction that comes about mainly through the influence of a third factor,* the spontaneous activity of the unconscious, which is individually different in each situation because it is spontaneous, then therapy cannot be taught as can most crafts and disciplines. It cannot be codified into repeatable techniques. The efficiency of the therapist will depend upon his awareness of the true agent, the unconscious, and upon his knowledge of its manifestations. What one must study, then, if one is to be scientific, are the manifestations of this third factor, which makes possible through its influence the therapeutic results. Therefore, what is especially taught, studied, and learned at the C.G. Jung Institute is knowledge about the manifestations of the unconscious as related to the therapeutic situation.

This body of knowledge, with amplifications from contexts in other fields of study, is the principal content of what is taught at the Institute in Zurich. It is a body of knowledge both vast and only partly organized. It consists of Jung's writings, his privately printed seminars, and research and studies done by collaborators and pupils from 1902 to the present day. This is the written content of analytical psychology, the core of the study program. It is transmitted mainly by means of lectures, by seminars with small groups of students, and by individual reading.

Often the manifestations of the unconscious cannot be understood because of the limitations imposed by consciousness. At best, they are partly understood in terms of personal memories and associations. To get at their fuller meaning, they need to be amplified beyond the label of meaninglessness given them by an uninformed conscious mind. Interpretation of the psychic contents, images, patterns of behavior will require—in order for the interpretation to be scientific and unbiased by the personal associations, analyst and analysand—knowledge of parallels and analogies. In fact, if the therapeutic influence of the unconscious is misconstrued owing to too personal a view of the manifestations, the whole healing process can be jeopardized. The more objective the Jungian analyst, the more objective his knowledge of the processes and images. He must know as much as possible in order to understand as fully as possible the material presented to him in the therapeutic situation. Learning these parallels and analogies by working on comparative material from folklore, fairy tales, myth, ritual, literature, religion, traditional symbolism, etc., that is, the method of amplification, the second main part of the study.

The term "medical psychology" covers the third area. The subjects include: psychopathology; its broader extension into syndromes, methods, treatment, diagnoses, aetiology, etc., or the study of psychiatry proper; and theories of neuroses, that body of clinical data and hypotheses as it has developed in Western Europe and which forms the main historical root of the psychotherapeutic profession. That knowledge of this field is demanded should be self-evident. Analysts' responsibility to their practice and to their profession requires that they be familiar with the pathologies of psychologic life. Further, they must be able to communicate with their colleagues in the operational system of medical psychology. Lectures are given regularly in these areas. Candidates are required to attend—the only obligatory lecture course in the program—three semesters of clinical visits where psychiatric cases are presented and discussed weekly. Freedom of attendance indirectly stimulates the teachers and raises the quality of the seminars. It is not found in the practice of American psychoanalytic institutes: "The lecture courses in Psychoanalytic Institutes, while again allegedly for the students' benefit, no longer have to depend on making the subject interesting and profitable to the student: attendance at these courses is *compulsory*" (Szasz 1958, 601).

To test what a candidate has learned, oral examinations are held in these areas: basic principles of analytical psychology; association experiment and theory of complexes; theories of dreams; theories of neurosis; psychopathology; general history of religions; psychology of fairy tales and myth psychology of primitive peoples. These eight examinations together make up the *propaedeuticum* and must be successfully completed before a candidate may do control case work. To test the integration of this learning with trainee's practical ability and psychological maturity, the final or diploma examinations are held at the end of the training course in the following areas: symbolic material from the individuation process; interpretation of dreams; interpretation of a fairy tale or myth; interpretation of pictures from the unconscious; practical case interrogation; psychiatry.

A candidate must in addition submit a diploma thesis that, too, is designed to show the integration of learning and individual ability. This piece of research also serves the purpose of extending further the field of analytical psychology. (In addition, lectures but no examinations are offered in special areas of psychology related to the main work, e.g., psychosomatics, child psychology, animal behavior, test psychology.)

The main areas of study—analytical psychology, amplification, medical psychology—were considered by Jung to be essential for analysts working along the lines he developed. Each time the study program came to his attention, he held fast to these areas. This occurred at least three times: in 1939, when the first ideas for the Institute were discussed; in 1948, when the Institute was founded; and again in 1959, when the subjects for examination were reconsidered.

Following Jung, we may assume that this body of knowledge is unconditionally necessary; whether it is sufficient is another question. I believe that other areas that might be included (physiological psychology, academic psychology, biological and genetic aspects of psychology) must remain supplementary because of the time limits imposed by the main program and because these subjects can be studied at the universities. Here it is well to remember that the study program is postgraduate. It is required in addition to the doctoral speciality already achieved. The doctor's degrees in economics, law, literature and philology, education, medicine, biology, theology, philosophy, and psychology (the faculties from which the candidates have mainly come) already show the highest academic competence our universities can bestow. It is not the task of the Institute to give a general education, even if the well-educated man perhaps makes the better therapist. But it is its task to provide the means for trainees to fill out the holes in their previous education. Thus, those who have never worked in hospitals, who have had little to do with the sick, who are unfamiliar with the special position of the professional therapist, need clinical experience. On the other hand, the medical people often need that background in the liberal arts, particularly the history of culture, which is throughout involved with Jung's approach to psychological problems. And, since all, when they finish training, have the title of psychologist, familiarity with the issues and terms of psychology (academic, experimental, historical) might be a desirable addition.

So much for the content. The method of learning—particularly lectures and examinations—can be questioned upon the ground that postgraduate study is rarely characterized by these school-type procedures. However, the method has proved itself and has strong justifications.

Lecturing is often the only way in which recent advances in the tremendously varied areas necessary to the study of analytical psychology can be imparted. And lecturing is a forte of the Institute. In the past twelve years, nearly 150 people from the world over have given regular courses or special lectures at the Institute. It is a rare thing for students in a speciality (analytic psychology) to be offered such a broad and unspecialized program. Jung (1943, 83) wrote: "Although we are specialists par excellence, our specialized field, oddly enough, drives us to universalism and to the complete overcoming of the specialist attitude, if the totality of body and soul is not to be just a matter of words." This opportunity to meet personally with analytical psychologists and others who are authorities in their related disciplines is important for that *extension of consciousness* necessary for the psychotherapist. Jung often found the cause of neurosis to lie in the contemporary narrowness of consciousness, its loss of cultural and historical perspective, its rational specialization.

The examinations for the diploma perform a function similar to that of English Bar examinations or American "medical boards," even if not recognized yet by state licensing laws. Professional qualification today requires standards beyond the subjective attestation of a training analyst, as in the "prehistoric period." The examinations offer objective criteria for judging proficiency, and they set minimum standards for an incredibly heterogenous group of candidates. They provide a focus for study and a disciplined vessel within which to work. And, on another level, they have the effect of an initiation.

A balance must be kept so that examinations do not usurp the important roles of the personal analysis and the control case work when proficiency is judged. *The function of examinations for psychotherapists is primarily one of standard-setting rather than of candidate-judging.*

There has been a gradual increase of emphasis upon practical seminars in the study program, beginning about 1955 with the control case colloquium and the clinical visits. Training will benefit from this trend toward research seminars and group work. More time given to objective amplification of candidates' own and of their control case material (even if it must be at the expense of listening to lectures) will develop the candidates' individual investigative abilities, opening the way for creative advances in our field.

Control Casework

After a candidate's successful completion of the *propaedeuticum* and upon a letter of recommendation from the training analyst, the curatorium can permit the candidate to take his first case. Cases are distributed partly through the Control Case Clinic under the supervision of the president of the Institute, and partly through personal relations, i.e., from one's own analyst, from friends, from analysts of friends. There is also the possibility of working with institutionalized patients in nearby mental hospitals.

There are no rules concerning how many cases may be taken at the beginning, but it is usual to start with one or two and perhaps to carry as many as five or six toward the end of training. There are also no rules as to which training analyst must control the candidate's cases or in what manner this control is to be effected. Candidates attend the weekly control case colloquium (conference) in which they present their cases under the supervision of a training analyst or an experienced medical analyst. Rules govern the numbers of cases (minimum three) and hours (250) the candidate must have in order to be eligible for the diploma; also the method of reporting monthly to the secretary of the Control Case Clinic the numbers of cases and hours, the amount in fees collected (which must be turned over *in toto* to the clinic), and the name of the supervising analyst for each case. Further, it is required that each case be written up (two cases reported on at length) and submitted to the curatorium before application is made for the final examinations.

There is no single supervisor. Candidates must have worked with three analysts in all, two of whom (male and female) are their training analysts and the other performs at least one control. It is possible, therefore, to do the major part of one's control with one's own training analysts. This would seem again to concentrate things in the personal analysis. It is counterbalanced by the study program through which a candidate gets known as well to other staff and curatorium members, e.g., through the control case colloquium, the diploma thesis, written papers for seminars, examinations, and written control case reports.

I believe that the main reason why no more rules have been laid down about supervision is the general consensus that candidates are best left alone to find their own way with their cases, so that as soon as possible they becomes aware of their own style and their own blindness. The least help is the best help. It is more important to develop a style out of one's nature and experience than to learn techniques. Technique is picked up in the control sessions, in the group colloquia, in the case material seminars, and of course from one's own training analyses. But only that which is picked up (integrated) is effective, not what is indoctrinated. Tight supervision might hinder the development of style, which could be ruinous if we take the practice of psychotherapy to be an art as well as a science. Too much control might only relieve immediate insecurity, preventing more profound constellations. Often, therefore, candidates relieve the insecurity in their personal analysis. But this, too, belongs, because their case work is a most important part of their life problems at the moment, and so will appear naturally in their personal analysis.

What goes on in the control sessions depends entirely upon the control analyst. Some may demand from some candidates full written reports—even verbatim—and at least one weekly session for every two hours of case work. The other extreme is for candidates to see their control analysts, as they would visit a tutor or research supervisor, for a report every now and then (monthly perhaps or less frequently), or only when things seem stuck. There is no limitation upon what personal problems of the candidates may enter into the discussion, although the procedure to my knowledge generally accords with Fordham's description (1961), that is, if the supervisor is someone other than the personal analyst, only bits of analysis are done and they refer generally to the countertransference situation in the control case.

The training process that I have just described can be criticized in many ways, for there is no claim that things are perfect; in basic attitude it belongs, however, within the tradition that has grown up in Zurich. The main aim is to leave the responsibility as much as possible to the individual candidates and to step in and correct only where danger or damage seems to begin. Thus the problem of intervention on the part of the control analysts is nicely managed. On the one hand, the supervisors' self-restraint is an *acte de confiance* toward their junior colleagues; on the other hand, the supervisors' intervention accords with the professional ethos of responsibility toward the analysands. In considering the role of control case work in the final assessment, *the therapeutic success is never the whole story.* Therefore, the additional reports (which might best be written), from the leader of the weekly control case colloquium, is also valuable in the assessment of ability, since these colloquia bring out other aspects of the candidate: openness to criticism, management of case presentations, insight into cases not one's own, etc.

Recently, it was decided to state in the regulations what has more or less been the practice, namely: candidates are asked to do a good part of their control work with an analyst who is not one of his personal analysts. This concentration of supervisory authority may increase the sense of responsibility of the control analyst concerning the future practice of the candidates.

It is in keeping with the principle in Zurich that at least three analysts are responsible for one candidate.

Emotional Climate

This phrase is taken from Thompson (1958). By it she means the atmosphere of the psychotherapeutic training institute, "which has many of the qualities—both good and bad—of a close family group." Broadly, I take it to cove all the relationships to be found in any academic or group research setting complicated by the problems of transference and counter-transference. Power struggles, favoritism, parental projections, nepotism, intersibling rivalries as well as many of the phenomena studied in animal behavior (peck order) and group psychotherapy, are all part of this emotional climate. It sounds hideously high ransom to pay for the release of the candidate from a single analyst, the prehistoric system of master, mentor, and supervisor in one. Yet in the light of experience at the Institute in Zurich, we might reappraise the question of emotional climate.

Several factors seem to save the emotional climate at the C.G. Jung Institute from being as destructive as Thompson finds elsewhere. One is surely the *spiritus loci*: Zurich and Switzerland—Forel, van Monakow, Bleuler, Pestalozzi, Flournoy, Rorschach, Brun, Adolf Meyer, Szondi, Piaget, Daseinsanalysis, Jung, etc.—an objective tradition in psychology that goes beyond the personal. A second is the introverted, tolerantly democratic, and profoundly individual attitude of the Swiss, which has as corollary a certain reserve toward group activities. A third is specific to the Institute; training is only one of its activities. From the point of view of numbers involved, it is a lesser activity, "adult education" being its first concern, with research, publications, information, and social relations also playing roles. The fourth, again peculiar to the Institute, is the international and interdisciplinary spirit of the place. The relations of the students with each other are full of fruitful projections and are psychologically stimulating and broadening. The good talk, the freedom and enthusiasm, the long-lasting friendships that develop, all are the mark of Zurich and are difficult to describe. The many sorts of attitudes and people under one roof contrast with the uniform limitations of clinic, university, department, etc., from which the candidates have come. This again makes for individual relationships freer of power and group motives. A graduate in Jodhpur, another in Los Angeles, and a third in Copenhagen can hardly help training analysts with their power struggles against their peers; nor can training analysts in Zurich wield much influence over their trainees' future miles away.

Besides these factors that contribute to the positive emotional climate, one more must be mentioned: the *multiple analysis* approach to the transference. A candidate must work with at least three analysts in all: one of the same sex, one of the opposite, and one control case supervisor. (One may work with more than three, but not fewer. The moment of transition to a second analyst occurs only with the advice and consent of the first analyst.)

Does multiple analysis "water down" the transference or play off one analyst against the other, or worse, can the candidate "hide" by escaping from one to the other? This is not the place nor am I the person to deal properly with the theory and practice of multiple analysis. But in so far as it relates to the emotional climate of the Institute a few observations are called for. So let us try the last two questions first—*in relation to the emotional climate.*

Resistance takes many forms, and candidates can make use of any training system to serve their resistances. However, the involvement of the candidates with each other and with the staff gives ground for mutual projections and *corrections* of these projections. The atmosphere of the Institute itself discovers a candidate to himself and to his analysts. I believe the term "transference dilution" (cf. Fordham 1961), like the term "lay analysis," is loaded. It sets up a false question, a *petitio principii.*

Conclusion

After twelve years, the experiment of an Institute for research and training in analytical psychology has begun to build up a tradition. This tradition works importantly in the relation between junior students and senior ones and in turn with the graduates. Graduates are beginning to take part in training, as teachers, examiners, and analysts. What goes on at the Institute in Zurich, and the attitudes it conveys, are rooted in a healthy *spiritus loci*. This *spiritus loci* can also be said to be the spirit of Jung; the facets of his work and personality are reflected in many directions by those of his pupils and collaborate who form the corpus of the Institute.

The topic of emotional climate could occupy a paper at least as long this one, which has been limited by trying to cover the whole program. The negative aspects of power belong to the same realm of Caesar as one's institutions, and they must be lived with. It is plain that all relations bounded by four walls have their shadow side. But these power issues are not the focus of attention so long as there are more fundamental things at stake, namely the gigantic and paradoxical task of developing an Institute and training candidates based on the psychology of Jung with its extreme emphasis on individuality, and at a time both unpropitious and urgent. The power problem comes to the fore, it is my guess, when an institute is losing vitality and purpose. This is hardly the case in Zurich, which now, at thirteen, is just entering a new cycle of growth.

The present shows the following developments: expansion of the lecturing staff, an increase in numbers of qualified applicants, more emphasis upon control case work and clinical experience, a trend toward more research and practical working groups, the founding of a dream, picture, and film archive.

The future will depend not only on the past tradition and the present developments, but upon the lively, dedicated spirit in which all the activities of the Institute are carried on. This spirit would seem to flourish best in the Institute as it was conceived—small, private, free, international, interdisciplinary, low-budgeted, and loosely organized, providing a platform for all in the field to come and do their work and have their say.

Bibliography

Balint, Michael (1948). "On the Psycho-Analytic Training System," *The International Journal of Psycho-Analysis* 29

Fromm-Reichmann, Frieda (1949). "Notes on Personal and Professional Requirements of a Psychotherapist," in *Psychoanalysis and Psychotherapy: Selected Papers,* edited by Dexter M. Bullard (Chicago: The University of Chicago Press)

Ekstein, Rudolf and Wallerstein, Robert S. (1958). *The Teaching and Learning of Psychotherapy* (New York: Basic Books)

Eliade, Mircea (1951). *Le Chamanisme et les techniques archaïques de l'extase* (Paris: Payot)

Fordham, Michael (1961). "Suggestions towards a Theory of Supervision," *The Journal of Analytical Psychology* 6, no. 2

Jung, C.G. (1943). "Psychotherapie und Weltanschauung," *Schweizerische Zeitschrift für Psychologie und ihre Anwendungen* 3. Translated as "Psychotherapy and a Philosophy of Life," in *CW* 16: *Practice of Psychotherapy*

———. (1944). *CW* 11: *Psychology and Alchemy*

———. (1946). "Psychology of Transference," in *CW* 16: *Practice of Psychotherapy*

———. (1951). "Fundamental Questions of Psychotherapy," in *CW* 16: *Practice of Psychotherapy*

Kerényi, Karl (1956). *Der Göttliche Arzt* (Darmstadt: H. Gentner)

Maeder, A. (1900). "Der Archetyp des Heilers und die Heilung," *Antaios* 2, no. 4.

Meier, C.A. (1949). *Antike Inkubation und Moderne Psychotherapie* (Zurich: Rascher).

Newton, Kathleen (1961). "Personal Reflections on Training," *The Journal of Analytical Psychology* 6, no. 2.

Piers, Gerhart (1960). "Report on its activities," The Chicago Institute for Psychoanalysis

Plaut, A., (1961). "A Dynamic Outline of the Training Situation," *The Journal of Analytical Psychology* 6, no. 2

Szasz, Thomas (1958). "Psycho-Analytic Training," *The International Journal of Psychoanalysis* 39

Thompson, Clara (1958). "A Study of the Emotional Climate of Psychoanalytic Institutes," *Psychiatry: Journal for the Study of Interpersonal Processes* 21

2

JUNG'S CONTRIBUTIONS TO "FEELINGS AND EMOTIONS": SYNOPSIS AND IMPLICATIONS

At the turn of the century, when Jung began to write on psychology, there were no clear distinctions among the various components that had been grouped, or discarded, in that bag called "the affective faculty." From the time of the Enlightenment in Germany (eighteenth-century writers such as Moses Mendelssohn, J.N. Tetens, and Kant), the soul was divided into three parts: thinking, willing, and feeling; the cognitive, conative, and affective faculties. Into the affective faculty was thrown everything that did not fit into thinking or willing. Thus, it embraced desires, drives, and impulses as well as intuitions, instincts, moods, sensations, and of course, feelings, emotions, affects, and passions. Different psychologists at different times would rescue this or that piece of the affective faculty, such as sensation or impulse, and incorporate it into their system of thinking or willing. But fundamentally, this third region of the psyche, like Plato's third class of men, was inferior; the model on which it was conceived echoed the ancient trinitarian division of the soul, the lowest aspect of which was associated with what was below the diaphragm, especially the liver. Furthermore, this hag of feelings was always in opposition to thinking, or, as Mendelssohn said at the beginning of the modern tripartite division, "We no longer feel as soon as we think." By the way, the opposition between thinking and feeling is still found in the scientistic psychology without heart and the romantic psychology without head. Jung, too, as we shall see, presents thinking and feeling as opposed functions; but his psychology, having for its overall aim the union of opposites in the soul, does not rest in this split between head and heart.

Modern Theories of Feeling

The lack of differentiation in conceptualizing the affective faculty and its functions betrays a lack of differentiated experience of these processes themselves in the collective psyche of Western nineteenth-century man, who after all is simply describing himself, painting his own portrait, in his theories. It was as if feeling and emotion had lost touch with consciousness, or had fallen into the unconscious. Therefore, it is no surprise that the most acute differentiation of feeling and emotion was made by psychiatrists in their investigations of the unconscious and their descriptions of psychopathology. The invention of that language, mainly in clinics and asylums throughout the nineteenth century, encompassed a wide range of the passions of the soul, but from their obverse, abnormal, unconscious side. While nineteenth-century academic psychology was making acute observations in regard to thinking processes, sensation, perception, and memory—feeling and emotion were still largely in a bag. Some psychologists, mainly German (Lersch, Bollnow, Krueger)[1] believed that this bag must be kept closed. The affective realm belonged inside, in the depths of the person. To open it to thought would kill the very object under observation. "We no longer feel as soon as we think." In other words, in the nineteenth century there was a problem of feeling and emotion, not only academically but conceptually. The conceptual problem expresses a psychological problem, a feeling problem of the human soul. It is a problem we are not done with even today.

Jung's Feeling Function

Jung clearly separated feeling from the other affective processes and so helped to reinstate it. In his *Psychologische Typen* (1921), he defined feeling as a distinct function of consciousness, placing it on a par with thinking. We shall return to his definition of feeling.

Jung came upon the role of feeling also experimentally. His earliest descriptions of feeling stem from his association experiments, which he devised and performed during the first decade of the century. In these experiments he sometimes found affective reactions to stimulus words, such as "yes," "bad," "I like," rather than ideational associations

---

1. See James Hillman, *Emotion: A Comprehensive Phenomenology of Theories and Their Meanings for Therapy* (London: Routledge & Kegan Paul, 1960)., ch. 9, for examples.

in the stricter sense. These affective reactions judged the stimulus word, qualified it with a subjective appreciation, and established a connection between the individual and the stimulus by means of this subjective appreciation.

In attempting to give full recognition to these affective reactions, he began to formulate his theory of types in a paper read in 1913 at the Psycho-analytical Congress in Munich. This first formulation made one basic division between thinking, introversion, and *dementia praecox* on the one hand, and feeling, extraversion, and hysteria on the other.[2] This simpli-fication was transformed in his final elaboration of feeling as it appears in his 1921 major work, published in English in 1923 as *Psychological Types*. I quote now from that work the essence of Jung's definition of feeling:[3]

> Feeling is primarily a process that takes place between the ego and a given content, a process, moreover, that imparts to the content a definite *value* in the sense of acceptance or rejection ("like" or "dislike"); but it can also appear, as it were, isolated in the form of mood, quite apart from the momentary content of consciousness or momentary sensations.
>
> ...feeling is a kind of *judging*, differing, however, from an intel-lectual judgment in that it does not aim at establishing an intel-lectual connection but is solely concerned with the setting up of a subjective criterion of acceptance or rejection. The valuation by feeling extends to *every* content of consciousness, of whatever kind it may be. When the intensity of feeling is increased, an *affect* results, which is a state of feeling accompanied by appreciable bodily innervations.
>
> ... Feeling, like thinking, is a *rational* function, since, as is shown by experience, values in general are bestowed according to the laws of reason, just as concepts in general are framed after the laws of reason.
>
> Naturally the essence of feeling is not characterized by the fore-going definitions: they only serve to convey its external manifesta-tions. The conceptual capacity of the intellect proves incapable of formulating the real nature of feeling in abstract terms, since think-ing belongs to a category quite incommensurable with feeling...
>
> When the total attitude of the individual is oriented by the func-tion of feeling, we speak of a *feeling-type*.

2. C.G. Jung, *Collected Papers on Analytical Psychology,* edited by Constance E. Long (London: Baillière, Tindall and Cox, 1916), 402.

3. C.G. Jung, *Psychological Types or The Psychology of Individuation,* translated by H. Godwyn Baynes (New York: Harcourt, Brace & Co., 1923), 543–47; cf. *CW* 6: 724–29.

The feeling function is that psychological process that evaluates. Through the feeling function we appreciate a situation, a person, an object, a moment, in terms of value. A prerequisite for feeling is therefore a structure of feeling memory, a set of values, to which the event can be related. As a process that is always going on and that gives or receives feeling-tones—even the feeling tone of indifference—the feeling function connects both the subjective "me" to the object by imparting value or "importance" (cf. Whitehead), and the object to the subjective "me" by receiving it within the subjective value system.[4] Feeling, therefore, functions as a relation, and is often called "the function of relationship." Because it relates us, it has to do with adaptation—extravertedly to an environment, or introvertedly to our subjective *milieu interne.* Through feeling, subject is related to object, to the contents of his own psyche as values, and to his own subjectivity as general feeling tone or mood.

As a process feeling requires time, more time than is needed for perception. It behaves in the same way as thinking, rationally organizing perceptions. It is coherent, if not systematic. The ability to handle a problem or talk with a person in the right way shows a rational discrimination, and an adaptation to what is needed leading to correct conclusions. Yet the entire operation may not be intellectual. One says different things to different people according to the values of the situation, and according to the requirements of the other person and one's own objective psyche as subjectively felt. These answers to questions may not be either truthful or correct in the logical sense, but from the point of view of feeling they may be exactly right. When a child asks for an explanation, an answer may be given from thinking or from feeling; at times, a story that answers to the anxiety in the child may be "truer" than an intellectual explanation of causes. To hit the mark truly does not mean always to tell the factual or logical truth. In therapy, a problem may often be relieved by absurdities of anecdote or parable rather than by relentless analytical pursuit. Often the whole picture of harmony is more important in resolving a conflict than either logic or facts. The function of feeling then creates a situation in which viewpoints may reasonably blend even though the opposing logical and factual issues have not been settled, and may even have been compromised. One may be irrationally at odds with an appointment or

---

4. Alfred North Whitehead, *Modes of Thought* (New York: Macmillan, 1938).

an outer obligation, yet in tune with one's own values and mood. To do something when you "don't feel right" may be more irresponsible and destructive than failing the commitment. On waking in the morning, feeling tells us how things are with us regardless of the outer rationality of weather, time on the clock, duties of the day, state of the body. And above all, feeling provides the order and logic for love. Let us now look at some implications.

First, in Jung's use the term *feeling* differs sharply from other ways in which the word "feeling" is used, such as feeling certain, feeling something is in the air, feeling something is fishy, rotten—all of which belong to what Jung calls the function of intuition. So, too, feeling comfortable, exhausted, or feeling the texture of cloth, refer to the function of sensation. In this or that individual at this or that moment, feeling may be muddled with intuition or sensation, but by definition feeling is distinctly other than sensation and intuition.

Second, feeling is a *function*. A function (from *fungor*) acts, performs, operates. A function is an activity, a process that goes on during a period of time. It has consistency, continuity, and identity. As such, it can be a function of the ego-personality. Feeling is an instrument by which events are shaped and colored and with which we evaluate experiences. We have it in our hands to use: by means of the feeling function we make ethical and aesthetic judgments, develop a hierarchy of values, elaborate manners and taste, carry out intimate and social relationships, and experience religious life.

Third, feeling as a function differs from *feelings as contents*. This distinction between the feeling function and feelings is of major importance in Jung's work and has major implications. The feeling function may evaluate thoughts, objects, psychic contents, or events of any kind. It is not restricted to feelings. The feeling function feels (appreciates and relates to) not only feelings. Feeling is not limited to feelings any more than thinking is limited only to thoughts. We may feel our thoughts, discover their value, their importance. So, too, may we think feeling and about feelings—as we are doing, for instance, in this symposium. Feelings themselves—irritation, enjoyment, boredom—may be handled and adequately or inadequately, valued positively or negatively by the feeling function. We may be fittingly bored or wrongly and badly bored; we may be well irritated or poorly irritated. The organization of feelings depends less on the feelings than it does upon the function.

Fourth, in Jungian psychology a great deal is made both in theory and in practical work of *inferior functioning*. The feeling function may be dominant as in the feeling-type, or it may be less developed and inferior. It may be a typical way in which the ego-personality functions, or the feeling function may be affect-charged and rather ego-alien. Inferior feeling refers to the inadequacy of the function. Inferior feeling botches up values and makes the wrong feeling-judgments. It performs wrongly, or rightly at the wrong time. Its timing is off. It does not inform the person how he feels about this or that, whether he likes or loves, whether he is adaptively related to what is taking place outside or inside. He can feel sad only when he falls ill, or feel happy only when given recognition. His feeling depends on the performances of his body, or the actions of others. His own function seems not to be present. His work world has no feeling (moral or social) consequences. Even such positive feelings as love, joy, or giving, may be handled inadequately by an inferior feeling function so that they are misplaced, inappropriate, and destructive. Our love is autoerotic, our joy unenthusiastic, our giving inconsiderate. An analogy may be made with thinking: inferior thinking may be reflecting on such major ideas as God, the nature of matter or energy, or the interrelationship of cells. But these ideas, in themselves positive and significant, may be handled in a mystifying, confused, even archaic way, revealing the inappropriateness and inadequacy of inferior thinking, even if that is at times originally creative.

But, *fifth*, inferior feeling is not to be confused with negative feelings. Negative feelings are those either inwardly experienced as bad and painful, such as guilt, boredom, fear, or as socially condemned, such as hatred and envy. Just as positive feelings can be mishandled by an inferior feeling function, so can these so-called negative feelings be expressed appropriately and adequately. Think of Jonathan Swift and what he did with his negative feelings of hatred and misanthropy. Therefore, from this point of view, we might say that there is no feeling that in itself is negative. Much depends on the way in which feeling functions with it. The psychotherapeutic, even cultural, problem is not the problem of negative feelings—hatred, aggression, envy, and the seven deadly sins that we bring originally with us into life. Rather, the therapeutic and cultural problem concerns the development of the feeling function so that it becomes an adequate container, or channel, or mode of operation for these feelings.

The general inferiority of this function in our society has many sources: our emphasis upon intellect, our competitive educational system, the lack of cultivation of the feminine virtues in man and woman, the decline of feeling systems such as religion, morals, aesthetics, manners, friendships; loss of interest in personal essays, letter writing, and diaries, and in loving rather than its technics and legal programmatics.

Sixth, an education of the feeling function is possible. Because the education of feeling is largely absent in our usual education, it has become a main theme in therapy, whether in groups, in sensitivity training, or individual analysis. This education begins with the function of feeling itself, just where it is. If you permit, it is an education through faith, faith in the function itself, which can develop if allowed to be exercised. Therefore, the education of feeling means foregoing the familiar condemnations of its inferiorities from above by our superior thinking. It begins with the courage of the heart: to like what one likes, to feel what one feels, to refuse what one truly cannot abide. It requires admission into consciousness and the re-evaluation of so-called negative feelings. Although the education of feeling may begin on this level of highly personal feeling reactions, eventually discrimination becomes more objective and the personal factor recedes.

Seventh, and finally, feeling plays a *central role in Jung's psychology.* We cannot read Jung with the intellect alone. Conscious comprehension of Jungian psychology means feeling comprehension as well. All the principal conceptual symbols—introversion, complex, shadow, self, synchronicity, for example—are experiences of feeling. A complex is a felt reality. A symbol is not only a sense image with intuitional and intellectual content; it presents itself as value and as a living relationship, evoking feeling.

Emotion and Affect

We come now to emotion. Jung uses the term more or less interchangeably with affect. A distinction between emotion and affect, partly based on Jung, was made by Ernst Harms at the 1948 Mooseheart Symposium.[5] I, too, differentiate emotion and affect. In my book, emotion and affect

---

5. Ernest Harms, "A Differential Concept of Feelings and Emotions," in *Feelings and Emotions: The Mooseheart Symposium,* edited by Martin L. Reymert (New York: McGraw-Hill, 1950), 147–57.

are differentiated. I conceived emotion as a total event of the personality activating all levels and therefore a symbolic kind of transformed consciousness with "body" in it. Emotion is thus less than normal unemotional consciousness because it has levels of affect that narrowly intensify awareness, and yet more than normal unemotional consciousness because it is a heightened total condition. Affects, on the other hand, I conceived as not total, but partial, primitive, and relatively unconscious. Simply: affect lowers the mental level to what Janet would call *la partie inférieure d'un fonction*, whereas emotion raises, transforms, and symbolizes. Emotion is essentially a purposive creative state that has affect within it.

The image of the centaur expresses what I mean. In Greek myth, the centaur, half-man, half-animal, instructor of Achilles, Jason, and Hercules, i.e., heroic consciousness, as well as Asclepius, i.e., therapeutic consciousness, and an inventor of music and medicine—indeed a high state of emotional awareness—is also the creature used for capturing wild bulls, or the blind impulse of affect. The whole man, at one with body consciousness, or in a state of emotional being, overcomes the affects.[6]

Jung does not distinguish in his definitions between affect and emotion.[7] His distinction between feeling and emotion/affect is mainly quantitative.[8] Feelings become affects when they release physical innervations.

These physical innervations, which characterize affect in distinction to feeling, are important in Jung's thought in two ways. First, the physical component of affect makes possible the measurement of the complex with physical methods (psychogalvanic phenomena). Secondly, Jung's view of schizophrenia, which goes back to the early years of the century, also requires this physical quantitative view of affect. Jung suggested that

---

6. [Hillman refers here to a specific centaur: Chiron, who is differentiated from other centaurs in that he is less wild and more civilized, more intelligent and rational. Chiron is an immortal healer who is struck by a poisoned arrow and unable to either die or recover, caught in a perpetual state of woundedness. As such, in the context of this essay, Hillman is referring to Chiron as an image of a dominant, developed, or "educated" feeling function, differentiated from his fellow centaurs in his sensitivity, sophistication, and dedication to teaching and alleviating the suffering of others. It should also be noted that the asteroid Chiron features strongly in astrology as a marker of trauma, woundedness, or interpersonal and spiritual sensitivity.—Ed.]

7. Jung, *Psychological Types*, 541.

8. Ibid., 522.

the physical innervations or affective charges bound up with the psychic factors in a repressed complex could ultimately act as a toxin inducing physiological changes resulting in schizophrenia.

Jung's Concept of the Complex

Clearly, Jung's theory of affect cannot be separated from his theory of the complex. And his psychology was called at the beginning not analytical psychology but complex psychology, attesting to the central role that in his view the complex plays in the human psyche. A complex may be defined as a group of psychic contents intertwined in a specific pattern and cohesively united by a similar and ambivalent affective tone. They are affect-laden. The ambivalence is experienced as compulsion and inhibition, as desire and anxiety. Complexes, like affects, are ego-alien; we experience them as intruders. We not only have them, but they have us, dominating us, driving us, inhibiting us. The personal aspect of the complex consists of events of my personal life—associations, memories, habits, and the like. The archetypal core of the complex is both an instinctual pattern of behavior and an image idea. For example, the mother complex affects the ego with desires for incest, with bad-tempered, demanding, indecisive moods of lameness, with omnipotence urges and desires for sexual prowess, and with longings for liberation and transcendence. These affects are presented on a fantasy level by symbolic ideas and images such as the dragon-hero fight, the wounded hero, the mighty phallic lover, Jesus the truth-bringer, etc.

Perry's "Affect-Ego"

The latest Jungian contribution to the theory of emotion was made quite recently by John Weir Perry.[9] His ideas are relevant here. The complex always constellates the ego in a specific way; by affecting the ego it gives us an "affect-ego." For example, when the mother complex has me, my ego may act the weak and wounded son-lover. When the father complex has me, the ego is caught by the image and affects of the son in one of its forms: dutiful prince and successor, rebellious father killer, tricky Tom

9. John Weir Perry, "Emotions and Object Relations." Paper read in 1968 at the Fourth International Congress on Analytical Psychology, Zurich, and published in *The Journal of Analytical Psychology* 15, no. 1 (January 1970): 1–12.

Thumb who will not grow up. The generation struggle today is loaded with affect-ego problems, the sons constellating the fathers, the fathers constellating the sons through these archetypal complexes so that perception of each other is affected and distorted into pre-existent archetypal images. The patterns of affect in suppression and in rebellion going on around us are so universally similar—both in behavior and in ideational image—that they seem stamped from one typical, or archetypal, pattern.

Thus the complex is paramount in Jungian practice. An affect is always presumed to contain an archetypal core that reveals itself in specific patterns of behavior and specific images of fantasy. We go avidly after these fantasies and images (via dreams, say) in order to discover what complex is constellated, what archetypal pattern is being enacted. Then we compare the motifs of the complex with objective psychological material; that is, we amplify the motif beyond its personal associations, seeing the personal family fights also in view of the specific symbolic patterns of the Mother and Son-Lover or Father and Son struggles, etc. So, we look at affects with a mythic eye, as fantastic symbolic role-playings of the person, which are necessary to the personality as a whole, and purposive even if ego-alien at the moment of occurrence. We regard the stimuli that discharge an affect, even if coming from without and seemingly, trivial and incidental, as necessary to a person's mythic pattern of life, else they would not affect him. Thus affects have a survival value. Furthermore, we consider changes of mood and expressions of affect as belonging to personality transformation, and that this process of transformation could not take place without mood and affect. Thus, important for our approach is the intrapsychic origin of mood and affect; and the question of how mood and affect arise from wholly inner self-steering fantasies.

There are other aspects of Jung's theory of emotion that we shall have to leave aside, such as the Shadow or the Anima. The "Anima" in particular (the feminine aspect of the man) is the archetype involved with the irrational and moody complexes of the male personality. (I have taken this up in some detail in relation to affect in the last chapter of my book *Insearch* and also in *Anima*).[10] We must also leave aside the implications for

---

10. James Hillman, *Insearch: Psychology and Religion* and *Anima: An Anatomy of a Personified Notion* (Putnam, Conn: Spring Publications, 2014 [1967]).

parapsychology of Jung's view of emotion. His theory of synchronicity, an a-causal connecting principle for the explanation of meaningful coincidences, also involves his theory of emotion.

Implications for Therapy

We can, however, discuss the practical implications for therapy that Jung's view offers. This seems most relevant, since therapy involves everyone dealing with the problem of his own emotional life. We are all in therapy with ourselves, interminably. The perennial problem of emotion—to use the phrase of Magda Arnold—is not theory-forming, but "how to live," or "how to be" in Joseph Conrad's words. How can we survive, and how can the world around us survive, our affective attacks; how can affect become emotion, without which we cannot survive? The great conundrum of affect is the double-bind: "Thou shalt not repress," and on the other hand, "Thou shalt not act out." So what are we to do with our affects? I may get rid of them neither by repressing them within nor acting them out.

This leaves but one choice: living affects in,[11] keeping them, holding onto them with all the intensity they bring with them, in order to gain their secret, their image, their fantasy, their purpose in my life. If held and watched and felt, the affect will ultimately reveal its image, i.e., the other side of the complex (on the hypothesis that the image and the affect are aspects of one complex). By living-in the affect, by concentrating upon it, by fantasying the terror, the hatred, the lust right through to the end—neither repressing nor acting out—by dreaming the dream along in the phrase of Jung, one does answer Conrad's question "how to be" with Conrad's own answer: "Immerse yourself in the destructive element." For then, experience shows that the affect will, with grace, transform itself into emotion; through the vigil one has kept with it, there has been added consciousness to what was hitherto blind. By having lived close to it, one

---

11. [Here we can respect the introverted, internalizing attitude that Hillman is describing while also recalling his later move in expanding imaginal reflection into the world as a form of extraverted depth. In these later essays, Hillman furthers Jung's efforts to overcome Cartesian dualism (inner versus outer)—via concepts such as synchronicity and the psychoid layer of the unconscious—by recognizing the presence of soul in the world, and psyche as an imaginal field that includes both mind and matter, and that renders both introversion and extraversion as inherently psychological attitudes.—Ed.]

has joined with it. No longer man wrestling with wild bull, we have a new kind of emotional awareness, man and animal nature joined, the Centaur. Thus can affect transform us, rather than we it; it transforms our life and our awareness into emotional and symbolic experience. What hitherto was a symptom in our case history, to be dealt with or explained, now, with grace, is psychologically integrated, part of experience, and built into our soul-history.

In Hindu esoteric psychology (Tantra), in that system called the Kundalini Yoga, the place of affect is the imaginal belly, between the navel and the solar plexus. The area would include the liver of Greek antiquity, and the upper colon of eighteenth-century psychiatry, so long considered the "locus of insanity." This region is described in the Kundalini system as a seething cauldron, a place of fire, and there the god, Rudra the "howler," abides. But this place is also called "filled with jewels." Affects, much as they may howl, burn, and stew, are nothing to "get rid of"; with abreaction, behavior therapy or tranquilizers, for that would be to get rid of the potential jewels. If contained psycho-logically—held, kept, lived-in, and above all *valued with feeling*—the pas-sion can transform into valuable psychological treasures, those diamond bodies of indestructible psychic experiences.

3

SOME EARLY BACKGROUND TO JUNG'S IDEAS: NOTES ON *C. G. JUNG'S MEDIUM* BY STEFANIE ZUMSTEIN-PREISWERK

Since the publication, fifteen years ago, of *Memories, Dreams, Reflections* (MDR),[1] Jung's autobiography recorded and edited by Aniela Jaffé, there has been little work on Jung that extends our knowledge of his early life. The first published letter is from 1906—when Jung was 31. Notable exceptions by two medical historians are Henri Ellenberger's chapter on Jung,[2] which investigates source material firsthand and Hans Walser's paper,[3] which reports on crucial events in Jung's career around 1911–12.

Now Stefanie Zumstein-Preiswerk has published a short, popular, semi-fictionalized biographical sketch of Helene (Helly) Preiswerk,[4] the mediumistic girl with whom Jung did his parapsychological investigations that became the subject of his 1902 doctoral dissertation, "On the Psychology and Pathology of So-Called Occult Phenomena." The author is a blood relation of both Jung and his first cousin Helene (Helly). All three descend from the same ancestor, Samuel Preiswerk-Faber (1799–1871), who was Jung's mother's father and Helene's father's father (as well as being the principal control voice in the seances). *C. G. Jung's Medium*

---

1. C. G. Jung, *Memories, Dreams, Reflections*, edited by Aniela Jaffé; translated by Richard and Clara Winston (New York: Vintage Books, 1989); *Erinnerungen, Träume, Gedanken* (Zurich and Stuttgart: Rascher, 1962).

2. Henri F. Ellenberger, *The Discovery of the Unconscious: The History and Evolution of Dynamic Psychiatry* (New York: Basic Books, 1970).

3. Hans Walser, "An Early Psychoanalytical Tragedy: J. J. Honegger and the Beginnings of Training Analysis," *Spring: An Annual of Archetypal Psychology and Jungian Thought* (1974): 243–55.

4. Stefanie Zumstein-Preiswerk, *C. G. Jung's Medium: Die Geschichte der Helly Preiswerk* (Munich: Kindler, 1975).

attempts to recapture not only Helene but the milieu of the family of Jung's mother, and by consequence, a piece of Jung's psychological atmosphere during his student years.

Owing to the fictionalized way the book is presented, it is hard to discern new material from hearsay, gossip, or invention. It comes, as the author says, from her father (Helene's elder brother) and her mother (Helene's best school friend), as well as from other relatives of the Preiswerk and Jung families. She also relies upon biographical accounts already published by Oeri,[5] Steiner, and others listed in her bibliography. There are several appendices, long notes, old family photographs, and family trees. She also makes use of, and gives a personalized twist to, many passages from Jung's writings on his medium, and pieces together facets of the autobiography (MDR) to reconstruct—even with imaginative conversations between the persons long dead—the figure of Helly and the family world of C.G. Jung between 1887 and 1903. Clearly, the book is not intended as a scholarly biography, despite the research offered. Rather, it bears the stamp of personal family memories, fantasies, resentments, and cannot be read as a distanced historical account.

Despite these disclaimers, the book holds interest to the student of Jung's thought, for these were the years when "Jungian psychology" was germinating. On the dust jacket of her book is this sentence from Ellenberger: "This germinal cell of Jung's analytic psychology is to be found...in his experiments with his young medium cousin, Helene Preiswerk."[6]

Of course, Jung's psychology springs from wider intellectual and experiential ground than offered by Helene Preiswerk. Oeri says he was a young man packed with ideas. His youthful interests ranged through philosophy, theology, and natural science, and for them he had other proving grounds (his friends in the Zofingia student club) than his medium. Yet, by reading Zumstein-Preiswerk's chapters together with all else that we have of that time, one may espy what Ellenberger means. The dissociability of the psyche, the projection of the repressed, the relativization of the ego, the psychology of the transference, the autonomy of the

5. Albert Oeri, "Some Youthful Memories of C.G. Jung," *Spring: An Annual of Archetypal Psychology and Jungian Thought* (1970): 182–91.

6. Ellenberger, *The Discovery of the Unconscious*, 687.

complex—more, the very reality of the psyche—first concretely evidenced themselves to Jung, neither with Bleuler at the clinic, nor with Freud, nor during his "Confrontation with the Unconscious," but through his cousin. Jung himself wrote in 1935:

> This idea of the independence of the unconscious, which distinguishes my views so radically from those of Freud, came to me as far back as 1902, when I was engaged in studying the psychic history of a young girl somnambulist. (*CW* 7, p. 123)

And later:

> Just as the Breuer case we have discussed was decisive for Freud so a medical decisive training experience observed underlies my own views. Towards the end of my medical training I observed for a long period a case of somnambulism in a young girl. It became the theme of my doctoral dissertation. For one acquainted with my scientific writings it may not be without interest to compare this forty-year-old study with my later ideas. (*CW* 7:199)

This report aims to pass on to English-language readers some of the background to Jung's early years and early work that can be dug out of Zumstein-Preiswerk's book. I am not in a position either to check on her sources or to transmit her fictionalized style; I am merely setting forth (by transferring to page numbers in her book) some notes and implications that might be of particular interest for students of Jung.

Spiritism in Jung, his Ancestors, and his Basel Milieu: One of the author's main themes is that the Jung family—maternal and paternal—was psychic or spiritistic (16–17). But as good a case could be made in reverse; from the information she presents there were as many family members who were rational, sceptical, and scientific (114–15). Jung's personality No. 1— and not only No. 2—has its ancestral background.

To go further, some historical-minded Jungian student ought to do a doctoral dissertation on Jung's doctoral dissertation, so as to analyze the soil from which his work grew. Jung himself records (*MDR*, 98–99) that occultist phenomena described in a book he chanced to come upon in his student years "were in principle much the same as the stories I had heard again and again in the country since my earliest childhood." His most avid—but of course not his only—reading during university years was in spiritualism (ibid.). Zumstein-Preiswerk says that Jung pressed spiritualistic books on his friends (n. 38) and inscribed an edition of

Justinus Kerner's *Seherin von Prevorst* to Helene for her fifteenth birthday in November 1896 (68).

Kerner (1786–1862) was so widely read that in his dissertation Jung refers to him *en passant* without exposition of the book's contents, as if it were common currency (16). Zumstein-Preiswerk also says that table-turning and seances had become the vogue in Basel as elsewhere in Europe at the end of the last century. Jung observes in his dissertation how the medium performed much like Kerner's clairvoyant.

Freud's basic ideas have been placed against the sexual repression and attitudes toward children of Victorian Vienna. Jung's basic ideas about the autonomous complex and its personification might equally be placed against the spiritism of the 1890s. This move would give an added perspective to the origin of the complex theory, the association experiments at Burghölzli presenting only its scientific-empirical elaboration.

By this I am not suggesting that the occult is at the root of Jungian psychology. It is even questionable if it was the occult as such that drew Jung as much as the fact that here was an area tabooed and repressed by the accepted materialism of his day. As his friend of that time, Oeri, says:

> …he had courageously schooled himself, intensively studying occult literature, conducting parapsychological experiments, and finally standing by the convictions he derived therefrom, except where corrected by the result of more careful and detailed psychological studies. He was appalled that the official scientific position of the day toward occult phenomena was simply to deny their existence, rather than to investigate and explain them. For this reason, spiritualists such as Zöllner and Crookes, about whose teachings he could speak for hours, became for him heroic martyrs of science.[7]

The occult as such was never even in his student years the main occupation of Jung. His interest then, just as much later in regard to flying saucers and synchronicity, lay in puzzling through to a *psychological understanding and scientific formulation* for events that lay outside the normal range of academic interest, but not outside the normal range of human experience. What he sought and achieved, already in his doctoral dissertation, was the integration of the parapsychological within a broadened psychological theory.

---

7. Oeri, "Some Youthful Memories of C. G. Jung," 187.

Jung's Mother and the Seances: The first seance took place on an evening in June 1895 (53). Carl was still 19, Helene 13. Jung's mother took part— it was in her living room. All persons present, except for Jung, were female (74). They sat around a table which she had inherited from her father. This table later cracked in two, as did a knife that Jung's mother had also inherited from her father, Samuel (n. 44). As the author points out, the statement in *MDR* (105) that the table came from the paternal side must refer to the father's side of Jung's mother, not his own father.

The author also corrects the impression (*MDR,* 107) that the seances with the medium went on for about two years and were experiments in the academic-empirical sense. She says (93) that they were carried on intermittently between 1895 and 1899 and that they were mainly confined to the family circle, except for occasions (92) when Jung brought along school-friends. Jung himself emphasizes the "family romance" character of the medium's communications in his dissertation (*CW* 1: 63f.), a fact to which the author gives much personal import. Moreover, she says that the sessions were embedded within a host of other parapsychological phenomena: precognitive dreams, spontaneous psychokinesis (table- and knife-breaking), xenoglossia, trance states, etc.

About Jung's mother we read in the Swiss edition of *MDR* (406):

> My mother often told me how she used to have to sit behind her father when he was writing his sermons. He could not bear it that, while he was concentrating, spirits went past behind his back and disturbed him. When a living person sat behind him the spirits were scared off.

Jung's mother supported his work with the occult. This side of Jung, and of Jungian thought subsequently, finds its source in his personality No. 2, which Jung closely associated with his mother. And, as I see it, the occasional factionalism that breaks out regarding the main direction of Jungian psychology can be derived from opposing Jung's two personalities, or the "father complex" and the "mother complex," an opposition that leads to a one-sided scientism oscillating with a one-sided occultism, science and the occult constellating each other. Jung himself not only resolved this sort of opposition in the theory of complexes with its two sources in science and seance. But he moved beyond the simplistic questions of rational versus occult in his psychology of the image. His notion of psychic reality as first of all based on the immediate datum of the image ("image *is* psyche"—*CW*13:75) frees us from nineteenth-century kinds of questions. An image is neither rational nor irrational, to be captured neither by scientific methods nor occultist, but calls first of all for imagination.

The Nietzsche Problem: At the time of the seances, Nietzsche was alive. His *Zarathustra* appeared only some ten or fifteen years previous. Jung's autobiography tells how important Nietzsche was in Jung's youth as a frightening warning to him about personality No. 2 (*MDR*, 102). Zumstein-Preiswerk (82) quotes the version told her by her mother (Helene's close friend) of a seance concerning Nietzsche. Helene reportedly spoke with the voice of her and Jung's grandfather. The voice called out to "Carl" saying that Nietzsche had a pact with the Antichrist and warning against Nietzsche's teachings. (Cf. *CW*1:50—52, where "N" would refer to Nietzsche.)

It is here implied that the medium picked up Jung's own subliminal thoughts and emotions and announced them to him. Much later (during the 1930s) Jung returned to the Nietzsche problem in a major work, his "Zarathustra Seminar." There he analyzed with No.1 that No.2 aspect that long ago had been represented by Nietzsche. What one learns new from Zumstein-Preiswerk's book is the *consistency* in Jung's concerns. His turmoil over Nietzsche was founded not only on psychiatric and mythological (Dionysian)[8] concerns, but it, too, had an ancestral root in the religious convictions of a family spiritus rector that had been voiced long before through Helene.

The Medium and the Repressed: In defense of his dissertation against a review by Hahn, Jung repeats his main thesis regarding occult phenomena: "in a nutshell the splitting off of psychic functions from the ego-complex...and consequently the strong tendency of the psychic elements toward autonomy" (*CW*1:159).

Toward the end of his life, and the end of his autobiography, Jung returned to the questions posed by occult phenomena ("On Life after Death," *MDR*, 322), saying: "In most cases where a split-off complex manifests itself it does so in the form of a personality, as if the complex had a consciousness of itself...I dealt long ago with this phenomenon of personified complexes in my doctoral dissertation."

---

8. Cf. my "Dionysius in Jung's Writings," *Spring: An Annual of Archetypal Psychology and Jungian Thought* (1972): 191—205. Reprinted in *UE*6: *Mythic Figures.*

The messages that came through Helene during the seances were, in Jung's view, from beyond her ego complex, and this beyond was literally projected as "The Beyond." But the material she transmitted in trance state was especially personal, about family matters, giving good ground to his hypothesis that repressed complexes belonging to the medium's personality form the content of the spiritualized voices. For instance, two of the messages concerned the fates of Helene's sisters, Berthi and Dini. The former had gone to Brazil and given birth to a mulatto [i.e., biracial] child (54);[9] the latter, infected by her syphilitic husband (51), had had two miscarriages and a premature son who died shortly after birth (54, 57, 66, 87). Such knowledge of the family shadows was probably a heavy burden for a child, and it forms a main content of her messages.

Another more obscure personification is "Conventi" (CW 1: 60). He was a poltergeist whom Helene supposedly succeeded in banning from the Jung house through various rituals. "Conventi" was, according to Helene, an "Italian murderer" (67). She had been particularly fond of the Italian Renaissance, believing at certain moments that she had lived then as a Princess engaged to Ludovici Sforza. As I have discussed elsewhere,[10] Jung had at least four crucial dreams and experiences in an Italian setting. There is an "Italian" conundrum in his biography, epitomized by his awe-filled statements about Rome and his fainting while buying a ticket to go there (MDR, 278–88). If Jung's life presents a "myth" for our times, as several writers on Jung suggest, then part of understanding this myth requires a deeper exploration of its "Italian" aspect. It seems that some of this had already been foreshadowed by Helene years earlier.

Carl and Helene: For the obvious sake of discretion and medical rectitude, in his dissertation and in the autobiography Jung had disguised the identity of his medium. Zumstein-Preiswerk, however, in her wish

---

9. [In a note to his dissertation, Jung mentions Spinoza's "hypnopompic vision" of a "dirty black Brazilian" (CW 1, p. 59 n. 49). [Both Jung's comment and Hillman's outdated term "mulatto" equate racial diversity with the family "shadow," which is an essentially racist attitude. As Hillman says in a later essay, "White casts its own shadow" ("Notes on White Supremacy: Essaying an Archetypal Account of Historical Events," *Spring: An Annual of Archetypal Psychology and Jungian Thought* [1986])—Ed.].

10. Cf. "Plotino, Ficino, and Vico as Precursors of Archetypal Psychology," in my *Loose Ends* (Dallas: Spring Publications, 1975), 160f. Reprinted in *UE* 8: *Philosophical Intimations*.

to lay matters bare also seeks to clarify ambiguities that the disguise may have necessitated. Helene did not die at age 26, nor did her character disintegrate toward the end (MDR, 107). She died two days before her thirtieth birthday, and on the basis of relatives' remembrances and evidence of Helene's handwriting, the author asserts there was no unusual deterioration.

Helene had been one of Jung's childhood playmates (17), and Jung did not know any girls other than his cousins until 1891 or 1892 (aet. 16 or 17) (MDR, 79). Carl was six years and three months older than Helene.

After the seances were concluded, and Jung had gone on to medical school and then Burghölzli (December 10, 1900), Helene and her elder sister Emmy moved to Paris. In the summer of 1902, the year of the publication of his dissertation, Jung went to Paris to study under Janet. Helene was then working in the fashion world as a seamstress near the Madeleine (100). Jung sought her out, accompanied her on an excursion to Versailles, drove with her in a two-horse carriage and, on her twenty-first birthday, took her and two of her sisters to the theater (102). A facsimile of his note to her is appended in the book. It has not been published before. In my translation it reads:

> Paris II.I.03
> rue Casimir Delavigne
> Hotel des Baleens
>
> Dear Helene!
>
> Since this evening I am back in one piece at my hotel and want to ask you if during the week you really have no time evenings. I'd like to chat with you and fix a date for theater. If you don't have time, then I suggest next Sunday evening at 7☐ in front of the Sarah Bernhardt theater. They will probably be doing *Théroigne de Méricourt,* which is very beautiful. *Résurrection* at the Odeon is rather grander and *Le Joug* at Mme. Réjane's funnier. I'll go along with whatever you wish. I'd like very much to see you once more this week, for a week from Monday, that is on 19-I, I leave for London. From there I probably will go over Ostende straight home for my coming wedding on 14-II.
>
> Wouldn't it be possible for you to be at the Madeleine Wednesday evening at 8 ¼?
>
> Please, send me a little note about both suggestions.
>
> With cordial greetings
>
> Your cousin Carl

Would you like to go once to the Grand Opera? That would be really splendid.

Jung returned to Switzerland for his wedding in February 1903; that same autumn Helene (with her sister Vally) opened a fashion boutique in the Aschenplatz in Basel (104). In the spring of 1905, Helene received this note:

> Dear Cousin, may I make your acquaintance? Carl told me lots about you. I also heard that you turn out ladies' clothes with real Parisian chic. Unless I hear from you to the contrary, I'll come by for a fitting.
>
> Emma Jung-Rauschenbach
> (106, my translation)

We do not know if this was the same dress that Jung saw in the dream-vision of his wife after her death. She was "wearing the dress which had been made for her many years before by my cousin the medium. It was perhaps the most beautiful thing she had ever worn" (MDR, 296).

According to the Swiss edition of MDR (406), Jung first met his wife-to-be in 1896, during the time of the experiments and soon after the death of his father. He says she was then about 14 (which was also about Helene's age who was some six months Emma Jung's senior). Jung was "at once absolutely certain" (406) that she would be his wife.

There is another sudden impressive encounter with a young girl told in Jung's memoirs: the Catholic peasant girl with whom he talked while on an excursion to the Bruder Klaus hermitage. As with the first meeting with his wife, here, too, was a "feeling of fatefulness" (MDR, p. 79). As we know from Jung's later writings, this sort of experience occurs when the anima is constellated.

I would hazard the suggestion that because, as he says on this same page, he had not known any other girls save his cousins, the encounter with the peasant girl near Flüeli and with his wife in Schaffhausen—both while on excursions—represented the exogamous, or "stranger" (CW 16: 438), anima image.[11] We may surmise that an endogamous aspect

---

11. I am grateful to Aniela Jaffé for recalling another similar incident involving the "stranger" and exogamy. "At a festival in Zofingen, while dancing in the grand Heitern Platz, Jung fell seemingly hopelessly in love with a young lady from French

had perhaps been carried by Helene, his cousin on his mother's side. For it is also, according to Jung's later theory, that the first anima figures are endogamous and closely associated with the mother.

Transference and Kinship Libido: These reflections on the anima bring out in my estimation one of the main implications of Zumstein-Preiswerk's book. The book intends toward the view that Jung's own latent occultist capacities were experienced through their embodiment in his younger cousin. The author (p. 36) calls attention to Jung's own spiritistic capacities as witnessed throughout the autobiography. It is implied that Jung later integrated the gift of his endogamous anima, no longer requiring that it be experienced through projective rapport with Helene.

By rapport I mean the close sympathy bordering on undifferentiated *participation mystique* between experimenter and his subject, which is a part of the necessary conditions for successful work in the parapsychological field. That Zumstein-Preiswerk turns this rapport between Jung and Helly into a suppressed love story, with Helly pining to death, tubercular like an operatic Mimi, may be required by her style of telling the tale but it is not required for our understanding of this background to Jung's work. Love is only one way of experiencing *participation mystique*; insight is another. Jung himself mentions (*MDR*, 50–51) his gift for *participation mystique*, connecting it with his personality No. 2 and with his mother. He recognized both the value of such close rapport for insight and its danger for undifferentiated identifications. Hence, he is supposedly the first to have urged on Freud that the analyst be analyzed, and throughout agreed with Freud about the importance of transference ("The main problem of medical psychotherapy is the transference. In this matter Freud and I were in complete agreement"—*MDR*, 212). That there was "transference," "*participation mystique*," or "love" between Jung and his medium is only to be expected.

This returns us to another of the seed ideas I mentioned above that are to be found in these early years: Jung's view of the transference. If we look at his essay on that subject—published in 1946, fifty years after the seances with his cousin!—we see that he bases transference phenomena upon kinship libido, or the endogamous urge that tends toward the sister and is

---

Switzerland. One morning soon after, he entered a shop, asked for and received two wedding rings." (Oeri, "Some Youthful Memories of C.G. Jung," 186).

socially organized through cross-cousin marriage systems. His early experiences and "The Psychology of the Transference" (CW16:431-49) should be placed side by side. For there we read that kinship libido is the instinct, "which serves to hold the family together," as it is also the basis of the *opus major*, the alchemical conjunction. When the anima is unconscious, he says, it appears as a projection and "the carrier of the anima-image is distinguished by magical characteristics." Yet, through these magical projections, "psychic existence becomes reality" (CW16:431-38).

There is a half-spoken accusation in *C. G. Jung's Medium* that Helly died for love of Jung (110) who had left her behind and to die when he no longer needed her for his work. Here, I believe the author, through sympathetic identification with her subject, has become entangled in the sympathetic magic of transference and the transference problem of her ancestors.

When we are invited to see Jung against the background of his relation with his medium, then we must go further and see them both against the background of those times. Social history would tell us of the *Schwärmerei* of young girls for older males in the family, of the inordinate respect shown by the less educated for the more educated, of the experimental subject's desire to please the man of science. The syndrome of the age—and Charcot, Freud, and Breuer were also in its coils—was hysteria.

For understanding the Helly portrayed in this book, again Jung on the transference is helpful. He writes of the longing created by the endogamous tendency and the necessity of its internalization through sacrifice (438). He says further: "If, however, the projection is broken, the connection—whether it be negative (hate) or positive (love)—may for the time being collapse so that nothing seems to be left...Sooner or later, here or in some other place, it will present itself again, for behind the [transference] problem there stands the restless urge towards individuation" (447). This book presents the transference problem eighty years later in a new place—or rather, personalistically displaced. For the ethos of the personal relationship between these two first cousins in their teens and early twenties cannot be faulted, nor should it be measured by standards of today. That individuation took one course in his life and another in hers also cannot be attributed to their relationship.

But above all, their personal relationship cannot be held to account for the transpersonal phenomena, later to be called transference, the idea of which was then completely unknown. (The "history of transference"—from

Bernheim and Charcot, through the agonies of Breuer and Freud, and the tragedies of Jung and Honegger, as well as its appearance in spiritism between the 1880s until about 1915—is still to be written). What this relationship does help account for, however, is some of the background in Jung's experience for his idea of transference. Further, we can see the way his process of individuation consistently interiorized phenomena of his youth, transforming them into late psychological theory.

However, if we read about the early years of Jung's personal life in order to understand the later years of his theoretical life, we have the cart before the horse, and are working reductively, personalistically. To understand early Jung, we must read late Jung. To understand events of 1896, we must turn to his writing of 1946.

The Goethe Legend: In a seven-page, small-print appendix, the author attempts to lay to rest the legend that Jung was a descendent on his father's side from an illegitimate liaison of Goethe's. She goes to some pains to reconstruct both the impossibility of the affair in Goethe's life at that time and the need for this legend in Jung's family. (The whole issue had already been carefully dealt with by Aniela Jaffé [*MDR*, 35n.1]. However, the appendix does remind the reader that Helene, in one of her trances, presented herself (through her larger personality, Ivenes, [*CW*1:63]) as having been seduced by Goethe. By thus impersonating Jung's legendary ancestor, she enacted a piece of the Jung family myth, again emphasizing the kinship libido between them.

This legend is important—as legend. And as legend it is not meant to be proved or disproved, but psychologically understood. The statement by Jung that "My godfather and authority was the great Goethe himself" (*MDR*, 87) is not to be taken literally: godfather as ancestral sire. The Goethe story shows the importance of family legend as a means of "mythologizing" (Jung's term) the burdens of inheritance, and the legend shows the autonomous psychic need for ancestor worship. An individual fate requires more than the individual to carry it; it calls up legendary figures, "ancestors." Jung himself has now become one of these legendary ancestors—witness two subtitles of recent biographies: "His Myth for Our Times" (Marie-Louise von Franz)[12] and "The Story in Our Time"

---

12. *C.G. Jung: His Myth in Our Time* (New York: C.G. Jung Foundation for Analytical Psychology, 1975).

(Laurens van der Post).[13] This returns us to our starting point in these notes: the interplay between fact and fiction.

❀

The book could lead the reader astray into that fruitless question that besets the rational mind reading any biography: how much is fact and how much is fiction, and where the line between them? But the entire question of biographical accuracy is one not only of fact, or history, but also one of imagination that feels into the case at hand.

How accurate Zumstein-Preiswerk is in her *Einfühlungsvermögen* is for the reader to decide. But the question of historical accuracy is not of main interest.

There have been other attempts to lift the disguise from figures in the past of depth psychology. Freud's "Anna O." or Bertha Pappenheimer is only one well-known example. From the beginnings of psychotherapy, case histories required a new style of writing, a new fictional form.[14] Jung's disguise of Helene into the "S.W." of his dissertation is neither an assault on her character nor a distortion of "facts." It is, rather, a mode of fictionalizing required by the new field that had to develop a new form of writing about psychological persons. As Freud said at the beginning of his first major case presentation, this kind of writing is close to the *roman à clef*. It is curious to see that Zumstein-Preiswerk's attempt to set the factual record straight makes use of even a more fictionalized mode.

This says something about psychological writing. It is not "scientific" or "historical," but "legendary," or better, it is most scientifically historical (ethically honest and objectively accurate) when it takes full account of the personifying, myth-making imagination. Somehow we in depth psychology have to learn that the psyche, as Jung says, "mythologizes" and, in doing so, it continually factualizes fictions and fictionalizes facts.

Whether Helene is worth the book, or the book this review, is questionable. For surely it is not Helene Preiswerk who is fundamentally of interest, it is C.G. Jung; and she has been rediscovered only because of him. One could easily lose the sense of proportion and forget the immense

---

13. *Jung and the Story of Our Time* (New York: Pantheon Books, 1975).

14. Cf. my "The Fiction of Case History" in *Religion as Story*, edited by J.B. Wiggins (New York: Harper Colophon, 1975), 123–73.

difference between them, even then in their youth. For the giftedness of a medium and the giftedness of a Jung bespeak two very different kinds of gift. If it is true that Jung derived much from working with Helene, how much more did she derive from working with him? But this the book overlooks in attempting to vindicate her at his expense, a vindication not required in the first place.

What does remain of deepest interest—and we can thank *C.G. Jung's Medium* for reminding us again—is the importance in the origin of depth psychology of these unusual women, whether those investigated by Charcot in Paris, Bernheim in Nancy, Freud in Vienna, or Jung in Basel. It was they who embodied psychic reality. And it was this fascination with the "magic" of psychic reality as embodied in these young women, such as Helene Preiswerk, that bespeaks the anima that was emerging via these pioneers of medical psychology into our age of psychotherapy.

Connections and Separations

4

FRIENDS AND ENEMIES

Introduction

Our theme, Friends and Enemies, is not a topic of the day. It is not a subject exciting attention either among psychologists or the literate laity. As collective cultural phenomena, part of the repertoire of the contemporary man, Friendship and Enmity have fallen into disuse. This is, of course, nothing new to us; like the fading arts of conversation, letter writing, telling of tales, and walking, there is neglect of the arts of friendship and enmity—and there is occasional complaint. The latest—probably familiar to you—is that from C.S. Lewis in his *The Four Loves.*[1]

Proving the decline is hardly necessary. We need only recall the role friendship played in antiquity: Plato, Plutarch, Seneca; Aristotle's *Ethics,* which gives two of the ten books to it; Cicero's long treatise. Again it was a topic of the day in the Renaissance and the Romantic period, times marked by the friendships of great men as well as by an interest in friendship itself. And enmity, too, from that described in the Elizabethan theater to the rivalries of the nineteenth-century industrial robber barons, has shown a corresponding decline. Just as we need not make out a case to show the decline, so, too, we need not occupy ourselves here discussing the historical, social, and cultural aspects of this decline.

What interests us about this falling off in friendship and enmity, is how it might be tied up with the general theme of the Shadow Problem. I mean by this: might it be possible that topics that concern psychologists so much—things like transference, ego development, homosexuality, power; resistance and hostility—could be thought about again in terms of this rather old-fashioned frame: Friends and Enemies.

---

1. C.S. Lewis, *The Four Loves* (New York: Harcourt Brace, 1960), ch. 4: "Friendship."

Objections might be raised right here at the outset. Granted that the topic does not receive attention in the daily world; but analysts, and especially Jungian analysts, do give attention to it and some of their work might be taken as attempting its revival.

Unfortunately, I do not think this is altogether the case. Jung's work on the shadow illumines friendship and enmity from a new direction; but our theme as such is not given much attention in Jung's works. Harding's *The Way of All Women* takes it up,[2] and there is a chapter devoted to friendship in Bertine's *Human Relationships*.[3] But psychologists, Jungians included, seem to approach the subject either from below in terms of projections, shadow, dependency or from above on a moral uplifting level of "relationships." Psychologists find friends to be really necessary; one cannot live in a vacuum; friends and enemies help us realize our shadows, discover projections, and our feeling function, and so on. I think just this sort of removal of the stuff and gut of friendship and enmity to the level of relationships, this psychologizing, has helped in our time to increase the intellectualism, the autoeroticism, and the suspicion that make friendship most impossible.

I regret using Dr. Bertine's book, for which I have great respect, as point here, but this passage may show what I mean.

So begins the part on friendship: "The subject of the present chapter leads to the heart of psychological relatedness as a conscious achievement." To friendship she gives top value, and she defines it more or less with the following passage:

> When I speak of psychological relationship, I mean one in which there is not only affection but understanding also, and a serious attempt to become aware of the real nature of the libido constellated in the situation, such as shadow reactions, hidden or half-admitted personal motives, complexes that may distort, type differences that may becloud, and archetypal patterns that may influence the mutual feelings and reactions. This effort to become conscious in the living situation is important that communion may be released from needless interference and the relation may thus attain its full potential of development.[4]

---

2. Mary Esther Harding, *The Way of All Women* (New York: Harper & Row, 1970).

3. Eleanor Bertine, *Human Relationships: In the Family, In Friendship, In Love,* with a foreword by C.G. Jung (New York: David McKay, 1958).

4. Ibid., 193.

This is a noble aim indeed, and the very core of "conscious relationship," but is it friendship? As long as we are figuring out what is going on in a friendship, and having it for the sake of our own process, and examining personal motives, complexes, types, projections, etc., are we not just increasing intellectualism, autoeroticism, and suspicious distrust? This may not be the meaning Dr. Bertine meant with this passage, but I do believe that analysts in encouraging relationships are, at the same time, doing their bit against friendship.

A look at the two words might help bring· out what I mean. *Friendship* has its root in the old Teutonic and old-English *freojan*—to love. The equivalent in the Romance languages is *amitié*—from *amicus, anare,* again: to love. The background is the same in Greek: *philos.*

Relate on the other hand has a major group of connotations that give it an intellectual cast: to recount, tell, narrate; to refer back, to something in law; to refer to a book; the particular way in which one thing is thought of in connection with another, as in logic.

We have relationships, and we can relate. We have friendships, but we cannot friend.—The only verb that applies (unless we want to drag in "befriend") is to love. Friendship touches something: less conscious, less moral, less verbal; it is an emotional event.

As such, it is something simpler than relationship. As Thomas Aquinas says it: "Friendship is love simply speaking."[5] It happens as love happens and has something unconscious about it. It goes beyond relationship; or relationship, as a conscious piece of work in the sense of Dr. Bertine, is a step toward it, is necessary for it. But friendship is the finer, because it is the more simple, more emotional.

To use a tale from the Master: when a group of us went out to Jung's house as students, he veered away from the main point of our seminar and spoke about the necessity of working day and night at becoming conscious of everything, and then he said, there is a time when one becomes unconscious again, but then in the right way. I think this is what I mean about relationship and friendship, and that carrying on the conscious effort too long, relating too strenuously, kills friendship.

So, not only by writing, and talking about relationships and relating, and by not writing and talking about friendships and loving, do analysts

---

5. Thomas Aquinas, *Summa Theologica,* I–II, q. 26, art. 4.

contribute to the decay of friendship, but they seem to neglect enemies and hating—in their writings at least—altogether.

In the passage quoted from Dr. Bertine, only one half of the theme is taken up. What about the other half: enmity? Here we come upon something curious: How many analysts have ever heard an analysand refer to someone in a dream or in his life as an enemy? We do not like Smith or Jones, he may be a rival in a job or another member of a triangle, but there is not that sense of personal complicatedness, of unremitting, fateful bound-upness that "enemy" implies. We have interiorized our enemies, and we fight them in a peculiarly personalized way as the body, the animus, regressions, power drives. But the implacable hatred and sense of keenwittedness (Plutarch declares that enemies keep us on guard and sharp), the constant struggle with the outer enemy seems to occur only in family problems—with the parents or brother-in-law, or wife, or her lawyer. Perhaps, one must be altogether redeemed from the family, not just to have friends, but even more, to have enemies. Perhaps enemies require quite a bit of ego development, and the ability to have enemies might be a sign of a sound ego. The reverse might also be true. Family problems become overloaded with inauthentic love and hatred, because there is so little other personal opportunity for these emotions in our times.

How many marriage problems—the enmity that develops, the daily hatreds, quarrels, feuds, battles—could be due to enmity finding no other outlet? And how great are the demands of friendship made from husband or wife, demands that ought perhaps not be so concentrated in one place? The fear that all outside relationships weaken the marriage is true enough in the early years when "forsaking all others" is the code. But is marriage the place for every aspect of human love and hatred? Marriage has become burdened by the retreat from other forms of relating. So long as all intimacy among the same sex is hounded as "homosexuality," and all intersexual intimacy is taken only as a prospective "affair"—because of the decay of friendship—marriage has become the only safe place; it must carry everything. Marriage expectations—constant confidences, comfort in trouble, complete understanding, mutual stimulation and sharing—prove illusory because these are rather the expectations of friendship. Marriage requires some persona, closed districts, and barriers of defense, while it is friendship, according to the ancient writers and modern ones (the Germans, Bacon, Emerson, Thoreau), which offers total openness.

Continuing, I have wondered if analysts have taken enemies enough into account. Friendships might be encouraged as a "good" in the value system of individuation, but "enemies" one is supposed to be able to analyze away. They tend to be taken on the subjective level only, to be worked through as shadow projections, integrated. As if to say that one should make friends and integrate enemies. Right here, the analyst, if he takes up this position, prevents one of the ways in which tragedy can reach us. For the enemy, the personal antagonist who is an instrument of fate, is fundamental to the tragic sense of life. As I was working on these ideas, I read of two farmers near Zurich, feuding neighbors, one 59 and the other 66, who had been enemies for years. Finally, they exchanged words and had it out in a field; one strangled the other and was led off to the law.

Events like these are so rare in our civilization that we immediately presume something pathological, yet one also feels deep reverberations of something ancient and archetypal. What is the archetypal background of this basic form of interpersonal relations? This is, of course, a subject all in itself, requiring not only study of the concepts of friendship and enmity in antiquity—the way I have proceeded—but also its manifestations in biography, mythology, and literature.

One clue to its archetypal meaning is given by astrology. The seventh house or descendent is opposite to the first house or ascendent. It refers to the alter ego, the Opposite, thus to forms of *partnership* in marriage, society, and business. It refers, as the astrologer Alan Leo puts it, to Friends and Enemies, for the relationship with the Other can go in either direction even though it remains, whether friend or enemy, under the aegis of Venus.[6] This aspect of relationship is clearly differentiated in astrology from the fifth house and the eleventh house where other aspects of Eros appear, and with the eighth house and the twelfth where other aspects of Hostility appear. The seventh house concerns the other as peer, as fundamental opposite, either as partner or as antagonist, as the archetype of the fateful Other to whom one is married for life.

The companion, the partner, the antagonist, friend, enemy—are all faces of the Other, and the other in the last instance is also the Self.

---

6. See Alan Leo and H.S. Green, *The Horoscope in Detail,* Astrological Manuals No. IV) (London, 1906), ch. 8: "Love and Marriage. Friends and Enemies."

Jung puts it like this: "I conjecture that the treasure is also the 'companion,' the one who goes through life at our side—in all probability a close analogy to the lonely ego who finds a mate in the self, for at first the self is in the strange non-ego. This is the theme of the magical travelling companion."[7]

The personal yet *impersonal* aspect of this Other, this "impersonal Other," is fundamental to an understanding of it. Our friends are not those whom we might wish to have as friends ideally chosen. They are those who happen to be one's friends; people who fell into one one's life due to circumstances. And this, often like much else of our fate, has its origins in childhood. So that even when we begin a new friendship later on in life, there comes a time when that, too, gets to be rooted in childhood, through confession and traveling back together into each other's is past.

If we take the other as fortuitous, as necessity, not a matter of choice, then it can't be shaken off or laid aside at will. And there remains a strong bond between the two that calls for mutual obligations. Marriage formalizes these obligations; so do business partnerships. In antiquity, friendship and enmity were also so formalized with customs. Scholastic philosophy differentiates at least twenty-nine kinds of friendship, as, for instance, blood kinship, friendships among pilgrims, among warriors, among civil citizens, between man and God, between equals and unequals; useful ones, pleasurable ones, and so on. These definitions provide frameworks, similar to the rules in the Chinese *Book of Rites (Liji)* between brothers and between other family members.

This obligation between friends helps account for the feelings of frustration and betrayal, of paradise lost, when we meet again an old friend who has not moved along the ways we have moved. Each differentiation in the ego requires a corresponding differentiation in the other, whether between friends or between opponents like Holmes and Moriarty. Thus, as we grow, we spur our friend or enemy to grow too. His failure to keep up is bitter.

Aristotle writes:

> But if one friend remained the same while the other became
> better and far outstripped him in virtue, should the latter treat

---

the former as a friend? Surely he cannot. When the interval
is great, this becomes most plain, e.g., in the case of childish
friendships—if one friend remained a child...while the other
became a fully developed man.[8]

This implies that it behooves us to make new friends, since friends are
a good and old friends can fall away, But the point we have been laboring
is that friends can't be "made"; we make relationships, but friends happen.
Or, rather, they can happen if we can recognize the feelings of friendship when they arise, and fulfil the obligations of friendship so as not to
destroy or lose what is happening. Hence it would seem that the art of
having friends is an awareness of friendship feelings by the admission of
friendship love, which too much psychological acuity can kill.

At this point, let us build a platform so that we can take off from here
for the next stage. The platform has these main planks: Friendship and
Enmity are basic to human life. They have fallen into disuse, or into the
unconscious. Thus we are not sure how to be with friends or enemies, nor
are we sure in our feelings about when, or when not, friendship or enmity
is actually going on.

The next stage then is this: Can this disused capacity be dug out and
freshly developed, and how?

Now one of the several rules in depth psychology concerns just those
abilities or contents that are not being employed by consciousness. They
are said to undergo alterations. They become first of all shadow problems,
that is, they become more childish, more sexualized, more brutish, familial, compulsive, sentimental, automatic, labile, ambivalent, symbolic, and
so on. In short, they begin to get nasty.

So when we begin to dig out our capacity to have friends and enemies,
we shall find this capacity encrusted over and mixed with the shadow
problems of the day.[9] Separating things out of the shadow, of course,
requires getting the feel of the different strands, and being able to recognize each thing for what it is. Otherwise, we are likely to call friendship *in
statu nascendi* something else and miss it altogether.

Not recognizing it falsifies it, and is perhaps, too, one reason why
some knotty issues seem so irreducible; it might be genuine friendship

8. Aristotle, *Nicomachean Ethics* 9.3.

9. [See Hillman's essay "Jung's Contribution to 'Feelings and Emotions'" in this
volume for a discussion of this capacity.—Ed.]

or enmity burgeoning. Thus this basic pattern of relationship might be taken into account as well as those others like parent-child, teacher-pupil, doctor-patient, lover-beloved, siblings, which get so much more attention.[10] It is to this task, the task of differentiating friendship and enmity from what it appears as and looks like and gets muddled with, that the second part of this talk will be devoted. And the special fields where our theme is relevant are homosexuality, aggression, transference, and training.

Homosexuality

The awakening of love of a man for another man today is a highly problematic matter. At once a feeling of this sort gets named homosexual, and unless the man is a practicing homosexual, or has come to terms with his own homosexuality in a sophisticated and analytical way, he is afraid.[11] He stamps down on these feelings; and not taking pains to differentiate what is felt, he calls them what the jargon of the day calls them. Recognizing *non*-homosexual love is then the task; and it is easier to recognize homosexual feelings first, because they are set in a more differentiated system of signs and signals. There is a language, mannerisms and manners, a "gentleman's code" if you will, which gives one the chance to recognize in oneself and others what is going on. (This is brought out in case reports, in the sociological studies of homosexuality, and in the micro-analysis by Ray Birdwhistell in Pennsylvania.[12] For instance, one can look at a stranger in the eye only for an exact length of time, a few seconds, else it is an advance, sexual or aggressive.)

Thus the differentiation of the feelings of friendship bear paying attention to, or they get mislabeled and repressed, and can then become just what they were not intended to become—sexualized, owing to this repression.

The first and evident difference—that of sexual contact—is not really, very useful at the beginning when the feelings awaken and when, as we

10. [See Gustavo Barcellos's *The Sibling Archetype: The Psychology of Brothers and Sisters and the Meaning of Horizontality* (Thompson, Conn.: Spring Publications, 2016).—Ed.]

11. [This paper was first delivered as a lecture in October, 1961 at the Analytical Psychology Club annual conference. The current version was completed in 1962.—Ed.]

12. Ray L. Birdwhistell, *Kinesics and Context: Essays on Body Motion Communication* (Philadelphia: University of Pennsylvania Press, 1970).

said, because of repression and shadow contamination, they might well have a sexual cast. In antiquity, much attention was given to the difference. In discussing the Academy and education in Greece, opinions have gone between two extremes. In the nineteenth century, the *paiderastia* side of relationships was covered over, for instance, by Benjamin Jowett, Plato's major English translator. In this century, there is a tendency to reduce all forms of love, including friendship, to sexuality. This position was advanced by the Epicureans, who found friendship fundamentally a form of sexual attraction and the desire of love to be due to the accumulation of semen.[13] One is reminded of Freud's early theories expressed in his letters to Fliess.

Whatever the practices in Greek social life, the philosophers continued to strive at differentiating friendship love from homosexual love. For Socrates, all physical love was base; ruled by the vulgar side of the goddess; celestial love, ruled by the lighter side of the goddess, was friendship. Thus love in the physical sense, rooted in the desire for procreation, was not really love. Love and friendship were opposites.[14]

Plato, too, sought reformation through education and through law, in order to elevate homosexual love into friendship. Aristotle separated the two even further: finding love to have a natural basis (procreation), he was even more severe on pederasty. For him, friendship had nothing to do with homosexual love. For Aristotle, friendship consisted in loving, and loving in a personal, intimate way. Aristotle succeeded in joining opposites that Plato held wide apart. For Plato, there was on the one hand personal, bodily love, and that was homosexuality, and on the other hand impersonal ideal love, rational love (later called Platonic love), for the Eidos, Beauty, the Good. Aristotle laid the groundwork for the modern view of friendship by stating that friendship was personal and intimate, but also noble and rational, beautiful and good. For Aristotle, it was "one soul in two bodies" (Diogenes Laertius). Because friendship love was already in the union of the soul, the bodily union was not relevant. This was an important advance on Plato, whose famous image of two halves roaming· the world looking for each other implied two bodies and two souls, requiring soul union concurrent with bodily union.

---

13. Lucretius, *De rerum Natura* IV.
14. Xenophon, *Banquet,* 8.10.

I believe this notion of rational love, both personal and intimate, yet still not sexual, is what we boggle at today. We can't conceive of the personal and intimate between two men without suspicions of something else. Take this passage from Thomas Aquinas: "The lover is not content with superficial knowledge of the beloved, but strives for intimate discovery and entrance."[15] How does that strike our modern ear?

If we use C.S. Lewis as guide to English notions of friendship, then my guess that the personal and intimate is too sticky for moderns seems right. He uses this image: Lovers stand face to face and gaze into each other's eyes; friends stand side by side and face down the same road. Friends share interests; lovers share each other.

Lewis says:

> In a circle of true Friends each man is simply what he is: stands for nothing but himself. No one cares twopence about any one else's family, profession, class, income, race or previous history. Of course you will get to know about most of these at the end. But casually. They will come out bit by bit...never for their own sake.[16]

This sort of "pub" friendship seems particularly English; Santayana's years among the Anglo-Saxons put him in the same vein. He says that a friend is not the keeper of his friend's soul.[17] Intimacy is out.

The Romantic notion of friendship would have none of this. Intimacy was all. This line appears most lately in the Existentialist Ludwig Binswanger, who also uses the image of looking into each other's eyes.[18] He finds this not at all unbearable, but the very hallmark of friendship. Let us recall—"And the Lord spake unto Moses face to face, as a man speaketh unto his friend" (Exodus 33:11).

Well, where are we? What are the criteria of friendship that mark it off from homosexuality?

First of all, the sense of *urgency*. Friendship, according to the ancient writers, though a great joy, was never ruled by what they called the

---

15. Thomas Aquinas, *Summa Theologica*, I–II, q. 28, art. 2.

16. Lewis, *The Four Loves*, 70.

17. George Santayana, *The Life of Reason or The Phases of Human Progress* (New York: Charles Scribner's Sons, 1921), 152: "He is distinctly not his brother's keeper, for the society of friends is free."

18. Ludwig Binswanger, *Grundformen und Erkenntnis menschlichen Daseins* (Zurich: Max Niehans Verlag, 1953), ch. 1.

involuntary appetites. It was a bond formed in freedom; unlike erotic love with its compulsion. The hours and hours friends spend together do not have to mean disguised, latent homosexuality, when we remember that in antiquity, friendship called for actual living together.

Secondly, there must be an *equality* of interest in each other. Friendship develops *au pair;* there is not the suddenness of falling in love, where the other might be quite indifferent, thus becoming but an object, an image carrier.

Third, there is an obligation between friends; constancy is perhaps the best word, while homosexual love is supposedly characterized by fickleness and promiscuity. Feelings of affection that continue, even when the friendship itself has loosened, or even after one member has died, represent typical friendship phenomena—and must not be cast down as "sentimentality." Gertrude Stein's famous phrase would not suit· Aristotle, Cicero, or· Seneca. She says: "Before the flowers of friendship faded, friendship faded."[19] For the classical authors, friendship was not so fickle that it faded. Those that do fade, as those made in childhood, nevertheless demand attention for the flowers. Aristotle says, one must keep remembrance of the former intimacy and feel an obligation to the former friend, even with attempts at reform, and come to his assistance as one would help one whose physical property is in danger of bankruptcy.

The friend is thus a tie to one's past and roots one in reality, while homosexual love lives mainly for the present. Whereas homosexual love delights in youth, the cult of the body, and so fears aging, friendship was always regarded as the virtue of maturity.

If the key to the ancient notion of friendship is a rational and voluntary kind of love, the model of which is the love of God of the philosopher (not of the passionate mystic), then I believe we are speaking of the characteristics of the *anahata* region of the Kundalini Yoga. Friendship would then be an affair of the heart, and above the diaphragm, where events may pain more but burn less. It remains a physical, bodily reality—so that friends well enjoy proximity, eating, living, drinking—all activities together. They embrace on seeing each other again, and even hold hands in some cultures; but the emotion is from the chest rather than the pelvis.

19. Gertrude Stein, *Before the Flowers of Friendship Faded Friendship Faded, Written on a Poem by Georges Hugnet* (Paris: Plain Edition, 1931).

And it would be the analyst's job to hold himself from labeling these emotions, for they may get permanently damned below the diaphragm, prevented thus from being expressed in the region of their goal.

Aggression

It may be evident to my elders and betters, but it has only just recently dawned on me that in today's world there is more room for acting out sexuality than for acting out aggression. Adler and power get less attention than Freud and sexuality. The ancients recognized both equally, calling them the irascible and concupiscent appetites. But today repression is rather one-sided, and we are more likely to find ourselves locked up for assault and battery than for fornication or adultery.

At the same time that individual aggression is banned and lived vicariously through mass entertainments or disguised in symptoms, it appears in collective life as a mark of the times.

I am obliged to tie this problem in with my theme, and to find cause for the decline of individual (that is, personal) and the rise of collective (that is, impersonal) aggression in the decay of enmity as a fine art. It is not altogether dead; there is a revival moving upon us, and as usual through the back door of Eastern cults, e.g., judo and karate; and from below, in the peculiar codes of gang honor and the loyalties of delinquents.

The rigorous laws that obtain in most nations against laying hands on another person, the scarcity of practicing witches who can put a spell, and the banning of the duel have caused a great gap. Not only have we lost someone upon whom to vent physical violence, not only have we lost one of the ways of measuring ourselves, but we have lost sets of skills and rituals for developing the art of aggression, for managing hostility. This is also true in the nonphysical media: there is a falling off in cursing, satire, lampooning, yellow journalism of the scurrilous, libelous sort, political scorn, and even in vituperous scientific, literary, and religious argument.

The decline in enmity cannot be due only to Christian ethics. A more Christian age—say Elizabethan England or Renaissance Italy—saw also more enmity, and more awareness of its rituals and skills: poisoning, plotting, imprisonment, ransom, revenge, family debts, and blood feuds. Nevertheless, when comparing Jewish, Greek, and Roman attitudes with the Christian, we find nothing in the older traditions like "turning the other cheek." The maxim in antiquity was: "Do good unto your friends and evil unto your enemies." Ludovic Dugas, whose work on this subject is most thorough, finds that antique morality does not seriously consider charity in the Christian sense.[20] It accepts wholeheartedly the right to hate one's enemies.

Plutarch's treatise on the usefulness of enemies (*Moralia*, II) brings this out. Hatred is the other side of love, and one cannot renounce hatred without renouncing love. Although hatred is an evil, it is the condition for the greatest good—a necessary evil required for love. There was furthermore a sort of psychological hygiene in those notions: according to Plutarch, each of us has a certain amount of hatred and jealousy in our hearts, and it is best to let this out on our enemies. He says that skilled gardeners plant garlic and onions besides violets and roses to draw off the malodorousness, Acting out enmity is a catharsis. Consciously carried out evil in accordance with arts and rituals, like sticking pins in a fetish, prevents the accumulation of it in the unconscious.

Of the more common inimical motives, *jealousy* and *revenge*, at least, are worth a closer look. Jealousy is one of the few last places where meeting the personal opponent is still admitted in our culture. Skills and rituals still obtain there: spying, private detectives, even homicide as *crime passionnel*. The theme occupied the ancients, and the French moralists in the eighteenth century, as well as the tragedians. To see it in this light, as a phenomenon in itself of majestic terror, as a form of enmity, might be more valuable psychologically than trying to reinterpret jealousy with our contemporary kit of hidden dependencies, instincts, power drives, possessiveness, Oedipal flashbacks, sexual inadequacies, and the like. It is altogether possible that one is jealous not only because of the woman in the case but also because *we need an enemy*, an enemy to contend with day and night, in thought and action—the "other" who both sets the limits to my life in its inmost and wounding point, and yet who challenges me to my utmost potentiality.

In considering vengeance, we are brought up against the conflict in moralities mentioned before. Is it Christian? Is it a virtue or a vice? We find St. Thomas sayings, "Vengeance is a special virtue." He is able to come to this conclusion after a careful bit of reasoning. He writes:

20. Ludovic Dugas, *L'Amitié antique* (Paris: Félix Alcan, 1914).

> Vengeance consists in the infliction of a penal evil on one who has sinned. Accordingly, in the matter of vengeance, we must consider the mind of the avenger. For if his intention is directed chiefly to the evil of the *person* on whom he takes vengeance and rests there, then his vengeance is altogether unlawful: because to take pleasure in another's evil belongs to hatred, which is contrary to charity whereby we are bound to love all men...If however the avenger's intention be directed chiefly to some good, to be obtained by means of the punishment of the person who has sinned...then vengeance may be lawful.[21]

He separates the personal from the impersonal aspects of vengeance. The man whom we punish with revenge is merely the means, the instrument of evil. We are not out to get the man who is our enemy, to put him down because he is he; neither is it a personal matter with the other man in the jealousy triangle. Yes, it is personal in the sense that it is he as he, but it is impersonal because we are meeting there the evil he represents, the position he upholds. In theological language, it is his sin we are fighting. Ultimately, the contender again becomes not this man here but the great adversary, the devil.

Both jealousy and revenge involve one's sense of personal worth and dignity—not prestige. Prestige is of the anima, who can be stung and then become waspishly vindictive. But the man goes beyond this by incorporating these affects of injury into a masculine code and scheme of action. He takes a stand. Thus for jealousy and revenge to move us, we must first have loved someone and stood for something. We must have a position and awareness that there are positions diametrically opposed. This goes against the idea of understanding the other. In fact, the other cannot be understood, and that is just why he is the other, and any failure to accept this is a failure in carrying the tension. The other is a threat, and revenge means carrying this awareness constantly, that same constancy as in friendship. It is living a conscious paranoia—if you will. It might even be that had we more chance for conscious revenge, we would have less paranoid suspicions, querulousness, litigations, counterplots, and petty vindictiveness.

This bears on analytical practice in the following way. Expressions of hostility in "negative transference" are not to be worked through only in

---

21. Thomas Aquinas, *Summa Theologica,* I–II, q. 108.

terms of parental hangovers and resistances. In our time, analysis is one last place where we can maintain and develop a hostile relationship. It is the place where enmity can flourish. We can have an enemy, confront him regularly, and have it out. The affects of jealousy and revenge, of hatred and aggression, by being contained in the analysis can develop, from mere acting out, to skills and rituals, and eventually to the deeper meaning of the tragic sense of being "cabined-cribbed-confined" by the other. In the end, it can come to the realization that the analyst is not you, is truly another, and his influence, his spirit, is enemy to your own. This would be a *via negativa* to individuation, as part of the process of *separatio* and *distillatio* of one's own essence. Might it be that the companion, the secret sharer who was first projected upon the analyst—might also be the secret enemy, the great opponent, the great or last enemy, the Devil or Death with whom one strives as Jacob or Job, whom one can never conquer but with whom one must forever contend?

Ego Development

Before we finish off with a bit about transference and training, we might mention again the relevance of our theme for ego-development.

The egocentricity of creative people is well known—also their desperate hatreds and enmities. As ego development hardens, we should expect enmities to increase. If we take analysis as a creative art, or at least partly so, then enmity among those who practice it is to be expected. It belongs to the properly hardened ego. Even those close to the Self, as lives of saints and sages show, retain implacable hatreds. They fight evil and evil fights them to the end. They do not sit on a rosy cloud of love, understanding all, pardoning all.

I noticed in the cases of three young men, one Swiss, one English, one American—one 24, one 27 and one 29—that soon after they had begun their analysis (within the first four months in each case), they had all managed to get themselves into a fight. One picked on a hotel porter and then a movie usher; another quarreled with a taxi driver· and gave him a beating; the third fell into argument with a stranger on a safety island waiting for a tram, and they exchanged punches. All three of these young men had not had any fights for years, not since they had been schoolboys. This acting out of hostility, the psychopathic shadow or what you will, went along with an increase of awareness of themselves, of their own identity, which they weren't going to let anyone push around. Such enemies are primitive; they do not represent challenges to principles or to a code of honor. But somehow for these three young men, having it out, physically, was an affirmation of their own identities. They had to meet the other to find themselves. Further, it challenged their will to win and the ability to take risks. This aspect of ego development has to do with the capacity to handle one's emotion; to be willing to stand for the emotion and risk consciously its consequences. In all three cases, the fights went parallel to handling emotion in other situations: sexual relations, with the parents, with the boss.

Transference

The question before us is: how can we notice when an analytical relationship is becoming a friendship? And another: could it be possible that the emotion of friendship could lead the analytical relationship out of some of the transference/countertransference blocks? This would only be possible if we could see some of the emotions occurring as being authentic to friendship, and further, that friendship is as basic as transference and cannot be reduced to it.

The inability to separate is supposed to be a sign of transference. Yet Aristotle says that friendship withers from separation. Like any faculty, it must be exercised. The difficulty in separating from an analyst has, of course, many grounds. But I would here propose this additional one: genuine friendship emotion. And I believe the desire to do something together—found a club, a clinic, a journal—is a classical manifestation of friendship longings. Friends form groups. This is a hallmark of friendship described again and again from the Pythagoreans to C.S. Lewis. Friends join eagerly with others who share the same point of view. The groups that different analysts have formed, and the enemies they have constellated, from Freud and Jung on, need not be judged always as unresolved transferences. They might be honest-to-God friendships and enmities.

A third place where we might push back, the borders of transference, from usurping too large an area concerns *need*. An analyst who feels joy in the company of an analysand can kill this spontaneous demonstration of need for friendship in himself by calling it countertransference. (The patient kills his joy in a similar way.) This need for friendship has always been recognized as part of basic human needs for the life of virtue. Of course, it can be argued that this need must be met elsewhere—not with analysands. But what about this? If love arises, friendship love, then there it is. Can it or should it be analyzed away?[22]

We are referring here—and this qualification is important—to late stages of analysis, or advanced stages of transference, as for example in the training situation. In the latter stages, especially, two people are supposed to be equals. The two partners might feel that until real equality has been achieved in the relationship, it cannot be a friendship. This is partly illusory. In antiquity, there were strict rules about the relations of friends who were not equals. Equality of friendship has another meaning than the equality arising from social position, activity or passivity, power, age, or natural gift. Cicero defines carefully the duties of the superior and the inferior in a friendship. Thus, the analysand need not strive to equal his older, wiser, more affluent, and influential analyst in the field of their mutual interests in order to achieve equality. The relationship between peers meant for the ancients moral peers. It was a psychological equality. Reinterpreted, it refers to a relationship between two egos in terms of the Self; an equality in the relationship to the Self, not limited by the outer conditions of the egos.

Equality forces intimacy. Intimacy, coming from one side only, distorts the friendship trying to emerge. The demand for intimacy from the analysand and the desire to talk of himself from the analyst, I would tend to see as signs of burgeoning friendship. The analyst can help as midwife by being more revealing about himself. Intimacy must come slowly—too much too soon is as inappropriate to analysis as it is to friendship. Plutarch tells us to be very careful and judicious when choosing a friend, but after the choice is made, then to be completely open and trusting—and truthful.

---

22. [Cf. John Ryan Haule's *The Love Cure* (Thompson, Conn.: Spring Publications, 2023 [1996]), which argues that love in many ways must be constellated, but not literalized and enacted. The "unitive moment" must be followed by the "disunitive moment" in which the analyst and patient reform their separate ego identities following the dissolution and merger that occurs in a loving encounter. Love is only dangerous when it coagulates into literalized sexuality.—Ed.]

If we take analysis as a way of entering into friendship, and the analyst as an eventual friend, the choice of analyst and the way in which the early stages are carried on can be related to Plutarch's observation. Hesitation, uncertainty, scrutiny, and suspicion belong. Resistance to intimacy, to revealing oneself all at once to a stranger who might as well become a foe as a friend, shows good feeling—surely more feeling for the fitting than spilling it all out in a group or from a couch.

Thus, in advanced analysis, when separation is difficult, when there is a joint urge to undertake something together, when there is a joyful need to see each other, when there is equality in the relation to the Self (this of course is highly variable), when there is a demand for increased "intimacy and entrance"—we would have signs of friendship. And these signs may appear long before all transference has been ideally resolved.

I believe that recognizing friendship and seeing how it differs from transference will help us all in a very dark area, so that we can encourage the one and analyze the other.

Training

In antiquity, teaching was a conversation between friends. For Plato, teaching was a generation through the spirit, and love was the principle of this generation. For Socrates and for the Stoic academy, teaching was a form of loving, and friendship was the *conditio sine qua non* of teaching. One teaches others because one loves them, and one teaches only those one loves. Teaching can only be on a friendly, intimate, confidential basis. And finally—it was the Epicureans who brought this out—loyalty to the sage-teacher, a loyalty of friendship; assured loyalty to the doctrine and the school. And this loyalty was reinforced through joint celebrations. The birthday of Epicurus was celebrated each year, and there was a banquet on the twentieth of each month.

Those friendly discussions among intimates, exchanges of ideas and sympathies, investigations through dialogue of objective questions of common interest, were not enough. The masters, Socrates especially, influenced the development of their pupils by the example of character. They lived the representative life and practiced what they preached. Thus there could be no withholding of information about the master's life; for true teaching, his life must be an open book. There is a passage in the apocryphal Platonic dialogue *Theages* that shows the *mana* personality of the teacher:

I will tell you, Socrates…what is incredible, upon my soul, yet true. For I never yet learnt anything from you, as you know yourself: but I made progress, whenever I was with you, if I was merely in the same house, without being in the same room, but more progress, when I was in the same room. And it seemed to me to be much more when I was in the same room and looked at you as you were speaking, than when I turned my eyes elsewhere: but my progress was far the greatest and the most marked whenever I sat beside you and held and touched you.[23]

If teaching depends on friendship, then the development of friendship becomes the key question in developing one's school. The Greeks recognized this and devoted much consideration to the nature of friendship and the ways in which it could be developed. Because teaching so involved love, it could not, of course, be recompensed with money. Thus, one and all, Socrates, Plato, Aristotle, and Xenophon attacked the teachers who charged a fee. These were the Sophists; "Wisdom must be given as love and cannot be sold," says Xenophon.[24] Teacher and pupil were not in a free relationship of buyer and seller, but involved through natural feelings for each other in a liaison. There was a clear distinction between the professional teacher and the teacher in his academy, which reminds us of the Ashram atmosphere.

So we see that many of the issues of today—positive transference and training, of loyalty to a group and its founder, the personality of the master, the question of magical effects, the problem of fees—all were recognized before. We might ask the past what it can tell us to help sort out some of these questions that still are involved in training today. I am assuming that training is teaching—but I imagine that we will agree on this. Training for the profession of analyst is closer to what goes on in today's academics—the universities. Then teaching aimed at the development of self-knowledge, justice, and virtue, rather than mastery of intellectual contents.

I believe that the main point here touches what I have been pleading for all along: recognition of the role of love. We are told that we cannot train another without loving that other and without his loving us. If the analyst's eros is not up to the job, then he will try to avoid admitting it

---

23. Plato, *Theages* 130d–e (trans. W. R. M. Lamb).
24. Xenophon, *Memorabilia* 1.6.13.

into the training situation. But it must be admitted, and this leads the trainer and the trainee to begin their friendship through mutual admission of their own inferiorities. This further implies that friendship actions may be begun before transference issues are all cleared up.

If we follow the old sages to the letter, there can be neither fees, nor secrets, and one must live together in a communistic Ashram or Kibbutz. Modern depth analysis has brought a refinement of this cult-forming tendency. Fees, privacy, and physical distance provide limits—but it might be that some of the intensities of nearness and intimacy (and escaping fees by meeting outside the appointment) for trainees could be looked at as expressions of developing friendship. Then they might be encouraged for they would be indications of that love necessary for training.

(A postscript on physical "togetherness" in training belongs at this point. I touched on it briefly in an article in *The Journal of Analytical Psychology* while describing the emotional climate at the Zurich Institute.[25] The model for the dancing, eating, traveling, partying together mentioned in that article is something quite basic to training conceived as we are doing here. It is a well-known motif in esoteric teaching: the Zaddik dancing and singing with his pupils; Ramakrishna dancing and singing with his devotees; the Zen masters having their apprentices cook for them, their eating together; the Guru and pupil bathing together, on pilgrimages together...This is a neglected and important theme that we must leave for now.)

Conclusion

Now we are at the end: I have tried to present something different or new. Nowadays, one is more likely to find something new by rummaging around in the past. There are two ways of connecting the past and the present in psychology. One is to take bits of the past and look at them in the light of modern psychology, Jung's work on Alchemy and Mythology is an unsurpassed example here. Another way—the way I have been going here—is to take bits of modern psychology (homosexuality, aggression, transference, training) and look at them in the light of the old philosophies

25. James Hillman, "Training and the C.G. Jung Institute, Zurich," *The Journal of Analytical Psychology* 7, no. 1 (January 1962): 3–19 [and in this volume].

and customs. It is quite possible, I believe, that a great deal of what we are discovering in our work is simply old commonplaces that have become lost. If so, then it might be better to call things what they once were called than to give them new—and sometimes pathologic—names.

"Friends and enemies" is another way of saying "love and power." Perhaps they cancel each other out; as mutual exclusives: where love is, there is no power and vice versa. But, perhaps, too, they are mutually necessary. We cannot love unless wo stand somewhere and are someone; to stand and be is also to stand against and to put down those who would interfere with your way and your love. The cynic might say that our friends are our only real enemies, and one ancient Greek has even said: "Regard your friends as eventual enemies" (Dugas). The optimist—and as an American I am entitled to be that—might put it round another way: regard your enemies as eventual friends.

5

SCHISM
AS DIFFERING VISIONS

You may recall, as I do from school days, the sad, sweet passages toward the end of Shakespeare's *The Merchant of Venice* (where Lorenzo and Jessica tell each other of mythical lovers from the Classics), and Lorenzo saying:

> In such a night
> Stood Dido with a willow in her hand
> Upon the wild sea-banks, and waft her love
> To come again to Carthage.
>
> (Act 5, Scene 1)

"Parting at the seas' edge," says Gaston Bachelard, "is at once the most tearing and most literary of good-byes." It is a perennial image—to be found again at the opening of John Fowles's *The French Lieutenant's Woman*, the heroine roaming melancholy on the wild sea-bank—perennial image because it is a perennial experience. Between us two lies now an ocean, depths of salt, cold, and darkness. Though easily bridged today by phone cable and jet plane, still, out of one world there are now two, continents far-flung, oneself now an island, apart.

Such is parting; yet this is not quite schism, which means a special kind of parting, the worst perhaps: splitting. An ugly word that, something we ought not do, split or be split, or split things and people off. Schism means cleaving, cutting like a cleaver, the knife, severing. Consequently, it is bad for integration, for it is hardly a whole-making thing, favoring growth and synthesis and those other goals at which we work. Thus schism is one of those phenomena that requires a fresh look to see what it is all about and whether anything might be redeemed from it; it is another of those phenomena in need of some saving by means of the usual psychological question that differs from the moral question—and let us keep those two approaches quite distinct. The moralist asks what can we *do* with the will about schism, while the psychologist asks reflectingly, what *place* has it in psychic life at all; what is its necessity?

Reflections

When we think of schism—especially those of us here with theological interests—our minds reverberate with the great schisms of Christianity. Our first thought of schism is in terms of religion, and that is how the word has come into usage. "Schizoid" and "schizophrenia" are much later, and weaker, terms. Here, the notion of the general, of common sense is not so far off. We may appeal to that figure so dear to British lecturers, the "plain man" of "common sense" who understands schism as having to do with *doctrinal splits;* and for once the "plain man" is right on. For, as we proceed into this question of psychological necessity, we shall come to recognize that indeed the theological metaphor and framework is psychologically fundamental.

But first something of the emotions. You notice that the Conference is entitled "Relationship-Parting,"[1] and I have all along assumed that the topic dealt me is the dirty one, the radical unambiguous parting, irrevocable, the most tearing and the most literary, that is, passionately intellectual, a position at the sea's edge, the "drear and naked shingles of the world" (Matthew Arnold), out of earshot, excommunication. Schismatic parting is filled with rancor, bitterness: I hate you and your position, your thoughts, and above all, your blindness. What splits us now is not a higher fate and necessity, but evil; onto you falls the darkness because you no longer share my vision and cannot see where you have fallen. In Your parting from my position you have brought me doubt, *Zweifel,* devil. No wonder that one tradition holds that all divisions are the work of the Devil and that devilry enters religion mainly through schism and heresy.

A schism may have to do with one God or three, with Protest or Popery, with Christ as man or Christ as God, with national or international communism, with kinds and times of baptism, or theories of the libido, of art, cosmology, education, economics... whatever the contents, the stuff over which the split occurs, these are not themselves, psychologically, the cause of the cleavage. As psychologists, we are not taken in by the relative

---

1. [The Annual Conference of the Guild of Pastoral Psychology, Oxford, 1971. —Ed.]

value of the arguments, on which side truth lies, or deviation, or evil; nor are we taken in by the strength or weakness of the people, their merits, their personalities. Our interest lies, as psychologists, in the phenomenon itself—schism—the extraordinary passion with which it is charged, and the specific quality of this passion, so tearing and so intellectual. Such exorbitant pledges—like Freud and his circle and their common signet rings—the megalomanic thunderous curses, anathema, the tortured heretics, the detailed doctrinal defenses and programmed revenge, promulgations of positions, intellectual gyrations to assure one's rightness, the other's wrongness: these intensities indicate something more at work than either the struggle of personalities or a contest of ideas.

In searching for the place to put schism and the affects it generates, we shall avoid the rubric of *growth*. Indeed, it would be comfortable to place it there: growth is such a generous, warm notion, taking care of everything as "natural," as belonging to the development of personality. Psychology does so enjoy this new conceptual device of the Great Mother and her Child, who sees all psychic change as development and every process a sign of growth. This philosophy turns us all into infants again, and, though supposedly a good condition for Christians and for Romantics, the philosophy or fantasy of growth makes psychology both maternally materialistic and childish. Growth is indeed an appropriate vision and necessary metaphor for children, but in an adult growth also means aggrandizement, overweight, overpopulation, overkill, cancer, escalation, proliferation. So that growth has become the foolish metapsychology of fat men in a declining culture. For let us be reminded squarely that we in this room are not growing like plants and children, but, as the Buddha said, we are decaying, and our brains, like a deciduous forest of flaking cells, are paralleled in psychic process by narrowing of horizons and shrinking of possibilities, even as we change: the rule of Saturn extends daily in the psyche, bringing narrowing limitations in many senses, including the inevitable symptoms and irreversible signs of physical and psychological decay. Change, yes, schism brings, but change is not necessarily growth. To ignore the limitations and insist on growth (as with Teilhard de Chardin, for instance), to speak of the expansion of consciousness, of growth toward individuation, of development toward larger synthesis of wholeness, is to deceive ourselves by placing events that have to do with the soul of mature men and women and their deaths against an unfitting archetypal background of growth and life.

So, to see schism as a biological process—the schizocarp splitting for seeds, ground splitting as grasses push up, cells splitting for new generation—would indeed place the fracturing affects of schism against an unfittingly optimistic back ground. The Great Mother who favors biological metaphors, seeing things as "only natural" meaning "comfortable," takes out the sting, allays the sharpness of the knife, lulls us into assuming that the hatred is merely a reflection on the unwitting personal level of an impersonal necessary process in nature. So they deceive us, the psychologists of growth, when they say: things must divide in order to grow and the pain is of parturition, the destruction really a creation in disguise. Do not focus on the cleavage, they say, but on what is coming forth from the cleft, the child without history, without past, without any concern for what was split so that it might be born. Forward, onward, upward.

Similar to the delusional background of growth and just as inadequate is the background of *separation*. We are familiar—especially in England owing to the influence of John Bowlby, Melanie Klein, and the *Klein* Jungians—with the psychodynamic idea that humans begin in a state of fusion with mother, or collective unconscious, or self, and then separate; they cleave apart from that which they had been cleaving to. First fusion, then separation in order to find identity and individuality. Schism would thus be a radical attempt at individual identity by means of parting and separation emotions. We must split from the original ground, whether this be actual mother and breast, or internal symbolic mother and breast, or dragon monster, darkness, collective unconscious, or self. Schism is taken to be a necessary step of ego development in the process of individuation.

Let us pause over this one; let us think, and feel, just what this psychodynamic fantasy of individuality means, for does it not imply that individuality is a separated, isolated, split-off condition in its origins? Does it not also tend to characterize the ego in its development as schizoid, that its strength partly depends on its separatedness, and that its reality principle is partly one of insular competitiveness, paying your own way, being your own man, a Hobbesian vision of all against all, of radical independence, dependency overcome. After all, the hero with his knife as a metaphor for a "strong" ego facing "hard" problems in a "tough" world also is a metaphor for an ego who cleaves and cuts, at whose very essence is separation and parting, the theme of this conference.

Is it then a wonder that we are so obsessed with "relationship" and with fantasies of merging by falling: into love, into depression, into illness, into Self. And is it really surprising that there is today a movement toward communal togetherness, groups, and the blurring of consciousness's sharp edges that classical analysis diagnoses as "weak ego." If the new ego is blamed for its penchant toward fusion, was not the old ego schismatic, having for its metaphor the separated independence, the *opus contra naturam* of Prometheus and Hercules, of St. George and Christ—who, too, brought a sword.

No, we shall keep away from these two interpretative backgrounds to the questions of schism. Neither growth nor separation is satisfactory. The first makes schism too pleasant, the second, too much in keeping with the heroic—and cruelly schizoid—metaphor of individuality. These two ways of understanding schism would blunt its subjective pain.

The psychologist is obliged to be a phenomenologist, to take things as they appear as authentic and real, and to stick with them. Let us not associate away from the pain of schism, nor amplify it into something else, but remain, existentially if you will, in its presence. There is nothing more objective than its own intense subjectivity; when it hurts, it hurts, and we betray the hurt by moving away from it. All we can do is to let the archetypal background to the savagery, bitterness, and tearing present itself.

Already we begin to see that *schism can present itself according to different visions*: from within the cosmos of the Great Mother it is a biological necessity, a manner of growing. Yet, if principally a doctrinal, intellectual matter, then maybe schism has little to do with maternal metaphors of botany and vegetables, and we must search for other visions of the cleaver, e.g., the Hero with the knife, or the Great Enemy and divider, or, another, the dismembered Dionysos, the divided/undivided as he was called. One phenomenon, in this case, schism, will have various possible mythical perspectives in an archetypal psychology.

Returning to the earlier question—what place has schism in psychological life, what is its necessity—we may note a similarity in the various schism metaphors, whether vegetative, psychiatric, parturitional, or even geological where a schist refers to crystalline rock that is easily split into layers. Common to the metaphors is the one *becoming many*; the one breaks in to a dyad, a polarity, or a polycentric field. Doctrinal divisions can be taken in the same way: the single unitarian monotheistic vision resolves into several. Another god is born, the God of the Many.

If we continue within our *theological fantasy*, then the word "schism" does, as the dictionary says, appear mainly in contexts of Christian thought—and we know why. Schism reflects the inherent capacity of any unified doctrine reinforced by a monotheistic vision to fragment, to reveal the many that are potential in the one. Employing a *psychiatric* fantasy, schism means latent psychosis (schizophrenia), reflecting the psyche's potential for splitting into inherent components, losing its coherence and modes of communication between parts, ending the rule of a strongly ordered ego. Within a *mythological* fantasy, schism refers to the absence of Hermes-Mercury, or his concretization. The interpenetration of archetypal perspectives ceases, or has become concretized into self-isolating units, each promulgating its own doctrine. The mutual entailment of the gods breaks down, and when they can no longer speak with each other how can we?

The main writings on schism in the early Church were by Cyprian and then later by Augustine. Each wrote of the phenomenon in treatises called "On Unity of the Church" (*De unitate ecclesiae*). *The idea of schism made sense only within the perspective of a prior unity.* In Augustine's words (*Contra epist. Parmeniani*), schismatics are those who "have cut themselves off from Unity." Whereas heresy has to do with sacrilegious *teachings*, "you are schismatic by your sacrilegious *separation*" (*Contra Gaudentium* II, x; italics mine).

Thus in Christianity, the word schism received a value not usual in earlier Greek philosophers whose polytheistic psychology perhaps allowed them to take it as a fact of natural life, e.g. Plato (*Phaedo*, 97a, 101c) as a parting of paths, and Aristotle (*History of Animals*, 4.7.8) as a cleavage in a hoof. Schism is not a threat, not an abnormality when roads divide or hooves are cleft, but within the cosmos of unity schism is indeed a passionate dangerous issue, the very worst that can happen. And we note that in the history of the early Church the controversies of schism were all in regard to the *symbols of unity*: authority of the Bishop, Eucharist and sacraments, role of Rome. These were not theological disputes only, only concerned with the relative value of certain dogmas; they were transposed at once into the question of unity, the unity of the Church and of God, because within that unity still lay the ghost of polytheistic paganism, the threat of the gods of the many, monotheism's "latent psychosis."

Thus Henry the Eighth's refusal to comply with the rule of Rome, symbol of unity, had to lead to the schismatic reaction of the Pope ("schisma patimus, non fecimus," the English were fond of saying). Although there were economic and political reasons for Henry's actions, his "case" provides a notorious paradigm for the curious intermixture of personal anima psychology and doctrinal schism. The unified doctrine of the Church did not have room for all the requirements of Henry's soul. Nor would Anne Boleyn comply: she would not become a mistress to the throne, but of it. Something had to give; something had to split. Henry held together, so what gave was the unity of marriage and the unity of the Church. The *causa efficiens,* the immediate impetus that carried Henry into his perilous theological course, was his passion for Anne Boleyn.

We may suspect that the anima has much to do with schism. As envoy of life, whenever situations become too principled—monolithic, monotheistic, monogamous—spiritually *one*-sided in other words, this archetypal factor will appear to cause correction through trouble-making, by awakening passions. And these passions must appear also in the spiritual, doctrinal realm, for it is there that she is particularly enclosed. Were it merely a matter of emotion versus reason, love versus duty, or anima versus spirit, we would not be involved with schism, because a schism must split intellectual principles, creeds and codes, by envisioning doctrine differently, by meeting doctrine with doctrine in its own area of spirit. Henry did not fight Rome only in the name of the heart, for love, but in doctrinal language of theological dispute involving the best minds of Western scholarship; hence, a schism.

So, when you or I get into those tearing conflicts over ideas and we are then judged by perceptive colleagues in terms of the anima—he gets into such anima rages; his anima does all his thinking; it's all because of the women in his life; he loves the vanity of scandal—these perceptions will not do. Certainly the anima has put emotion into the ideas, filling them with life; but surely, too, the passion has been transposed to an intellectual realm where the conflict of people has become the schism of ideas with transpersonal, historical significance.

In recognizing the archetypal factor of the anima in these splits we do her a service by adding to our knowledge of her. Besides the anima as mediatrix between what we understand and what we do not understand, as representative of life, as carrier of nature, beauty, tradition, and psyche, we may add the further essential function of the *anima as troublemaker*, as cause of dissent between man and man, man and woman, man and himself. Moreover, since this is the manner in which anima mainly appears—in the messes we get into, the moods, arguments and foolishness—we are again obliged as psychologists, before condemning and setting out to correct with therapy, to enquire what point to this trouble, what intention this division. If the anima is an archetypal factor, then the trouble she is making is not merely emotional but also theological, that is, archetypal.

Henry's conflict was focused upon divorce, and divorce is indeed one of the ways that schism today reaches us as a vivid, threatening experience. Where there was one, joined in marriage, held in a golden ring, all others forsaken (neglected, abandoned), there shall be divorce into two. Marriage is split, and split marriage, like a split Church, is an impossibility. The monogamous view of marriage corresponds with the monotheistic view of God; it is therefore not surprising that so much theological writing so concerned with unity was on this theme of marriage. Divorce in human life alludes to the possibility of schism in God. Polygamous and promiscuous are Old Testament metaphors for polytheistic.

Marriage—even secular by registrar—has a theological background. It, too, is formulated by law and into a credo of words, and in this formulation divorce is psychologically inherent. For, if my thesis is correct, the more we rigidly insist upon unity the more will diversity constellate. The forsaken "other" must inevitably appear: the repressed return.

The situation that then occurs is called a *triangle*, but the triangle is after the event. First the unity of marriage has constellated the "other," and only after the other has had his or her effect does the triangle appear. Until then, the marriage conjunction has served as a defensive or transformative mandala, keeping out all others, providing a set of habits, a delusional or transformative system in which the force of love could be contained. The third releases love from this psychic structure. The mandala breaks. For a while everyone seems crazy, and also is crazily searching for new systems and justifications to encompass the energy. We study theories of love, use novels and films as models, put it all into the money complex, talk to friends and analysts and ministers, turn even to the Bible to build for ourselves new defenses, new structures.

The triangle necessarily releases a host of demons, because it breaks up unity of psychic structure and its pairings of balance and compensation. The "other" represents "all others," reminding us of the latently split nature of the psyche into multiples.

Psychology has said a great deal about individuation *alone*—the one to the One—and of individuation in the *dyad* (or *quaternio*)—relating, pairs, conjunction—but the triangle is where the demons are: immense psychological energy in rage, jealousy, anxiety, delusions. We might look again at all triangle relationships—of couples and the child, of couples and the affair, of couples and the analyst, of mother-daughter-son-in-law, etc.—through a model that does more justice to the passions displayed. Why do mother and father manage all right until the son enters the room, or why must a patient in analysis spend so much fantasy energy upon the analyst's wife or previous patient? Freud's original metaphor (Oedipus) was triangular. And this remains the only metaphor psychology has had for matters of extraordinary importance. Something archetypal is taking place that has an intensely separating effect on a prior unity, yet seems to increase the flow of energy through the parts. One vision no longer holds things together, yet there is a holding together with intense differentiation through so-called negative affects.

The questions raised by the schism of divorce need new ways of reflection. The triangle provides one, but it, too, needs a perspective freed from our former models of unity, models that do not leave enough space for understanding polyvalent multiplicities.

❧

Returning to Dido and Aeneas, this time Virgil's, we find an episode—indeed tearing and literary—bearing directly on our theme. You may recall that Dido was the Queen of Carthage, who fell in love with Aeneas. Now Aeneas was a child of Venus, and was afflicted and persecuted by Juno. The conflict in Aeneas, and between him and Dido, begins in heaven as a conflict between Juno and Venus. Dido's love grows while Aeneas and his men, beaten in war, fatigued from travel, rest in Carthage. Venus fears that he may not be received well there and then that he will dally there, which could mean forsaking his goal, Italy and the founding of Rome. Juno, however, is quite pleased with the development (Dido's passion) originated by Venus in order to assure Aeneas a safe haven.

Juno wants to make political capital out of it, saying to Venus: "Where is our rivalry taking us? Would it not be far better, by arranging a marriage, to seal a lasting peace? You have got the thing you had set your heart on: Dido's afire with love, wholly infatuated. Well then, let us unite these nations and rule them with equal authority." So, she arranges that during a storm the lovers shall meet in a cave where Juno will unite them in lasting marriage. "Venus," says Virgil, "made no opposition to Juno's request, though she smiled at the ingenuity of it."

All happens as Juno plans. The lovers meet in the cave, each coming with his own vision from his own goddess. "Dido recked nothing for appearance or reputation: the love she brooded on now was a secret love no longer; Marriage she called it, drawing the word to veil her sin."[2] You know how it ends, as echoed in *The Merchant of Venice*: Aeneas never saw his love and union with Dido as marriage for he was a son of Venus, and Jove and Mercury reminded him of his destiny, so that he says to Dido when they divide: "His orders: I saw the god, as clear as day, with my own eyes, entering the city, and these ears drank in the words he uttered. No more reproaches, then—they only torture us both. God's will, not mine, says 'Italy.'" Dido, having seen another vision prepared by another god, rightfully rages in despair, curses, and finally kills herself. "We make our destinies by our choice of gods" (Virgil). That schism, so literary, so rending and at the water's edge, represented the entire complex of hatred and rivalry between Rome and Carthage, Europe and Africa. The legendary Dido, her face on Carthaginian coins, had become the archetypal image of the trouble-making anima, inspirer of war.

Thus when people fall in love, not only eyes, lips, and hearts meet, but theologies. We come to the encounter not only with love but also with an *idea* of love. Juno and Venus are two ways of loving and also *two philosophies* of love stemming from different archetypal perspectives that do not agree—partly because, by the way, Aeneas did not give Juno enough recognition (Book III). We bring into a situation a subjective factor "made in heaven," that is, we bring with us a perspective archetypally governed

---

2. Passages quoted from Book IV of *The Aeneid of Virgil*, translated by C. Day Lewis (London: Hogarth Press, 1961).

by a suprapersonal dominant that forms our idea in accordance with the logos of that *theos*. We come with a theology.

In Classical theology (what we call mythology), one of the divinities who gives most trouble of the sort we today call "anima" is Aphrodite (Venus). In her way she governs several schisms. Due to her, Paris chooses against Athene and Hera, a choice among archetypal perspectives resulting in that epic account of splittings, the *Iliad*, upon which much in our culture rests. Aphrodite also gives Hippolytos hell (by means of Phaedra), dividing him from his comrades and his one-sided pursuit of Artemis, and she gives the women of Lemnos hell by visiting them with a bad smell, dividing them from their men and turning them into Amazons. In each case, Aphrodite insists upon her portion of human attention that a goddess deserves. Helen, Aphrodite's human incarnation, is an instrument that launches a thousand ships, and, through the affects she constellates—like the anima troubles (as psychologists would call them, had they Henry Tudor in analysis) between Rome and England—a historical schism is prepared, forcing the gods apart. Aphrodite and Ares (Venus and Mars) are secret lovers, i.e., they merge with each other, so that love's honey and war's gall are tastes not as distinct as we might suppose.

When Jung writes that the anima and the old wise man archetypes have a close, sometimes indiscernible relation, we see this working itself out in theological disputes. They begin as anima contention and rivalries, with scheming, pique, insult, revenge. (The Donatist schism, so important during the fourth century, began partly owing to the intrigues of Lucilla, a historically obscure, enigmatic woman friend of the rebelling Bishops.) Issues of personal vanity and desire turn finally into doctrinal positions about the nature of man, God, and the universe for which men kill and will die. But the ideas are present at the beginning as are the affects to the end.

If I were to attempt a fundamental statement about the intention of the anima in this trouble-making, it would be in terms of Jung's description of her (together with the animus):

> They are quite literally the father and mother of all the disastrous entanglements of fate and have long been recognized as such by the whole world. Together they form a divine pair...the anima

wears the features of Aphrodite, Helen (Selene), Persephone, and Hecate. Both of them are unconscious powers, "gods" in fact, as the ancient worlds quite rightly conceived them to be. To call them by this name is to give them that central position in the scale of values which has always been theirs whether consciously acknowledged or not. (CW 9.2: 41)

In the same work (CW 9.2: 427), he correlates the anima/animus with polytheism, the self with monotheism.[3]

In other words, the conflict brought by the anima has as its background the *multiplicity of the psyche*. Multiplicity is absolutely basic in Jung's description of the psyche. Psychic structure is polycentric. It is a field of many lights, sparks, eyes; its energy is scattered into constellations, like a starry sky. Jung does not depart from this description though, at times, he worries over plurality (CW 12: 105, 156), his introverted temperament, I suppose, preferring the monistic tendency (CW 6: 536). Because the anima is the mediatrix between the discrete personality and its collective, archetypal background, *she becomes the representative of multiplicity*, who splits us up by sowing divisions, thereby reminding us how complex is totality.

The reality of our wholeness is therefore not to be confused singleness, or unity, or a monotheistic description of totality, because as Jung says: "Reality consists of a multiplicity of things," while the unity of the *unus mundus* must remain "a metaphysical speculation," a "hypothesis" (CW 14: 659–60). The polycentricity of the psyche, its many constellations with their many foci, were represented once by a polytheistic pantheon and by the animation of nature through the personification of nymphs, heroes, spirits, daimons, and the like.

Should we take a standpoint exclusively from any single one of these configurations and behave mimetically to only one archetypal pattern, that is, should we act monotheistically, we have already performed an excommunication by cleaving ourselves off from communion with the many forms. Then the goddesses in their variety, epitomized by the promiscuity of Aphrodite, insisting on plurality, embroil us in situations in which other standpoints must be recognized, creating those doctrinal

---

3. For a discussion of this theme, see my "Psychology: Monotheistic or Polytheistic," *Spring: An Annual of Archetypal Psychology and Jungian Thought* (1971): 193–208. Reprinted in *UE* 1: *Archetypal Psychology.*

divisions we refer to, after the event, as schisms. Schism seems hardly possible in a polycentric universe. The quarrel of the gods is not schism. But in any system whose stress is on unity, as the Church with its one creed and one God (even in three persons), schism is inevitable, as if the monolith, Petrus, on whom it stands is potentially a geological schist.

When I say "forcing the gods apart," I refer to a human fault. By insisting on clarity of borders, proper definitions, we make divisions. In a sense, we bring about the quarrel of the gods through our one-sidedness, which we ennoble by calling it choice and free will. When we insist upon concrete, literalistic enactment of the myth to which we happen to stand closest, then, by choosing one pattern in our enactments, we become one-sided. We become psychologically monotheistic. This one-sided choice can occur even in a polytheistic religion where it is called henotheism.

There is a difference between monotheistic *religion* and monotheistic *psychology*. The first is a belief, and the second an attitude. We may have one without the other. Judaism, for instance, seems more monotheistic in religion than in psychology. In Judaism, God is not defined and the Torah may have 600,000 faces, one for each Jew in Exile. The content of belief is left suspended, uncodified, and the psyche is free to fantasy. The volumes of Jewish commentaries exhibit the endless fantasies. None are heretical. Although the religion remains monotheistic, the psychological attitude within it displays all the variety of multiplicity. Schism is rare (except for that major one, Christianity).

By psychological monotheism I refer to the literal attitude toward psychic events, which tends to exclude their speculative, mythical play, their 600,000 faces. One vision dominates, attempts to extend its system to make "unity"; the one converts, integrates, and swallows the many. Like Dido, we see only the constellation that we are in, the vision that both makes us see and blinds us. In contrast, the polytheistic attitude recognizes from the outset the polyvalence of psychic structure. Borders are ill-defined, so that flow and interconnection between archetypes and imagery stay open. "The fact is that the single archetypes are not isolated from each other in the unconscious, but are in a state of contamination, of the most complete, mutual interpenetration and interfusion."[4] One

---

4. "Archetypes of the Collective Unconscious," in C.G. Jung, *The Integration of the Personality,* translated by Stanley M. Dell (London: Kegan Paul & Co., 1940), 91.

cannot say that this activity or image always belongs to this or that god, for the gods are not so clearly defined. We are not sure that it is an "anima mood" or an "animus attack." One cannot really be certain where love and hatred separate because Mars and Venus do intertwine. Imagination speculates rather than fixes into concepts; borders dissolve. The gods imply each other. Thus, we have such difficulties with the Greek religion: the gods blend into each other, not keeping to distinct the spheres that we, with our literal monotheistic consciousness, expect from them. We want irreconcilable opposites that require transcendent functions, grace, and synchronistic magic to synthesize. We do force the gods apart.

The gods are forced apart by our strong ego stands. They create between the gods a no man's land marked out by psychiatric diagnoses. To take a position between and among the gods, where they interpenetrate and interfuse, is to be in a "borderline state," the possibilities of which have been denied by the heroic ego's insistence on well-defined positions.

Conclusion

The psychological significance of the polycentric structure of the psyche, and its reflection in pagan polytheism, goes perhaps further than we are able to realize. If there are truly differing visions of one and the same event, and if these visions are given by differing archetypal perspectives, we have to reconcile ourselves to differences more profound, and to separations more divisive, than those of sex and age, of nation, culture, and class, of attitude and type—all these are social, historical, or biological givens, but they are not made in heaven. Inasmuch as man is created in the image of God, we are created in the image of this or that face of God, or this or that god, and our createdness is not only a one-time historical event but also a continuing metaphorical event offering possibilities of interpretation and enactment.

As we are made according to a divine image, so our images are divine. In our imagination we reflect the different divinities of the imaginal realm. In our subjectivity we are governed by a multiplicity of factors, each with its eye shining through ours. And, as the gods demand that they be not neglected and forgotten, they insist stubbornly upon their being seen according to their own eyes, each according to his or her own light. To look at Aphrodite only from the viewpoint of Artemis may bring us disaster, as to Hippolytos. What is Hermes to his brother's vision but a cattle thief, and what is the Dionysian perspective to the Apollonic but a hysterical rout without distance, form, or proportion. I may not analyze anima behavior only from the viewpoint of the heroic ego on its career, nor may I look at the exhilarations of spirit only from the perspective of the mother who will condemn it as a puer inflation to escape from her complications she calls "the mother complex."

Each of the archetypes will be seen, even if they, like the gods, drive us to rupture, madness, and suicide in order that we give them their due. We see them though but darkly, in the mirror of our subjectivity that is limited to only this or that face, knowing only in part, restricted by the mytheme in which we are and the god we have chosen or that has chosen us.

I cannot change my vision as a matter of opinion, nor be proved wrong, nor be argued out of a position. I can, at best, not excommunicate, giving recognition to a reality that consists of a multiplicity of things. I can, at best, recognize that our visions, like those of Dido and of Aeneas, are archetypally given, and that our personal tragedy is partly because we have not seen the other's god, since we worship at different altars. Once the shift of vision from one myth to another, once I have been cre- ated through the vision of another god, in that god's image, there is no return and I shall see phenomena differently, now by means of the logos of another *theos.*

Though the visions may be incompatible, *they do not require the animosity of schism.* We may after all stay together in hatred, just as we may separate in love. Psychology usually puts hatred with parting, love with union, but is this not too easy? It is easy to leave you in hatred, and easy to stay with you in love. But the reverse of these pairings is that psychological art we call "consciousness." It is a consciousness that inhabits borders, at the seas' edge.

So, you and I cannot agree, and neither of us is right or wrong since each archetypal perspective has its justice. We can but strive against each other, parted, agreed to disagree, without the luxury of knowing that one of us is closer to the truth. There are many mansions and a house divided does indeed stand, even in hatred. The necessity of schism? *To end the illusion of unity,* of any delusional system that does not give place to the distinctive multiplicity of the archetypal powers affecting our lives.

Finally, then, to resolve the question of schism by placing it within this cosmos of multiplicity, let me quote a passage from "Sermon IV" of Jung's *Seven Sermons to the Dead*:

> For me, to whom knowledge hath been given of the multiplic-
> ity and diversity of the gods, it is well. But woe unto you, who
> replace these incompatible many by a single god. For in so doing
> ye beget the torment which is bred from not understanding, and
> ye mutilate the creature whose nature and aim is distinctiveness.
> How can ye be true to your own nature when ye try to change the
> many into one? What ye do unto the gods is done likewise unto
> you. Ye all become equal and thus is your nature maimed... The
> multiplicity of the gods correspondeth to the multiplicity of man.[5]

---

5. "Septem Sermones ad Mortuos" (1916), translated by H.G. Baynes, in C.G. Jung, *Memories, Dreams, Reflections*, edited by Aniela Jaffé (New York: Pantheon, 1962), 385–86.

6

EXTENDING THE FAMILY
(FROM ENTRAPMENT TO EMBRACE)

Believing himself dying of monoxide poisoning in his hut near the South Pole, Admiral Richard E. Byrd penciled, as a last act, a message to his wife, one to his children, and another to his mother. Recounting his ordeal in his book *Alone*, published a few years later when he was 50, Byrd wrote:

> At the end only two things really matter to a man regardless of who he is; and they are the affection and understanding of his family. Anything and everything else he creates are insubstan-tial; they are ships given over to the mercy of the winds and tides of prejudice. But the family is an everlasting anchorage, a quiet harbor where a man's ships can be left to swing to the moorings of pride and loyalty.[1]

I feel the Admiral was not expressing only the sentiments of his 1930s, upper middle-class, Virginian culture, nor do I believe this faith in family as supreme value was only the necessary accompaniment of heroic consciousness. The hero, immersed in an epic as was Byrd in his polar night at death's edge, locates himself inside an ancestral line. The heroic ego becomes an extension of a larger will that is anchored in the sense of belonging and serving nourished by family ties. Beyond both the bourgeois and the heroic is the primordial metaphor of Family itself, as an everlasting anchorage to which one forever belongs. We are born into a family and, at the last, we rejoin its full extension when gathered to the ancestors. Family grave, family altar, family trust, family secrets, family pride.

Our names are family names, our physiognomies bear family traits and our dreams never let us depart from home—father and mother,

---

1. Richard E. Boyd, *Alone* (New York: G.P. Putnam's Sons, 1938), 179.

brother and sister—from those faces and those rooms. Even alone and only ourselves, we are also always part of them, partly them. There is no escape from family; and it is this *amor fati,* as the Romans called love of fate, that Admiral Byrd recognized, turning the entrapment in the shelter that he believed would be his tomb into the quiet harbor of family, the isolated man joining the wider body, turning the vice of no-way-out into a virtue in this final recognition.

This precisely is the gist of this article: to turn the vice of entrapment in the personal family into an archetypal recognition of family as the supreme metaphor for sustaining the human condition.

The Battered Family

Where does family fit in the modern myth of individual independence? That myth says, home is what you leave behind. Moving on means moving out. You can't go home again—unless after failure or divorce. Admiral Byrd's safe anchor feels to many like an albatross. Women want careers, downtown, where the action is. Men long for something more, undefined, but most surely *not* more family. Marriages and family foundings, especially foundings of large families, are more and more countered by separations, living apart, single-parent households, divorces. Generations divided; children in day care; elders in Arizona. The place where one is most likely to be killed is at home, both perpetrator and victim, family members.

Yet family has been battered by more than these sociological developments. It has taken an even worse beating from the notion of development itself. Nothing has abused the family more than our psychological theories of development, with their myth of individual independence.

Family, so goes the developmental tale, is only the beginning, a necessary evil, which like all beginnings must be left behind. An adult has grown up, declared his independence, and his life and liberty are dedicated to the pursuit of his own happiness. In the United States, a newborn infant is believed to be so symbiotically fused with its mother that every effort must be made to develop its ability to separate, to stand on its own as early as it can. In Japan, a newborn infant is believed to be so utterly alien that every effort must be made to enfold it within the human community as early as possible. Two opposed trajectories of development. Neither is right or wrong. Both are living myths, "myths" because they are lived unconsciously as truths and have long-term consequences.

Psychoanalysis has swallowed whole the myth of individual develop-ment away from family. Everyone who buys an hour of analysis buys into this myth called "strengthening the ego." The first steps of any cur-rent treatment in mental hygiene (brain washing?) uncover the family romance, as it is called, which, in the widest sense, refers to the damaging fantasies arising from an individual's relations within the family. Notice here the focus on the independent ego; the family represents merely the limits imposed by genetic nature or environmental nurture, a restrictive influence on personal growth. Other cultures would not imagine the indi-vidual over and against family. Where other cultural myths dominate, an individual is always perceived as a family member. Our myth, however, insists that ego is strengthened and full personality achieved away from familial ties and pressures.

Psychology has even invented secondary embellishments to make its myth of individual independence more compelling. (Otherwise a per-son might naively suppose that the family pulls and pressures are what other cultures regard as filial bonds, kinship love, family pride, parental sacrifice.) Therefore, psychology has discovered an entire demonology within family. Byrd's safe harbor is packed with the irremediable envy of sibling rivalry between brothers and sisters, castration threats by fathers, disguised cannibalism by sons, devouring mothers and schizogenic mothers, as well as omnipotent, amoral, polymorphous perverse chil-dren. These are only some of the denizens of the deeps in family life. Of course, therefore, maturing, coping and handling have come to mean freedom from family. And, of course, psychology finds itself justified to go right into the home to exorcise by means of family therapy the crea-tures that its myth has created.

Is it too much to assert that the most devastating effect of Western psychology is neither the reductive sexualization of the mind nor the pseudoreligion of self-centeredness, but rather its deliberate rupture of the great chain of generations, which it has accomplished by means of its myth of individual development toward independence? Not honor your father and mother, but blame them and you will come out strong.

A Jewish joke says it best. Three mothers from New York retired in Miami Beach are comparing the love of their sons. The first says: "You know my car, the Jaguar? So who paid for it? My son." The second says: "You've been to my apartment. You saw the Chagall on the wall. Who bought it on Madison Avenue and schlepped it down here? My son." The third mother then says: "My son—he goes to a psychiatrist on Park Avenue four times a week, for the fourth year already. Eighty dollars each visit. Eighty! And what do they talk about? Me!"

Psychology's demolition of the family—whether by uncovering vipers in the bosom of its love or by urging independent individualism—succeeded at least in demolishing the bourgeois, sentimental fantasy of family that had, in fact, mastered children, oppressed wives and sisters, and kept men enslaved to their repressions. Pious attempts to restore the Norman Rockwell tousled and freckled family portrait have fallen to the incredible statistics of abused and molested children, battered wives, and infirm elders brutalized by their own kith and kin. That paradigm of family—more German even than Anglo-Saxon—ensuring church attendance, child discipline and ethical culture, and orderly, home-cooked, *bürgerliche* meals exists only as a fundamentalist nostalgia for the nineteenth century.

Family Problems

The overwrought, exhausting difficulties that consume family life indicate that something important is going on. Any big emotion signals value; the task is to discover the gold in the sludge. Let's see what we can recover from five typically emotional moments in family life.

False identity: During childhood, traits of personality are identified and one's identity begins to form partly in accordance with the perceptions of others. "Gilly's a real tomboy, a string bean who only has time for animals." (Will Gilly ever marry? Will she become a lesbian or a veterinarian?) "Billy can't keep out of trouble. I can't trust him out of my sight." (Will Billy ever hold down a decent job? Might he end up in prison?) "Milly was the quietest baby, always smiling and such a charmer." (Will Milly stay home with her parents, keeping them happy, or get pregnant at 15?)

From these sorts of family fantasies two contradictory clichés emerge: "No one knows you better than your family" and "My family can't see me at all." The division of "goods" between Gilly, Billy, and Milly keeps them in family-determined roles that seem, as time goes on, to be false identities. Was I really a tomboy or was I only living out what my mother wanted to be herself? Am I really a charmer or was I only placating my father?

Discovering whether these perceptions are true or false, that illusion of finding a real identity independent of the family fantasy, is far less rewarding than is the recognition that within the family a personal myth begins to take shape, the myth that forms one's identity. By identity here I mean identifiable reactions, habits, styles. One finds oneself inside a myth that is neither true nor false but simply the precondition for fitting one into the family drama as a recognizable character.

Moreover, if there are no pronounced family fantasies, the drama doesn't work, and we flounder about in that strangely loveless limbo that psychology calls an "identity crisis." Family love expresses itself by means of these fantasies of "what I want you to become" and "what I am proud of you for." These fantasies of identity show that someone is noticing traits, habits, styles. Whether a person lives into the myth or rebels against it, there must first be a myth.

Relatives and In-Laws: Most lives are spent among likes—similar budgets, similar age spreads and gaps, similar tastes and vocabularies. The people whom we choose to be with do not truly force us beyond our usual psychological boundaries. In the family, however, just where you might expect to be with those most like you, you encounter instead a collection of the strangest folk! At any large family gathering there come together the most extraordinary behaviors and most incompatible opinions, yet all this is in the same clan.

Voltaire supposedly said, "Nothing human is alien to me."[2] Relatives and in-laws provide the opportunity of extending our human understanding to what strikes us as alien, indeed. Where else, how else would one ever spend an evening with a man from Orange County who pays dues to the Klan, or with a math professor who interprets signals from outer space, or a junkyard dealer who did time in the state penitentiary. And the manners, the clothes, the bodies!

This is more than "alien," Voltaire. This is downright outlandish, freakish. Here we realize that large family affairs, rather than being scenes of convention, are actually performances of high comedy, outrageously funny, which also serve to encourage one's own peculiarities.

After all, as an in-law and relative yourself, you, too, appear, and are, rather freakish to the others. The attentiveness you pay to the in-laws

---

2. [This quotation is also attributed to Terence: "Homo sum, humani nihil a me alienum puto" (I am human, and nothing human is alien to me).—Ed.]

and relatives at such reunions works both ways, for rarely are you yourself heard out so patiently, with such curiosity. Family seems to evoke a profound curiosity in each of its members about the others, especially the more distantly related or more peculiarly entwined. Gossip abounds; people spill the beans and try to catch up on what has happened "since we last met"—a catching up that goes beyond recording births and deaths. Shadows come rushing out of the closet and join the party without moral opprobrium. A large family reception receives, *in magnificentia et gloria*, all shadows; all events, whether good news or bad, associated with family members, are magnified and glorified, thereby extending the size of the family's heart. The measure of a family's magnanimity is not what it gives to charity but rather its capacity to shelter the shadows of its members. Charity begins at home. We each feel this heart extending when, for instance, a little pride arises over the naming as "best insurance salesman in the county" a seemingly unremarkable young man who is, nonetheless, married to your great niece.

The Family Dream: A widower, getting on to 70, dreams: "I see a strange old family photograph, the whole clan, both sides. I recognize the faces even though I don't know or never saw some of these people. I somehow know the story of each one in the picture. It is amazing to see them all lined up like a school-class picture, or for getting an award. I am there, too, in the picture. Then, as I look at it, the faces seem to change, not grow older or anything, just seem to get clearer and sharper and even begin to move like they were talking or like a home movie."

A young woman in her early 20s, soon after having moved out on her own, dreams: "I am in a room on X Street (old house where we grew up) with my family—my little brother, sister, stepmother, and maybe my father—but it is not really them, or both them and not them. Everyone is just sitting there as if forever."

Why does her dream distinguish between the actual family of memory and a family "that is not really them"? Who is this ghost family in her dream? And who is the enormous family of faces ("both sides") that are coming to life in the old man's dream? Today, psychology answers, these figures are the family images who are composed of your subjective impressions and feelings, and these, the dream says, may be distinguished from the real members more realistically. But can there be so sure a distinction between memories and images? Do we not always experience "little brother," "step-mother," and the ambiguity of "father" both as the individuals they are and in terms of the hyperimportance given to them by these mythic roles?

Leaving home, as this young woman was doing, invited a new perspective toward her idea of family, a new distance beginning to separate within her awareness between what she could leave behind and what she would always carry with her as if forever. It is as if only by accepting "for forever" these fateful images of little brother and stepmother, etc. that we can see them not merely as them but as images within the imagination.

Similarly, the old man begins to watch the entire family come to life, himself as one of them, in his dream. As he ages, the family becomes more mythical (faces he never actually knew) and more honored (as if for an award). The dream opens him up to the family as a large populous story, shot through with personal memories yet extending beyond them into pure imagination: their talking in the home movie of the family soul.

Family Meals: The sign "Home Cooking" might still bring in some customers, but for many the family table was the place of trauma. Studies in family disorders accuse the evening meal of being a major focus of household tension. Here, at table, family fights over money, politics, or morals are most likely to break out, and later eating patterns—the rhythms of chewing, swallowing, breathing, and talking; the intermissions between silence and noise; the very notion of what constitutes "good" food—take on their definitive forms. Here, too, gross food disorders like anorexia and bulimia often appear first. Whether the atmosphere at meals boisterous and competitive, or chaotic with phoning and TV, or gravely formalized, tension is always on the menu.

Tension at the start of a meal belongs with the instinct of appetite. Just go to the zoo at feeding time and watch the animals pace and snarl, or ask a good Italian waiter about getting the *prima* (first course) on the table quickly. Meals are meant to start fast and conclude in digestive leisure. Tension, therefore, belongs to the moment of sitting down at table, and not only for animal reasons. Tension arises as an unconscious recognition of the sacramental nature of this family act. Grace overtly acknowledges the sacramental tension, and so do all the many rituals that go with family meals: fixed places and dinner "on time," the rituals of clean hands, of setting places and clearing the table, and the endless attempts to modify the tension with light music, dimmed lights, and rules concerning what is appropriate to talk about at table. All this elaborate etiquette, and every family will have some rituals even if utterly disguised as "just dig in," attempts to propitiate the archetypal forces that gather invisibly around the family meals and are ready to explode civilized conventions at the most innocuous provocation.

Going back home: Whether from prison camp after a war or just taking the bus home for Thanksgiving, homecoming is fraught with dreadful anticipation. Opening the front door releases overwhelming emotions—and also the counterforce of repression against those emotions that so often characterizes the stifled atmosphere of returning.

Here we must remember that going home is always going *back* home. Returning is essentially a regressive act in keeping with an essential function of family: to provide shelter for the good regressive needs of the soul. Everyone needs a place to crawl and lick his wounds, a place to hide and be twelve years old, inept and needy. The bar, the bed, the board room, and the buddies do not meet the gamut of needs, which always limp along behind the myth of independent individuality. Something always remains undeveloped and this piece needs to "go back home" as country-and-western lyrics often enough affirm.

Going back may mean sleeping till two in the afternoon, or taking refuge in the bathroom, crying with mom in the kitchen, or just complaining as do the grandparents who fall ill during every visit. Going home, at whatever age, offers going back, regression. And the fight against family during these return trips is, therefore, a displacement of the fight against regression. We don't want to admit the weaknesses in our characters and the hungers in our desires. We don't want to admit that we have not "grown up," and so blame the family both for bringing out our worst and then for not indulging it enough. Meanwhile: that strange sense of consciousness ebbing away, going down the family drain.

The debilitating energy loss strikes everyone alike as if a communal power outage. Everyone caught in repeating, and resisting, old patterns. Nothing changed, after all those years! No one can get out even for a walk to break the spell, the whole family sinking deeper into the upholstery (and TV has little to do with it and may even be, in such moments, the household god who saves). These moments attest to the capacity of family for sharing—French anthropology used to speak of a *participation mystique*—in a common soul or psychic state, and for containing the regressive needs of the soul.

No one is at fault, no one is kicked out, and no one can be helped. In the paralysis lies the profound source of acceptance. Grandpa can go on grumbling, brother attacking the administration, sister introvertedly attending her exacerbating eczema, and mother go on covering up with solicitous busyness. Everyone goes down the drain because family love allows family pathology, an immense tolerance for the hopeless shadow in each, the shadow that we each carry as permanent part of our baggage and that we unpack when we go back home.

These five bad moments are symptomatic of what lies at the root of family problems. Not the failure to "relate," not the breakdown of the old patriarchal model, not even the incurably freakish, especially depressive, pathologies that make their home at home, but rather the root lies in the archetypal nature of family itself. As an archetypal reality, the experience of family feels so often "unreal" because family is permeated through and through with external exaggerations, and impossible too-muchness or mythic dimension, which is the stuff of the symptoms we suffer and also the stuff of much of Western culture's stories, novels, and dramas. And this mythical exaggeration is at work in even the most conventionalized, urban, eat-and-run, unconnected, first-name parents, upward-mobile, areligious unit of consumers called "family." Family is less a rational place than a mythical one, and the expectation of finding rational reality at home is precisely what makes us condemn it as "unreal." Attempts at unambiguous communication, reasonable discussion of problems, and structuring a new paradigm all overlook the fundamentals at the source of family life: the deep-seated and indestructible complexes of the psyche—once called demons, ghosts, and ancestors—whose places is in the home.

Family in a Word

The notorious nuclear family of statistics, sermons, and advertisements—two parents, two siblings, a family car, and a pet—does not correspond with the Latin word from which family derives. "This famous word... is inseparable from the idea of land settlement, and is therefore essentially *das Hauswesen,* the house itself, with the persons living in it... And thus the religion of the *familia* will be a religion of practical utility, of daily work, of struggle with perils...; it is not the worship of an idea of kinship."[3]

---

3. W. Ward Fowler, *The Religious Experience of the Roman People: From the Earliest Times to the Age of Augustus* (London: Macmillan, 1911), 70.

Familia, familias to the Romans meant primarily "a house and all belonging to it," "*the slaves in a household, a household establishment, family servants, domestics* (not = *family*, i.e., *wife and children)*" [Lewis & Short, *Latin Dictionary*]. Neither parentage nor descent, not even bloodkinship within the clan for which the Romans had the word *gens*, determined the use of the word *family*; place did. By Romans, here, I mean the entire civilized Western world and its language that lives on in our Latin roots.

Because *familia* connoted a physical house and all belonging to it as goods, fortune, inheritance, the more accurate part of the fantasy of the American nuclear family may be the station wagon and the household pet. In fact, a domesticated animal was considered often a familiar. Living together in familiarity is a psycho-economic organization—such is the meaning of family. Even the Greek word *oikonomia* (from which come economy and economics) means household management or keeping house. The family is a function of the house, rather than vice versa, where "house" is the concrete container of multiple familiarities and intimacies, the domesticated (*domus* = house) world of belongings—what belongs to us and to what we belong—and where belonging also means what is fitting, appropriate and customary.

This etymological revelation suggests a father brought a sense of family, giving primary emphasis to the idea of a supportive psychic system under the same roof, whether farm, keypads, or a condominium block. This broadest sense includes the notions of service and participation, a membership investing in and benefiting from a larger household. Filial piety and brotherly love seem irrelevant to this household, yet it does include all the things belonging to an estate: animals, goods, and furnishings. Your family is your furniture in more than a metaphorical sense. Little wonder that such bitterness can erupt over dividing the family dishes after divorce or death; or that dreams of the old family car can continue to haunt long after the car itself was trashed. The family soul includes far more than a few nuclear people of the ad. It includes all that background in the ad. The setting of the TV sitcom—stairs, couches, and lamps—is as much a part of the family as the characters who crack jokes.

Family may not so much derive from the bourgeois class's devotion to property and the guarantees afforded by the laws of ownership. Rather, those bourgeois values may be derived from the soul of the *domus* and its belongings, asking for permanent structures of caretaking. Perhaps the property class and its laws were created by a need of property for ownership, things wanting to belong. At least, the word *familia* invites these reflections about the psyche of the property.

Various gods and goddesses lived with the ancient family: *Vesta* at the hearth (*focus* is the Latin word) who must be acknowledged first and daily else the central bonding flame might go out; Janus at the gates so that one remembered the different faces required for inside and outside; the three different gods of the doorway (of the door, the hinges, and the threshold) who prevented bad spirits from entering the domestic interior; the Lar or Lares who were the ever present and remembered ghosts of the household's dead. (Food falling to the floor at a meal wash at once taboo, belonging now to these familiars of the underworld.)[4] And there were the Penates, or the wee ones of the cupboards, without whom Old Mother Hubbard might find not even a bone. The ancient home gave plenty of place to the invisibles that live in a family, propitiating and domesticating its demons, which it acknowledged as rightfully belonging.

Above all these laws Juno (Hera in Greece) who presided like a stately, powerful Roman matron over the psychic and material well-being of the household. In Juno was combined instinct and institution: marriage both as that coupling urge for permanent bonding and as a societal stability. The regular order of life within the household and within the bodies of the women in the household was regulated by the calendar; the first day of each month, the Callens, was dedicated to Juno. Little houses made of clay with devotional objects in her cult, and heroes of myth—and most great Greek heroes were sent on their way because of Juno—we are recognized as such not only by their deeds but also by the trophies they brought back home. Ulysses felt himself a failure because after a twenty-year absence he arrived home unclothed and without spoils. His family, by the way, included his old nurse and his old dog. Again, that emphasis upon ties beyond blood, and upon animals and things.

Re-Visioning Family for Adult Life

Much of what is said about family reflects the viewpoint of the child, family as either positive nest or negative cage. Even the political notions of

---

4. [Cf. Velimir B. Popović, "Hekate, or On Being Trivial in Psychotherapy," in *Archetypal Psychologies: Reflections in Honor of James Hillman*, edited by Stanton Marlan (New Orleans: Spring Journal Books, 2008), 369–95. Popović explores the underworld aspects of Hekate, including her role as the goddess of table scraps.—Ed.]

family consider the institution through the same eyes of childhood, the right wing insisting upon its stabilizing, the left on its inhibiting, effects. In fact, many of the dilemmas we have touched on so far, and our own mixed feelings about our families, arise because we remain in the perspective of the child, longing for home and rebelling against it.

We can move this ambivalence by moving out of the childhood view. What then is family in adult eyes, for adult life? What does it signify for a person passing age 45 or 50? Where and how does it matter even after the developers have torn down your childhood home and neighborhood, after your parents are buried and lawsuits have split you from your brothers, after psychoanalysis has revealed the corruption, hypocrisy, and exploitation in the family's heart, and even after the family that you yourself may have parented is broken up or so distorted beyond recognition as "yours" by serial marriages, step-siblings and vicarious offspring? Let us try to find some values by extending the notion of family beyond what a child can imagine.

The Vertical Family: As one ages, interest grows downward toward the descendents, the features and characters of grandchildren and their children. At the same time, interest shifts backward to forebears, genealogy—where we all came from, how we got to settle here, memories and tales. Eudora Welty's *Losing Battles*, a superb novel of a single family birthday party, condenses the vertical extension into the image of the tiny red-headed love child dashing out of the opening pages at dawn and ancient Granny in her chair, carried about, remembering, forgetting, nodding off, stalwart and ridiculous—the two pivots of the vertical dimension of family, each somewhere beyond the reach of actuality but perpetuating by implication family back into the darkness of the unknown ancestors and forward into unborn days to come. Gabriel García Márquez's *One Hundred Years of Solitude* imagines the lives of all the ancestors and descendants into similar patterns with similar lives, the great hundred-year tree and hundred-year war of family beyond ones personal life. The stitched and framed sampler of the family tree, "the evening with the photograph album" as T.S. Eliot calls those remembrances,[5] dilates the focus of life beyond a solitary and lonely self. Instead, I am one figure in the tapestry,

5. , "East Coker," in T.S. Eliot, *The Four Quartets* (New York: Harcourt, Brace and Company, 1943), 17.

maybe off a little to one side, yet ramified into a huge social structure with a part in the history of my region and its people.

Here we encounter the Chinese idea of longevity, not merely as an actuarial statistic that announces my life expectancy. Rather, longevity can connote an extended consciousness downward into my children's children and backward to the ancestors. Tribute to them, even our commandment to honor thy father and thy mother, "lengthens" life, a longevity of imagination embracing centuries.[6] The more we are able to enter the heart and mind of the children's children, and the unforgivable shadows in the mindset of our parents and their parents by understanding the ways in which they perceived and valued the world, we extend our span. Each child ruled out, each parent cut off, is a lost limb of imagining power and thus shortens life.

Nepotism: One ramification of the tree is that voice of influence called nepotism. "I have an uncle in the business." "My wife's sister works for HUD, maybe she can do something." "Harry owes me one; my father helped his father when he was really down." It doesn't matter how you look, what you can do, where you went to school, or even if. It is enough to be related, and if one must choose between efficiency and loyalty in hiring and firing, then loyalty, blood—loyalty, first.

Much of the world runs this way—not only the Church of the Renaissance (from which we have the term) or the "family" as the Mafia is still called today. The loyalty of nepotism is neither that of love nor friendship. It has nothing to do with personal relations. Instead, this vice teaches the virtue of the primacy of family feeling over any individual member, where family feeling is a code of conduct, a religion even, because it is a commitment to death. Nepotism that exalts family above all powers on earth. It says no claims of law or love or a personal conscience take precedence over family.

Genius and Fama: the Roman marriage bed was called the *lectus genialis,* associating it with the family genius, the generative soul power in the core of the family. "Genius," says Fowler, "would be that soul of a man which enables him to fulfil the work of continuing the life of the *gens*

---

6. [Cf. Roberts Avens, *Imaginal Body: Para-Jungian Reflections on Soul, Imagination and Death* (Washington, D.C.: University Press of America, 1982), in which Avens explores the distinction between personal immortality, or literal eternal life, with an imaginal connection to the invisible realm, an "eternalizing" imagination. — Ed.]

[clan]."[7] (I would add "soul of a woman, too.") Though in later Roman meetings, *genius* become a highly individualized guardian spirit (like our angel), it nonetheless arises in and speaks for the generative power of the familial soul. Since the genius takes care of you, you must take good care of it.

During the Renaissance, this careful relation with one's invisible spirit appeared in the concern for *fama* or reputation. One was enjoined to do everything possible to magnify, or save, one's reputation, which functioned as an almost autonomous being, like a genius, spurring character to noble aims. Today the drive to succeed, to please the family, to honor and carry on the family name, still motivates our contemporary careers. Even if perfectionistic and overdemanding, this inherent desire of the genius of the family may at times sustain a person when individual power fails.

Service: Domestics, servants, and slaves belonged to the Roman family and, as metaphors, still belong to the contemporary meaning of the word. Attempts to liberate women from the household service or adequately recompense them for it, as well as the advertising of labor-saving devices and products that free one from the household drudgery, give backhand recognition to the fact that where there is a family household there is slavery. In one way or another, we are each slaves to family.

The idea of family service, however, extends beyond the maintenance of its property, the heirlooms and records, keeping anniversaries and celebrations, beyond the daily labor devoted to the well-being of the household, those chores that belong to "homemakers." One also serves an invisible family, as if an archetypal force. With the passing of time a sense of its power grows within one's psyche, like the movements of its skeleton inside one's flesh, which keeps one in servitude to patterns entombed in our closest attitudes and habits. From this interior family we are never free. This service keeps us bonded to the ancestors. How we are able to live these habits and attitudes, and inherited propensities to specific diseases, our own morbidity, provides each person with an individual way of honoring "our fathers and our mothers."

Humor and Fate: Enough has been written about family as fate. The genealogies in the Bible—the tales of Genesis and Exodus are one after

---

7. Fowler, *The Religious Experience of the Roman People,* 75.

another family stories; the curse of the House of Atreus releasing one Greek tragedy after another; the history of Western "civilization" from the Roman empire through the First World War as a succession of murderous rivalries between royal families. It is as if history is simply family writ large, and fatefully. But not necessarily tragically; because, even if family is fate, it is also a laugh, the experience of *The Human Comedy*, as Balzac called his encompassing series of family novels. Family remains the source of world humor about mothers-in-law, poor relatives, wedding nights, fading minds, and deathbed scenes. Fate cannot be carried without humor; nor can family; so that perhaps the greatest or all gifts that family offers to adult life is the dignity it grants, even as it pokes fun at, the ridiculous plight of old age.

By extending family into a fullness of meanings, I have tried to remind our highly individualized and rationalized consciousness that profound significance resides in all aspects of family, especially those that are intolerable and generally condemned. I have tried to show that family is a sustaining institution not just because of blood ties, procreation and childbearing, or because it supposedly fosters the virtues of mutual respect and responsiveness and thence bourgeois respectability and responsibility, or because it is said to provide the social and economic structures upon which civilized decency depends. These are the conventional and literalized meanings of family that have kept its imagination far too narrow. I have instead been attempting to present family as supreme metaphor for our life on earth because it presents that force of human attachment to a dwelling place, of domestication of the savage and the nomad, of honoring the invisible, the demonic and the dead, of making intimate and familiar and "owned" the persons, animals, and things of this world, taking them home to the hearth, ourselves as long-term caretakers in bondage to our fate on earth, playing out the comedy of human continuity.

7

LOVING THE COMMUNITY AND WORK
FROM *THE RAG BONE SHOP OF THE HEART*

Dogs bark at people they don't know.
(Heraclitus)

The poems in this section speak in different ways about being in community. All the ways make a similar assumption: we don't so much build communities as we are already built into them. Just by being here in the world, our life is with others. And it is in this communal context that work belongs. By throwing yourself into a task, you take part in the world, give it your gifts, and bring it your love. Work may call for muscle, know-how, and a sweet hand, but, as soon as we are engaged with other people, something else more important is required, as William Stafford says in the first poem. All mutual relations depend on "awake people be[ing] awake...the signals we give...should be clear," otherwise we don't know who the other person is or let the other know who you are.[1] To love is to talk right. This clarity may be more essential to living and working with others than strong feelings and kind flowers.

So the first way of recognizing community is through work. Work is often coupled with love as its opponent or substitute, as if each were an escape from the other. But this coupling means that work and love are equivalent passions, that work is another mode of desire, a form of love itself, else work could not substitute for love. Freud thought the purpose psychoanalysis was to resolve the twin problems of love and work, again suggesting they are of the same nature. Both give joy, put you in "the high seat," as Gary Snyder says, quickening your senses so that the truck's

---

1. William Stafford, "A Ritual to Read to Each Other," in *The Rag and Bone Shop of the Heart: Poems for Men*, edited by Robert Bly, James Hillman, and Michael Meade (New York: HarperCollins, 1992), 233.

Polished hubs gleam/And the shiny diesel stack/Warms."[2] Work helps "shake off this sadness" (Unamuno).[3]

When work is imagined different from love, work becomes a grueling job. We have to push ourselves to do it for money or to climb the ladder, and we have to look elsewhere for community. We forget that all work always implies other people. Jobs express communal needs. They say, "help wanted," you're needed. And a man's identity comes as much from what is wanted from him by others as from his own self-generated desires.[4] Therefore, those writers say, don't sit around waiting for inspiration, that "winged energy of delight" (Rilke).[5] "[S]tart then, turn to the work" (Unamuno); "Whatever you can do,/or dream you can, begin it" (Goethe).[6]

A second way of community derives from an alert sense of social justice. Lorca's furious, bitter, ideal Spanish passion is also compassion. Compassion is communal eros, being others, for others, toward others. Lorca who was seized and shot by Franco's fascists, spoke his love as outrage. "The mountains exist. I know that." (Don't tell me about calm serenity and inspiring heights.) "But I have not come to see the sky./ I have come to see the stormy blood." He speaks for dead pig and lambs and ducks, and all else that is murdered so that our civilization may go on as it is. This style of communal love attacks

> ...all those persons
> who know nothing of the other half,...
> of these empty offices
> that will not broadcast the sufferings.[7]

All this was written long before the deceits of the Gulf War, the conspiracy of Irangate and the subversion of the Constitution and the secretive statism of corporate America (which Lorca calls "New York"), which pays the hit men of species, soils, cultures, and children the world over

---

2. Gary Snyder, "Why Log Truck Drivers Rise Earlier Than Students of Zen," in ibid., 241,

3. Miguel de Unamuno, "Throw Yourself Like Seed," in ibid., 234,

4. [*The Rag and Bone Shop of the Heart* is a collection of poetry intended to address issues relating to men and masculinity. As such, the language in this essay is deliberately gendered. —Ed.]

5. Rainer Maria Rilke, "Just as the Winged Energy of Delight," in ibid., 236.

6. Johann Wolfgang von Goethe "Until One Is Committed," in ibid., 235.

7. Federico García Lorca, "New York," in ibid., 244‒45.

(with the acquiescent complicity of taxpaying citizens). Of this terrorism, Lorca writes in terrifying lines with a terrible love. Men building community through recovery groups and personal support sharing may learn from Lorca another approach to community love.

That genius of enlightened rationalism Dr. Samuel Johnson, drinking dish after dish of tea in his candlelit chambers while inventing the dictionary of the English language, declares in a few terse words a conclusion similar to Lorca's: men are bound together by feelings of brotherhood. Within all community flows fellow feeling. Only when we are asleep are we alone, said Heraclitus.

Alfred Adler called fellow feeling *Gemeinschaftsgefühl*, which has been translated into "social feeling" and "community feeling." Adler, who originated psychoanalysis along with Freud and Jung, considered *Gemeinschaftsgefühl* ("the feeling of intimate belonging to the full spectrum of humanity") to be the dominant motive of life, as basic as Freud's sexual drive and Jung's urge toward meaning. For him, "A man of genius is primarily a man of supreme usefulness."[8]

So, third, the brotherhood of community arises when men can do useful things together. Jim Heynen conveys this fraternal feeling in his description of boys saving pheasants during an ice storm.[9] Boys especially feel the binds of brotherhood. Psychology calls this elemental association peer pressure; sociology, gang behavior; anthropology, the young male initiation group. These are ways that academic language can cover over the deepest emotion of "intimate belonging" that urges men to join together.

When this primary feeling is distorted by violence, by ideology, or by exploitation, that is, by leaders who cheapen and betray the emotions of brotherhood, it can turn nasty and fascist. But in the depths there remains a love *with* others that shows as love *for* others and carries all teamwork from sports, group music, and construction to the gritty loyalty of a platoon under fire.

James Wright's account of his Scout troop evokes the perennial boy interior to every man.[10] This boy still remembers the nicknames and off

---

8. Alfred Adler, *Problems of Neurosis: A Book of Case-Histories*, edited by Philippe Mairet (London: Kegan Paul, Trench, Trubner & Co., 1929), 35.

9. Jim Heynen, "What Happened During the Ice Storm," in ibid., 249–50.

10. James Wright, "The Flying Eagles of Troop 62," in ibid., 251–52.

peculiarities of his old companions, still thrills at recollections of their common adventures. For then were the first stirrings of deep friendship, group loyalty, and the mysterious free happiness that comes with doing things with other men. The two poems that follow, by Robert Francis[11] and Kenneth Rexroth,[12] move the sense of comradeship from young boys to old men, their reminiscences, delusions, sadness, and insane exhilaration in simply being together. "We are comrades together./Life was good for us," says Rexroth, "[L]et us journey together," says Thomas McGrath.[13]

11. Robert Francis, "Waxwings," in ibid., 253.

12. Kenneth Rexroth, "For Eli Jacobson," in ibid., 254–55.

13. Thomas McGrath, "Epitaph," in ibid., 256.

8

MARRIAGE, INTIMACY, FREEDOM

The force of the title—these three little words "Marriage, Intimacy Freedom," like those other three words, "I Love You," strike such deep chords. What an extraordinarily powerful fantasy is here at work! How much longing is stirred! O, if only...

I say fantasy with deliberate purpose, for we each know from the facts of our lives that Marriage is often dull, banal, and also a crux of agony; Intimacy brings us to stammers, complaints and tears; and Freedom, as Erich Fromm said fifty years ago, is one of humankind's greatest fears.

So the actualities of marriage, of intimacy, of freedom as events we try to live in, practice and clarify in concepts are quite distinct from the hopes and longings generated in the soul by the fantasies of Marriage, Intimacy, and Freedom. Just here is the mystery: the strange disjunction between Fact and Fantasy, and just here is the misery, trying to force the facts to fit the fantasy, or sardonically abandoning the fantasy altogether.

We shall have to ask what does the soul want that it sets us so on expectation's edge? What is this response in the heart that brings us to long for a new marriage, a better marriage, a different marriage, more true intimacy, and for freedom? Why these three terms? Why not three older Republican ones—Marriage, Children, Family? Or newer ones: Relationship, Divorce, Selfhood; or just two: Intimacy and Freedom; why throw in Marriage?

Might there be a way to maintain the ideal fantasies toward which we long when we hear these words without succumbing to the difficult facts in which the words are embedded, especially the facts of marriage?

In responding to the three themes of the title, I beg incompetence. It is as if I strayed into a dream where I must discuss in a foreign language a topic about which I haven't a clue. Freedom? I am Mr. Bourgeois, guilt-loaded with obligations, reduced by anxieties about promises and schedules, chained by habits and taxes and stick-in-the-mud routines, hemmed in by the conventions of consumer values, cosmetic appearances, and hypochondriacal worries. Freedom!

As for Intimacy, I run from it. It's none of your business. I often pronounce in print against contemporary cults of intimacy, the sharing, confessing and revelatory glimpses of inconsequential childhood. I consider our civilization to be caught up in the minutiae of intimate biography, people wanting to gossip about themselves (not even about their neighbors) and then calling this gossip "recovery." All this intimacy in a world where there are dire and desperate public matters waiting.

Marriage—I've tried it. Indeed, I've been married more years of my life than I've been single, and those were the main mature *conscious* years. But I haven't a clue what makes it work and not work, discern which is which, or whether that word "work" is applicable at all.

Perhaps I hesitate to discuss marriage because I look to the Greeks for archetypal patterns. Except, perhaps, for Philemon and Baucis, horror stories: Clytemnestra; Medea and Jason; Phaedra and the mess in that household; Priam and his concubines; the frustrated husbands of the *Lysistrata.* Think of Socrates and Xantippe. As for that pop version of a devoted couple (Penelope and Ulysses), he caved in with Calypso for seven years while she was entertaining in their house innumerable nameless "suitors." Besides, is that a marriage when the couple are apart for twenty years! The great goddesses—Artemis, Athene, Aphrodite, Hestia—stayed clear of marriage, while the marriage of Persephone and Hades was spent one third of the time in Hell, among specters of the dead and no daylight.

Solon the lawmaker is said to have refused to set rules for marriage. He was so down on it that he regarded woman a dead weight on a man's life. Plato and Lycurgus took marriage only as duty; their laws insist men marry for the state's sake, and they order punishment for those who marry late or never. Plutarch warns of money marriage and uses the image of chains for a marriage to a rich woman. Besides these cautions for men, feminism has well laid bare the misery of marriage for women in antiquity.

Zeus and Hera, however, offer a more complex and entertaining story. Cheap editions that tell us he was a philanderer, a real "animal," and she a furiously possessive virago, miss the fact that together as a syzygy they present the archetypal tension, so crazy to live, of all our three themes. They do have intimacy, but her idea of marriage is set against his idea of freedom; while her idea of freedom is to do her own thing all by herself apart from marriage. Our human limits do not let us hold what Zeus and Hera can combine. They go on eternally in their bind; we divorce. So, I want to find other patterns, other myths. For once to be free of the Greeks.

We are already into one of our topics: Freedom. Let's go on with it. How do we usually imagine it: a bird's wing, Hermes's light heels, flitting, puer, trickster escapes, escape artist, unhampered libidinal arousal. Unimpeded, uninhibited, unpredictable, untrammeled, unbound. Don't fence me in. Free-wheeling, free-loading, freebooter. Is this the vision of freedom informing the minds of the founders of our Republic?

In his recent book, *From the Wrong Side*, Adolf Guggenbühl-Craig entitled a chapter "Creativity, Spontaneity, Independence: Three Children of the Devil."[1] He lays out quite ruthlessly how dangerous and anti-social are these shibboleths of current humanistic psychology. He shows how our devotion to independence denies the simple truth that we are each deeply and necessarily dependent on one another and, I add, the environments that sustain our lives. He also makes clear that the spontaneity of freedom may be cruelly destructive. Many acts of violence—rapes, beatings, suicides, homicides—occur suddenly, spontaneously. Free acts. What the French call *l'acte gratuite*, may arise as an impulse from the savage soul, undomesticated or demonic. To be free is not necessarily to be good.

Yet what does the soul—which speaks sometimes most accurately in the depths of language—want with that word Freedom that sets off such expectations? What sort of preposition accompanies and influences Freedom? Freedom *from*—from fear, want, and oppression, such as enunciated by the Charter that established the United Nations after World War Two? Or is it freedom *of* choice, opportunity and movement or access in today's political language?

Or, is it rather Freedom *to*: to do as I like, to hire whom I want, to tell the boss to shove it, to go where I want, to marry whom I please—a freedom of agency in the empowered and recovered adult of therapy?

1. Adolf Guggenbühl-Craig, *From the Wrong Side: A Paradoxical Approach to Psychology* (Putnam, Conn.: Spring Publications, 2014) [1992].

Or, fourth, is it possibly Freedom *in*? This seems moronic or oxy-moronic, for the fantasy of American, epitomized by Texas, freedom is "don't fence me in." "In" means within limits or constraints of any place, time, situation, condition, such as in the kitchen, in an hour, in a conversation, in a marriage.

This fourth preposition, "in," rather than freedom of, to and from, suggests that the joyful expectation arising in the soul when the bell of freedom rings is nothing other than living fully in the actuality of this or that situation, as it is, which gives to that situation wings, freeing it from the desire to be elsewhere, to escape from it, to want more, thereby sating the soul's desire with the fullness of the present. How do we say it? "I love what I'm doing...I'm fully in it." "I'm really into Tex-Mex cooking; my new computer; repainting the house." Is this compulsion? Addiction? Or is it the freedom given with passionate love?

Here, by the way, is what the soul, via its invention of language, says about freedom: the Indo-European root of "free" is *pri*, love, from which, Freya, the Nordic-Teutonic goddess of love, Fria, Friday Free-day, just as Liberty the Latinate equivalent, comes from the Italic god Liber, who blended with the Greek Dionysos, the free-flow of liquid saps contained in the plant world, the sexual stuff in the marrow of the animal, the liberal loosening within any moment, place, or condition, the moment we feel how we love it and it loves us. Yes, a liberal must be a big spender and free lover just as the right-wing declares. Etymology is also politics.

By locating the source of freedom in the love goddesses Frigg and Freya and the figure of Liber, I am de-coupling the idea of freedom from the human individual. I am de-humanizing it. That historical location of freedom with the personal "me," for all its liberating and dignifying advantages, has also resulted in Western competitive atomism, each of us straining for esteem and empowerment by asserting his and her rights. Such free individuals like free radicals, combine into no communities until forced by a social contract that protects that person's freedom in exchange for submission to the contract. Otherwise life would be brutish, nasty, and short (Hobbes).

Logically, then, freedom *from*, *of*, and *to* depend on the prior preposition *in*—buying into the contract, being in the *polis*. Only then are you free from fear and able to do what you can. Participation in the collective affirms your actual self, which I have defined elsewhere as the internalization of community. You are your city. So collective participation, *pace* Jung, is not the price of freedom but its true ground. Freedom is assured less by exercising your individual will in distinction to all others and more by belonging to the other. Myths express this innate belonging as brother-sister marriage; for instance, Zeus and Hera. Our marriage ceremony calls it "cleaving," "til death us do part."

Belonging inherently in the other could also be called intimacy as described by the dictionary: a deep and extensive familiarity with; close; thoroughly mixed and united. I am implying now that our marriages can be relieved of that defensive stance of a nuclear twosome, defending privacy against collective infringement. Two homesteaders on the prairie, away, alone, apart, shotgun cradled, standing guard. That steadfast marriage implies a bad world.

Inherently separated individuals cannot "marry" without giving up their individualistic definition of freedom. So our marriages don't "work," and neither does societal freedom. The more "freedom" our nation advocates, the more we invent regulations of it: wiretapping, security surveillance, anti-Freeman measures, more imprisonments per capita than any nation on earth, longer school hours and curfews on youth, more credentials and permits and licenses, as well as politically corrective pressures of every sort that curtail and inhibit. We are caught in an unfixable dilemma: the more we affirm personal freedom the less of it we have. The more we demand guarantees from society, the less we feel freedom to be our own. What begins as personally innate and inalienable has come to depend on impersonal and alien systems.

I think this distortion of freedom derives from those three prepositions we already mentioned—freedom from, of, and to. For these prepositions tie freedom with choices—as if more choices, the more freedom; tie it with need gratification—as if the faster and fuller a gratification, the more freedom; tie it with opportunities to enact fantasies—as if the more we can do, the freer we are. Surely, an exhausting program of multiple choices, speeded satisfactions and hyperactivity. Rather like American consumerism, which fosters neither marriage nor intimacy.

The only way I can imagine fixing the unfixable is to connect freedom with that fourth preposition, in. Only by shifting the idea of freedom to a base in myths and figures of the soul, as a cosmic ferment innate, might freedom be realized in its original sense of an ecstatic, orgasmic potential that vitalizes any choice, satisfaction or opportunity. This libidinal notion of freedom was developed by the Freudian left of Reich, Marcuse, and Norman Brown, and witnessed long before it entered their minds by Christian, Sufi, and Hasidic mystics in their exalted and tortured delights.

Freedom as the inmost juice of intimate love, the goddess Freya in any moment able to bless any situation, leads us straight to Intimacy as the place where freedom can fully flourish. Opening the heart, the belly, the mind, via the mouth. Don't stop flow. Released libido—libido from *lips* [Greek], downpouring, outpouring. "I have never said this before." "Tell me, say anything you want." "I feel freer than ever in my life." "Do whatever you want with me." "Let go, let go." These are the speeches of intimacy—and of freedom. No wonder Freud's "talking cure" worked in nineteenth-century bourgeois Vienna: it offered freedom and intimacy both. To say whatever comes into your mind without restraint invites Freya onto the couch. Of course what came out was erotic, sexual. Not the later Apollonian analysis of the speech or an Oedipal *heureskein* (figuring out your past deeds to "know yourself"), but Liber loosed, the loosening of the mouth as wine and whiskey loosen the tongue. Aphrodite loosening the girdle; Dionysos, "the Loosener." (And Dionysos, you will remember, was both Lord of Souls and only god, other than Zeus, who had one wife, Ariadne, with whom he stayed married.)

Therapy supposedly gives you leave to be just as you want to be, utterly free, and supposedly loved for you as you are. This word "leave," to have leave, to take leave, to go on leave or on liberty—all lead back to the same meaning of love. For the words "leave" and "believe" are cognates of love. Intimacy gives leave to state one's love and one's inmost belief. Do you see why it is easy to fall in love with therapy, with the therapist? And why when you fall out of love with the therapist, you no longer believe in it?

That intimacy has a sexual meaning is archetypally and mythically appropriate. "Did you have intimate relations?" asks the trial attorney, the news reporter. Intimacy meaning sexual relations; genital relations; intercourse as communion of the liquid sap of life. "Free," from Freya and Frigg; those Norse goddesses derive their names from the same Indo-European root, *prij*, love, and *prij* is also the root of prick and Priapus. "Friend," too, comes from this root, that friend with whom you can be truly intimate.

Freya travels in a carriage pulled by pussycats. Other names configure her as a fertile sow, as liquid manure, and the riches of the fecund earth of horse stall and barnyard. Intimacy invites in the vital sweet and smelly fantasies that are the inward riches of freedom.

These goddesses of freedom, Freya and Frigg, also provide the blessings of marriage in Norse mythology. Imagine: freedom and marriage under the same aegis! Within this configuration a stable marriage would be indeed a stable marriage. Marriage thus becomes the place of both freedom and intimacy, the place where permission is given for the prick, the sow, and the pussycat, where "you have my leave" to be as you are, a leave that is the essence of love. To grant leave is to give love. The blessed state of matrimony therewith blesses all the priapic barnyard liberties of intimate life.

Well—so it might seem from the etymology and the mythology, but we do not live any longer among the Vikings, or the peoples of Italy for whom Liber was a friendly force. Dionysos has become a drunk, an unstoppered tongue at an AA meeting. Our language has been Christianized along with our lands and our customs. So, when couples try to shed that Christianization in order to follow their bliss by living out the pagan myths—as did D. H. Lawrence and Frieda (*nomen est omen*)—they may find themselves more likely wracked on the Cross than frolicking with Frigg.

Marriage today owes more to St. Paul than to Freya, Paul who said it is better to marry than to burn. Marriage is where the fires of ecstatic freedom dampen into the pallor of ash, where intimacy is only a carnal necessity for procreation, and where the passion of extramarital and premarital fantasies of intimacy and freedom are burned away. Marriage as burn-out. Marriage as the big chill. Which then leads to the idea of personal freedom as escape from marriage. Robert Stein in his classic book *Incest and Human Love*, and in his several writings in issues of the *Spring* journal, calls this urge—and problem—"de-coupling."[2] De-coupling offers a fantasy of intimacy *outside* of marriage in such extramarital places as the therapist's office rather than under the comforter of the marriage bed.

Stein, a lovely man and a boldly original and sensitive therapist, said for years that the basic problems we meet in therapy, the basic messes

---

2. Robert Stein, *Incest and Human Love* (Putnam, Conn.: Spring Publications, 1988) and *Love, Sex, and Marriage: Collected Essays of Robert Stein* (Woodstock, Conn.: Spring Journal Books, 2001).

of human lives, begin in marriage. I agree with him because marriage, which is an archetypal mess to begin with, as a conjunction of incompatible opposites, is made yet more insupportable by our repressive negativist Pauline version of this conjunction. The blessed—and wherever there are blessings there are cursings too—state of matrimony is theologically cursed from the start. Even its intimacy has been lessened; so often what one brings to it from the most sacred place of the soul is feared by the other as a threat. "I could never tell this to my wife." "My husband simply doesn't want to hear about such things…"

We hold back from each other and suspect each other instead; thereby a cold bed of marriage becomes a hotbed of jealousy. We forget that marriage, by its very oath of better and worse is a sanctuary where exposure is not only allowed but absolutely mandatory. Thus, Felix Pollak's poem, "The Dream."[3]

> He dreamed of
> an open window.
> A vagina, said
> his psychiatrist.
> Your divorce, said
> his mistress.
> Suicide, said
> an ominous voice within him.
> It means you should close the window
> or you'll catch cold, said
> his mother.
> His wife said
> nothing.
> He dared not tell her
> such a
> dangerous dream.

We keep our marriages going by repression. No wonder freedom and intimacy become its opposites.

Finally, now, I believe that beyond Marriage, Intimacy, Freedom, there lurks a fourth and hidden term. For a Jungian, there is always a hidden fourth. Within and behind the aspiring expectations of the soul is a

---

3. Felix Pollak, "The Dream," in *The Rag and Bone Shop of the Heart: Poems for Men*, edited by Robert Bly, James Hillman, and Michael Meade (New York: HarperCollins, 1992), 432.

haunting sadness from which our three themes offer seductive solutions. I am referring to the human condition of loneliness.

We have been living in a century of increasing loneliness borne out by demographic statistics that show the breakup of large families living together, the divorce rate, the women who must work to maintain the nation's unjust trickle-down economics, alienation of adolescents, prolongation of existence for the aged, separatist racist practices, tremendous mobility of the population, and all the other sociological statistics testifying to loneliness. The current idealization of "community" and the therapeutic shibboleths about "relationship" bear further witness to an underlying isolation of individuals.

Isn't this loneliness cosmological? Doesn't it come with our *Weltbild?* Like atoms rapping in a void: we may be attracted and repelled to one another, but we are inherently unrelated. Isn't our loneliness epistemological? For we are but a pair of perceiving eyes, protruding from a processing brain observing a world we inhabit though not necessary to it. Loneliness comes with how we have mapped the territory, so loneliness can hardly be remedied by personal measures. No marriage, no intimacy and no exercise of personal freedom can reach its roots that extend throughout Western cosmology.

And so, your loneliness and mine tell of a more fundamental separation—that exile from the cosmos itself, from the gods and *daimones* and ancestors, and from the rituals that keep the world, that is also their world, intimately shared. Inside your and my desire for relationship is that longing for relationship with them, while our call for community yearns for communion with them who sustain life, give our lives their myths, provide its truths, inhabit its nature, and govern its works.

They do not guarantee blessing—again witness the Greeks. Destruction and disaster also issue from their hands. And, they are certainly not free in any drive-by or any Texan sense of freedom, for the gods too are bound by cosmic order. At least, however, intimacy with them ameliorates the yearning that we bring to the fantasy of marriage and which its facts do not assuage. Just this loneliness, this search for sheltering union, as Robert Stein revealed so poignantly in his writings, makes our all-too-human marriages fall apart and enlarges the delusion that to be "unmarried" is to find intimacy and be free, both.

Though I cannot fix what is wrong or state what is right, I may at least plead for that little preposition *in*. The more we stay in and the further we go in, the more freedom we may find and the more gods we may discover. The *in*side of marriage would be like that startling depiction of Socrates at the end of Plato's *Symposium* (217*a*), a dialogue about love and intimacy. The "ugly" casing of the human (Socrates) has "little images inside…so godlike, so golden, so beautiful and so utterly amazing."

This is the intimacy we covet and may find—intimacy with them "so utterly amazing," and also with them in their monstrous shapes, relieving the personal of demands to cure marriage of its peculiarities and pathologies. You can't cure the gods—so lay off trying to change your partner. Intimacy with them invites a freedom of commerce between their world and ours, between human and inhuman, between fantasy and fact. The impersonal inhuman immortals take up rooms in the personal frailties of the human household, sharing bed and board, and boredom, freeing the householders of working so hard at the marriage. I think this is what the married soul most wants.

*Personifying
or Imagining Things*

9

A NOTE ON STORY

From my perspective as depth psychologist, I see that those who have a connection with story are in better shape and have a better prognosis than those to whom story must be introduced. This is a large statement and I would like to take it apart in several ways. But I do not want to diminish its apodeictic claim: to have "story-awareness" is *per se* psychologically therapeutic. It is good for soul.

To have had story of any sort in childhood—and here I mean oral story, those told or read (for reading has an oral aspect even if one reads to oneself) rather than watching story on screen—puts a person into a basic recognition of and familiarity with the legitimate reality of story *per se*. It is given with life, with speech and communication, and not something later that comes with learning and literature. Coming early with life, it is already a perspective to life. One integrates life as story because one has stories in the back of the mind (unconscious) as containers for organizing events into meaningful experiences. The stories are means of telling oneself into events that might not otherwise make psychological sense at all. (Economic, scientific, and historical explanations are sorts of "stories" that often fail to give the soul the kind of imaginative meaning it seeks for understanding its psychological life.)

Having had story built in with childhood, a person is usually in better relation with the pathologized material of obscene, grotesque, or cruel images that appear spontaneously in dream and fantasy. Those who hold to the rationalist and associationist theory of mind, who put reason against and superior to imagination, argue that if we did not put in such grim tales in early impressionable years, we would have less pathology and more rationality in later years. My practice shows me rather that the more attuned and experienced is the imaginative side of personality the

less threatening the irrational, the less necessity for repression, and therefore the less actual pathology acted out in literal, daily events. In other
words, through story the symbolic quality of pathological images and
themes finds a place, so that these images and themes are less likely to be
viewed naturalistically, with clinical literalism, as signs of sickness. These
images find places in story as legitimate. They *belong* to myths, legends,
and fairy tales where, just as in dreams, all sorts of peculiar figures and
twisted behaviors appear. After all, "The Greatest Story Ever Told," as
some are fond of calling Easter, is replete with gruesome imagery in great
pathologized detail.

Story awareness provides a better way than clinical awareness for
coming to terms with one's own case history. Case history, too, is a fictional form written up by thousands of hands in thousands of clinics
and consulting rooms, stored away in archives and rarely published. This
fictional form called "case history" follows the genre of social realism; it
believes in facts and events and takes all tales told with excessive literalism. In deep analysis, the analyst and the patient together rewrite the case
history into a new story, creating the "fiction" in the collaborative work
of the analysis. Some of the healing that goes on, maybe even the essence
of it, is this collaborative fiction, this putting all the chaotic and traumatic
events of a life into a new story. Jung said that patients need "healing
fictions,"[1] but we have trouble coming to this perspective unless there is
already a predilection for story awareness.

Jungian therapy, at least as I practice it, brings about an awareness
that fantasy is the dominant force in a life. One learns in therapy that
fantasy is a creative activity that is continually telling a person into now
this story, now that one. When we examine these fantasies we discover
that they reflect the great impersonal themes of mankind as represented
in tragedy, epic, folktale, legend, and myth. Fantasy in our view is the
attempt of the psyche itself to remythologize consciousness; we try to
further this activity by encouraging familiarity with myth and folktale.
Soul-making goes hand in hand with deliteralizing consciousness and
restoring its connection to mythic and metaphorical thought patterns.

---

1. [For a full exploration of this idea in the work of Freud, Jung, and Adler,
see James Hillman, *Healing Fiction* (Thompson, Conn.: Spring Publications, 2020
[1983]).—Ed.]

Rather than interpret the stories into concepts and rational explanations, we prefer to see conceptual explanations as secondary elaborations upon basic stories that are containers and givers of vitality. As Owen Barfield and Norman Brown have written, "Literalism is the enemy." I would add: "Literalism is sickness." Whenever we are caught in a literal view, a literal belief, a literal statement, we have lost the imaginative metaphorical perspective to ourselves and our world. Story is prophylactic in that it presents itself always as "once upon a time," as an "as if," "make-believe" reality. It is the only mode of accounting or telling about that does not posit itself as real, true, factual, revealed, i.e., literal.

This brings us to the question of content. Which stories need to be told? Here I am a classic, holding for the old, the traditional, the ones of our own culture: Greek, Roman, Celtic, and Nordic myths; the Bible; legends and folktales. And these with the least modern marketing (updating, cleaning up, editing, etc.), i.e., with the least interference by contemporary rationalism, which is subject to the very narrowing of consciousness that stories themselves would expand. Even if we be not Celtic or Nordic or Greek in ancestry, these collections are the fundamentals of our Western culture, and they work in our psyche whether we like it or not. We may consider them distorted in their pro-Aryan or pro-male or pro-warrior slant, but unless we understand that these tales depict the basic motifs of the Western psyche, we remain unaware of the basic motives in our psychological dynamics. Our ego psychology still resounds with the motif and motivation of our hero, just as much psychology of what we call "the feminine" today reflects the patterns of the goddesses and nymphs in Greek myth. These basic tales channel fantasy. Platonists long ago, and Jung more recently, pointed out the therapeutic value of the great myths for bringing order to the chaotic, fragmented aspect of fantasy. The main body of biblical and classical tales direct fantasy into organized, deeply life-giving psychological patterns; these stories present the archetypal modes of experiencing.

I think children need less convincing of the importance of story than do adults. To be adult has come to mean to be adulterated with rational explanations, and to shun such childishness as we find in fairy stories. I have tried to show in detail how adult and child have come to be set against each other: childhood tends to mean wonder, imagination, creative spontaneity, while adulthood, the loss of these perspectives (cf. "Abandoning the Child"[2]). So the first task, as I see it, is re-storying the adult—the teacher and the parent and the grandparent—in order to restore the imagination to a primary place in consciousness in each of us, regardless of age.

I have come at this from a psychological viewpoint, partly because I wish to remove story from its too close association with both education and literature—something taught and something studied. My interest in story is as something lived in and lived through, a way in which the soul finds itself in life.

2. James Hillman, "Abandoning the Child," in *UE6: Mythic Figures.*

10

SEX TALK:
IMAGINING A NEW MALE SEXUALITY

Men are not talking to each other about sex, at least not hetero-sexual men. Women talk—in detail!—yet the few men who talk about sex talk only with their women partners. With each other, sex talk becomes adolescent boastings and action-packed machismo. How can a man learn, or teach, about what really happens and might happen if he keeps secretive and dumb about genital intimacy?

Dumb sex is cultural. Our white American speech doesn't provide good words for genitals and intercourse—and hardly any phrases about places, rhythms, touches, and tastes.

Listen to the marvelous language of foreign erotica: jade stalk, palace gates, ambrosia! Compare these with cock, prick, dick, nuts, balls; with suck, jerk, blow, yank; and with gash, bush, frog, slit, clit, hole. A Chinese plum is to be deliciously enjoyed; our cherries are to be taken, popped, or broken. Suppose we were to call him, as he once was named, Jolly Roger or Little Johnny Jump-up, or happy warrior, smiling wand, black magic, or Purusha who is smaller-than-small and bigger-than-big.

Our Puritan prose cannot encompass the sexual imagination to which great temples are built in India. Our imagination reinforces the image of lovemaking as a heroic performance, that hard-rock fantasy of sex. Yet performance heroism makes impotence all the more threatening—and inevitable. This hard language at the core of our sex talk makes us ignore that times of lassitude and gentle reluctance are also divine, for in these moments, imagination swells the body with reverie and longing.

Confidence in male prowess doesn't require talking big or even be-ing big as much as letting our flaccid sexual speech become more redo-lent and swollen. Purpling. This means talking more concretely and with more pleasure about sexual fantasies. For the sexual acts themselves de-pend on imagination.

I find three dominant modes of imagining reality now. One is the heroic: screwings, chasing, shooting. Another is the romantic fantasy of fusion, where the two become one, riding the rhythm so that the cock belongs to both, or to no one. But fusing can turn suddenly into terror and be felt as loss of phallus: she took it; consumed it. Romantic enchantment becomes bewitchment by female power.

A third mode holds desire within mysteries of initiation, invoking the dark gods—both in their wild animal and little child shapes. A kind of neobaroque theater of the sublime—a strange beauty of terror, awe, and play together—the sexual body and the emotions of love meet at the risky edge, promising neither heroic victories nor completely satisfying unions. Here is a wider devotion to the animistic or animalistic powers on which sexuality always depends and urges toward; not secular humanism but the Mysteries.

11

FOREWORD TO *INSCAPES OF THE CHILD'S WORLD*
BY JOHN ALLAN

Though you and I once were children and may now be parents, and may even be dedicating our working lives to the care and counseling of children, we hardly know them. What really is a child, this state called childhood, or adolescence, and who is this particular child now in my charge? Why do children seem a people apart—as we say "men, women, and children"? Why so fascinating, enraging, wondrous, and incomprehensible?

The smaller the child, the more this is the case. The Platonists, and the Romantics who followed them, had a theory to account for our feelings of the child's strangeness, its peculiar terrors and pleasures. The child's soul descends, they said, from another archetypal world, entering this world trailing clouds of glory as it comes (Wordsworth). A being close to angels, it arrives knowing everything essential. Or, as we would say: its collective unconscious is replete with primordial awareness. This angelic guise was demonstrated by pointing at the child's skin when a baby, its face when asleep, its smile, its startling inventive freedom. The angelic guise became a standard icon in graveyard stone and nursery-book lithograph during the last century especially. Only in this century of our Western history has the child been overburdened with carrying the "bad seed" of our civilization's disorder. Today, children everywhere are worried about and need "help," from infant massage to play therapy to corrective lessons. Something is always" wrong" with them.

The soul's difficulties with its descent into the world show up in counseling as "adjustment disorders," or worse, as autism, mutism, attention deficit, anti-social behavior, and the other ills cataloged in our textbooks of abnormal psychology. From the Romantic perspective, the counselor serves as a midwife to the psyche—a role Socrates imagined for his work, guiding the child into the world without too much loss of its remnants of mythic memory. Or, to use another simile from classical Greece, the counselor is like a *paedagogos,* a slave or servant who walks along with a child to school.

School tries to put the child's psyche within the mind of practical reason: clock time, factual truth, and a xerox notion of images, i.e., accurate reproduction. What you draw is what you see. School defines "realism" as photographic realism and tests the child's sense of reality in the hard schoolyard of competition. Coping before hoping. Realism, however, ever since Plato and still in philosophy today, refers to realities of invisible forms that are innate and pattern the actual world. A classical realist would say the child brings reality with him or her, a reality that today we call fantasy.

The child's fantasy is still in thrall to the "thing of beauty [that] is a joy forever," as Keats said. As he also said, this beauty is truth. Or, let us say, according to the Romantic vision beauty is the interior truth potentially available to the child to keep it on course. Beauty is as much a guide as reason, discipline, and psychological know-how. The child's need for beauty as guide suggests the arts take primary place in the teaching and counseling of children. After all, the arts at least refer to beauty and must keep it in mind; whereas psychology, education, and social studies seem completely unconscious of its importance in moving the soul deeply, so that beauty has become the Great Repressed in the training of professional counselors. The arts take primary place for another reason. They bridge between the child's first world of imagination and the actual world into which it descends, thereby providing a hands-on way of healing the most fundamental cleavage in human existence.

The daily pressures of work make us forget that the child as symbol, and actual children too, always evokes the twin possibilities of terror and joy, extremes at the outer edges of the curve of normality. The child enters the world still open to emotional intensities beyond the usual. This confronts the therapist often with emotions long dormant, even extinct, in his or her own soul. Those who have most to do with children seem to have lost the feeling for the child's terror and fascination with terror and, even more, to have lost the child's extraordinary possibility for joy. Instead, we meet children with worried concern, therapeutic goodwill and professional smiles, but few laughs. We would bring the child under the normalizing shelter of the bell curve: nothing to extremes. Keats, Blake, and Whitman, however, insist on the wildest joy.

Freud did too. He saw the child's sensuous delight in all things as a polymorphous sexual libido. The child enters the world packed with the pleasure principle, a roly-poly of desires for what the world offers. Like a goat's kid, the child dances with surplus exuberance; like a kitten it explores everywhere and takes sudden fright; and like a piglet, how good it all tastes! The world is a good place to be—when, and only when, the imagination with which the child descends is still alive enough to imbue the things of the world with the child's vision of beauty.

Not its innocence makes the child's psyche so susceptible to corruption of its desire, but its attachment to beauty. Eating disorders, media addiction, hyperactivity and victimization by exploiters are based in the child's native desire for beauty in this world comparable to the richness of its fantasy in the unconscious soul. Exploitation could not occur if a child entered the world a mere *tabula rasa* void of any prior delight in and recognition of sensate images. So, the disorders of sensationalism reveal the child's innate aesthetic response to the world as a place of pleasure, in which all things are desirable. *Schlaraffenland* and Paradise are where we begin, and the child will live in a cargo cult of consumerism when the fantasies of the extraordinary that fill its soul are not given imaginary and imaginative response by its adult guides.

But many adult guides who meet the disturbed child are themselves disturbed by their training. We have been initiated into the myth of developmental psychology: that all life moves in one direction starting in infancy (but not before, not beyond). Moreover, the simplistics of our myth say that this one-way direction in time is causal: a person is caused by history, and the earlier the history the more powerful the cause. So, childhood has been declared the source of all our disaffected behavior. This tale told by dynamic and developmental psychology says childhood is basically miserable. Every therapy session searches memory for traces of unhappiness. We do not turn there for beauty and joy, but to uncover the curses of abuse, shame, and fixation on that abuse and shame. Bad mothers, absent fathers, and envious siblings are the demons and ogres in psychology's fairy tale. This script curses the family with a psychology of blame instead of honor. It also curses the pleasurable world and the origins of the libido in sensuous joy. No wonder that actual children become so anesthetized that they are content with the pseudo stimuli of TV, so that by adolescence they have to shoot up to feel. They sit in classes without motivation, walk the streets in sullen rage, and seek desperately for sensuous transcendence in sounds, speeds, and sex for an altered state of mind as an alternative script to the soulless and joyless dealing, handling, coping, managing life as a program of practical reason. Unconsciously, they recollect something else, something more, which they would find again, sometimes by suicide.

To get some of this off my chest, or out of my heart, and to offer a *vision* of children, I welcomed John Allan's invitation to write a foreword to his book. As his colleague, his friend, and now his publisher, I am enthused by his book. It is important. He shows a way that is practical, sober, and unassuming for the great escape from reasonable realism, backward and inward to the inscapes of the child's soul by restoring the authenticity of the child's own visionary activity. He gives detailed instructions for coaxing the child into its inscapes, into the forgotten terrain of its interior knowledge, the recovery of which is healing. He knows the children and their plight; he knows the imagination and its force; and he also knows the counselors, their encouraging tendencies and their possible wrong reactions. For, after all, the counselor is obliged to engage in a world of witches and wizards, of violent wars and drowning babies, of quicksand and pathetically withering flowers, a world from which his or her training has yielded little more than alienation. To engage in the child's fantasy requires one to be engaged by one's own. To enjoy one's own dreams and be comfortable in one's own inscapes should be the first requirement for working with children. This book makes this requirement a pleasure, for John Allan leads the reader into the forest, gently, and with the practical know-how of a naturalist.

The beauty of the book lies just there. It gives the reader the inscape without heavy theoretical equipment, without psychodynamic bulldozing. It is a book without argument—for the imagination doesn't argue—a book without accusations against social forces, bad parents, the curse of poverty. Sure, all that is always present: ugly abuse, crass stupidity, misfortune. Yet, through it all we watch the actual display of each child's fantasy, telling its stories and painting its pictures as it slowly disengages from the mess in that process we call therapy. For me, the prime virtue of this book is its good sense. John Allan is not, like me, an intoxicated Romantic. Nor is he out to attest to the archetypes developing into the

Jungian Self. He wishes to—and does—lay bare what actually happens with schoolchildren when their inscapes are wisely received and allowed to form. If we must use that abused word "creative," then here is witness to its simply happening. All the while the prose is straightforward, the information comprehensive, detailed, and instructive, packed into the pages, with little fuss. As Allan says in his Introduction, he wanted to be a forester. In this book, he is taking care of the trees.

For a good example of his know-how, turn to Chapter 8, the case of the five-and-a-half-year-old psychotic girl, Luci. She comes with a dream of having visited the "dead land"—"no people, no fires in the fireplaces, no food in the refrigerators, no beds in the bedrooms, and no furniture in the living rooms. Outside there are no flowers, no grass, only rocks." Luci's psyche is in the wasteland of a "deep depression," as Allan says. But notice, he does not jerk her out of it, console her with mothering, or fear for her dissolution. The image tells him where she is, and he enters that place with her and speaks with her from within the inscape, trusting that a *vis naturalis* (a natural life force) is working its way within the psyche even in the "dead land" or mythical Underworld, in the shape of images and the colors of feelings.

Another hint we may gain from the book concerns interpretation. When and how do we interpret a child's images? Allan suggests that at certain moments the counselor make "linkages...from the drawings to the therapeutic relationship or world situations." He gives this example:

> I see the helicopter pilot is repairing the hole in the road...I wonder if at times you feel I'm like that pilot helping you mend some of your hurts.

Here we watch the way interpretation acts as a bridge between worlds, teaching the practicality of metaphor for helping the descent from images into experiences. For the child here learns how one and the same image— helicopter pilot repairing holes, i.e., whirlybird man or sky hero performing the archetypal task of shoring up human culture—is at the same time concerned directly with the personal fate of the child himself. The holes are not in the child or made by the child. He is not they, any more than the pilot is he. Nor are the holes directly the result of past abuse any more than the pilot is the present representative of the helping therapist. These implications of the image are drawn from it by interpretation. The image itself, however, remains intact as the actual healing factor because it gives the child a way of picturing in metaphorical terms his drama, fostering his imagination to go on the road of his life and meet his plight by the innate means of "dreaming the myth onward," as Jung defined his therapeutic method.

Interpretation exercises our metaphorical thinking, that capacity to realize on several levels at once. We learn to grasp that the exotic world of symbolic scenes and the painful world of human relationships can be in continuing relation.

Despite Allan's advice regarding interpretation and the book's many demonstrations of it, he does maintain, in accord with the Jungian view, that imaginative expression in the presence of the counselor with no interpretation helps children release some of the power of symbols and their emotions at a critical moment in their lives. Again, we see his reliance upon the child's own psychic images, what Jung calls the symbolic process of individuation, a deep-rooted autonomous activity that strives like the energy in a tree or the instinctual vitality in any living form to maintain its integrity in face of its destiny—even if that destiny be early death due to illness or accident.

I would also point out that this integrity in the practice of counseling begins with the respect Allan shows for the integrity of the images themselves. If we reduce the images back to our assessment of the child's personality (his violent hostility or her mute fright) or to traumata suffered by the child from the environment, we are not recognizing the full authority of the images in shaping the child's destiny. We are not allowing what the child brings with him or her into the world, in the Platonic and Romantic sense of an innate capacity to form life in accordance with imagination (or, as Jung wrote, "fantasy creates reality every day"). Our task is to nurture the child by nurturing its inscapes.

For instance, Allan emphasizes "talking about the content of the picture in the third person ('I notice you've drawn a big gorilla; I wondered what the gorilla is thinking...feeling...and planning to do next')."

Had Allan said—and here I am inventing a scenario—"I guess that gorilla reminds you of your father when he gets in that 'state' after drinking," or had said, "I guess that gorilla is how you feel when you tear up your room and want to beat up on your little brother," then the gorilla would have lost its potency as a living being of imagination and been reduced to a mere component of the rational world, explained as a function of personality (the child's rage) or a residue of experience (the child's terrifyingly drunken father image).

Instead, Allan invites the gorilla to step out of the drawing and speak. This gesture toward the image respects its autonomy. The gorilla becomes a partner in the counsel: child, counselor, and gorilla. The two persons turn directly to the personified image for understanding why it has appeared, what it feels, how it plans to move; thereby the child—and the counselor—can possibly foresee in which direction within the crisis of the child's destiny the next phase might go.

The invitation to the gorilla to speak is so radical that it moves to counseling itself outside our culture into other times and places, and into another myth beyond humanism. In the Middle Ages, this turn to the image would be demonism; in Victorian anthropology, animism. But in ancient Egypt, Greece, and Rome, and among Eskimos, South Sea Islanders, Native Americans, and West Africans, the recognition of the image as a living intelligence that plays a governing role in our soul life is simply a basic truth. "Animism" is our Western way of saying that images, places, precious things and natural phenomena are animated, which literally means *ensouled*. So, it seems, that by means of the art of therapy with disordered children, our disordered civilization may be taking its first steps toward the restoration of the sense of a world alive, and that the child appearing in your next counseling session may really be a missionary from heaven.

Pathologizing or Falling Apart:
Transitions and Transgressions

12

THE COURAGE TO RISK FAILURE

It is beyond an honor to speak to you today. It is a surprise—and an irony. This is the first high-school graduation at which I have spoken, to which I have ever been invited. More, it is the first high-school graduation I have ever attended. I never graduated from my high school in New Jersey. Something came up, there was a war on. I saw a chance to avoid that last half of senior year, those final exams—especially Latin and Math—and I jumped into college. Then, they called it nicely "acceleration." My principal summoned me into his office—I do not suppose Dr. Mattern uses that sort of old-fashioned terror—to warn me of all the risks, worst of them being without a high-school diploma I could never teach in the State of New Jersey. His prophecy was right, I have never taught in the State of New Jersey. *Pace*, Mr. Principal, and wherever you are, look at your boy now!

The risk is always to be taken. A risk refused is life refused. And there are always risks available. One does not need to search them out, chase them with glue bottles, pep pills, and kicks. I am my own risk; you are your own risk. There is enough in us and about us, if we are engaged, involved, to make each day a very risky matter. We make our own risks, and as such create our own lives through the risk we take.

Risking is today called "the courage to be." This "courage to be" means to stand for what one is—your gifts and stumblings, your public strengths and private sins, your own individual nature, which is simply your example of human nature. As well, the courage to be means to stand for what one was: the past from which you came, your family and the style of your family, your ancestors, the beliefs and traditions of your part of the country, your special background, the quirks of accent and regionalism, the accidents that came your way, the dreams that drive you forward. And the courage to be means to stand for what one wants and aims for. Being yourself includes also your hopes, the star you stretch toward, the moral principles that belong to you, the ideals, the goals that come disguised in fantasies of how it may one day be.

In my work as an analyst, a psychologist, the people I meet are struggling to be, to find what they are meant to be, struggling, wrestling with how to be. And no one can tell them, just as no one can tell you, fundamentally in the deepest sense, where the heart is, where the courage comes from, where risks are given assent. One cannot be told. One creates oneself, one's own way of being, one's style.

School prepares with knowledge so that risks can be weighed on a larger scale than the petty one of just "me" and my meager experience. School gives the wider perspective. One learns other words in other languages, other ways of perceiving and expressing what would otherwise be a single, one-dimensional fact. One gains a historical depth toward issues for decision, and models of men and women from history and literature who can be patterns and pointers in forming one's own way. A statesman, an author, a figure in a novel returns in our dreams, giving a hint of how life might be lived.

School also gives the tools of numbers and information with which to cope. Risks can be taken with more calculation, with more awareness, one goes girded and forearmed. Yet the true risk, true adventure always has in it the unforeseeable, where there is no answer until the adventure is begun and the answers only come through the experience itself. No one can ever tell you "how the water is": temperature, chemical analysis, hydraulic flow, handbooks on swimming, color films, even memory. No, you must get in yourself: immersed, surrounded, wet.

So that the courage to be means finally nothing less than full commitment and involvement in life, over one's head in the current. The current, let us note, is more than taking part in activities, being in and with it, where the action is. The it, let us note, that one is with and the it that one is in may not be for each alike. What one has to get with is for each different. For some of you, it may be the great mainstream; but for others, full commitment may be to an inner world of thoughts and moods and imaginings often grossly misunderstood by others; Or full involvement may mean the commitment of service to another person, without holding back, without fear of submitting, of being weak and dependent, without reserving judgments, but the courage to be in love. There is no comparison of risks; only of the way we take them. There are no insurance brokers who can give the odds in advance. And there are odds. There is always a risk of failure involved with involvement.

So when we draw our profiles in courage, the darkness against which the profile stands out, which makes the profile possible at all, is the backdrop of failure. If the urge to move forward, to succeed, is only to keep away from failure, the fear of falling flat, of being let down in love, set back, dropped out, then the urge to success is questionable. How do we judge the go, go, go man on the run: is he running toward success or away from failure?

Success opposes, denies failure. Success moves toward security. But the courage to be, to take risks, includes insecurity and remembers at each turn that failure is a real possibility.

We sometimes forget that failure has two sides. The unconscious puts another face on things, gives them another meaning. A failure throws the train off the track, closes a door: bursts the river levee. But a derailment also starts a new chain of events in an unexpected direction; the closed door means one is forced to find another way through; and the flood may change the river course and bring new life to dry land.

Some of the most eminent people in history failed at all their attempts, only to be led through their failures to their own real calling. Many of the political leaders today spent years in jail or underground. Many of the writers had books rejected again and again. And is there any way to know about love except through the anguish of failure?

To avoid a risk because it might lead to failure is to miss the meaning of risk. It is just the possibility of failure that gives the risk its kick, its genuine authenticity, which we recognize by the emotions of thrill, anxiousness, and joy. And it can be in such small steps: simply saying aloud what you think; simply saying no when you mean it; simply the extra step of trying harder or the extra abandon of letting go.

What may seem a failure from the standpoint of success may turn out quite otherwise. So it is foolish to compare or to judge those who seem to have failed. What may seem first to be a reverse may be no real reverse at all—only a detour, an off-beat path. And the man or woman who travels the side roads may not move too well on the throughway, but they know the countryside and the lay of the land. When emergencies come, and the cars above break down or crack up, the one who has already been ditched, bogged down, stalled, has the wisdom and patience to cope. School should have taught you not only how to make success but how to take failure. But school, too, often gets at us through the fear of failure, and then the capacity to take risks, instead of encouraged and expanded by school, shrinks.

This shrinkage in the courage to be we find all about us: don't get taken, play it safe, keep it cool. But playing safe is soon the end of playing, and the cooler we keep, the colder we grow. Then especially we need the courage to take a risky step out of a pattern of closing in.

As I said, we do not need to search out risks. They are at hand at every moment. The risk now, today, is to seize the day, this day of your final completion of compulsory education, the obligations to the system set by society. This moment is a modern repetition of the primitive initiation rite, where you move from one stage of life to another, leaving what is only expected of you to explore the open land of choice and risk, where you can no longer be compelled by law to learn; but where you may follow your own stream where it takes you. It is usual to give caution and warn of responsibility at these rites—to beat the heavy drum. Yet the ancient meaning of this day is to re-affirm not only your place in the long tradition, your belonging to society and your membership in it, but also your free individuality, that your mind is your own, your body is your own, your heart is your own, and your will is your own. And the day is not only serious, sentimental, and solemn. To take it only as such is to avoid the risk, the full involvement of your moment and the courage to be your age, which makes the day as well a day of choice, high jinx, and joy.

13

LIFE AND DEATH IN ANALYSIS

In our talk this afternoon, I shall not be careful in my use of terms concerning analysis. Were I to be careful, I would have to define analysis; but you know better than I do that we do not have a single definition that is acceptable to all of us who work in the field. This has to be so, because when we are actually at work, we do many things and are many people. I may be giving therapy or counsel, teaching, advising, analyzing, interpreting, directing conscience, caring for soul, reacting, nonreacting, interacting, not interacting, and so on.

We could only define analysis if we knew what we were doing; but we do not know what we are doing, and we can never know, since it is an activity like painting or writing poems in which the unconscious continually intervenes and prevents us from conscious knowing that can be formulated in definitions.

However, I do regard my principal task as an analyst, and particularly as a Jungian, as being involvement with this unconscious side that prevents my clarity and my knowing. Just what do I mean by that? What is the unconscious side of the person's psyche? Do we mean a state of unconsciousness like sopor or coma? Or do we mean a kind of behavior like highly affect-charged, or just its opposite, habitual and, therefore, unreflected and unconscious? Or do we mean—and I think this is how I shall be tending to see the term—a hypothetical region, a topological description, a section of the human being that is outside my awareness but acting through my actions, thinking within my thoughts, motivating my will, affecting my feelings, and above all, through complexes and fantasies influencing my imagination and my way of perceiving myself and the world?

So it is to these fantasy complexes, these mythical parts of the person, that my attention is mainly focused when I do analysis. I am less interested in his daily case report: the fights with his wife and the trouble with his son, and the symptoms that appear and disappear and reappear—the personal interactions. Oh, yes; these are there in the foreground, of course, and they are pushed on us all the time. But I am after the background; not the case history and its progress, but the soul history in its process.

Or I might, in another way, say that analysis is a concern for personality transformation; and "personality" here means a vessel or a great mask like the Greek persona or actors wore in the drama, and through which the god speaks. The mask is not a thing I put on to meet the faces that I meet, but rather would be the necessary role one plays, the die into which one is cast or the part one plays, so that the voice of the god within the soul, within the psyche, actually can speak; and through this force of the godly within the soul, the personality is forced in to existence as a carrier of something beyond itself.

Now, the soul history of personality is revealed mainly through dreams, which usually circle around certain experiences or themata; and they leave out entire areas of a person's remembered life, of his biography. For example, supposing I spent six summers in a camp as a boy, and during twenty years of recording my dreams I never dreamt of any of this. Or that I have fourteen cousins, and I have only dreamt of one of these cousins in all those years; or that I traveled in many countries, and only three or four of these countries come back again and again as themes in my inner mythology while others are dismissed like that. That my dreams continue to center on certain people, places, scenes, and colors, rewoven and interwoven into a mythology of my own soul. This is the difference between my outer case history and my inner soul history.

It would seem that life, or outer case history, is more and more directed from within by the soul history. When things matter, it is because of the inner aspect. This inner aspect of experience, the feeling that it is mine and important, and something to do with my fate; that I may even have a moral and immortal objective that is religiously concerned, and not just an event or an accident (although accidents can be very important)—this is what I refer to as a sense of soul.

Naturally, the questions of life and death will be of great importance to this sense of soul. And it seems that when one gets to this place in analysis or in a deep talk with another person—and it certainly doesn't have to be during office hours and analytical deep talks don't only have to occur with analysts—those issues will come up in a deep talk. These issues of soul and its destiny and the problem of death come up. They come up in other ways long before we are open to this sort of discussion.

But first let me interpose just one observation: These deep conversations are not meant in an academic or philosophical sense. One doesn't have to have read Plato on immortality of the soul in order to get to the soul and its religious concern, its concern with morality. One doesn't have to be involved with philosophy and have deep ideas that you've taken from somewhere else. Everyone of us will die and everyone of us has been with death in some way or another. And on these deep levels of soul, we are all in communication even if our individual case history of class, color, religion, education, and so on keeps us far apart. On the level of the soul, we are all the same and can all talk. On conceptual levels, we may differ; but not on symbolic levels, not on the levels of fantasy and myth. We do not differ on this level from other ages of history and other peoples who also were involved just as we are on this level of the soul, with how to live and how to die; and why we live and why we die; end what happens at death and after death; and what is the relation between living and dying. It is only our clinical jargon and our academic conceptualizations and our sociological terms and our ridiculous anti-historical pride that separates us from the other person. It's not the client who is not suitable for therapy because be has not the educational level, but it is the therapist who is not suitable because he hasn't the symbolic level.

The matters of life or death, or what we might call the philosophical questions, the questions of meaning, are central and vital to the soul. These have always been the main issues of the psyche throughout all the cultures and all the ages. The matters of life and death may, therefore, be said to be the main concern of the soul. Its other face, its other principal concern, is, of course, love; the context of human life and the conduct of human life among humans. But this other main concern of the soul—love, to give it a name—is not separable from the issues of life and death.

The soul has, then, at least two faces: spiritual and erotic; a face of meaning and a face of love. These are interwoven so that if one is damaged, the other suffers. If we have lost meaning, if life and death do not hold together in a philosophy or a *Weltanschauung*, then love does not function; and if we have lost connection to love, meaning falls apart.

These matters of life and death come up naturally in analysis, not only because they are verbal questions and/or interesting ideas; but rather, it seems to me, as if the phenomenon of analysis itself seems to constellate such questions. It is as if analysis—this deep discussion; not always so deep, but this discussion as I am presenting it—this discussion of two people in two chairs laying their souls bare, two people intensely concerned with fundamentals and asking the unconscious voice to come in, too, and have its say; by asking for dreams and asking for emotions and asking for fantasies and reacting to and from this level—this peculiar ritual, which has been created in the last sixty years and didn't exist before and which we call analysis, draws not only the soul to show itself in the face of love (or what is unfortunately and hideously called "the transference and its erotic aspects") but also to show its passionate concern with matters of meaning.

So dreams pick upon symbols and use the language of very deep meanings in the sense of eternal meanings, eternal archetypal themes that, if followed and not reduced to something else, believed in, submitted to, lead to fundamental issues of life and death. Now what leads in this process is often something rather absurd and obscure. At first, it may seem to be the analyst who is the leader of this psychological process; or, as he was called in ancient times, the "psychopompos," the leader of the psyche or guide of souls. The leader of the psyche, or the leader of the soul, comes up in dream images: or the land into which he is leading is like Purgatory or an unknown country, or Australia, which is "down-under," or the Lost Continent, or some other place across the seas; and the leader function comes up as a white hunter in Africa, or a conductor on a train, a man in a mine with a lamp on his hat.

The leader or guide or guru is often first thought to be the analyst, just as the other aspect of the soul uses the analyst, too, as the lover in order for the experience of love to be let out and set alive.

But after a while, one realizes that it is not the analyst at all, but that the psyche has in itself a function, who is imaged in some sort of a figure, that leads it into fundamental problems of meaning, into unknown land, into questions of why one lives and what death means; and these questions are phrased in such a manner that they are highly obscure, absurd, paradoxical. It would seem from the empirical witness of watching this occur in analysis that the individuals involved are led or forced to work out a philosophy of life. This issue can become so urgent and pressing that the issue of life and death indeed becomes a matter of life and death, and here the suicide problem often begins.

Suddenly a person has, in a sense, not only begun to question life but has entered death, and has been led by this function within himself (projected, perhaps, on the analysis, carried by the analyst) to set out ever more profound questions. This function doesn't let him go, isn't satisfied with simplifications and cheap answers and reductions, and consciousness begins to question its own roots. This has an effect for the moment, perhaps for some time, of laming the personality. Everything is questioned; nothing stands up at all anywhere. This leads one against the stream and one has, in a sense, said "no" to life.

Now this questioning of life, which is an opposition to life, is destructive to life as it is and, therefore, is the death aspect of growth. This push within the psyche that is essential to personality development shows itself as well in the traditional forms of personality development, all of which have a death aspect.[1] In other words, personality development goes by way of dying. It is not a continual expansion of more and more light, more and more life but, rather, a series of dyings, and analysis as a methodical adventure of personality transformation is always a series of deaths and dyings, a prolonged breakdown, a drawn-out suicide.

Traditional cultures speak of the stages of life or of life organized through phases. The turning points of these stages or crises usually follow a path of biological development; that is, there is supposed to be a first half and a second half of life; or life is divided into youth, middle-age, and old age; or it's divided into four stages of man, or seven, or ten, or twelve. There are examples of all kinds of thought in this field, but the important thing is not so much the separations but the transitions between stages. These are sometimes called in anthropology "rites of passage" or "initiation rites" or "sacraments." In each of these transitions, the essential thing for the personality is its movement. The personality with which one is identified now, here; the me that is as I am, and this is where I am now—here; this, which is built on continuity, built on habit, built on memory—all the things that have brought me up this far—this dies. The external identity, the thing that I'm identified with, is killed or is slain or dies.

---

1. "So we live, and are forever leaving" (from Rainer Maria Rilke's eighth *Duino Elegy,* translated by A. Poulin, Jr.).

Now from this point of view, suicide can be seen as a hasty attempt to move from here to there, to go through; or it can be seen as a rite of passage. It can be seen as an expression of the urgent need transform personality as an expression of the development that would bring what is hitherto unknown, unconscious, and new into consciousness.

It doesn't look this way, of course. It shows violence and it shows dis-order and it shows confusion, or it show regression into nothingness.

But it can also show, in these forms of disguise that make it appear to be anything but development, something so pressing and so urgent and so terribly real to the person's soul that it is no use to attempt to block it without realizing that the destruction of self is first of all a statement of radical transformation. It is the most radical way the me of here-and-now can become the not-me. The conscious personality can become the wholly other and unconscious personality.

Suicide is the ultimate trip out from here to there. It would take us too far to go into the archetypal background of analysis as a transforma-tion of soul. It would be too much to go into the questions of the rituals of death and the ideas of dismemberment in so many of these rituals in initiation rites, or the role of death in various disciplines that are involved with the development of personality, such as Yogi disciplines or spiritual disciplines in the Church, or in alchemy, or the initiatory death and tor-tures in puberty rites, or the death in the mystery religions, which were concerned very much with dying in one stage of life in order to enter the next, or the shamanistic flight completely out of this world, which is a kind of archetypal background of the trip, or initiation experiences, or the descent into hell, which confronts the hero in many examples of his development in fairy tales, in folk tales and myths.

All of this seems to be perhaps irrelevant, but most of the world we call underdeveloped takes its orientation from this kind of thinking; and most of the personality in us that is underdeveloped takes its orientation from this kind of thinking.

Our dreams and our unconscious fantasies show this. An examination of all these patterns of changing personality, or developing the soul, so that it, too, has a developmental history, not just an external case history, would show a striking insistence upon death experiences. It would also force us to the conclusion that interference with this death experience by preventing it, by finding it faulty reasoning, by misunderstanding it as a pathological social condition that needs to be cured, would deprive the soul of its very chance for transformation.

As the critical moments of the transformation process in tradition involve death, so, too, do these critical moments within analysis involve death. Because in analysis we are primarily concerned with these transition phases. We are involved with the unfolding of a life through these dyings. So a person is stuck in childhood or stuck in his early marriage fantasies or stuck in the expansion aspect of his career. In each case, something begins to die away, no longer to function; and the identity of that personality, the being of himself dies so that the next phase of his life becomes possible. Just as the crustacean once a year moves out of the structure that he has built up, crawls out of his shell and sheds that mass of armor, and lies like a vulnerable mass of jelly on the bottom of the sea, so do we die and dissolve before we can create out of ourselves new constructs and a new house for the psyche within which we can then live again.

What dies in these situations is our ego hang-ups, our ego identifications, the hardness of the ego, the order that we have set up for ourselves, the continuity and identity and habit—all these ego virtues. It is as if the psyche is not all ego, as if there is something outside of the ego that wants this death, something outside of the ego, other than the ego, seems to remain during this death and is, so to speak, reborn during this death.

The fact that the ego dies in analysis, but that other psychic processes both direct this death and are there throughout death and after it, points to the fact that the ego is not the center of the personality, but that there is something that transcends the ego and is superior to it. What we call this other is less important than that we experience it, and that the experience of it comes most vividly, it would seem, in analysis, through death experiences.

❁

Now we go on to the question that there is another aspect of death within analysis that we ought not to avoid, and that is aggression. You are all very familiar with the aggressive component in suicide, a component that has been formulated as killing oneself, killing a significant other, or as being killed by another. However we put this, we have to enter into the problem of aggression of killing and being killed, of some kind of savage, murderous, destructive component; and we have to examine our views of this part of the psyche.

If we look around us, we find that this component, which we can call for the moment aggression or destructiveness or evil, is not—and I repeat, is not—fully faced and accepted as a psychic fact by the major views in our field. The refusals are many. I think the neo-Freudians generally refuse the death instinct and its ramifications in the area of destructiveness. Konrad Lorenz and the animal behaviorists do not come to terms with the evil in man. Sociology and other psychologies see such behavior disorders as derivative of fear and frustration, of negative experiences with the mother or with society, and so on.

I can't discuss—I'm unable to, haven't the ability to discuss —in detail these theories of aggression. I only want to point out the thinking they have in common, which is that they fail to help us understand the fact of the aggressive component in suicidal death; und we need a way of coming to terms with this aggressive component if we are to come to terms with suicide. If suicide has an aggressive component and one is killing and destroying, and this killing and destroying is viewed on these models that refuse to allow an ontological position to killing and destroying, which can only see killing and destroying as some form of warped derivative reaction formation, then we can never come to the deepest acceptance of suicide as a problem. We will judge the suicide because of our judgment against, or our warped view of, the aggressive aspect. We will see suicide as illegitimate und warped.

The suicidal person is getting back at someone. Or he plays a game of revenge, is murdering, or is vicious. Often he is acting out against his analyst. (I'm talking, of course, always within this limit: "Life and Death in Analysis"; where it seeps out into other areas, I'm glad but now I'm pulling it back.) His analyst represents the leader of his own psyche into its depths and into its exploration of death, as we discussed.

Regardless how we interpret it as an act against the analyst or a way of destroying the psychic function or image the analyst carries, we still need to face *per se* that the psyche, the human soul, has in it the capacity to kill and destroy; and even if we say that aggression can be twisted into perverted forms because of fixations or early frustrations or whatever other things we want to attribute this to, we have still to recognize that the human soul is not just passively twisted but actively twists, and that the psyche has the capacity to kill and to delight in killing. The history of mankind from Cain and Abel (which was the first thing that people did when they got out of the Garden of Eden) is a history of murders and wars. This is an ontological reality and killing within the soul, as a reality within the soul, is recognized by the Ten Commandments as a perpetually eternal fundamental human possibility: given with man's existence, always there, and not a derivative of something else.

Now, this is tough; and the only place, it seems to me, where this reality of evil within the human soul and within the universe is given full credit in psychology (it is in philosophy and in religion) is in Jung's psychology. In the last years, it seems the Jungians have become obsessed with the concept of evil.[2] It seems there is not a semester or term at the Jung Institute in Zurich that does not deal with evil or Satan or something on the problem of evil, the problem of the shadow, the problem of this part of life.

The Jungian view, it would seem to me—and I suppose other Jungians might have other views—is that the potential, not only to react aggressively but cruelly and sadistically, the capacity to enjoy enmity and to have enemies, to live and be hostile, to war and to destroy, is fundamental and innate, not only in man as a disposition, but as part of the reality of existence.

In other words, I think the Jungians take the devil seriously and regard the destructive aggression that is expressed often through suicide as an expression of this evil, an evil that can not be dismissed through sociological, or biological explanations à la Lorenz, or as psychological reductions to what happened early on, or to sociological misfortunes, and so on. It is fundamental, as the devil is fundamental and not derived; the devil is not only an absence of good or a privation or a shadow that ultimately really works for good (although we don't see it).

---

2. See Adolf Guggenbühl-Craig's writings on killing and being killed and on the shadow aspects of psychotherapy in *From The Wrong Side: A Paradoxical Approach to Psychology,* translated by Gary V. Hartman (Putnam, Conn.: Spring Publications, 2014 [1992]); cf. also *Evil,* edited by the Consortium of the C.G. Jung Institute Zurich, translated by Ralph Manheim and Hildegard Nagel (Evanston, Ill.: Northwestern University Press, 1967).

I don't believe that we can take the aggressive hostility that is expressed in analysis without a very deep acceptance that evil exists in the world. In my book on suicide,[3] I'm afraid, I did not present enough in my view against suicide prevention. I did not present enough about evil that can express through suicide as murder and killing. If in that book I tried to show how one can in analysis get inside the soul and understand it from within and that this understanding can make the actual suicide superfluous and unnecessary because of the death of the psyche has been achieved and accomplished within the soul so that it doesn't have to be concretely lived out in the world, I should also have discussed the importance of getting inside the aggression, the killing, and the murder that is implicated in suicide.

I can never come to terms with this aspect if I regard it as an aberration, a derivative of frustration or other things. Accepting suicide as a legitimate possibility as I did there, or even accepting the symbolic meaning of entering death for the sake of transformation and that suicide is an expression of the transformation drive, still leaves something out; and that something is the violence or the evil of the aggression or the murder that, too, must be taken as fundamental to human beings and also as a legitimate possibility of human nature.

If I don't take this position, I'm still outside and judging the person, and I have not come to terms with the destructive face of the creation and of the creator who made this creation.

By accepting evil, please understand, I don't mean condoning it, any more than I mean by not being for suicide prevention that I'm for suicide. I'm not for or against suicide. Only what does it mean in the soul? So with the evil that may be behind some suicide, I am not for it by accepting its reality; I am not embracing it. I am not for the devil by saying, "Yes, I believe the devil is real." I'm not for the atomic bomb or the concentration camps or other aspects of destruction and murder just by saying, "I accept these things as real and true and there and fundamental facts."

So we can't come to terms with the destructive violence and the destructive cruelty by denying its basic reality. We can only come to terms with this part of the problem of suicide. We can only deal with

3. James Hillman, *Suicide and the Soul* (Thompson, Conn.: Spring Publications, 2020 [1964]).

the devil if we begin by admitting his existence; that there's something demonic, savage, terribly difficult and self-destructive. That's why we have got such a problem. Admitting his existence is not giving the devil a ticket into the world. That isn't the point, I'm not condoning it. I'm saying that my hatred and wish to kill and revenge are fundamental realities. Now, what is to be done with this? This is where it all begins. The real problem is: What's to be done? How is it to be handled? Where does one go next in the struggle with evil? This, then, is an altogether new problem. This approach does not try to get rid of the causes of evil through psychological insight or social reform, because the causes of evil have to be laid to something eternal, always there, ontological; as laid, for example, to God himself. This opens a new vista into the nature of being and sees the destructiveness of killing oneself and even of all aggression in a very troubling light, to which I do not have a solution. But I am very pleased to present this as a fundamental problem.

❀

There's one little thing left, which is tied in with the title of this talk. We've been talking mainly about analysis in relation to the theme of the meeting. I want to turn specifically now to the idea of life and death. It's a curious thing, and it's been noted from very easily cosmologies or primitive mythologies of how the world came into existence. It's in Indian philosophy and in Greek philosophy and in the beginning of men's thinking about the world and how it is that things are put (also about fundamental issues) as a polarity.

For example, good and bad, high and low, male and female, dark and light, and so on. Now the opposition of these principles has been raised to be a basic law of the universe in many, many systems of thought: Chinese Taoism, or in Aristotelian thought or Hegelian thought. There is a polarity between which they operate.

Even our religious culture, the Judeo-Christian one in which we are involved, begins when God creates a world by dividing upper and lower, and separating darkness from light, and calling one half of the system good (the light side).

The immense range and complexity of biological life is also divided into polarities of male and female. There are very, very few exceptions where this polarity doesn't hold in biological classification. This polarity of male and female or of any of the basic polar oppositions, such as dark and light, red and green, old and young—this thing can not be reduced to the simplifications of just electrical poles (from where we get the term "polarity") of positive and negative. There is something qualitatively different between the two poles.

Life and death comprise one of these polarities. But we have split it apart by our antithetical thinking, by the way we think. Our Western, Cartesian kind of thinking has split this apart, so that where life is, as it has been said, death is not; and where death is, there is no life. You can find positions that describe: We can not talk about death because as long as we are alive, we know nothing about it. Absolutely split apart; opposites.

Now in this way the polarities have been turned into logical contradictories. "It" becomes "life and death," becomes "they"; and they are split apart, and they are mutually antagonistic and at war. This tearing apart of things that originally belonged together is an especial phenomenon of our time. Black and white—who says black and white are opposites? Or queer and straight, or hip and square, or young and old, or advanced and backward? And all the walls and borders and solutions of problems by making splits even sharper, keeping things clear.

The origin of this problem within the ego and the way the ego is developed in our society—a whole other scene, and we can't do that now. But I want to point out that there are other ways of thinking about polarities such as life and death besides "where life is, there's no death" and vice versa.

⌒⫯⌒

14

COMMENTARY TO *KUNDALINI:*
THE EVOLUTIONARY ENERGY IN MAN
BY GOPI KRISHNA

On a hot day in the early summer of 1952, I remember going to the house of Gopi Krishna in Srinagar with my wife and two friends, Gerald Hanley and F. J. Hopman who has done so much to see that this book finally reached the public. We were all living in Kashmir and had come upon the work of Gopi Krishna at a local fair where a pamphlet of his poetry with a brief account of his experiences was distributed by one of his followers. I went on the visit out of curiosity, sceptically, critically, expecting a mountebank, ready to argue, disprove, and later perhaps laugh.

I recall the heat, the flies, and my shirt stuck with sweat to the back of an old leather armchair. He sat on a cot, reposed, round-bodied, in white, smiling. The look of his skin seemed different from others I had met during the past year in Kashmir; then I thought he looked healthy, now I might say he glowed. I remember the simplicity in which our conversation took place. Above all, I remember the eyes of the man: friendly, luminous, huge, softly focused. They attracted and held my attention and somehow convinced me that what was happening in this room and with this man was genuine. I visited him several times for talks before we left on a pony trek to Shishnag and then the return to Europe. Because one or two unusual events occurred to me in the high mountains after meeting with Gopi Krishna, I tend to regard him as an initiator and a signal person in my life. Our meeting went deeper than I then realized. His eyes first led me to trust my own sight, my own convictions, beyond my trained sceptical Western mind. This was itself an initiation into actual psychological work that I only later took up.

So it is with reverence to him and to the culture from which he has risen that I add these short comments as an act of gratitude. It is my intention neither to explain nor defend what Gopi Krishna has written, but only to relate, where I am able, some of his experiences to Western depth psychology, especially to the process of individuation as described in the analytical psychology of C. G. Jung.[1]

---

1. [See Diana Swain, "Re-Visioning Kundalini: Exploring Kundalini Experiences

Commentary to Chapters One and Two

Our text opens with a classic example of the meditative technique. Whether for Eastern or Western psychology, the prerequisite of any human accomplishment is *attention*. All tasks to be mastered demand the focusing of attention. The ability to concentrate consciousness is what we call in Western psychology a sign of ego-strength. Disturbances of attention can be measured by the association experiment, which Jung developed to show how the ability of the ego to focus upon a relatively simple task (the association of words) can be impaired by unconscious complexes. The assiduous, prolonged discipline of attention to a single image (the full-blooming, light-radiating lotus) is as difficult as any concentration upon a learning task in an extraverted manner. Whether introverted or extraverted, whether Eastern or Western, we may note at the beginning the significance of the ego, that which focuses, concentrates, attends.

The many-petaled lotus at the crown of the head is a traditional symbol of the Kundalini yoga. In the language of analytical psychology, the attention of the ego is fixed upon a self-image in mandala form. The ego has chosen its image according to the spiritual discipline, just as in Christian meditation there is the Sacred Heart, the Cross, the images of Christ, Mary, the Saints, etc. Rather than discuss the objects of concentration (comparative symbolism), let us note briefly in passing the difference of technique between *active imagination* and yoga discipline. In spiritual disciplines, as a rule, the attention is focused upon already given or known images (in Zen Buddhism, there may be no images but a *koan*, or an object). In each case, the focus of attention is prescribed, and one knows when one is wavering or "off." In active imagination, as described by C.G. Jung, attention is given to whatever images or emotions, or body parts, etc. "pop into the mind." Rather than suppressing the distractions, they are followed attentively. The method is half-way between the free association of the Freudians where one leaps freely from one image/word/thought to the next with no idea of the goal and the traditional spiritual discipline of rigid fixity upon a given image.

from a Jungian and Archetypal Perspective" (diss., Pacifica Graduate Institute, 2018). Swain argues that Kundalini is both accessible and useful for many Westerners, counterbalancing Jung and Hillman's position on the subject. See also Ida Chi Lachiusa, "The Transformation of Ashtanga Yoga: The Mythopoetic Journey from Body to Psyche Among Female Survivors of Relational Trauma," (diss., Pacifica Graduate Institute, 2015).—Ed.]

Active imagination develops a more personal psychological fantasy. (The lotus is after all a highly impersonal image that any adept anywhere could focus upon unrelated to his own personal psychological makeup. It is not "his" lotus but "the" lotus.) Active imagination is concerned with the ego's relation with, and personal reactions to, the mental images. The emotional involvement with these images and their spontaneous reactions back are as important as the nature of the images themselves. If the quality of a free association can be judged by its uninhibitedness (lack of suppression), and the quality of a disciplined meditation can be judged by its unwavering fixity and undistractedness, the quality of active imagination can be judged by its emotional intensity, which is given by the opposition between the ego position of the conscious mind and the various figures, images, and intentions of the unconscious psyche. Hence, it is called *active* imagination in that the ego not only attends, not only suppresses what does not belong (as in a spiritual exercise), but actively takes part in the drama or dialogue that unfolds by asking questions, experiencing emotions, pressing toward solutions.

Furthermore, one aim of active imagination is often rather extraverted. I mean by this that one seeks through the meditation the counsel of inner figures concerning practical personal problems, whereas spiritual disciplines attempt to surmount (crown of the head) a world that gives rise to such personal problems and in which no permanent solutions can truly exist. In active imagination the counsel is sought not in terms of should I do this or that action but, rather, what attitude is correct, what complex is constellated. Spiritual discipline, on the other hand, aims toward the divine and the transcendence of attitudes and complexes.

Again and again we shall come to passages in the text that emphasize the enormous *physical cost* of the experience. It is important to realize, and we can be grateful to our author for never letting this fact slip, that transformation of personality is exhausting. Consciousness alone consumes hundreds of calories a day, and the intensity of introverted discipline requires as much energy as extensive extraverted mental activity. Outstanding in the work as we go through it is the importance of the body. In spite of the seventeen long years of discipline, the author suffered a severe disorientation of consciousness. We cannot put this down to a neurasthenic constitution or a neurotic hypochondriasis. It is as if the one thing he did not expect was the degree of physical cost, the actual organic events. In this, our author is a modern man, for it is the problem of us modern men to connect the body again with the spirit, rather than identifying spirit with soul or mind, to the detriment of body. The emphasis upon the body in what follows is nothing else than a description of the meaning of incarnation of the spirit in a modern example.

From the personal, analytical point of view there are certain observations one could make concerning the *family constellation* of the author, which may have had some bearing upon the archetypal eruption. From the beginning there was a spiritual ambition. His old father led the way in this direction and our author's desire to prove himself to his mother is a dominant theme. He was the only son, carrying the psychological burdens from both parents.

His own recollections of *childhood* bring out two facts that belong to his own "personal myth." The first is the experience of having almost died and having been saved by a wonder. The child-in-danger motif is part of the mythologem of the savior-hero. It establishes chosenness; one has in childhood met the powers of darkness and been rescued from them by supernatural forces. The gods single out at an early age those who are to carry consciousness further. The miracle of consciousness is frail at the beginning and can easily be snuffed out. Moses, Christ, Dionysos, Hercules are examples of the child-in-danger.

As a child he had the experience of questioning himself in that utter overwhelming way that we find in the Buddha (when he was considerably older). Or, in modern times, Jung's description of his early years in his autobiography, *Memories, Dreams, Reflections,* iterates this motif of sudden devastating awareness.[2] This same question lies at the root of all philosophy and it had the same shattering effect upon Descartes, but again at a later age.

Gopi Krishna's early dream can be reduced in banal terms to a wish-fulfillment. He found in his dream a world "the very opposite of the shabby, noisy surroundings in which I lived." Yet how little this sort of interpretation tells us! It is a compensatory wish fulfillment surely, but it transcends the personal. It is archetypally compensatory, completing the world picture of earthly reality by an equally powerful reality of the unearthly. It is a wish-fulfilment not in the language of the world, but of a *Weltanschauung.* As such it is a statement: "Look! You are not what you think you are. You are not only what your surroundings make you. There is more to reality than what

2. C.G. Jung, *Memories, Dreams, Reflections,* edited by Aniela Jaffé; translated by Richard and Clara Winston (New York: Random House, 1961).

is given socially and externally. You have another personality altogether different from the one you take for granted as 'you.'" (I refer the reader again to the number one and number two personalities Jung writes of in his own life in *Memories, Dreams, Reflections*.)

It is therefore little wonder that with this archetypal background to his life (the father/mother constellation, being saved from early death, the childhood awareness of self, the dream vision) that he could not read enough of symbolic, mythic material. The *Arabian Nights* and fairy tales connect personalities number one and number two. Fairy tales tell universal truths; they are archetypal accounts of how the personality meets and overcomes its own dangers. They speak in the language of symbols directly to the soul. The fairy tale is not a substitution for reality but is a necessary nourishment for the world of psychic reality.

Lastly, in regard to the *author's personal psychology*, we find two further rather typical facts. The failed examinations cut Gopi Krishna off from a substitute career in which his spiritual aims could have become an intellectual or academic ambition. This sort of failure is often to be found in biographies of unusual people. It is signal, preventing the personality from developing along collectively approved lines. After the examination failure, there was only one way to go: his own. Failure as such does not give logic to this decision; rather the failure is symbolized into a parting of the ways, a fateful annunciation, so that it became clear to him what his call really was. The call was then finally announced in the author's thirty-fifth year, that is, at the midpoint of life, after having discharged his extraverted duties (education, work, parents, marriage, children, society) and the introverted obligations of the ego (to establish a living contact with the unconscious, the development of a subjective point of view, a *Weltanschauung*). Too often, in the West, we fail to realize that even in Eastern disciplines the spiritual life is not meant as an escape from the worldly life. There is a *karma* to be fulfilled on earth, within the *dharma* of necessity. In fact, it would seem that the development of awareness requires a very solid basis in reality: an embodied personality in the daily world and an ego that can submit to its own unconsciousness. We can be grateful to our author for showing us in careful detail the ordinary outer context and inner milieu in which these extraordinary events took place.

Commentary to Chapters Three and Four

We encounter here a term central to the theories that Gopi Krishna discusses more fully later. This term is *prana*. He defines it as a subtle life element and compares it to a fluid and to electricity. He further gives it a materialistic description: "an extremely fine biochemical essence of a highly delicate and volatile nature, extracted by the nerves from the surrounding organic mass. After extraction, this vital essence resides in the brain and the nervous system... it circulates in the organism as motor impulse and sensation."

It would take us far afield to discuss in an adequate way the comparable ideas in Western psychology. I have already given some attention to the history of the idea of psychic energy as a circulating flow within the organism in Chapter Six of my book on emotion.[3]

Prana is both a superintelligent cosmic life energy and the subtle biological conductor in the body, that is, it is both a universal life force and a physiological actuality. It is both immaterial and material, both independent of here-and-now yet inextricably interwoven with the life of the body. As an energy endowed with intelligence, *prana* compares with our similar notion of spirit.

Western psychology used the same model of thought from the earliest of Greek ideas until the end of the eighteenth century. But we no longer use this model of thought in describing psychic energy. In the West, energy is either material and, therefore, nervous energy that can be measured and is reducible to electrical or chemical descriptions, or it is an immaterial principle called the soul or mind or libido or *élan vital*, which has no physical description. Freud, in his early thinking, tried to connect the two by deriving libido from sexual liquids. Reich tried to connect psychic energy both to sexual physiology and to a cosmic orgone energy in the universe. We are unable to conceive of a unified energy principle since we suffer in the West from the Cartesian division of experience into material and mental.

Now, the value of Gopi Krishna's account of *prana* lies less in the traditional description of it—which one can find, as he says, in Hindu thought and Yoga texts—than in his own experiences. His actual *experience of enlightenment* on the first day (the first page of this book) was of the flow into the head of a living liquid light. In other words, what was called in Greek, Arabic, and

---

3. James Hillman, *Emotion: A Comprehensive Phenomenology of Theories and Their Meanings for Therapy* (London: Routledge & Kegan Paul, 1960).

medieval thought the "breath," "the animal spirits," or "spirits of the soul," and corresponds in description with *prana* and with the circulating light in Chinese yoga and alchemy,[4] was spontaneously experienced as such, as a living liquid light, by our author. It is important to note that he was astonished by what happened and that he attempted to fix his attention upon it, as one would observe carefully a spontaneous event occurring in a routine laboratory experiment. He did not make it happen, nor could he make it happen at will. The identification of his consciousness (the watching, attentive ego) with the light yielded a supra-personal experience (outside and above his body) that accords with the theory of *prana* as a universal energy unbounded by body.

We may gain a glimpse of how enlightenment can be accounted for psychologically. I do not mean explained, only "given an account of." Evidently, there is an archetypal experience of the circulation or flow of light that has been formulated in many cultures and times into various terms we now call "psychic energy." The flow of this psychic energy in its totality is the entire psychological self, or the Self. When the partial system of the ego is released to, identifies with, or is overwhelmed by, the self, an experience of enlightenment ensues. This is what Gopi Krishna describes. The immersion of the ego in this stream of light is a common theme of religious mysticism, and also of psychopathological derangement.

Our author was at once confronted with this problem, and the major part of the book deals not with the experiences, but with their *integration.* The road to the enlightenment experience has been made much shorter with modern hallucinatory drugs and other techniques. The real issue is how to integrate these experiences, how to live with them, how to keep them from overwhelming the body and external reality, how to translate them into awareness and human service, how to ground them in the world—in other words, the "return," how to return with them to the human condition.

The first sign of disorder in the flow of light was the turmoil of "sinister light," "particles of an ethereal luminous stuff," the "shower" or "waterfall spray" effect. Intuitively, Gopi Krishna knew that it was not right. Comparable effects are noted in states of psychological dissociation, in which con-

4. See Richard Wilhelm, and C.G. Jung, *The Secret of the Golden Flower: A Chinese Book of Life,* translated by Cary F. Baynes (London: Kegan Paul, Trench, Trubner & Co., 1931).

sciousness appears to break up into multiples of itself, disintegrating into sparks, *scintillae,* fragments, or hosts of tiny insects. From the Hindu point of view the turmoil could be attributed to a state of mind called *vṛtta* ("whirling motion"), that is, the self, or light *per se,* is not disordered, but the state of mind of the attachedly observing ego is still affected by hyperactivity. And this we have in the author's statements that he was searching, questing, questioning, examining, reading, writing letters, worrying, etc. It is the *introspective* worry itself that we might interpret as *vṛtta* and that splits up experience into an anthill of particles.

In addition to the fear of madness, the inner derangement of mind, other events occurred that we call in the *language of psychopathology,* "depersonalization," "disorientation," "alienation." The sense of belonging to his own body here-and-now and the feeling connection to his own family were among the first attachments to go. These secondary symptoms, as well as those of roaring or other sounds and visual distortions that our author describes, belong, too, to the symptomatology of various psychopathological states called, e.g., paranoid, schizophrenic, epileptoid. One might well imagine that had our author presented himself with this syndrome at a usual Western psychiatric clinic he would have been diagnosed in the way that he himself intuitively feared. From the psychiatric view, was this experience not a psychotic episode?

With this question we come to the heart of a Western problem. We have no other than these diagnostic categories for conceiving states of this kind. Alien and altered states of consciousness are the province of the alienist. Fortunately, Gopi Krishna had another set of concepts (Kundalini yoga) that could place within a nonpathological context what was going on. In so far as the awakening of Kundalini is not limited to the Indian subcontinent only, it is conceivable that some of the experiences described in Western psychiatric interviews could also be viewed as the beginnings of enlightenment rather than as the beginnings of insanity. (I think in particular of epilepsy and of Dostoevsky.) The touchstone, again, is the same: the way in which the personality handles the experience, the *integration* of it.

It is to our author's credit that he avoided psychiatry, and even medicine, when later he was to go through the feverish experience of being burned alive from within. Again, however, from the viewpoint of modern psychiatry such avoidance is typical of a man undergoing paranoid delusions. How close the borderlines are! How much depends upon the quality of the person and the way he grapples with the integration of his experience.

Sometimes, therapeutic psychology lays stress upon its therapeutic task at the expense of the psychological. Then we find that what a person has, his diagnosis, has become more important than who a person is. Psychology is obliged to put the who first, the psyche of the person, his soul with its qualities and virtues, its uniqueness as a moral being for whatever diagnosis it may accrue. Our author was holding to this position. He did not want to be treated, whereas to be "cured" of what he had would have meant loss of both who he was and why he was. As Agehananda Bharati points out, "if an adept seems to 'act mad' it is just because people around him do not see what it is all about, as they are lacking the adept's frame of reference."[5] Tantric preceptors deny mental disease en route to *samadhi* and warn the adept: "Do not think the mind is sick when there is *samadhi*." Therefore, Gopi Krishna was following the tradition by avoiding professional help, and by staying within the guidelines of tradition he guaranteed his own sanity. Professional counsel, whether medical or spiritual (guru or master) admits the views of another—and superior—into one's momentarily abject helplessness. At that moment of seeking help the relationship is not symmetrical: one is professional, the other at a loss. All the health is on one side, sickness on the other. In this condition, one too easily hears the collective voice in oneself that does not understand or believe, and so turns the matter and oneself over with suicidal relief to the professional. Gopi Krishna did not split the archetype of the healed one and the wounded one. He stayed right with his ambivalence, believing and doubting, feeling himself found and lost at the same time. This ambivalence was his balance. Had he been more sure, he might have been more deluded; had he been less sure, he might have turned himself in for professional treatment and had his doubts confirmed with a diagnosis.

Next occurs a passage that seems banal enough to skip over, but I believe it deserves a comment. I refer to the information that so reduced was our author in all activities that he took to *walking*. I have found in my own work with people that during periods of acute psychological pressure, walking was an activity to which they naturally turned; walking not just in idylls of the woods and mountains or by the sea, but simply around the city for hours in the early morning or at night. Prisoners circumambulate the yard, animals exercise in their cages, the anxious pace the floor. One goes for a walk. Man

---

5. Agehananda Bharati, *The Tantric Tradition* (London: Rider & Company, 1965), 290.

is *homo erectus;* he is in his element when vertical. More, the agitation of the whirling motion of the mind is placed into an organic rhythm by walking, and this organic rhythm takes on symbolic significance as one places one foot after the other, left/right, left/right, in a balanced harmony. Thus the wild spiritual adventure within takes on the deliberate movement of the pilgrimage, even if only around a confined space. So in dreams, the symbolism of walking rather than driving or being driven in a vehicle, or even riding a bicycle or an animal, is an "improvement." It reflects man's contact with the earth directly, his freedom to wander up and down it, and his continually alternating standpoint of left/right, left/right.

I see no reason why we cannot accept our author's own view of the heat episode. Can our psychology provide a better explanation of it? It can be compared with some of the wrong turns in alchemy in which there is too much sulfur, and the work is burnt black; or where the fire itself (the inner heat, or *tapas*) is not kept at a low slow temperature but rages up too quickly; or in the language of Christian mysticism the fires of Hell, the scorched *siccitas.* In psychological practice, comparable experiences are sometimes referred to as unexplained psychosomatic fevers.

An interpretation of the shift from the right-sided *pingala* to the left-sided *ida* can be made in this way: habitual consciousness attempts to integrate a new experience in its manner. Despite the shattering of the old vessels (mind, orientation, physical strength, feeling connections, body image), the emotional basis of his masculine consciousness remained intact. This habitual canalization of his energies we might call *pingala.* We may make a comparison to the sulphur in alchemy as the principle of masculine will that must be sublimated by connection to the unconscious (mercury) and joined with its opposite, the feminine principle of salt. The channel through which his will, his control, his ambition, the structure of his energy itself had to be altered. The new wine required a new bottle. The shift from the right to the left side meant an abandonment of his former personality and his identification with what had held him up for the first thirty-five years. No wonder he was laid low; no wonder it was a death experience! The left side of *ida* is appropriately feminine, just as it is in Western symbolism. It is the side of softness, where the heart is, and it belongs to the moon. We would call this redemptive cooling grace of *ida* the first appearance in our text of the archetypal effects of the anima.

Commentary to Chapters Five and Six

We meet in Chapter Five the *ideational context* of our author's experience. This cannot be overestimated. Our author did well to place it at this point, because it is the supporting frame that kept his experience from going wrong. He had developed subjective anchors during the first part of his life. He had practiced yoga, but the practice itself was not enough. For a Westerner, even more, the practice of yoga is not enough. Yoga is based on a philosophical system of ideas, a *Weltanschauung,* a way of viewing self and world, and this must be operative in a critical time as that context of meaning on to which one can fall. This context of meaning made it possible for Gopi Krishna to comprehend and thus to further and to integrate what was happening to him. Again, to our loss in the West, we are so lacking in an adequate context that we do indeed go to pieces at the eruption of the unconscious, thereby justifying the psychiatric view. Fortunately, Jung's analytical psychology gives in its account of the process of individuation a context within which these events can be meaningfully comprehended. Fortunately, too, Jung studied as a psychologist this branch of yoga. He called the Kundalini an example of the instinct of individuation. Therefore, comparisons between its manifestations and other examples of the individuation process (e.g., alchemy) provide a psychologically objective knowledge without which there would be no way of taking hold (comprehending, *begreifen*) what is going on. Very often, therefore, it is of utmost value during a period of critical psychological pressure in which the unconscious boils over, to provide the sufferer with psychological knowledge. His experience needs to be confirmed with objective material much as the yoga disciplines provide, showing that what he is going through is appropriate and belongs to the process. The analyst is called on to confirm the other's experiences through his own, and what he has gained from working with others; as well, he has at his disposal knowledge of the process in general as described in mysticism, rituals of primitives, mythologies, spiritual disciplines, and works such as this by Gopi Krishna.

Our author stresses the *evolutionary importance of the events,* and indeed calls his book "The Evolutionary Energy in Man." I do not wish to contend this point. It is a favorite idea of many, including Teilhard de Chardin. This much, however, can be said: there is evidently an archetypal connection between profound mystical experiences of this sort in which one's own consciousness has evolved and personality developed, and the idea that the same experience is fundamentally possible for all men and, therefore, meant for all men.

Religious experience of this sort brings with it the gift or curse of messianism and prophecy. Psychologically, it was evidently valuable for our author to feel that what he was going through was not only personally meaningful but that it had as well a universal meaning. Experiences of the Self have this universality. We often then speak of inflation when the ego does not integrate the cosmic idea but takes it at face value. And perhaps it is meant to be taken at face value. How is one to know? Enough for our purpose to recognize the appearance of a sense of transcendent purposefulness as the events unfolded, and that this transcendent purposefulness was interpreted by our author in the traditional manner as a call.

There are many references to *diet* in the text. Of course, they can be said to represent the obsessive concern of the highly intuitive person with the sensation details of life, especially life of the body. I recall a paranoid patient at Burghölzli, the subject of whose conversations with me was on the one hand abstract mathematical theories and visionary poetry and on the other the system of his food intake—how many slices of bread to eat at lunch, the nutritive value of tomatoes, etc. But diet cult cannot be reduced to compensation alone. The popular press gives accounts to fascinated readers exactly how, what, and when the great men eat. The great are often obsessed with diet. Food after all quite simply means world, and one's eating habits represent one's habitual way of taking in the world. Gopi Krishna clearly had to stop feeding himself in his former way. This shift of attitude toward food reflects a shift from the outer to the inner aspect of life-in-the-world, called in Hindu terminology a shift from the *sthula* to the *sukshma* aspect.

He writes: "This happened time after time as if to impress indelibly upon my mind the fact that from now onwards I had not to eat for pleasure or the mechanical satisfaction of hunger, but to regulate the intake of food with such precision so as not to cause the least strain on my over-sensitive...nervous system." In other words, genetically the most fundamental instinct, the lowest level of psychological life (the oral stage) was also now in service of the ongoing process.

He approaches his diet with "precision." The mention of that word in this context indicates to me the differences between a wrong and right kind of compulsiveness. Precision about psychic life—whether in exercises and diet of the body, in details of dreams and fantasies, in the elaboration of imagination into art—points to the way in which the drivenness of obsessive compulsion can be overcome from within by its own principle. Like cures like. The psyche has an affinity for precision; witness the details in children's stories, primitive rituals and primitive languages, and the exactitude with which we go about anything that is important. Precision is not a preserve of natural science nor is the precise method to be identified with measurements only. Our author realizes that to change his style he must be precise about every detail. He will now approach his diet with refined detailed attention, with the repetitive and ritualistic concern of a violinist who would change his fingering or a boxer aiming to speed his counterpunching. He shows us another way of transforming obsessive compulsion, not by letting go and taking it easy, but through the positive virtue that lies within the compulsiveness. Compulsion can be seen as precision miscarried, a ritualistic behavior gone astray that asks to be set precisely right.

The changes taking place during this initial period of recovery affected principally the *body*. So, too, during an analysis we find all sorts of symptoms cropping up, sometimes symptoms of the most serious sort, synchronistic with dynamic changes in the analytical process. Alteration of consciousness does not leave the body out. How much more helpful it would be if we could understand these body changes in the way in which Gopi Krishna did, as necessary preparations for enlarged consciousness. If the body is the carrier of consciousness, it too must be altered. Yet, though Gopi Krishna understood this, each alteration he sensed brought *fear*. It seems as if there is a deep animal fear, a kind of biological resistance, to these changes, as if the body would rather not leave the paths of its instinctual ancestry. The animal in us shies and panics.

Perhaps this tells us something about symptoms. Perhaps they have to do with the fear of change and thus represent the conflicts caused by the new man coming into the old vessel of the body. By this I do not mean that with "re-birth" all symptoms disappear. But I do mean that the symptoms occurring concomitant with psychic change are protective as pain is protective. They hold us down and within our slow evolutionary patterns of the body without whose fear and symptoms we might go up and out of the body altogether in some foolish liberation above all symptoms that would actually be suicide.

A major change in body concerns *sexuality*. A re-organization of the sexual impulse would seem required for every transition in planes of consciousness. Initiation rites at puberty, and marriage rites, as well as the vow of chastity for those entering religious orders, all point to the importance of sexual changes in connection with changes in states of being. The Kundalini serpent power is supposed to lie curled asleep at the base of the spine in the region of coccyx, anus, and prostate; opinions differ as to its exact locus. It is intimately connected with sexuality, so that the transformation of sexuality through internalization becomes a necessary activity, even the major opus in the discipline. This is an idea can be found in yogic, alchemical, and shamanistic practices. It is also the basis of Taoist sexual practices.[6] Freudian analysis, too, can be seen as a ritualization of sexual life for the sake of its transformation, especially since in its orthodox form "acting-out" is discouraged during an analysis. The principal idea is simple: semen is that fluid in the body most highly charged with *prana*. Occult anatomy envisages a direct connection between the genitals and the nervous system, either via brain and spine or via the blood. Loss of seed means loss of that vital essence that is the source of the living liquid light. Semen must therefore be discerned and discharged upward rather than outward, thereby adding to the internal circulation of *prana*. Bharati speaks of the difference between Buddhist and Hindu attitudes. The former, as the Taoists, retain the semen; the latter discharge it (left-hand path of Tantrism) as sacrifice. In each of these varied traditions one idea stands out: the transformation of consciousness requires the transformation of sexuality that takes place through ritual.

Our text refers to unusual ferment in the genital parts and to the production of an increased abundance of semen. This runs contrary to the usual notions that yoga is an ascetic discipline through which the sexual impulse is depotentiated. Just not! And we can understand why chastity and continence and other sexual *mystitiques* (including the orgy and black mass) belong archetypally to the discipline of the "holy man." It is not that he has less sexuality than others, but more. (For example, an early sign of the call to shamanism among the Native American Mohave people is frequent childhood masturbation.) The "holy man" as "greater personality"

6. See R. H. van Gulik, *Sexual Life in Ancient China: A Preliminary Survey of Chinese Sex and Society from ca. 1500 B.C. till 1644 A.D.* (Leiden: E. J. Brill, 1961); Mircea Eliade, *Yoga: Immortality and Freedom,* translated by Willard R. Trask (Princeton, N.J.: Princeton University Press, 1970), and his *Shamanism: Archaic Techniques of Ecstasy,* translated by Willard R. Trask (Princeton, N.J.: Princeton University Press, 1972); and my own "Toward the Archetypal Model for the Masturbation Inhibition," given at the Third International Congress for Analytical Psychology in Montreaux, Switzerland, 1965 [and in this volume].

implies the endowment of greater sexuality; therefore, the transformation of it raises all sorts of problems, answers to which have been formulated in various esoteric techniques and disciplines, West and East, of which chastity and the ritual copulation of tantric *maithuna* would be opposite poles of the same archetypal formulation.

It is not infrequent in analytical practice that phases of obsessive sexuality (sexual dreams, fixations on the genitals, sado-masochism, masturbation, nocturnal emissions) occupy the center of the stage for a time. Reduction of these events to Oedipal conflicts is not alone sufficient. If a process of transformation is truly going on, then it will affect a person's sexual life, drawing his attention to his sexuality, and sexuality as such (which then takes on the numinous power of a god, formulated long ago in other cultures as the Lingam, or as Priapus). The ground of possibility for any transformation of sexuality is the recognition of it as an impersonal power. The *maithuna* aspect of tantric yoga makes this clear. It is not *my* sex and *my* pleasure and my orgasm; it is a force that flows through me, a force of play, joy, and creation. By separating the personal out of it, one can listen to it, obey or deny it, note its fluctuations and intentions—all of which means relating to it objectively. Once this step has been taken, the transformation at which our author hints, including seed retention, ejaculation control, and other practices described by Van Gulik and Gaston Maspero become less a matter of personal suppression, an adolescent battle between good and evil, than a detached game, at once religiously sacrificial and erotically educative.

In several places, we note our author's difficulty with *reading.* Not only could he not find the right material to study; he also could not concentrate. One of the first things that had to go was intellectual concentration. We call this in analytical work the *sacrificium intellectus.* It refers to the state when one is forced to abandon oneself to the ongoing process, as to a river, without knowing where it will lead, without having a chart of the course, without knowledge aforehand. The intellect can easily take over experiences and deprive them of their livingness. So in Freudian analysis the patient is generally not supposed to read psychology. In Jungian analysis there is no such rule, for when and what to read depends entirely on the actual situation. And it was a long time before the ability to read again returned to Gopi Krishna, indicating how strong the hold of the intellect can be, and in his case, what a danger it was. We must remember that he originally set out for an intellectual life from which he was saved by the examination failure. This points to a psychological truth: the greatest danger to our true calling, whatever it may be, is the one closest to it, the one that is the shadow of the substance. One is less likely to mistake green or white for true red, than rose, pink, or burgundy. Each contact with reading and intellectual formulation led him astray by endangering the process as an experience in the body. This body was his true teacher. He had to go it alone, but his body, like the dumb ass of St. Francis or the ass of Jesus in whose stable he was born and on which he rode to his last week and body's crucifixion, was his constant companion. Is that not the point of all this body obsession? Does it not say: we are animals with animal hair and teeth and gut. And this animal is a god as so many religious images the world over insist. The animals belong to divinities, who come in the shape of animals, who are animals, saying perhaps that it is the animal in us that is holy. Even the Kundalini itself is a snake. The animal that is divine is the wisdom of nature, or the wisdom of the body, that knows from primeval times with a knowledge that we cannot hope to emulate no matter what we read. Noah saved what was holy in the creation: life, the animals; the Torah came later. It is the animal in us who cannot read. The "serpent power" itself seemed to be demanding his obedience by preventing him from seeking another master with another kind of knowledge.

Some form of *confirmation* was needed. It was too much to go it alone. He had no master and was psychologically unable to read. Therefore, the letter of confirmation from the eminent master saying that what he was going through was authentic cannot be overvalued. The task of the Western analyst is often just that: to give an affirmation to the experiences that the other person is going through, to take them earnestly, to believe in his inner world and give credit to it. Above all, he mustn't be threatened by it or call it sick. This eminent master said that Gopi Krishna could be helped only by one who had already been there ("conducted the Shakti successfully to the Seventh Centre"). In Jungian analysis, we often say "you can only take someone else as far as you have gone yourself." This is a limiting statement and, if taken to heart, is quite depressing both for the student and the analyst. It also shows how all of us depend upon the very few real masters who have had to go so much of the way alone. It also makes us value what Gopi Krishna did on his own, and gives our text even further significance as a document that may be of use to others.

At the end of Chapter Six, our author raises in passing a question about his own *suffering*. When one reads the texts of mystics and holy men, as he did, one is struck by all the references to bliss and beauty. And it was the absence of bliss and beauty that made Gopi Krishna vacillate and doubt his own experiences. Again, we can be grateful to him for his honesty in recording the bitterness and burning of his own experience, and we can admire him for his absence of resentment. Suffering belongs. The visions in the desert of the Christian Saints, the dark night of the soul of St. John of the Cross, the terrible suffering of the Old Testament prophets, point to the necessity of suffering. To believe that it could be otherwise is—as we know from analytical practice—a remnant of childish idealism. In regard to the archetypal suffering involved in personality transformation, Western mysticism, patterned after the images of the Bible and Jesus and the Saints, might here have been of more value to our author than his own tradition. In this sense, his work speaks to today and is an excellent bridge to Western experiences in which the expanded or intensified consciousness coming through analysis does not rise as a lotus from a quiet lake, but is riven and torn by neurosis before any light dawns. Suffering ushers birth; the new child is born in pain; and the nails and thorns of the cross precede transfiguration.

Commentary to Chapters Seven, Eight, and Nine

In Chapter Seven, the text takes up *prana* again, this time more metaphysically. In Chapter Eight, we come to another of the traditional problems associated with mystical experiences and that is the question of *secrecy*. Our author was strongly moved not to tell anyone of what he was going through, not even his wife. Again, this rigid secrecy is typical of one in the throes of a paranoid delusion. To open the secret is in a sense what we call "reality testing." If it were laughed at, argued away, diagnosed as sick, a whole world would collapse. But more, there is something in the nature of mystical experiences that demands secrecy, as if the archetype behind the events that are in process needs a certain tension in order for it to be fulfilled. The alchemists envisioned this secrecy in their image of the closed vessel. In many fairy tales, the hero or heroine is ordered not to say anything until the ordeal is over. In the Greek religious mysteries, the participants were threatened with death if they told what happened. Initiation rites also require sworn secrecy. Secrecy intensifies, allowing what is coming to fruition to swell and grow in silence so that later it can be brought forth and shown. Secrecy is the ground of revelation, making revelation possible; what happens secretly in the wings, behind the scenes, makes possible the drama when the curtains open and the lights go up. The urge to withhold and keep back is part of being witness to the uncanny. What to hold back, when to tell, whom to tell, how to tell...these questions fraught with peril lie along the razor's edge between deluded paranoid isolation and individual strength, between arrogant private esotericism and uncertain loneliness of silence. Secrecy, as well, gives individuality; what everybody knows is no longer individual. Without our individual secrets we are only public ciphers.

He tells us in Chapter Eight that "at night I found myself looking with dread at horribly disfigured faces and distorted forms bending and twisting into awful shapes...They left me trembling with fear, unable to account for their presence." The encounter with distorted human figures in a night world seems another authentic necessity. It is evidently so important that Homer, Virgil, and Dante describe similar phenomena in the descent into Hades of their heroes. It is part of their journey. We find parallels in analysis. After a certain integration has taken place, there sometimes occur dreams of a hospital ward with ill and maimed, or a large photo of all the family members that oppresses the dreamer thereafter for days, or one's early school class, or club, appear en masse in the analyst's waiting-room. These shades, too, need transformation; they are parts that have not been redeemed despite the integration achieved by the conscious personality and its ego. Especially tormented in the Underworld are the unburied dead, those configurations passed away or repressed out of awareness but still not over and done with, hauntingly lingering at the threshold. The manifestation of these "awful shapes" reminds heroic consciousness that there are still shadows in the cave even if one has seen the light oneself. The psyche is separable; even if "I" have moved, there are some tormented "me's" left behind in hell. In Greek thought, the souls in Hades were regarded as moist, preponderating in the wet element of generation—life-giving moisture. Our author says these faces and figures eddied and swirled using the language of water for their motions. Perhaps these parts had not yet been through the cooking process, not yet been volatilized, and so they may herald a new descent into hell's torment and drying fires.

At this time, he notes that the "current" seemed to have as its aim the *liver*. The liver has always been an important symbol in occult physiology. As the largest organ, the one containing the most blood, it was regarded as the darkest, least penetrable part of man's innards. Thus it was considered to contain the secret of fate and was used for fortune-telling. In Plato, and in later physiology, the liver represented the darkest passions, particularly the bloody, smoky ones of wrath, jealousy, and greed that drive men to action. Thus the liver meant the impulsive attachment to life itself. From this angle, the renewed interest in the liver by our author could predict a revivification of general activity.

But if the currents that run toward the liver (and heart, too) indicate emotional activity, what about the pull downward of the shapes in hell? The two tendencies—downward to the disfigured night-world and outward into activity—are not as contradictory as they seem. In neo-Platonic thought the moist souls are precisely those that are still involved with the generative principle, the life cycle of binding *kleshas*. The souls in Hades want blood and eat red-colored food, i.e., they hunger for life. The activation of the liver may thus be seen as a movement toward feeding distorted fragments of unlived life that still longed to live, but in the long run of any Indian spiritual discipline must be yoked to the single aim of "pure cognition."

Commentary to Chapters Ten and Eleven

After the experience had calmed and his life returned to regularity, our author notes two remaining difficulties: he cannot read attentively for longer periods and he "continued to have a fear of the supernatural." He takes up this religious problem in Chapter Ten.

From the narrowly psycho-dynamic view, this *fear of the supernatural* is the result of repression. Anxiety is a manifestation in consciousness of a fear of a return of the repressed, in this case, of the unconscious itself. But, beyond this, we may also say that fear is the appropriate reaction after any trauma—the burnt child fears the fire. That this fear focused especially on the supernatural implies a new awareness of the unconscious,[7]

---

7. [It is worth noting that Hillman would later move beyond the term "unconscious," opting instead for broader language, including the underworld, the soul, imagination, the metaxy, *mundus imaginalis*, etc. He also made the move of assigning

a new relation to it, a new orientation of consciousness toward whatever lies outside its ken. As modern readers we can identify with our author. Until his experience, and even in spite of a deeply religious attitude, our author was not afraid of the gods or of the other world. He longed for it and worked daily to reach it. His religious attitude was comparable to the Western man's collective church-going belief. But now, having had a taste of this other world, he is in fear and trembling of anything that has to do with it. More, he is enraged by the usual sort of faith (people coming from places of worship, the usual pious literature, etc.). He finds himself "devoid completely of every religious sentiment," and cannot understand this "alteration in the very depths of my personality." He is in a God-is-dead phase.

From the experience one gathers through working with Western practitioners of organized religion, this turn of events is not unusual. A true face-to-face encounter with the numinous shatters all previous religious ideas. Sometimes analysis releases a genuine religious experience, and when it occurs in a clergyman, it seems to conflict with rather than support his previous training and system of beliefs. This is an astonishing state of affairs. Orthodoxy has always recognized this possibility and therefore warned dogmatically against individual experiences through visions and dreams. The mystic is not welcomed within the councils of collective religion, and one of the first acts of Jesus (cleansing the temple of money changers) was performed in rage. Moses is moved by rage to smash the holy tablets, and the prophets could also—from the collective viewpoint—have been called "devoid completely of every religious sentiment...rank atheists...violent heretics." The true coin drives out the false. Again, we have the psychological phenomenon that the greatest danger is not the opposite or contradiction of truth, but its nearest imitation. Pink sentimental religion threatens the real red thing more than does any antithesis.

The *alteration of his religious attitude* and his fear of the supernatural brought home to our author two lessons. First, a new appreciation of the values in this world (family, feeling connections, work and colleagues, health, the simple things); second, that the fear of the Lord is the beginning of wisdom. In other words, the fear of the supernatural has made

"unconscious" to the ego itself, stating that it is not the images that lack awareness but the very notion of consciousness as defined by the waking ego.—Ed.]

him aware of his own natural limits. The other world has become terrifyingly, experientially real; he has felt its power, not just known of it from books and teachings. He becomes the *homo religiosus* through the very fear itself, which is nothing else than awe, the primary religious emotion.

Now he can say that the movement to the other world is not a one-step matter. It is not crossing a threshold from a smaller room to a larger just like that. This is an old debate in spiritual disciplines. Is enlightenment achieved step by step as a pilgrim climbs that mountain? Or is it achieved in a break-through flash of illumination? According to the proponents of the second view, the first is impossible since we cannot achieve the eternal through a process in time. Gopi Krishna's observation that crossing the threshold is not done in one step implies that he however inclines to the first view, that enlightenment has a process character.

Our text next describes the first major transformation: *the extension of consciousness.* This was first experienced as a halo or luminous circle around the head, at the beginning dusty, later cleared. Onians, in *The Origins of European Thought,*[8] explains how the early idea of one's daimon or genius was imaged as a radiation around the head, and that seers could, of course, perceive this in another person. The saint is painted with a halo, implying that sanctity has something to do with illumination, with altered consciousness.

Gopi Krishna gives a clear account of this alteration. Consciousness and the "I" are no longer identified. The ego "instead of a confining unit, now itself encompassed by a shining conscious globe of vast dimensions." He struggles with formulation, simile, metaphor—a common difficulty in the description of this phenomenon, since the formulator (the ego) cannot grasp the totality of the event. In a nutshell, "There was ego consciousness as well as a vastly extended field of awareness, existing side by side, both distinct yet one."

This formulation is valuable for modern depth psychology. In our therapeutic work we aim at ego development, assuming that the development of ego and the development of consciousness are one and the same thing. Jung has shown that the ultimate development of the ego is its submission to, even immersion in the Self, much as Gopi Krishna

---

8. Richard Broxton Onians, *The Origins of European Thought: About the Body, the Mind, the Soul, the World, Time, and Fate* (Cambridge: At the University Press, 1951).

describes the "I" as immersed in the pool of light "yet fully cognizant of the...volume of consciousness all around." The problem in modern depth psychology is: how do we combine the idea of ego extension and development with the idea of extended and developed awareness? I mean by this: the two—ego and consciousness—are not the same; can they be developed independently of each other?

I think we come upon a main difference between Jungian analysis and all other forms of psychotherapy, and also we come upon a major similarity between Jungian analysis and Eastern disciplines. An aim of individuation-oriented analysis is the development of consciousness. In this process, the ego plays only one of the roles, since the consciousness of other archetypal components (anima/animus, shadow, mother and father imagos, and the self) is also an aim of the work. In contradistinction to other systems of therapy Jungian analysis may result in the extension of consciousness without any of the usual visible signs of ego development. The balance is delicate indeed: too little ego and there is no observer, no central point; too little consciousness apart from ego and there is too little objective field of awareness apart from subjectivity, too little impersonal sensitivity, too little compassion. For Western analysts, the distinction between ego and consciousness means a re-thinking of our therapeutic aims, especially those aims of contemporary "ego-psychology."

Alchemy gives us help in understanding the *whitening*. The "silvery luster," "whitish medium," "milky luster," "freshly fallen snow" are all terms we could as easily find in an alchemical text describing the wondrous appearance of the white phase. There, in alchemy, it occurs in the vessel and the language is chemical. They describe changes in which the substance so long worked over begins to whiten. (The earliest appearance of the white or anima phase, we may recall, came during the first burning fever reported in Chapter Four. There he catches sight of his small daughter Ragina, lying in the next bed, and considers himself through her eyes. He decides then not to treat himself from the outside [pouring cold water over his head] but to "bear the internal agony," which then leads to the intuition of rousing the *ida* channel and cooling himself from within. It works. The fire gives way to a "silvery streak" like the "sinuous movement of a white serpent in rapid flight." He then takes some milk and bread.)

Psychologically, this phase was prepared already by the shift from *pingala* to *ida*, that is, the change from a masculine to a feminine channel, the activation of the unconscious feminine side of the personality, or archetype of the anima. Gopi Krishna recognizes that the Kundalini is a feminine force, and he uses the image of the lively vital Shakti standing over the prostrate Shiva (who, by the way, in many pictures is passive but for his open eyes and erected penis). The shift from *pingala* to *ida,* which our author takes up only in a physiological way, means psychologically that the Shakti feminine power cannot be made to serve the masculine principle. The goddess is not activated to serve the man, but the feminine force or anima must have its own channel of activity, and man is only an instrument through which this force manifests itself. So, artists and writers put themselves at the disposal of the feminine muse, that white goddess, who shows herself, when beneficent, in beauty, love, and inspiration. Through the goddess, as when a man comes under her spell by falling in love (the most common of all experiences of the archetypal anima), things are "seen in a new light," one's "senses are sharpened," and the push of *pingala* seems irrelevant.

The Kundalini as feminine force evidently required for our author a feminine channel, even if in some accounts of its rising it supposedly ascends through a central pathway, Sushumna. This feminine channel for the feminine force has a wide complex of meanings in Tantric thought just as it does in our notion of the anima archetype. Bharati collects various meanings of the left artery or *ida* channel.[9] Curiously, we find one of these meanings is "the digestive power" hinting that by religious attention to his food intake and digestion Gopi Krishna may also have been paying homage to the anima. This corresponds with our ideas of the anima as intimately connected with the neuro-vegetative system. According to Bharati's translations the female pole can mean "wanton woman" as well as "nature" and "intuitive wisdom," but also it can mean "nonexistence." These aspects of the feminine are personified in Greek goddess figures where the not-being of Persephone is an essential part of her mother, nutritive nature, or Demeter, and where Aphrodite's wanton promiscuity finds place as does Athene's intuitive wisdom. This differentiation of the feminine is sorely lacking in our Judeo-Christian tradition that provides paltry examples of anima-consciousness, and these mainly secular and secondary.

---

9. Bharati, *The Tantric Tradition,* 175–77.

In psychological practice, the white phase refers to that period where a new feminine principle seems to dominate consciousness. There is more fantasy, the dreams are more vivid, there is less purposeful worldly action, there is more slowness, gentleness, even cool remoteness. The long period of intense suffering, depression, and worry (the nigredo) seems to slip away into a world of moonlight where everything seems redeemed and it is enough to have a sweet simple smile of peace and wisdom. One is more receptive, impressionable, sensitive. A new form of love comes to life, which at first is still romantic and wrapped up with oneself. Above all, this white phase, once the regressive virginal aspects are recognized, offers the possibility of carrying the seeds for the future in patient pregnancy.

Alchemy, too, gives parallels to the phenomenon of improved *health*. The white phase was one of the pre-forms of the final Philosopher's Stone and as such was a pre-form of the elixir of health. Although not immune, our author writes that diseases now were "distinctly milder in nature and usually there was an absence of temperature." The idea that the goddess in one form or another gives and takes away disease is widespread in India. In the West, some go to the shrines of Mary for cures. Implied is the idea that a developed relation to the anima, to the feminine principle, is an essential ingredient for health or wholeness. The feminine as such is said to be the principle of nature and life to which we can hardly relate adequately until we have integrated that feminine part of our own selves. Gopi Krishna makes this a central point of his work, recognizing from the first that the Kundalini is feminine, a goddess.

Commentary to Chapters Twelve and Thirteen

Unfortunately, we do not have the content of his *dreams*. We are told only of their vivid intensity, their sweetness and sublime beauty, and the concomitant heightened physiological activity, especially sexual. As mentioned above, the vivification of imagination belongs to the white phase, to the activation of the anima. It is remarkable how differently his process moves compared with what goes on in a Western analysis. For us, beautiful dreams are not enough. They must be recorded, worked on, analyzed, meaning extracted, integrated. For him, they needed only to be dreamt, felt, followed. Here we come to one of the ways consciousness and ego can be separated and developed independently. As long as we in analysis take up the dream in order to integrate it, we are extending the ego and identifying the extension of ego with the extension of consciousness. Our author did things another way. He let the ego sleep in its world of dreams; he observed merely what was going on, trusting (as one would in the white positive anima phase) and letting the process transform him. Rather than let his ego integrate the luminous other world, he let the luminous other world integrate him. His approach to greater awareness was just the reverse of what we assume in the West. We work at it; it requires intense activity. Gopi Krishna slept!—but at the right time and in the right way. Compare Bernard of Clairvaux's "alive and watchful sleep" that "enlightens the inward senses" (*Sermons on the Song of Songs*).

There is probably a great deal more to the interrelation of *dreaming and sexual excitation* than we today understand. Freud was the first to see intuitively a connection between the dream world and sexuality. He caged his insight within a strained mechanical system, almost destroying its value, but if we let it take free flight again we can speculate along the lines of our author's observations.

Assuming with Jung and with Gopi Krishna that Kundalini is the instinct of individuation, this instinct will have at least a strongly sexual component, if not an erotic base. Assuming, too, with Jung and with Gopi Krishna, that dreams play a major role in this process (mainly by preceding the level of awareness of consciousness), then we might speculate that what goes on in the dreams will be influenced by and reflect sexuality. Freud said this, of course, but he did not see the purposeful individuating aspect. Worse, he reduced the dream to sexuality, whereas Gopi Krishna sees sexuality in the service of the dream. Recent research in the physiology of sleep shows penile erections synchronous with dreams. In general, during periods of dreaming there is erection; during periods of non-dreaming there is detumescence. The experimenters speculate that the same biological system may be responsible for both activities. We would call this system the psychoid level; Gopi Krishna might call it Kundalini. Fantasy and sexual excitation seem to be two sides of the same activity. In Freudian psychoanalysis, fantasy is to be reduced to its sexual origins so that sexuality can serve its ultimately extraverted biological purpose. In Kundalini Yoga, it would seem that sexuality is to be converted in order to feed its ultimately introverted biological purpose. Jungian analysis might be said to take a middle position; sexuality flows on a sliding scale, at one time expressed mainly in images, at another time mainly in actions. In all three views, the sexual permeation of the unconscious is clearly affirmed.

A direct connection between brain and testicles via the spine is a physiological axiom in Indian, Chinese, Tibetan, Arabic, and ancient Greek medicine. We have no modern anatomical evidence for this connection. Rather than dismiss the idea as superstition, we may reinterpret it as a psychological truth, i.e., between the two creative centers of man there is a direct relationship; man's backbone holding him upright expresses this relationship between the two poles of his force.

The sexual union between head and genitals experienced physiologically by our author is presented in alchemy as the conjunction of male and female opposites (King and Queen, Sun and Moon, red and white, etc.). Often the metaphor of brother-sister incest is used. Psychologically, this conjunction means the union with oneself, self-fertilization, self-generation, and self-creation. The intensive prolonged introversion of one's libido, the devoted love that one lavishes upon one's own psychic life, the joyful acceptance of all biological desire and sexual excitation as belonging to and furthering the process going on in the psychic, imaginative world, endowing one's own genitals with the sanctity of a god—all this is meant by the union of crown and seed. The actual moment of the inner conjunction is said to be comparable to orgasm (see Chapter Fourteen). From this comes the divine child, the second birth of the new man.

We are, therefore, not surprised to discover our author experiencing himself as a "growing baby." Again his experiences were not in fantasy images or dreams of birth and infancy (as we often find in analysis) but in the organic experience within himself of these changes. He lived through the archetypal experiences, naively, in the best sense of the word, simply, naturally, unaffectedly.

As our author says, in the standard works of Kundalini and Hatha yoga, and in Chinese yoga as well, there are *chakras,* distinct centers of experience located in the body, each with an elaborate symbolism of color, number, animal, god, element, and body organ or system. Gopi Krishna did not have these experiences, although he explains how it might be possible for one to have viewed the circles of light as petaled *chakras.* For him there were no lotuses. We are reminded of his suffering. However, the organic experiences he sensed do correspond with the emphasis in these yogic systems upon *physiological reality* and upon the changes in vital centers and organs expected once the Kundalini is aroused and the light or breath is in circulation.

The question arises: did these events actually take place in his body, in his cells, nerves, organs? Or did they take place in the yogic body? Bharati says: "The physical and the yogic body belong to two different logical levels."[10] The *chakra* system of the yogic body is not supposed to have any objective existence in physical space. Yet the psyche insists on this body language and body experience so that what is logically impossible is indeed psychologically not only possible but felt to be true. Thus for Gopi Krishna this question does not arise. His experiences were definitely physical and in his body, his flesh afire, his organs affected, his appetites altered. *Prana* connects the two levels, which are really but one identity that our minds divide into two logics. Physiologists—and there have been some—may examine the physical body during *samadhi* for traces of its alteration and thus may demonstrate the effect upon the physical body of changes in the yogic body. But the psychologist starts with the psychic data that follows Gopi Krishna's report: his physical body was for him the *material place* of projection of immaterial events and there, in the "body," they were experienced by the senses and felt to be "real." Evidently, there must be some material place for psychic changes: the object of art, the alchemical materials, the physical body. In our Western tradition, we have come far in knowledge of the reality of the physical body and are comparatively ignorant of the reality of the body of the imagination. We do not understand enough about the effects of the imaginal body upon our physiology, not only in psychosomatic symptoms, but in all illness and its treatment. Our author's account shows how intimately the two "logical levels" merge in actual experience.

Because his report does not follow the standard examples of an ascent through distinct *chakras,* it is just that more valuable. The alchemists, too, complained that the literature was obscure and useless: no one could learn how to make the Stone from anyone else. Each had to do the work alone. So, too, in analysis, no two processes move in the same way, produce the same patterning of symbols and motifs, yield the same emotional experiences. Each case is individual and each relationship between analyst and analysand is different. In this sense it is always a creative endeavor. One

---

10. Bharati, *The Tantric Tradition,* 291.

must make and follow one's own way. The archetype of individuation may be said to be single, its manifestations multitudinous.

All the gods are within. This message is given by Heinrich Zimmer in his paper "On the Significance of the Indian Tantric Yoga." Within may mean: within the psyche, within the body, within the collective unconscious. Gopi Krishna makes it explicit that what happened to him was not an act of God, person-to-person as, for instance, such mystical experiences might have been taken by a medieval Christian. It did not come from without, but from within. The incarnation of these gods within is a terrible task, as our text has shown. "Whoever is near unto me is near unto the fire" is an apocryphal saying of Jesus. How are we to understand this incarnation? How are we to read the purpose of these events? What do the gods and goddesses want with us?

Commentary to Chapters Fourteen and Fifteen

In his description of ecstatic *samadhi*, our author says he was "living in a lustrous world of brilliant color." The extraordinary *visual experiences* of color and texture that are reported by Huxley in *The Doors of Perception*,[11] by those who have had LSD visions, by Zaehner in *Mysticism: Sacred and Profane*,[12] by Summers in *The Physical Phenomena of Mysticism*[13] confirm from different angles that what our author experienced belongs to this path. There are of course vast differences between the mysticism "sacred" of our author and mysticism "profane," by which, following Zaehner, I refer to technical chemical tricks "to get an experience."

Perhaps our contemporary greed to see (television, scuba-diving, photography, nudity, sight-seeing, LSD and mescaline) stands in place of the hunger of the soul for true visions. The prices on the art market attest to what man is willing to pay for true vision. Today, the hungry eye wants the beatific vision; we would see God's face, even if through chemical ecstasy.

Sacred mysticism recognizes the transformation of perception not as a separate visual experience, a kick or thrill, but as the outcome of a

11. Aldous Huxley, *The Doors of Perception* (New York: Harper & Brothers, 1954).

12. R.C. Zaehner, *Mysticism: Sacred and Profane* (London: Oxford University Press, 1957).

13. Montague Summers, *The Physical Phenomena of Mysticism* (New York: Barnes & Noble, 1950).

state of being. In alchemy this stage was referred to as the peacock's tail in which are "eyes" unfurled amid some of the most royally blazing colors known in nature. The Stone, too, was known as the tincture, which stained and colored any object it contacted. The return of vivid color follows the white phase. Psychologically, it refers to the return of health and vitality, joy in life, love for existence, the liberation of feeling beyond the personal immediate surroundings, the extension of sensation beyond the senses to the spirit of nature itself; whereas the spiritual world moves out from its shadowy existence as only a mental phenomenon and takes on the color of living reality.

Even in alchemy, this stage was followed by a new *mortificatio*, a new disintegration. There, it is difficult to tell why; here, we are given an insight. Our author, in his honesty, writes: "I was overjoyed at the glorious possibility within my reach now. There could be absolutely no doubt that I was the exceedingly fortunate *possessor* of an awakened Kundalini. It was only now that I could grasp the reason why...success...was thought to be the highest *achievement* possible...*the supreme prize attainable* at the end." He compares accomplished yogis with "mighty rulers and potentates." It was an "honor" that had been "bestowed on me."

The next paragraph begins: "But, alas, my good luck was exceedingly short-lived." From my italics above, it becomes clear just why: he had fallen victim to a new inflation. Little wonder after that blaze that he did catch fire himself. So again an even worse purge, an even worse "dying to everything" was necessary. (How necessary is suffering!) The peacock is also a symbol of vanity and pride; the tincture may stain the ego too, bringing to it the poisonous taint of revivified subjectivity that this world I perceive is mine, my reward, given to me.

The peculiar physical experiences belong to the death experience, and similar fits of jerking uncontrolled movements are reported in medieval accounts where these motions were attributed to a plague of devils. The experience is one of dismemberment, disintegration attested to as well by the Shamans as an archetypal event in their process in individuation (see Eliade's *Shamanism*). Psychologically, the central system of will that has the ego as its core falls apart into autonomous complexes. One is no longer in control of oneself, and the autonomic nervous system dominates the habitual system identified with the conscious will. One is indeed a victim of unconscious energetic centers, those devilish complexes, pulling every which way.

We cannot help but be enormously impressed with the overwhelming physical reality of Gopi Krishna's death experience. It confirms what I have tried to write about in *Suicide and the Soul* that only if the experience be totally convincing, totally "real," can a convincingly real rebirth follow.[14] Much as we may know this in advance, it is each time a terrifyingly threatening event—and it must be so, otherwise it would not carry the conviction of reality.

I am also enormously impressed that our author was saved by a dream, and such a simple one: a dish of meat. When he was first urged by an impulse to eat meat, he disregarded the unconscious suggestion perhaps on doctrinaire grounds, still convinced that his mild diet was the right one and that his appetite was a sign of greed (whereas his true "greed" was spiritual, as our italicized passages above show). This often happens in an analysis: the unconscious urges a step, an advance into health, which the conscious personality, still used to the limits of its neurosis, feels hesitant to make. But a forward step not taken when the time is there is the same as a step backward.

What does this meat mean? Is not meat a return to the human condition in its animal reality, the life of the blood, the instinct of involvement (hunting, struggling, killing)? Meat is the food of the hunter, warrior, chieftain. In alchemy, it would belong to the symbols of the rubedo, the red king, of masculine emotional strength. It is also the final integration of the mother complex, eating her as body.

Subsequent to the acceptance of meat, Gopi Krishna returns to the world of action, as a "chieftain," having organized a group for social work. He is thoroughly involved, not only with paper and ink as in his government office, but now on the plane of daily suffering—widows, refugees, war. The time of the return is traditionally critical. How does one re-enter daily life after the "great liberation"? After such experiences, how does one transfer the love and beauty and meaning to the other hours of the week? How does one bridge the gap between planes of being? If it is a narrow gate, an impossibly dangerous passage to cross the threshold into the releasing other world, how much more difficult to re-enter this known and confining world with all its pettiness and banal sorrows. For our author, the "return" seems to have occurred quite naturally. (Of

---

14. James Hillman, *Suicide and the Soul* (Thompson, Conn.: Spring Publications, 2020), 70.

course, in one sense he did throughout keep one foot well planted in this world with job, family, and diet.) His crisis was less an externalized one: "How do I enter society and the world of fellow-man bringing with me the gifts that I have been given?" His crisis came before, symbolized by the meat. Once that was eaten, his appetite "returned" and with it re-entry into the world in a new way.

The natural and easy flow back into the world, spreading himself thin over the troubled waters of social reality, to calm, soothe, bind up, again has a striking resemblance to one of the last stages of alchemy. I refer to the image of "oil." He describes his expansion of consciousness to extend "more and more like a drop of oil spreading on the surface of water." The Stone was said to have an oily nature, easily melted but not to be evaporated, staining (as a tincture) all with which it came in contact. "The development was gradual and the change so imperceptible" that he attributed it to general improvement rather than to a new principle at work. But just this imperceptible peaceful oozing rather than willing, this softening of friction rather than striving, this thick slowness that is yet lighter than water, is attached to it yet floats over it just this is the fat and oil of abundance, the joy and compassion of full being.

Commentary to Chapters Sixteen, Seventeen, and Eighteen

Verse comes naturally to those seized by what Plato called "mania" or divine frenzy. Shakespeare in one phrase joins "the lunatic, the lover, and the poet."[15] Lovers compose poems; mystics (the prophets, Blake, John of the Cross) use the verse form; haiku and Zen go together; and even some alchemists recounted their experiences in poetry. Those in analysis frequently find that only verse is suitable for giving form to what is going on-and this expression has nothing to do with art. Characteristic of verse is rhythm, the use of words for sound as well as sense, the symbolic cluster of meaning, brevity, and intensity. Verse has a ritualistic aspect. It is language as revelation, as pure symbol; echoed in it is the primitive throb of the dance, the ritual chant, and the nonsense of the child. It would seem to be the true language of the spirit.

That his verse came in many tongues is a fact not unknown to parapsychological research. In trance states, there are mediums who do speak in foreign tongues, even converse in languages they do not consciously

---

15. William Shakespeare, *A Midsummer Night's Dream*, Act 5, Scene 1.

know, nor have ever learned. These cases of glossolalia are evidence for what Ian Stevenson, who is the pioneering contemporary investigator in this field, calls reincarnation. Gopi Krishna would not deny this idea, but he finds another ground. His ability is owed less to a former incarnation than to his contact with the supersensible world through which all can be known. The great experience is set in paradoxes. This is typical of the indescribability of the highest mystical experiences. It is both "nothing yet everything," "immeasurable," "yet no bigger than an infinitely small point," "infinitely large and infinitely small at the same time." This is the Atman, bigger than big and smaller than small. From the topological view of the psyche, the ego focus is identified with its objective psychic ground. This totality is of course spaceless, timeless, extending everywhere unendingly and eternally present, in so far as the human personality when released of its limitations of circumstance is part of the same matter, the same energy, which makes up the whole universe. That especially the categories of spatial size are used for this description (rather than, say, categories of motion, nature, time, love, etc.) reflects the difficulties inherent in ego formulations of such experiences. The ego is bound to its body and this body has its definite spatial limits. Grand as we may imagine ourselves to be, we are but minute figures in a vast Chinese landscape, and placed not even in the centre of the picture. Transcendence of ego limitations is therefore presented by the ego primarily as a leap out of its spatial limitation given by the body's pounds and inches. (Distorted forms of this discrepancy between ego experience and body limitations can be found in every depression and inflation, when one feels smaller than small, or bigger than big.) I would also hazard the guess that space is the category appropriate to intuition (extension of vision, light, all-encompassing) and therefore preferred by intuitive types, which I assume Gopi Krishna to be partly on the basis of our author's own admittedly obsessive (at times) preoccupation with diet, body, sensation, and health, and his difficulties in regard to the factual order.

The experience itself was ushered in with "a cadence like the humming of a swarm of bees." The "bee-loud glade" (Yeats) is a favorite image in poetry and comes in mythology as well as in the Bible. But we must remember, in our text we are not dealing with images as in a Western individuation process reflected mainly in dreams, but with lived experiences. The whitening, the meat, the baby, the oil, were all actualities for our author. Because of this, we may gain some insight from his experiences into why the bee is a widespread symbol of natural wisdom. In addition to its natural intelligence and social organization used often as a metaphor for society, its conversion of nature into culture (honey and wax), its dancing, mating, feeding, building rituals, its death sting, its orientation ability—the bee sound (just as the numinous sound of the lion, the gander, the bull, etc.) evidently occurs, if we follow our text, at a special moment in the liberation experience. Perhaps it is the sound of a strata of instinctual earth wisdom, deeper than our mammalian blood, representing a spontaneous flight, wild yet ordered, of the collective spirit beyond personal individuality. The Pythian oracle spoke from such depths. Her psychic state was that kind of mania that Plato terms prophetic and that belongs to the god Apollo. Her answers were in verse, "some even maintained that the hexameter was invented at Delphi."[16] "Pythia" refers to "Python," the snake that Apollo killed and who resided in that place. She was, in other words, the daimon of the snake itself, the serpent power now in female form giving utterance to its wisdom. Supposedly, the serpent's bones and/or teeth were used for her oracles. And she was described in the Homeric hymn to Hermes as a "delphic bee."[17] Quite possibly, Gopi Krishna's experience of the bee sound in connection with his prophetic verse corresponds with the actual experience of the Pythian oracle so that through his account some light is shed on that ancient enigma.

After this last, highest encounter, the return itself is threatened. He abandons his work, identifies for a time with the *image of the holy man,* feels purged "clean of worldly love," and is ready to follow the traditional pattern of mystic seer, wandering, devoted only to the spirit. He views his attachment to the world as a weak spot in his system, but as we see later he is then reconciled with this attachment and in the last instance realizes its positive value.

The alternation of his states of consciousness throughout the years, especially the loss of heavenly joy time and again, is also described by the alchemists. They said the Stone must be coagulated and dissolved again and again. The more it alternated between these opposites, the more valuable it became. This lesson is hard to learn, for after every peak experience

---

16. E. R. Dodds, *The Greeks and the Irrational* (Berkeley: University of California Press, 1962), 92 n.70.

17. "Gedanken über die Pythia," in Karl Kerényi, *Humanistische Seelenforschung* (Darmstadt: Wissenschaftliche Buchgesellschaft, 1966).

one wants to "hold it," and after each valley experience one feels guilty, lost and humiliated.

Again we have evidence that the development of ego and the development of awareness are separate matters. His external ego situation, in fact, deteriorated in that he no longer had a job and was reduced to living upon the sacrifices of his wife, nor did he feel himself to be of any use even in the realm of therapy with all those who came with problems. Straightforwardly, he tells the limits of the enlightened one: such a one may be of value in teaching or helping others who are on the same path, but he is not a miracle man. To assume this role would be to misuse the experiences. This keeps our author from being a fraud and mountebank. He remains aware of his human limits and chooses to remain within those limits.

By giving credit to his wife, he acknowledges an archetypal aspect of this path. It is not taken alone; there is always the "other"—master, disciple, pupil, sister, wife, friend, beloved, who is the silent partner, who represents the human love and care, who carries the other side, gives encouragement by believing, and is the mortal twin to the immortal urge.

It could be argued again that this dependence upon his wife and family, his precarious health and his general ineffectiveness as both householder and as healer negates all that has happened, so that it becomes merely a psychic aberration. He admits that were it not for his mother and his wife, he would have died long ago. So what has this twenty-five years of ordeal really achieved? What positive results give evidence of the Great Liberation? Is he not just where he started: in the mother complex, a victim of mother matter, passive, delicate, dependent? How these destructive negative thoughts must have tormented him—or would have tormented his counterpart in the West.

However, within his tradition, this dependent relation to the Mother archetype is inevitable. Ramakrishna for example was always the devotee of the Mother, while the Indian Holy Man is ever her son in the sense of drawing sustenance from life and earth that is the cow that must never be harmed. Only in the West is this attitude questionable, for we tend to view negatively the realm of the Mother and to call that inevitable dependency upon the material limits in which we are set a "complex." We in the West are often too quick to condemn the "Mother," thereby cutting ourselves off from our own ground. Our author is neither paralysed by his passivity nor rebellious against it, and so he cannot be said to be caught in a complex. Rather, he lives the opposites. On the one hand, he is involved in the bold spiritual adventure, requiring the masculine virtues of endurance, courage, and individuality, while on the other he acknowledges without shame his weakness, sensitivity and physical limitations. He accepts the feminine root, not only of the Kundalini, but of life itself, thereby showing us a positive relation to the maternal archetype.

At the end of Chapter Eighteen, there is a passage that conveys what we might call his declaration of faith, remarkable for its simplicity. "I found that a man can rise from the normal to a higher level of consciousness by a continuous biological process, as regular as any other activity of the body, and that at no stage is it necessary or even desirable for him either to neglect his flesh or to deny a place to the human feelings in his heart." The same credo could apply to analytical psychology with a few exceptions. Rather than "biological" we might refer to the process as "psychological." We might interpret "flesh" and "feelings" with more liberality so as to include more shadows of the body and the heart. We might raise a question about the continuity of this process, since it also seems to have a discontinuous aspect that works by leaps and jumps and devolves backward on to itself. It can even devour itself so that the accomplishments of one phase of life may all be consumed in later errors. Our psychological process is definitely not progressive, ever upward and ever better, much as we idealize it and much as older people are obliged to believe. Jung gives us models for the completeness of consciousness, but these models are to be found more in his books than in his disciples. But then Gopi Krishna, too, points the way in his own person and his writings, not through training others. However, for our psychology the overriding importance in his credo is its emphasis upon an instinct of individuation (which, as I said, Jung called the Kundalini) and the process character of consciousness. This implies that something is meant with our psychic lives, our souls, and that this urge of meaning is a regular (continuous) function of our bodily nature. It is possible to each and does not deny the world and its life.

Commentary: Conclusion

All the gods are within. This message is given by Heinrich Zimmer in his paper "On the Significance of the Indian Tantric Yoga."[18] Within may

---

18. Heinrich Zimmer, "On the Significance of the Indian Tantric Yoga," in *Spiritual*

mean: within the psyche, within the body, within the collective unconscious. Gopi Krishna makes it explicit that what happened to him was not
an act of God, person-to-person, as for instance, such mystical experiences might have been taken by a medieval Christian. It did not come
from without but from within. The incarnation of these gods within is
a terrible task, as our text has shown. "Whoever is near unto me is near
unto the fire" is an apocryphal saying of Jesus. How are we to understand this incarnation? How are we to read the purpose of these events?
What do the gods and goddesses want with us? So many questions flood
in—metaphysical, historical, religious—that a psychologist is unable to
cope. We can only turn to the case at hand. Our author knows what the
goddess wants of him and the publication of this book is part of the purpose of that which he has been driven and led to incarnate.

The instinct of individuation, as the evolutionary energy in man, is
given to every man. Our author's experiences, he tells us, are possible in
varying forms to everyone. Furthermore, they are teleologically meant
for everyone. Our task is to incarnate the gods within. Having seen this
as the result of decades of wrestling with himself and these gods, he can
give us a golden vision of how things not only might be, but are meant
to be. Can we blame him for this vast speculation; is not this the stuff of
prophecy and vision, and is not our age deaf and dry to just such calls?
The relation of the one who sees the shadows as shadows to those still in
the cave is an archetypal problem. Our author has grasped the dilemma
and spoken out. Our author does not believe that it is enough for the
mystic "to work out his salvation with diligence"; he feels a call to call
others. In this respect, he is not to be regarded as a mystic nor is this an
account of an "experience" of which we have, due to drugs, more and
more at hand from every side. He presents himself as a modern teacher
and scientific inquirer into a realm that has been neglected and covered
over with accounts of "mystical experiences." He does not want us to take
this material as another variety of religious experience but as the very
meaning of human life itself.

The experience of himself as only a vessel through which the wind
of human history blows and from which the call to others sounds is

Disciplines: Papers from the Eranos Yearbook, edited by Joseph Campbell (New York:
Pantheon Books, 1960).

entirely in keeping with his point of view. As Professor Spiegelberg points out, Gopi Krishna never felt that what took place was personally his.[19] From the beginning he was a mere instrument; therefore, at the end, he is merely a mouthpiece of a vaster truth. The degree to which the ego personality takes part in these collective unconscious events determines their final shape. In the West, the mystic or artist to whom the extraordinary happens hammers the impersonal into personal form and presses his own vision upon archetypal patterns. The specific absence of personal form, the characteristic of impersonality, is the mark of the East. Yet, Gopi Krishna's biography is personal, and it is just this that makes it unusually contemporary and accessible. Just because this book from another culture is so accessible it meets us more than halfway, addressing to each reader a question about the nature of man. His question is the fundamental one. What could be more important to inquire about than the nature of man, his psyche, his spirit, his body, and the purpose of his consciousness?

Note

In addition to the works mentioned within the context of the Commentary, I would refer the reader to the *Collected Works* of C.G. Jung, vols. 11, 12, 14, and 16 in particular. Very valuable also is *Spiritual Disciplines,* a collection of excellent papers from the *Eranos Yearbook* (among them Zimmer on Tantric Yoga). For psychological background material, I read Jung's seminar on Kundalini Yoga[20] and his unpublished and privately circulated "Lectures on the Process of Individuation."

J.H.
Botorp, Hemsö, Summer 1965
(Revised *idem,* 1969)

19. Frederic Spiegelberg, "Introduction," in Gopi Krishna, *Kundalini: The Evolutionary Energy in Man* (Berkeley: Shambala, 1971), 5–9.

20. C.G. Jung, *The Psychology of Kundalini Yoga: Notes of the Seminar Given in 1932,* edited by Sonu Shamdasani (Princeton, N.J.: Princeton University Press, 1996).

⧸⊙⧸ ⧸⊙⧸ ⧸⊙⧸ ⧸⊙⧸ ⧸⊙⧸ ⧸⊙⧸ ⧸⊙⧸ ⧸⊙⧸ ⧸⊙⧸ ⧸⊙⧸ ⧸⊙⧸ ⧸⊙⧸

15

THREE WAYS OF FAILURE AND ANALYSIS

1. Failure in Analysis

We are each familiar with the failure of certain kinds of cases in analysis. Particularly difficult and unresponsive to successful therapy are people with styles of life in which homosexuality, alcoholism, or chronic depression are the major presenting "problems." To these can be added those with paranoid obsessions, the severe so-called character neuroses and people who have been diagnosed as sociopaths and psychopaths. That so many and so varied kinds of cases for which analysis may have been considered the preferred method of treatment turn out to be failures, gives cause for considering analysis afresh and in the light of these failures.

We are also familiar with another sort of failed cases, those in which a morbid cancer develops during the analysis, or which end in suicide, or where the countertransference reactions constellate such exorbitant fantasy and massive affect, or psychopathological lacunae, in the analyst that the case must be transferred or the analysis abandoned. Smaller failures perhaps go unrecognized—analyses that have as by-products estrangements within families, loss of extraverted adaptation, splintered friendships.

Through *clinical reflection* upon these various sorts of failures we may examine the kinds of cases that fail, or for which analysis fails, and we may bring our own failures as analysts to other analysts for scrutiny—all of which reflection attempts to correct present failures and minimize future ones. This manner of clinically reflecting is a function of the dominant empirical and moral theme of our culture: learning through mistakes, trial and error, getting better through working at it, if at first you don't succeed try, try again, in which the model is one of improvement away from mistakes, error, and failure, toward competence.

Failure in this metaphor is linked in a polarity with success, and we tend to measure failures normatively, that is as a privation of success. Failure is the obverse of successful treatment; success equals the minimum of failure. A successful analysis would then mean success with those areas of failure in the case—the dominating presenting complaints of homosexuality, alcoholism, delusions—and a failure would mean their continuation despite the personality development and insight gained through the analysis.

This model of failure, simple though it might seem, has nonetheless encouraged some sophisticated discussions of analysis. Existential analysis would do away with normative criteria of success and failure altogether. On the other hand, behavior therapy would consider failure wholly in terms of the normative criteria of positive functioning, making suspect the belief in analysis as a method of personality growth and increase of consciousness unless there is positive evidence of symptom elimination and relief of distress.

By what we define analysis will also define its success and failure: an analysis that aims for increase of consciousness or individuation cannot be judged a failure if it does not cure symptoms, and vice versa, an analysis that aims at removing a crippling phobia cannot be called a failure if it never goes into the patient's dreams, or integrates the phobia into meaningfulness.

Of course, this simple, normative model of success (as optimum health, psychic order or wholeness) neglects that success and failure may be conceived not as opposites or poles of a continuum but as an identity, so that *every analysis is both a failure and a success at the same time,* and every part of every analysis is both right and wrong, leading and misleading, constructively growing and destructively killing, implying that for analysis to succeed at all it must always fail.

2. Failure of Analysis

The inevitability of the first kind of failure opens a larger perspective, and we may move the question from specific failures in analysis to the general failure of analysis. Since analysis always shows certain sorts of failures, is there not something general about analysis that brings about failure, so that analysis itself may be considered a failure?

The literature shows that as there are discussions about the failure *in* analysis in certain kinds of cases, there are also discussions on the failure *of* analysis as a whole. Freud's late reflections on "analysis terminable or interminable" is the *locus classicus* for this kind of pessimistic consideration. Does analysis ever reach its end, in time or fulfilment? Is transference ever resolved, individuation ever achieved? Even if analysis does not satisfy the goal of cure, does it indeed yield enlargement of consciousness, depth of personality, finer love, better adaptation, significant life? If we look at the analysts, ourselves, as the paradigms for the process in which we sit for many years, what effect has analysis had upon our adaptation, our consciousness, our loving?

From another perspective, where are the validating statistics in regard to kinds of cases and kinds of improvement within such classes, and how may we ever formulate such statistics since nosological classifications into which we might class our cases are today all in doubt? Is "paranoic" a valid term with an actual referent? Where are the "manics" and "hysterics" of yesteryear? How can we assess success and failure of a treatment without agreed criteria for what we are treating, i.e., what is psychic illness and psychic health which gives meaning in general to an idea of "treatment."

The view that analysis in general has failed comes from critics from many sides. Experimentalists ask for public evidence of achievement; clinicians ask for evidence of improvement through analytical treatment; societal critics see analysis as the establishment's tool for maintaining our notions of sickness, of exclusive individuality, and of professionalism, perpetuating a system of bourgeois capitalism. Theologians and philosophers consider its failure more profoundly, regarding analysis to have an inadequate ideational critique and a suspect method that is more like brainwashing, or initiation into a religious sect than either a therapeutic treatment or an empirical science of personality exploration that it claims to be. It fails because its subliminal premises differ from its overt intentions. Finally historians (of ideas, social movements and medicine) see analysis within its setting of the twentieth century, as a response to a specific failure within that civilization, and that what was right for early twentieth century men is insufficient for us today.

Through just such *historical reflection* upon the failure of analysis we may recall that analysis did arise out of failure, in that it was a specific method for dealing with those peculiar kinds of cases that had failed to be understood, or even find a hearing by the prevailing system, e.g., the hysterics of Freud and Breuer and the schizophrenics of Jung and Bleuler. These were the medically and socially failed, and psychotherapy was invented as a specific response to these specific failures. If analysis arises from the maladapted, the peculiar neurotic discontents of our civilization who hitherto could find no meaningful place, the failed so to speak, then a third perspective opens in regard to the relationship between analysis and failure.

3. Failure as Analysis

Despite the critique of the first kind—that analysis fails in many specific instances—and the critiques of the second kind—that analysis as such is a failure—for me, and I shall assume for us preponderantly, the merits of classical analysis are so obvious that one need not dwell upon them. A panegyric here, or even an apology, is hardly in place, so let us turn instead to the defects of the merits. Let us take the clinical and historical reflection upon the failure of classical analysis one step further into an *archetypal reflection.*

By classical analysis, I mean a course of treatment in an atmosphere of sympathy and confidence of one person by another person for a fee, which treatment may be conceived as educative (in various senses) or therapeutic (in various senses) and which proceeds principally through the joint interpretative exploration of habitual behavior and of classes of mental events that have been traditionally called fantasies, feelings, memories, dreams, and ideas, and where the exploration follows a coherent set of methods, concepts, and beliefs stemming mainly from Freud and from Jung, where focus is preferably upon the unanticipated and affectively charged, and whose goal is the improvement (subjectively and/ or objectively determined) of the analysand and the termination of the treatment. This description leaves room for many versions of improvement—from alleviation of symptoms to individuation and mystical revelation. This description also leaves room for various aspects of Freud's and Jung's methods, concepts, and beliefs as they receive differing emphasis according to place, time, and practitioner.

An archetypal reflection upon the failure in and of analysis would leave untouched its definition, that is, we would not attempt to improve analysis in specific instances, nor redefine (update) it in general, so that it becomes a more adequate response to contemporary psychic ills. Rather,

I would suggest—and this shall be my final point—that analysis may continue as before even where it conceives itself not only as having failed historically and clinically, but as *being failure archetypally*; as being concerned with failure in the dictionary senses of failure: weakness, defectiveness, absence of victory, bankruptcy, deception, lack, and incompletion.

Failure would be regarded as one fundamental psychic factor in terms of which every man lives his life. Existentialism calls this category "scheitern," or the consciousness that arises from shipwreck. Alchemy has considered it under the rubrics of *dissolutio, mortificatio, putrefactio.* Buddhism speaks of inherent decay; D.H. Lawrence of the "ship of death."

Were analysis to be imagined in terms of its inherent failure (which merely parallels the inherent failure of every life) emphasis would no longer be placed too one-sidedly upon the integrative, increasing, enlarging, and upward-striving metaphor, the eros aspect of ever more unions, a metaphor that may be condensed into the keyword "growth" (which already has taken on overtones of escalation, proliferation and cancer). Instead, we would return to that tradition of the analysis of the soul that recognizes "two opposite propensities in the human frame; one constantly and uniformly tending to corruption and decay, the other to life and health"—a sentence from Ernst Stahl, the eighteenth-century German physician and philosopher who placed the soul at the center of his concerns. But the sentence might as well have come from Freud's contrast of Eros and Thanatos. Thanatos provides the archetypal reflection to our theme of failure.

When analysis follows the models of thought of nineteenth-century medical philosophy, its heroic and Great-Mother-Nature determined consciousness, then it will tend, as with Xavier Bichat, to define life as "the sum of forces that oppose death," and then it will consider the unconscious—as did Arthur Schopenhauer, Eduard von Hartmann, Carl Gustav Carus and even Henri Bergson, as an organic life force that develops and has, as Freud said, no negation. I believe that we still tend to view the unconscious in this nineteenth-century model, as the creative will of life slumbering in the soul, which unfurls into time and which if read rightly can keep us from failing.

Were analysis to take its historical origins (as a response to failure) also as its archetypal base, then its perspective might derive more from Thanatos and the statement of Bichat could be reversed. Analysis explores failure in terms of death, and it is called into existence as the psyche's preferred instrument to explore failure in terms of all the forces which oppose life, i.e., to look for Thanatos and its related archetypal dominants wherever life is blocked, defeated, bankrupt and failed.

This approach investigates (analyses) failure less to remove it for new growth, than to lead each mistake, error and weakness into failure (be "psychopompos" to it) by leading it to its final consequences, its psychic goal in death. Then every mistake of life, every weakness and error in and of analysis, instead of being set straight in repentance or wrung for its drop of consciousness or transformed and integrated, becomes rather the entrance to failure, an opening into the reversal of all values. Rather than as a block in Eros and the flow of life, we might consider failures as constellated, intended, even finally caused by the underworld which wants life to fail in order that other attitudes governed by other archetypal principles be recognized.

The gods then that we would consider to be the dominants of analysis would particularly be those who govern what the Romantics called the "nightside of the soul" (Fechner). Analysis would derive its attitudes from those archetypal dominants personified in the gods who have a special relationship with the invisible, underground nighttime world of death, terror, and tragedy, such as Hermes, Hades, Saturn, Persephone, Dionysos (Lord of Souls and source of tragedy), and especially the Children of Night described by Hesiod (Theogony): doom, old age, death, murder, destiny, fate, deception, sleep, dreams, quarrels, grievances, misery, nemesis. These personifications of Hesiod are the main content of analysis and they are partly what we today call failures since we have placed analysis among the healing, helping professions of positivism with its emphasis upon the gods and heroes of above, visible in Apollonic light, gods and goddesses of city, field, life, and deed. Even love we tend to conceive in the concrete manner of Aphrodite, forgetting the subtle intimacy of Eros and Thanatos, even their identity in Renaissance Neoplatonism.

We may do more justice with the failures in analysis and the failure of analysis when we consider analysis as a process in failure, and even individuation as a movement in the realm of Hades, invisibly, where the literalisms of life are reflected in the metaphors of death. Then individuation, the uniqueness of individual personality, will be recognized as Miguel de Unamuno characterized it in the tragic sense of life, which has its own joy, its own comedy.

When I am in despair, I do not want to be told of rebirth; when I am ageing and decaying and the civilization around me collapsing from its overgrowth that is overkill, I cannot tolerate that word "growth," and when I am falling to bits in my complexities, I cannot abide the defensive simplistics of mandalas, nor the sentimentalities of individuation as unity and wholeness. These are formulae presented through a fantasy of opposites—the disintegration shall be compensated by integration. But what of cure through likeness where like takes care of like? I want the right background to the failure of life; I want to hear with precision of those gods who are served by and thrive upon and can hence provide an archetypal background to and even an eras connection with the defeat, decay and dismemberment, because these dominants would reflect the *experienced* psyche (not in its Aristotelian conceptualization as belonging to life), but in the actuality of its only known goal that is also both its way and its substance, death.

16

A PSYCHOLOGY OF TRANSGRESSION
DRAWN FROM AN INCEST DREAM:
IMAGINING THE CASE

[T]he archetypes possess the quality of "transgressiveness": they
can sometimes manifest themselves in such a way that they seem
to belong as much to society as to the individual; they are therefore numinous and contagious in the effects.

(C.G. Jung, CW 10:661)

D
r. Gene Inborn shall be the patient's name, and we shall analyze
from my notes his dream of incest with his daughter. "He felt
appalled: shame and horror. No memory of any scene of sexual
act or its detail [although he was] sure it occurred, [and therefore he]
believes on waking that the details had been repressed." About the time,
he said, she seemed young, maybe around eleven, twelve, or fourteen.
Also, during the dream and while waking from it, he was troubled by the
to him appalling question as to whether he had committed incest actually
years ago and had no memory of it.

He worried these questions before, during, and after the hour:
should he check the facts with her? Would she remember what he
didn't; would she want to remember? If he did ask her for corroborating
evidence, would this be a seduction, even a compulsion to repeat, as if
to make actual in the present what the dream had raised as a possibility
in the past? Had he a "faulty" memory? And was the memory trouble
a sign of ageing, as the incest dream (the first reported in this case) a
beginning sign of a senile man's crazy sexual fantasies about young
girls? Was the absence of the sexual in the dream a disguise for the
absence of sexuality, i.e., impotence? Perhaps the dream was so appalling because he was "losing it"?

Dr. Inborn presented the image of a heavyset, bigfooted, slow, and
reflective man of depressive nature and rather obsessive. He had already

been analyzed twice, as a young medical resident and again in a training program. I was now his third or fourth analyst, and he was psychologically intelligent. He carried over into dreams the kinds of interpretive reflections that obsessed his clinical work. The daughter in this case had children of her own, a family he saw once a year at most. He felt fondly attached to her; and his dreams, where she appeared occasionally, showed her image to be a major soul carrier. According to his imagination of her, she read novels, went to lots of movies, wore all sorts of funny shoes, and there was always "music in the house."

The following associations also belong to the case. He remonstrated with himself for having been an "absent father." He never changed her diapers, never bathed her or spanked her, was usually preoccupied at her bedtime, though he sometimes said prayers with her in the dark. He did drive her to school for a while; they did play roughhouse when she had been in a tomboy stage, and earlier, when she was small, he had pushed her on the playground swings. He had few images of her, more generalized abstractions regarding her. He never had a sexual fantasy of her during those years nor later when she began to go out. He just shoved that out of his mind, or maybe thoughts of her with boyfriends never got into his mind.

Particularly this absence now bothered him. He worried that his having been an absent father was counterphobic to an incest wish or, worse, to a forgotten incest act. Maybe he was "wrong" about the memories of how he was and what he did when she was a child; maybe these memories were "just a reconstruction without a basis in fact." The dream worked in him obsessively as a trauma, even as it made him feel "somehow more alive." His sense of what was real, now and in the past, had been upset radically. So much for the case, now to the dream.

The dream presents four interlocked feeling thoughts: (1) "shame and horror," (2) no memory of an actual sexual act, (3) "sure it had occurred," (4) the question "whether he had committed incest actually" and yet had no memory of it.

This curious set of reflections and emotions encapsulates major theoretical issues raised by incest. By this I mean, primarily, the shame and horror and the acute conviction about its occurrence coupled with an unsure memory of actual details. I also mean the profound upset, the quasi-derealization and the obsessive turning of the questions. Even if the case of Dr. Inborn is not one of childhood, he is an "incest victim" inasmuch as he is both a supposed perpetrator and a person being abused in the present by the dream. So, I think we can draw from the imagination of this case ideas pertinent to a psychology of incest. And the psychology of incest from Freud and Jung onward, as Paul Kugler clearly and thoroughly has shown,[1] always challenges therapy to face the foundations of its thought.

If we follow the patient's approach, the emotions of shame and horror give the conviction that incest had occurred. *Post hoc, ergo propter hoc*: since there is shame and horror, there must be a shameful and horrible prior event to instigate these emotions. This leads to the belief that the sexual details were repressed and to the further troubling question that perhaps he might have committed incest in fact. Starting with shame and horror, he imagines forward to an incest scene and the fantasy of its repression. He invokes the figure of a censor and the idea of repression to support the shame and horror and the conviction that it had occurred. For one thing was "sure" in the dream: his conviction that it had occurred.

This approach gradually moves from what is there in the dream to a supposition[2] about what must be there (censor, repression). Or, rather, to a supposition about what is not there and why it is not there. He is explaining the dream before completing a thorough examination of the actual dream statement. *Not the actuality of incest is the main concern of an incest-dream analysis but the actuality of the dream,* what is actually there, and all of what is there. Not only does he not take enough of the dream into account, but what he does, he takes literally: shame and horror, the sure conviction, the troubling questions.

His approach shows what may happen when an interpretation is founded upon emotional literalism, or the naturalistic fallacy in the realm of emotions. Dr. Inborn is identifying his day-world ego with the dream ego's feelings and worries. He worries in the day world the same worries in the dream; he feels in the day world the same feelings in the

---

1. Paul Kugler, "Childhood Seduction: Physical and Emotional," *Spring: An Annual of Archetypal Psychology and Jungian Thought* (1987): 40–60.

2. Patricia Berry, *Echo's Subtle Body: Contributions to an Archetypal Psychology* (Thompson, Conn.: Spring Publications, 2017 [1982]), 72: "Under Supposition we might place any statement of causality, any 'because of this or that' interpretative move; likewise any generalization made on the basis of the dream, any evaluation, prognosis, any use of past or future tense."

dream. That these emotions are in the dream allows them to be *imagined*, to be seen through; but Dr. Inborn is not trying to see through. He is dreaming the dream along in its own emotions. Does not this emotional literalism keep a person unconscious because it keeps his day-world attitude in the stance of the unconscious dream? Then the dream becomes merely a syntonic support to already ensconced day-world attitudes. Because he feels the same shame, horror and sure conviction in the day as in his sleep, Dr. Inborn is still dreaming, and his interpretation is not so much a reflection as an unconscious defense against reflection, against seeing through.

Suppose we make a different move. Suppose we maintain the dream's paradox just as it is, true to the manifest content, sticking to the image. There is no sexual incident, yet there is conviction that incest has occurred. If we hold to both sides of the dilemma, then there is an occurrence without a happening, an incest with no event. Something happened that did not happen. So, what did happen? Not incest as event, *but incest as conviction, as belief.* The dreamer's certainty lies not in facts from the past but in faith from the dream. Incest did not happen in memory (no memory of it, he said, neither in dream nor in history), but it surely happened—in psyche. Memory and psyche have been rendered by the paradox into a contentiously troubling opposition. The dream seems to draw a dividing line between them; and the dreamer tries to resolve the tension by forcing one side to concur with the other: he supposes repression and forgetting in order to re-align memory, and he imagines literal evidence from a literal daughter to support the tenets of his faith.

The dream upsets Dr. Inborn's faith in his memory. It might be "faulty"; he is ageing, "losing it." The usual unquestioning faith given to memory when it is substantiated unconsciously by the reality of the psyche has been displaced to a conviction about incest, an incest without record which nonetheless surely occurred. Incest feels more real, more certain than fact. The dream that brings incest brings as well its own ground for certainty without historical or phenomenal foundation.

This paradox of the presence and absence of incest in the same image, this paradox separating memory and psyche, also joins them. So, the shame and horror in the dream belong to its paradox. The emotions pertain not merely to one side of the line, to the (repressed) memory of an incest act. They belong to the whole dream, to the presence and absence of incest, to the troubling opposition of memory and psyche, to the horror that one can be certain in faith without fact, and to the shameful fantasy of "losing it." The emotions corroborate not incest merely, but the excruciating dilemma released by the archetypal situation of losing trust in reality based on memory to finding conviction in reality that is "merely" psychic. For the dream has carried the dreamer into that no-place where psyche supersedes memory, where the dreaming psyche gives conviction. Dr. Inborn is inside the dream, initiated by the dream into "dreamtime"[3] where events are mythical and also real. As Sallust said of myths, they did not happen but always are.[4]

Since Dr. Inborn's worrying questions about "losing it" arrive with this dream, derive from this dream, we might ask why. Only this particular dream raises remorse over absent fathering and fears of impotence and ageing, evokes the thoughts of "faulty" memory and "crazy" fantasies. Why do these questions accompany this dream? Does incest as an archetypal phenomenon invite these demons in its train?

Here I must explain: to speak of incest as "archetypal" raises its value to a universal desire, recurrent, ubiquitous, emotionally-laden, richly symbolized, and inherently shameful as are all desires. "Archetypal" also affirms incest to be eternally present, always there (much as Dr. Inborn believes incest is there even when it is not actually presented in the dream). Its origin lies not in family or tribe; kinship structures may release or ritualize incest, but they do not originate it. Kinship structures and emotions may occur in biological, sociological and psychological families, and so incest may be released or ritualized in many sorts of kinship arrangements. What we see first in fact (kinship) does not mean prior in logic, for "archetypal" also claims that something can be logically prior to the conditions in which it appears even if it never appears apart from those conditions. Incest as "archetypal" can therefore be regarded as *sui generis*, irreducible, requiring its proper archetypal location in imagination apart from kinship libido, endogamy, regression and the Jung-Layard

---

3. Géza Róheim, *The Eternal Ones of the Dream: A Psychoanalytic Interpretation of Australian Myth and Ritual* (New York: International University Press, 1945). Cf. Jung on the Bardo state in *CW* 11: 837–56.

4. Sallustius, *Concerning the Gods and the Universe*, edited and translated by Arthur Darby Nock (Cambridge: Cambridge University Press, 1926), 4.9.

hypothesis of individuation as internalization through sacrifice.[5] Incest as archetypal prevents us from assigning it a purpose before we have bracketed out the various purposes incest and its taboo may serve in the humanistic contexts of biology, sociology, anthropology, etc.[6] We need to locate incest first in the imagination of its own appropriate sphere, that is, in the mythical context of divinities where it appears appropriate, even conventional, without the compulsion of desire or the frustration of taboo.

This account of "archetypal" permits us to introduce the term into this argument without begging the question. Our line of reasoning has said the dream brought the dreamer across the dividing line from natural, empirical, evidential faith into the substantial reality of dream as ground of conviction. The radical upset, the quasi-derealization experienced by Dr. Inborn, directly results from his crossing the line, the incest dream as transgression. His interpretation would keep him on the near side: hence he seeks literal evidence to dispel the appalling feelings concomitant with

---

5. *CW* 16: *The Psychology of the Transference*; John Layard, "The Incest Taboo and the Virgin Archetype," in *Images of the Untouched*, edited by Joanne Stroud and Gail Thomas (Dallas: Spring Publications, 1982).

6. "Archetypal" further implies that incest is considered a determinant in behavior even if this does not make the behavior determined. This crucial distinction is sometimes overlooked when justifying an action by claiming it to be "archetypal," therefore necessary, therefore inevitable.

That is why Jung so insisted archetypes are formal only and empty of content. Content depends on local conditions; the archetypal determinant is itself determined by its appearance as image. And images function as complex reflections rather than as mechanistic causes. Moreover, as Jung argued (*CW* 8: 235), the determinants of behavior are externally complicated by their relationships one with another, and thereby lose their compulsiveness. Or, as mythologists say, the gods never appear singly, always implicating one another, and so governing one another. Internally, archetypal determinants are further complicated by their polarity, that *coincidentia* of opposites where instinct and image, compulsion and inhibition, desire and shame, incest wish and incest taboo wrap around each other. You don't get one without the other—unless split apart by the old logic of determinism. Determinism deduces the actual world from logical necessities so that incest becomes an inescapable compulsion because it is logically necessary. Fatalism ensues—and psychopathy: any behavior justified by an appeal to archetypes. What is logical in mind has become mechanical in action. Against this determinism can stand only the split-off, inhibiting half of the internal complexity, a half now conceived as a separate principle, the will, which must not be determined at all but be free. But this is philosophy, and not the way myths think, imagination works, nor is it archetypal psychology.

transgression. Our interpretation affirms the far side or, more precisely, affirms the dream itself as the act of transgression, a moving across.

To where? Into mythical territory where incest occurs among divinities much of the time. In the Neoplatonic traditions, divine incest is the mode of divine interpenetration and cogeneration between likes, a figurative means of expressing the prolific permeation of eras through the cosmos unhampered by those dichotomies necessary for human limitation. Incest enacts cosmogonic eros. It is necessary to an erotic cosmology, that polytheistic participation of images, levels, and souls as families of relations, binding all things together in their desire for one another. Such is the case imagined archetypally, in its mythical philosophy, from within its mythical territory where the ruling powers that set limits themselves commit incest.

Greek and other mythologies say the primary limitation divides humans from divinity, mortals from immortals. Limitations appear in the human social context as proscriptions and taboos, their violation as *hubris.* Taboos keep humans in their mortal, nondivine place. Taboos are sacred, that is, given by the gods, just as incest is given with the gods. The taboo keeps humans safe from the divine world, restricting our sight to the near side of the line. Restricted to our human vision, our psychological understanding can only be humanistic. The transgression of incest becomes only a violation and its divine logic the projected fiction of our tabooed desires.

Freud took the transgression to be regression; Jung gave it the positive valence of progression toward self-union. Their dispute over the value of the transgression that irrevocably divided them—neither able to pull the other to his side of the line—expresses the transgressive psychology of incest and the very dilemmas regarding psychic reality forced on Dr. Inborn by his dream and on us by his case. Although the subject of the dispute between Freud and Jung was never settled—now it resurrects in the light-heavyweight specter of Jeffrey Masson—that dispute and its violent history states emphatically the transgressive nature of the subject.[7]

By this I mean drawing lines and crossing over the lines drawn. I mean incest breaks the bounds of thought and action in which it holds itself.

---

7. Jeffrey Moussaieff Masson, *The Assault on Truth: Freud's Suppression of the Seduction Theory* (New York: Farrar, Straus and Giroux, 1984).

The desire of incest is to violate its own taboo, yet this desire cannot be defined by the taboo. For, the incestuous impulsion of cosmogonic eros reaches toward intercourse with the other side, seeking the union of intimacy between familiar but separated natures. As it opens doors and mixes natures, incest simultaneously creates ever tighter inhibitions of privacy, secrecy, shame and isolating fascination. Even the Neoplatonic and mythical description is esoteric, that is, inhibitingly closed and private, although it speaks of incest as a cosmogonic connective.[8]

These paradoxical perspectives indicate that the incest taboo, too, means cosmologically more than prohibition for the sake of biogenetic breeding, kinship structures, and societal order. The taboo insists upon a distinction of realms, drawing a line, not only between interior and exterior as in Layard's propositions or between love and sexuality in Robert Stein's,[9] but also between kinds of imagination—mythic and historical, psychic and literal, archetypal and humanistic. By drawing these lines and simultaneously transgressing them, joining the very elements it keeps apart, incest disturbs a fixed cosmos, and generates a mixed one. We can never get a fix on it; surety lies in ambiguity, as the psychic insinuates its way into the literal "what really happened"—or whether. The very mixed-(up) condition of Dr. Inborn's mind resulting from his dream derives from the invasion of soul into reason, from the union of psyche with logic, or psychology, a psychology now arising from soul. And soul, by the way, according to most Neoplatonisms is a mixture, a *metaxy*, a middle (or muddle) ground. So, the patient's questions reflect the joining of differing realms and their differing logics, which clear answers would separate again, and the ambiguity increases if approached from one side only. It is this *joining in ambiguity* that we must insist upon, exemplified in the incest ambiguously committed by Dr. Inborn in his imagination, which commits him to imagination. *He has married his soul.* "Briefly stated, the [proto-typal] incest was not a casual affair, but a formal marriage. This point is of great importance since, so far as can be ascertained, no one has ever pointed out that all truly basic incest myths almost invariably pertain to incestuous *marriages.*"[10]

---

8. Cf. on Eros "the Binder" and the "Connectives": Hans Lewy, *Chaldaean Oracles and Theurgy* (Paris: Etudes Augustieniennes, 1978), 126–29.

9. Robert M. Stein, *Incest and Human Love* (Dallas: Spring Publications, 1984).

10. George Devereux, *Mohave Ethnopsychiatry* (Washington, D.C.: Smithsonian Institution Press, 1969), 360.

Does not this approach allow a fresh understanding of Dr. Inborn's worry over his faulty memory? Not so much his faulty memory as memory faulted *per se* when it is restricted to the a-mythical, only-human side of the line. The dream forces his mind to conclude a logical incest independent of appearance, a "mythical" incest without a when and a where and forces his memory toward redefining itself not only as a *record* of what once happened on earth but also as *reminiscence* of what always happens in soul.

Psychic reality substantiates itself: a dream, a thought, an emotion *are*. Psychic realities cannot be substantiated by outer facts. The soul provides conviction that is its own evidence. (Hence the unfalsifiability of delusions.) Dr. Inborn is of sure conviction. And so he has arrived at that place philosophers are often seeking: a self-evident surety, an unwobbling pivot for a world view. And he has arrived here via an incest dream. So, his worries about evidence emerging with that dream need to be considered in another light: not as added validation to an already sure conviction, but as symptomatic of transgression. The psychic contents of his questioning signify the metaphorical effect of incest upon him. Each word in each worry is symptomatic of crossing the line: loss of sexuality as physical in favor of "crazy" erotic fantasies, ageing with premonitions of "losing it," reflections about the impossibility of resolving his dilemma with recourse to fact, reservations regarding calling upon his actual daughter, the derealization of history or history as "just a reconstruction," as well as shame, horror, and remonstrations.

Of all these worries, that of the absent father deserves special attention. If we move that worry from a literal projection into the past to a metaphorical description of the present, Dr. Inborn is stating the absence of the old king, the voiding of his habitual approach to consciousness, which hitherto believed it makes psyche, it generates the daughter, soul, and is responsible for it, must lead, educate, and protect it. Instead, the dream incest says he is generating with soul in dream, now, in the present, an invisible mutual intercourse. Thus the sure conviction that incest is occurring is the very result of incest occurring, a faith given by anima[11]

---

11. On the faith given by anima, i.e., psychological faith as belief in the reality of the psyche, see Robert Grinnell, "Reflections on the Archetype of Consciousness: Personality and Psychological Faith," *Spring: An Annual of Archetypal Psychology and Jungian Thought* (1970): 35–39; also my *Re-Visioning Psychology* (New York: Harper &

as the old king absents his potency in favor of desire for the daughter, the generative receptacle who is "maybe eleven or twelve, or fourteen," this soul itself crossing the line into fertility. Yes, he is indeed losing "it"—his restrictive notion of empowerment; but he is also finding potency in the cosmos of invisibles whose attractive emissary is the daughter imago with many sorts of shoes and music always in her house. There is horror in that yielding of personal potency and a shame over the sweetness of feeling more alive given by crazy fantasies of erotic young girls.

❦

These elaborations on Gene Inborn's material merely carry on from this passage by Jung (CW 9.1:137):

> Just as the archetypes occur on the ethnological level as myths, so also they are found in every individual, and *their effect is always strongest*, that is, they anthropomorphize reality most, *where consciousness is weakest and most restricted*, and where fantasy can overrun the facts of the outer world. This condition is undoubtedly present in the child during the first years of its life. It therefore seems to me more probable that the archetypal form of the divine syzygy first covers up and assimilates the image of the real parents until, with increasing consciousness, the real figures of the parents are perceived—often to the child's disappointment. Nobody knows better than the psychotherapist that the *mythologizing* of the parents is *often pursued far into adulthood* and is given up only with the greatest resistance. (italics mine)

The way I have imagined this case suggests that the mythologizing propensity of the psyche "is often pursued far into adulthood" because mythologizing is a basic psychological activity that, try as we will, is never overcome; the psyche never fully yields to the delusion of an only-literal, only-factual reality. Myth-making, like dreaming, is always going on. The anthropomorphizing of reality, in this case, focused on Dr. Inborn's daughter: the archetypal incest imagined in the guise of a historical human. But daughter and father, too, form a "divine syzygy" that lies embedded within Dr. Inborn and his daughter, emerging in great strength with radical upsetting effects where consciousness is most

Row, 1975), 50–51; and *Anima: An Anatomy of a Personified Notion* (Dallas: Spring Publications, 1985), 111–13, passim.

restricted. What is this restriction? What is the condition of consciousness that calls forth the incest archetype?

We come to a conclusion beyond psychology, at that margin where depth psychology drifts into depth sociology, even world history. Jung says: "When a situation occurs which corresponds to a given archetype, that archetype becomes activated and a compulsiveness appears, which, like an instinctual drive, gains its way against all reason and will." (CW 9.1: 99). We saw in "the case of Dr. Inborn an obsessively compelling set of worries that would not let him go and a conviction "against all reason and will." To my imagination, this case mirrors the effect of the incest archetype in our time, our society, and our psychoanalytic theory. We are being abused by incest, in society, and in mind, body, and soul. Then, where is the weakness in the present "situation...which corresponds to [the] given archetype"?

The mythical and Neoplatonic settings for incest sketched above present its transgressive nature. That commingling and cogeneration become merely ambiguity and dilemma within the restrictive psychology of humanism. Since the essential desire of incest is ever-widening and ever-intensifying erotic connections, making intimate and familiar by mixing souls that prohibit each other, then the restriction of incest to a sheerly human understanding will only invite its abusive incursion. A world limited by the only-human constellates what is beyond the human: the more we personalize and literalize incest, the more we can expect an increase of its incidence in the literal world it is invading.

I am speaking here not only of the return of the repressed as a Law of Talion, but rather of incest desire as an archetypal necessity, a compelling instinct to transgress the all-too-human limitations on consciousness. A humanistic approach fails to meet the problem in its own terrain; incest calls our understanding to transgress its own limits, cross over into archetypal considerations, approach the presence of incest in the actual world by letting the imagination of incest mix up and reconnect consciousness beyond itself as it did in the case of Dr. Inborn.

Unless the transgression into mythical realities is followed, we remain in the only human restrictive weakness that constellates incest to overcome. By clinging to the facts of personal history, we deny the very incest, the transgression, which the facts would supposedly establish. The absence of facts that incited the imagination in this case can never be filled in literally, for that absence is the invitation to fill the mind in another way, beyond facts. Incest, as archetypal, transgresses; it "gains its way against all reason and will," moving against restrictive humanism's defensive dedication to literalism, historicism, and empiricism, which so disastrously menace the soul's animation of the world, its erotic commingling with all things. Will the soul concede the world? Will *anima mundi* let the world lie a poisoned corpse in a wasteland winter? I do not imagine the soul desires to be exiled from this world to abide on the distant side of the line in eternity with the gods. The soul seems rather to like it here and to be with us, often using strange, demonic, pathologized ways to force recognition of its desire.

Dehumanizing
or Soul-Making

17

THE BAD MOTHER:
AN ARCHETYPAL APPROACH

What follows takes up again a well-worn theme: mother and child. The mother archetype, the child archetype—depth psychology founds itself, and founders, usually, on these rocks. That life and depth psychology begin with mother and child says that we are in the rhetoric of beginnings, of foundational questions. That the theme is so well-worn says it has become unconscious again, laid smoothly in a groove, a grave. We do believe we know pretty much about it; read the psychological literature from Freud and Jung through Wickes, Neumann, and Fordham to Berry: we all do believe we know what's the matter with mother.[1]

If we can find a new twist in this basic theme and if, in particular, the bad mother can be re-visioned, then we may be re-visioning the basis of psychology and even life itself. Finding that twist is what we are about. We start with four assumptions.

First, there is an *experience* of bad mothering that badly needs to be understood as a psychological phenomenon in itself apart from norms about good and bad behaviors or acts of mothering. Even so-called good mothers experience themselves to be bad mothers.

Second, we can analyze this experience of bad mothering apart from empirical cases, phenomenological protocols, and sociological surveys. There are also archetypal structures in experience, and these may be scrutinized by an *archetypal method.*

---

1. Cf. "What's the Matter with Mother," in Patricia Berry, *Echo's Subtle Body: Contributions to an Archetypal Psychology* (Thompson, Conn.: Spring Publications, 2017 [1982]).

Third, we assume there is an inner child, an archetypal child *imago*, affecting each of us and so affecting every mother and mothering act.

Fourth, we can distinguish between the archetypal contents of mother and child as contents in a tandem and the archetypal structure of the *tandem as such*. Mother and child are not only each what they are, but they are as they are because they are locked together in a tandem that affects the nature of each.

We therefore need to look more closely at tandems if we want to understand any contents, such as mother and child, that are embraced by a tandem. These tandems—and I use this term for dyads, pairs, couplings, polarities, syzygies—whatever their contents, are affected by patterns of oppositional thinking such as dark/light, alive/dead, order/disorder, true/false, presence/absence, vertical/horizontal. Philosophers have elaborated further basic antinomies and have dissected oppositions into different sorts (contradictions, contraries, complementaries, etc.). Structuralists have located various kinds of oppositions in social practices and linguistic structures.

The mother-child bond, simply because the bond is a tandem, is subject to the influence of oppositional thinking, or "oppositionalism." This fact complicates whatever we say about our subject. Even if oppositionalism is not the only way in which reflective thinking proceeds (one can reflect in images, with feeling moods and by playing), nonetheless oppositionalism does affect the individual patterns and thinking about these patterns in any particular dual relationship between male and female, superior and inferior, young and old, and within the mother-child relation as well. Later we shall attempt to free the tandem from oppositionalism, but for now it is important to recognize that human behavior is subject to the transhuman structuring of archetypal configurations such as the tandem.

By placing the tandem relation in the foreground, I have reversed the usual approach of psychology, which generally considers the mother-and child prior to every other rubric. I want to show, however, that it submits to a category beyond itself. This metaphysical approach to an empirical problem—the experience of bad mothering—is a contribution of the archetypal viewpoint to psychology.

A meta- or superordinate factor appears also in the biological approach, to the mother-child bond. It, too, imagines the tandem, called "bonding," to be the determinant factor to which both infant and mother submit. Baby songbirds stretch their necks upward and open their mouths to reveal the yellow signaling spot that, anticipated by the mother's inborn release mechanism, releases the food in her beak into their throats. Lactation in the human mother coterminous with the neonate's search for the nipple is a further example of superordinate bonding—a coordinate pattern, delicate, complex, and of enormous durability, holding mother and child together in a single pattern of behavior that, following Jung, we may call an archetypal image of instinct.

Lactation is not a simple mechanism; mother and child are not unvaryingly in the service of that function. They each bring with them their individual idiosyncrasies. As contents they affect the relation—of course. And psychology usually locates the psychic structures that modify bonding within the mother *per se* or the child *per se* and their idiosyncratic interaction. I wish to add a dimension by locating the psychic structures which influence bonding within the phenomenology of tandemness. My point is that at any moment of mothering, or of "childing," archetypal twoness is at work, necessitating a rich phenomenology of ambivalence, bipolarity, tension that constellates oppositions of various kinds. Here, in the tandem, and not merely in the mother or in the child or in their superordinate instinctual interaction, the major psychological problems of motherhood and childhood begin.

The oppositionalism influencing tandems may take several forms. I shall single out one for our consideration: the child is imagined to be good, the mother bad.

❀

Unmeditated reactions of mothering are complicated by meditated ideas, or fantasies, about good and bad mothering. These fantasies differ from culture to culture, but whatever their content, fantasies remain constant norms in governing the conscious role model of mothering. These directive and corrective fantasies working within the mother as guilt have a major impact upon her child. A child grows within the shadow of the mother's guilt about mothering as much as within the mothering itself. The guilt regarding "how to be a good mother" usually derives from the archetypal Mother, imagined either as a woman's actual parent, her grandmother, or as normative ideals held up by the culture.

Owing to that either/or accreting to the tandem, tensions in the mother-child relation tend to be placed on one side or the other; either the mother is wrong or bad, or the child. Even if the symptoms—such as crass autistic or motoric disorders—appear only in the child, the actual human mother will assume guilt for them onto herself because of the archetypal ideal. The actual mother thus feels herself to be a bad mother.

The tandem itself reinforces this appraisal. If she is bad, then the child is good, offering a magical way of cure by belief in its goodness. This is, of course, a vicious circle, since the more good the child, the more bad she must be. The archetypal fantasies of the Divine Child—good, strong, and laughing—create an inevitable sense of herself as negative.

The archetypal tandem influences psychological theory too. Many schools have been caught in the same pattern of thinking as the mothers. The blame for the human condition is still laid upon the mother, her breasts, her habits during pregnancy, her caring during the first nine months, and so on. If the mother is held to be responsible, it, of course, implies that those who think this way have occupied the position of good children. Perhaps one reason why the theory of blaming the mother is so popular and perduring: it allows us psychologists the privileges of innocent childhood. The altar at which much of psychology worships is the shrine of the Negative Mother.

So, psychology finds a mother "never enough." If she is always present, then she is said to foster weakness, pampering, and dependency. If she nurtures with warmth and closeness, then she is called smothering and devouring. If she desires much for her child, fantasying its future from the reserves of her spirit, then she is dominating its life with her goals. If she is far-seeing, intuitive, and detached, then her prophetic wisdom is that of a witch. If she delights in life and the pleasures of the senses, then she is either seducing her children or depriving them of their lives by living so voluptuously her own. Whatever the style of motherhood, it seems cursed. What can a woman do? Whatever pattern of existence is hers, it becomes victim of the negative cast thrown by the archetypal factor of the negative mother. All the while she strives to enact the model of the good mother—being present to her child, nurturing, protective and attentive, sagacious in judgment, carrier of tradition, sensitive to the values of small signs in the bonding—inwardly she is haunted by feelings of inferiority and failure, or she defends brightly against her badness.

We are now ready to examine this experience of badness from three perspectives and to offer solutions to it. We may say first that the bad mother
reflects the *negativity* in the archetype itself. The phenomenology of the
negative mother has been laid out in detail by the Jungian school. Jung's
work on the symbols of the maternal libido (1912) presented the mytho-
pathological background of the negative mother and deliverance from her
through battle. In 1938, Jung composed his insights into a major essay on
the mother archetype. This has been followed by Neumann's mammoth
studies of the symbolic manifestations of the negative mother and their
psychological effects. Their work was supplemented by Esther Harding, and by H.G. Baynes and John Layard in England, and by the London school of Jungians, especially in regard to infants and ideas of the
mother-child relation absorbed from Melanie Klein, Anna Freud, Bowlby,
Winnicott, Fairbairn, and Guntrip.

In this plentiful literature, two dominant ideas stand out. First: the
human mother is not the same as the archetypal imago, although she is
influenced by it and is perceived by her child by means of it. Second:
the archetypal imago has a dual nature, two sides, positive and negative. Symbols and metaphors express this dual nature. The ocean that is
source of life also represents drowning in dissolution. Earth both supports us and buries us. Containers (jars, boxes, houses, institutions, cit-
ies) protect and also suffocate. The transforming vessel (alembic, oven,
bathtub) serves both the need for *temenos* and for narcissism. Those animals said by Jungian literature to represent the mother archetype show
the dual nature most clearly. The hugging, shaggy, loving bear is also
a clawing, crushing monster; the patient cow with its cud and udder
is also stupid, self-satisfied passivity; the nurturing wolf is at the same
time ravenous greed.

Jungian psychology considers the dual nature of the mothering experience to be archetypally given and therefore irreducible. You cannot have
a good side without the other. The moment mothering is constellated,
both sides are constellated. Nor is it possible to convert the negative into
the positive. The empirical mother's experience of her badness is an inti-
mation of the archetypal reality. Kali lurks eternal, so there will always be
urges to destroy the child. Child abuse, even an instinctual delight in it,
is given with the archetypal nature of mothering. The full experience of
mothering calls forth the urge to destroy the child, to feed off its life, to

turn it to stone, drive it mad, abuse or abandon it. This side of mothering appears in the stepmother of fairy tales.

Jungian therapy aims at making this shadow, this bad side, of mothering aware to the individual patient who is trying to deal with her feelings of hatred toward her child and her inferiority in regard to her only-positive ideal of mothering. By recognizing her fealty to a principle in which a dual nature is always present, she is less likely to fall into a vicious oppositionalism with her child (leading her to enact the cruel negative mother in sinister punishments or passionate outbursts).

By shifting badness away from personal identification and locating it in the negative side of the archetype itself, a Jungian therapy can alleviate torturing self-recriminations. Badness may not be condoned by this shift, but at least the patient can see its archetypal necessity. For archetypes are the superhuman carriers of collective consciousness, and so they help the ordinary human carry the superhuman burdens of life. (Archetypes all have a mothering function) As a universal human event, bad mothering belongs to any mother and to the Great Mother. This archetypal perspective leaves a mother less alone with her badness and, so, less driven to repress it and then forced to act it out.

Second, the bad mother, as an archetypal phenomenon, entails the good mother with it. If the first perspective located the experience in the negative side of the archetype, the second perspective relocates the negative itself in the conjunction of opposites within the archetype. Instead of opposing negative and positive sides and oscillating between feelings and behaviors called good and bad, we here understand duality to mean that there is always good within the experience of bad.[2]

Here I turn to the Buddhist idea of *Sunyata,* metaphysical emptiness or void. Against this background, the feelings of inferiority and failure—that one has nothing to give, that one is devoid of values, of love, beauty, and the positive virtues of mothering—take on a deeper significance. The guilt toward a fully positive image of mothering is emptied out, voided. This voids the positive image itself so that a mother can see through its idealized delusional aspect. This emptying out allows the guilt to shift. No longer is she bad because she failed the idealized image of the Good Mother. Now the idealized image itself, taken from her mother, her grandmother, her culture, shows its own vacuity. The idols

2. Ibid.

fall; the supportive saints fade. She awakens to see that good images have bad effects. And, as the good reveals its badness, so the deepest experience of her badness (her inferiority and failure) proves to be where her goodness actually resides.

I mean here that the sense of badness about her mothering is actual where she is close to that ground of being, the Great Mother, whose support appears exactly when she feels let down by all normative fantasies, all goodness gone. Where nothing sustains her, she finds Nothing sustaining her. The *Sunyata* as a metaphysical void becomes manifest in the absence of her personal will to do good and be right. In this emptied condition, she can be nurtured by moments of not being anything other than she is. Unmeditated reactions affirm the bonding.

Guilt, too, then finds a new location. Guilt—which forces literal actions of directing and correcting this or that instance of badness—becomes the inner voice of *Sunyata*: "I fail because failure is inherent in all my willed actions." They can succeed only when they come from the ground of emptiness, when I am grounded in an undefined, emptied-out mothering beyond all positivistic, technical notions of it. I abandon the search for how to be a mother. Sustaining itself sustains; in my absence everything in the world beyond me and outside of me carries my child. My very negativity is the *via negativa*, not only of mothering, but mothering to becomes a soul-making, a psychotherapeutic activity. Mothering becomes deliteralized from only the actual care of an empirical child to a path of deepening awareness into the sustaining goodness of the world.

Psychotherapy leads into *Sunyata* by letting go—not only of idealized norms, but letting the bottom fall out of therapy itself. Its corrective, constructive search fails. An utterly nonsupportive therapy. One falls into the lap of the bottomless ground. For only the abandoned child can be found by the mothering wolf. It is the abandoned child who discovers *Sunyata.*

Before proceeding with my main concern, the third perspective— the bad mother in tandem with the good child—we need to recall that child, like mother, carries symbols on its back. Child, too, is an archetypal metaphor, indicating both an actual young person and an aura of impersonal symbolic connotations. And, as mother can be abstracted into positive and negative, so child can be divided into the oppositions of childlikeness and childishness. Oppositionalism haunts the discourse of psychology.

According to the studies of Freud, Jung, Kerényi, Neumann, Brown, Campbell, and Bachelard on its archetypal phenomenology, we find these qualities and expectations in regard to the child. *Futurity*: the release of hopeful fantasies forward in time or beyond time; redemption of the present by rebirth into the future. "And a little child shall lead them." *Growth*: maturation as a developmental process with increase in size and differentiation of function. *Simplicity*: the child as primitive, natural energy, an intense seed of being. *Origins*: the small beginnings of any process, whether as beginning in a world beyond with innate knowledge of that beyond or in this world as the freshly novel and unpredictable. *Amorality*: the dedication to pleasure and polymorphous perversity, close to the animal and insane, and thus in need of baptism, initiation, and education. *Dependency*: weakness, exposure, abandonment—feelings that churn out the omnipotence wishes of heroics, magics, and make-believe of many sorts. *Joy*: a delight where self and world are fused: "the archetype of simple happiness" (Bachelard).

We are obliged to remember these archetypal implications of the child in discussions having to do with actual children and childhood. We must be careful in what we say about actual children until we can see them, and we cannot see them very dearly until we can see the notions that govern our modes of seeing, the archetypal projections that arise whenever the child imago is constellated. The history of ideas in depth psychology about children shows that they, like primitives, animals, artists, inventors, and the insane, have been forced to carry every sort of discarded and fantastic piece of the psyche that the "normal," "civilized" adult has excluded from his or her domain. By definition children are the archetypal minority group, whether idolized as perfect from the beginning or denigrated as bits of untamed nature needing a discipline to convert them to adulthood. We cannot see them for what they are until we can see what we consider "childish"—i.e., undeveloped, infantile, minor, dependent, immature—in our own minds, until we have taken back from children and childhood a variety of potentialities we as adults have disowned and placed in a special world called childhood.

Let us list these attitudes and behaviors of this special realm that supposedly belongs to children: spontaneity, creativity, playfulness, fantasy, wonder, curiosity; emotional vivacity in place of conceptual abstraction; need for sensual pleasure and immediate gratification of desires; thought processes that overcome natural laws, or what is often called magical thinking and a magical sense of concrete objects and actions; history legend rather than as factual past time; shyness and shame in place of mannered decorum; an eidetic imagination leading to easy familiarity with make-believe voices, faces, figures, and with animals and ghosts; rhetorical joy—hyperbole, singsong, alliteration, rhyme, onomatopoeic and apotropaic noises, story sequences, and the love of story. All this in one word, imagination.[3]

These traits, this imagination, belong to the child archetype and not literally to actual childhood and children. The literal identification of an actual person with an archetypal personification is *the* psychological error wherever we find it; femininity literalized and expected only from women; *senex* literalized only in old people, the dark shadow literalized only in dark ethnic groups.

Now, to the third perspective: the bad mother *arises within the tandem* with the good child. We shall no longer be speaking of the bad mother as a self-contained figure as was the case in the first two perspectives—both based on ideas of negativity within the single archetype. Now we look at the tandem that is superordinate to either mother or child and affects both. The tandem has this effect: qualities that the actual child receives from the archetypal projection impoverish the mother of those same qualities. Stated most extremely: what the child has and is, the mother has and is not.

Although coming into motherhood may expand a woman's existence in the directions found in the mother models of myth, culture, and family tradition, still, owing to the tandem with the child, motherhood also restricts her to a more singularly adult existence. She is expected to move away from imaginative attitudes and spontaneous behaviors that belong to the child archetype. She feels herself no longer allowed to be immature, undeveloped, infantile. The mother becomes separated from her actual child owing to her separation from childishness. She may resent her actual child for retaining qualities that she is now deprived of sim-

---

3. Cf. Christine Downing, "To Keep Us Imagining: The Child," in *The Goddess: Mythological Images of the Feminine* (New York: Crossroads, 1981); also "Abandoning the Child," in my *Loose Ends: Primary Papers in Archetypal Psychology* (Thompson, Conn.: Spring Publications, 2022 [1975]).

ply by her position in the tandem. Or she may attempt to recover these potentials by clinging to her actual child. Basic structures of bad mothering—rejecting her child, resenting her child, dependency on her child, and fostering dependency from it—derive from the empirical mother's relation within the tandem.

Moreover, she loses the ability to imagine a way out. Having lost the child, she has lost imagination, which would be the very way back to it. For instance, the radical change in sexual feelings after childbirth (a complaint of husbands about their wives) can be partly understood as an archetypal change, a shift in myth and a shift into a new tandem. The woman has lost her child by giving birth to it. She has become separated from her polymorphous perversity, curiosity, and spontaneity—the playful ground of sexual joy.

We are now able to draw conclusions for defining the "bad mother." So far I have restricted these observations to the experience of badness, without defining the content of badness beyond the acceptable conventions—such as, the bad mother rejects, demands, pampers, is guilty, self-centered, and the like.

I have refrained from defining the content of badness because a psychotherapeutic approach has to be assiduously careful about norms. Once we define just what a good mother is—nourishing soul, sheltering body, fostering spirit—we have only added to the guilt from which a mother already suffers for failing to live up to these norms. Norms in therapy become counterproductive to what they aim to establish. Norms are addressed to the will; they give it standards, and they lodge themselves in the superego. Yet it is precisely because the patient cannot redress her plight by will that she comes to therapy. The woman already has the best of norms which only make her feel worse. For psychotherapy, the issue is rather an analysis bit by bit of the experience of badness—when does she feel bad, what is her "lack," what are her "bad" acts, how are they performed, in what mood, to which child, how does she self-correct, on whom does she model herself? And, *who* tells her she is "bad": what voice? We look at the experience, its lived phenomenology, its images and voices, its mythical patterns.

The phenomenology of the experience of badness suggests images of its archetypal nature. But again we must be cautious and now for a theoretical reason. If the mother is a figure *in a tandem,* then we cannot adduce negative mother experiences only from the usual mythic stereotypes: Kali in India, Yamamba in Japan, Baba Yaga of Slavic or Frau Hölle of Germanic folktales. Plenty of child abuse here. These loathsome ladies bake children in the oven or eat them alive. They poison them, put them to endless sleep, turn them to stone. They do, indeed, frighten the daylight out of them. Plenty of grounds here for anorexia, dyslexia, school refusal, mutism, and eruptive violence.

Yet we may not draw our definition of bad mothering from these ladies because these terrible devouring petrifying negative mothers are self-enclosed prototypes. They stand alone. They are not figures in a tandem. So, just here, an archetypal approach differs from that of Neumann, Harding, and other Jungian therapists. They tend to read human behaviors in terms of single archetypal figures, reading myths with monotheistic consciousness. For them it is usual for an archetypal figure to be one and alone: Great Mother, Negative Mother, Divine Child, Puer Eternus, and the like.

Myths, however, take place in a polycentric field of persons. Myths are not merely tales about these persons but tales about their structural complications, their psychological relations. Mythical figures are in plots, as Aristotle calls myths; and human actions reflect not only the individual figures but also the *pathos,* the sufferings occasioned by the plots. In other words, to study how human nature performs its *imitatio* of the gods, we cannot confine our scrutiny to mythical figures; rather, we have to analyze, take apart, the interlacings of their plots.

Roasting a child in the fire is not in itself bad mothering. When Demeter roasts Demophoön, it is one thing, and should the witch roast Hänsel it is another. Good and bad depend here on the plot, the structure of the *mythos.*

Not that structure is prior to figure, prior to content—just to go on for a moment with archetypal theory. Rather, figure and structure are coterminous.[4] The very term "mother" takes its significance partly from the tandem with "child." Mother is subject to a psycho-logic of relationship

4. Cf. "An Approach to the Dream," in Berry, *Echo's Subtle Body.*

that is as primordial as the figures of the relationship. Mother isn't just mother: she is always in a plot with the child—now called "neurotic interaction"—and this determines bad mothering as much as does the singular figure of the Terrible Mother. A psychological structure is a relation, a configuration or plot.

This primordial complication of the tandem, this plot, is one way I understand Jung's emphasis—and Heraclitus's before him—on opposites. Figures and symbolic contents do not alone determine what happens in soul. They are subject to the tensions of relations that, when thought about abstractly, become "opposites." I prefer to derive opposites from tension, from plots, logical thinking from dramatic thinking, rather than the other way around. I really do hold that psychological relations precede philosophical conceptions in time and rank. Moreover, where the tension of opposites requires a language of overcoming, transcending, and conjoining, tandems and plots affirm relationships from the outset. We are always conjoined.

That we are always conjoined suggests a ground for the phenomenon of conscience. *Conscientia* is the Latin word for the Greek *syneidesis*, which, like "conscience," means "with-knowing," "together-knowing," an *eidos* shared in relation. The guilty feelings of bad mothering point therefore beyond their location in the subjective ego or superego; guilt derives complexly from our tandems, not simply from our persons. "Bad" feelings express the *agon* and *pathos* of the plots we are subjected to, those tensions of relations within and between the souls of human beings as well as between the human soul and the world soul. The tandem always forces us to consider an Other. Guilt reminds of this other, and conscience is the precondition of any individualism; the sense of badness is the price one pays for that neglect of the tandem reality of human affairs we nowadays call Ego.

Whether we call these complex tensions *plots*, or more particularly *tandems*, they organize events in definite patterns, subjecting human events to the priority of the image. An image is the intensification, the epitome, of the plot, because in it, structure and content, relations and figure, myths and persons commingle.

This view has immediate therapeutic bearing. An actual mother, seeking to rectify her sense of badness by modeling her dilemmas with her child on any single symbolic mother figure, cannot be sufficiently relieved.

Not she but the model is inadequate; her problems derive from the relation itself. She is right in saying that her problem appears only when she is with her child. She is suffering from the psycho-logic of the tandem that sets up badness as part of its plot.

Thus, bad mothering takes its definition from the oppositional effect of tandem logic. The dramatic tension with her child reduces to separation from it and loss of it. As child is equivalent with imagination, her language becomes unimaginative, imperative, abstract. As the child is growth, she becomes static and empty, unable to react with spontaneous novelty. As the child is timeless, eternal, she becomes time-bound, scheduled, hurried. Her morality becomes one-sidedly responsible and disciplinarian. Her sense of future and hope is displaced onto her actual child; thereby postpartum depression may become a chronic undertone. As her actual child carries her feelings of vulnerability, she may over-attend to it to the neglect of herself, with consequent resentments. Also, her thought processes become restricted to adult forms of reason so that the ghost voices and faces, animals, and scenes of the eidetic imagination become estranged and feel like pathological delusions and hallucinations. And her language loses its emotion and incantational power; she explains and argues.

Therapy derives from this description. And the first step of therapy is to view the tandem itself imaginatively, from the pole of the child rather than from the adult pole of oppositionalism, moralism, and hopelessness that immediately turns tandems into problems: good breasts and bad, positive and negative mothers, left and right brains. To experience a tandem as an opposition is already to be separated from the child. From the childish pole, the tandem is a see-saw, upsy-daisy/downsy-daisy, the eternal game of push-me/pull-you, offering endlessly pleasurable incentives.

So therapy with an actual mother is rapprochement with her archetypal child of imagination—through re-kindling fantasies, re-finding pleasures, releasing spontaneity, re-awakening dreams. It brings back the voices, the animals, and ghosts. Things take on names and faces. Therapy turns again to children's story, beginning with the patient's childish stories now going on, their shame and silliness, and the story of the patient's childhood. The mother's therapy begins in the tandem with her lost child of imagination, and her therapist is her actual child.

Though mothers know this and practice it playing with their children, even a momentary experience of bad mothering can set a woman back into the adult posture, its separation and loss. The movement in and out of imagination itself becomes a tandem.

※

I have offered three perspectives to the bad mother experience and suggestions for therapies implied by those perspectives. First, we saw the experience against the archetypal figure of the Terrible Mother. This perspective considers the experience of bad mothering to be given with the destructiveness of the archetype and therapy to be awareness of this archetypal necessity. Second, we saw the experience against the emptiness of *Sunyata*. This perspective considers the depths of one's failure to be the deeper ground of mothering. Therapy abandons supportive norms of good mothering in order to stay with the bad experience in which the deeper good resides. Third, we placed the experience within the mother-child tandem, claiming that bad mothering results from the impersonal logic of oppositions that accrete to tandems. Therapy is the recovery of the separated and lost child, the recovery of imagination.

A word in conclusion about my archetypal method. Rather than presenting a basic anthropology of the mother-child relation in terms of positivistic research or positive philosophical values regarding goodness and badness, I have attempted to enter that relation by staying with bad mothering as a primary datum. As an ever-recurring, ubiquitous, and emotionally important experience, it is assumed to be archetypally necessary. Positivistic approaches, as they harden their research results and strengthen their evidence into norms, make it harder for the individual woman to find necessity in her deviation from the norms that become more and more normative, leaving her less and less room for her increasing sense of badness. Positive research results tend to force practitioners to see "bad experiences" normatively, as pathologies, literally bad, to be done away with. The positivity in the method demonstrated here is therefore therapeutic rather than normative. Bad mothering finds place as an archetypal necessity in all three models. The method intends to result in an archetypal understanding of bad mothering that, like all deep pathologizings given with human life, belongs to the fundamental psychologic of human relations that are set within the *cosmoi* of archetypal patterns, patterns that force both necessity and compassion upon us.

A Coda on Education

Education of children, as Jung said in his lecture on this subject in 1924 begins with the education of parents and teachers, and it begins in lower education, not higher; in retarded, not advanced; with lowering our sights and their standards, down on all fours, with finger paints, with drums with bare feet; with slower days not longer hours; with tasting, not testing; with nonsense instead of jargon. Too much Rousseau and the sentimental education? Too much Rudolf Steiner, Free Schools, and Hippie happy kindergartens? Don't get me wrong: I am talking about us adults—not what children should be doing.

If nonsense rhymes and finger paints seem too childish, look at what we do now with the child—pouting resentments and junk food, passive-aggressive sport violence in front of the TV, buckets of popcorn, buckets of beer. The adult household with its apple toys, home as a radio shack, a fantasy island or closet of collectibles, its game rooms, its gimmicks and gadgets for building bodies as the imagination cheapens and blow-dries. Mary Kay and supermarket paperbacks. Meanwhile, growth, originality, and initiative, those primordial forces of the child, are consumed by that hyperactive omnipotence fantasy called "development"—whether personal, mystical, or financial, the project of oneself in space.

Nonsense rhymes and finger paints mean that I am not recommending the replacement of trashy *childishness* with higher forms of *childlikeness*, such as Bachelard's reveries toward childhood, Jung's divine child, Blake's innocence and delight, the Platonic child of wonder in the cosmos. A therapeutic education must beware of the ennobling course. Therapy is an education that works with equivalences, not conversions. It's a business of straight barter. We can't turn sinners into saints or dimes into dollars without shortchanging the Shadow. So, in exchange for fingering the push buttons, finger painting; instead of TV's nonsense language-game, Lewis Carroll; instead of Kodachrome, Easter eggs. The primitive barter of stupidity for simplicity—beginning where it's at.

Education, however, cannot stop where it starts. By definition, education must "lead out." It leads simple fantasy into imagination. The fingers themselves and the tongue, twisting along in its syllabic chant, want more than repetitions. The fingers and tongue find novelty by sophisticating fantasy into imagination.

We have come to that old conundrum, the difference between fantasy and imagination, and we can locate this difference now in the mother-child tandem. Fantasy is the activity of the motherless child; imagination is mothered fantasy: it is purposive, responsive, thoughtful. It mothers because it is child-focused—focused on the imagination. The key word of imagining is therefore not free but fecund, and its aim therefore is not exploring only but furthering, and the elation of fantasy is contained by consistency and carefulness. Child and Mother, both. To be led out to this *both*, we must make another psychological equivalence, exchanging the actual child as focus of education for focus upon imagination of the adult. We take childhood back in. This recovery of childhood from children gives them their chance at poise, dignity, and sobriety, their desire for reason and for duty, as we return to the closet of our childishness. This move is primary because the fantasy of educating imagination has all been put on actual children—what they should do for us. They have had to do what we as adults are not allowed (except in asylums and in that national asylum, California, the golden state of childhood), leaving us with an undernourished, deprived, mute, abused, and violent childishness, fit for *Pac-Man, Star Wars,* and *Halloween*—amusements of the adulterated mind.

This adulterated mind is the ultimate bad mother. By forcing childhood on children, we become bad mothers each of us. Each of us a "mothuh"—and this whenever, wherever, we take recourse in a nonimaginative response, in language, in administrative policy, in human relations, in shopping.

Daily encounters with the city of the world are imaginative moments to the child's mind. To the imagination, events are stories, people are figures, things and words are images. To the imagination, the world itself is a mother, a great mother. We are nestled in its language, held by its institutions, nourished by its things. The great mother complex that so afflicts our Western psyche—its dread and fascination with matter, its denial of dependency that we call Free Will, the oral craving of consumer economics as cure for depression—cannot be resolved by personal therapy alone. Personal therapy as cure, and that notion of cure itself, is an apotropaic defense against her—banning the city from the consulting room. The little mother of the consulting room can take care of us for a while, but outside lies the great wide world, and only the great wide world can cure us—not *of* the Great Mother, but by means of her, for the word "cure" comes from *cura,* "care." Like cures like because likes care for each other. The city itself mothers us once we recover the child of imagination.

We need but remember that the city, the *metro-polis,* means at root a streaming, flowing, thronging Mother. We are her children, and she can nourish our imaginations if we nourish hers. So, the *magna mater* is not the *magna culpa.* The actual blame for it all—the whole caboodle of down-town and the budget, of illiteracy and rearmament, ethical decay and ecological poison, the cause of the withering of our institutions—government, schools, family, trades and services, publishing and language—is the neglect of the city. And the city can be restored as mother by the child of imagination. Without that child we cannot imagine further our civilization or further our civilization's imagination, so that civilization itself becomes a bad mother, offering no ground or drink to the soul. Of course, the individual mother feels a failure. The experience of bad mothering is given with the civilization itself when the education of imagination is neglected.

So, to end where we began, with a classical, cyclical close appropriate to the rhetorical mode of the archetype we are invoking, the interminable mother: yes, restore the child to the mother, the imagination to the insti-tutions of education, including psychotherapy—more, to the whole city of the world—and indeed you re-vision the foundations of daily life.

18

YOUR EMOTIONS ARE NOT YOURS:
ARTS THERAPY AND THE DISABLED

The main materials of analysis since its inception with Freud are emotions: fear, paralysis, grief and depressions, dread and anxiety, anger, shame, hatred, and, of course, the complexities of love, desire, lust, jealousy, need, compassion, sympathy, obsession.

These states of soul, the material of any therapeutic session worldwide, were also once the subject of deep philosophical thought. Plato, Plutarch, the Stoics, St. Thomas, Descartes, Spinoza, and Hume wrote treatises on the various emotions, and if you look to Western theology from Jesus and Paul forward, with an eye to emotion you will find they too, the theologians, were most concerned with what to do with and about—and against emotion.

From an archetypal perspective, by which I mean that view that holds emotion primary and irreducible, universal and ubiquitous, of major value and of forcing unconsciousness on their subject, from this archetypal perspective, the disabled, the cognitively impaired, the recovering victims of bodily insults are not in a special class, for the common bond of emotions keeps us all alike, keeps us all equally sane and insane, victims of our rages and hatreds, of obsessive jealousy, of our shames and disgusts, our wild hope and longings. When Shakespeare's plays were performed at the Globe Theatre, royalist and commoner were amused alike; cripples, fools, scholars, monks, and soldiers all attended, wept and laughed, submitting to the same emotions.

We may be less able to enact an emotion, if disabled; we may be less willing to feel it, show it, speak from it—but the qualities of lust, grief, and fear belong to human heritage. Facial expressions of emotions studied by Theophrastus in antiquity and more famously by Darwin in Victorian times, still reveal universality in human features of happy smiles, sad frowns, glaring rages, blushing shames. To be in an emotion makes us most commonly human, and, as we shall see, beyond the human too. It is a pleasure—see, I smile—to return to this area, Emotion, thirty years after the publication of *Emotion: A Phenomenology of Theories and their Meanings for Therapy*—my first, big, thick, young man's pretentious assault on the field of psychology. I am happy here to return to this subject for two reasons: First, it offers me an opportunity to reflect on therapy as a whole from a most basic, let us say, archetypal, perspective, from the emotional base that belongs to common humanity, a base that is not technical, not metapsychological and part of some school, but simply "emotional." And second, I am happy to discuss emotion in Italy where, to our Northern and Western minds, emotion is expressed, developed, and fully alive. To our Northern and Western view, Italy means d'Annunzio and Bernini, Tasso and Anna Magnani, Visconti and Puccini, Caravaggio and Caruso. We like to ignore the oppressive, Saturnian restraints—that cynical and gloomy side of the Italian tradition. So, to talk of emotion in Italy to my naive American perspective is to bring my subject before the best audience in the world! I thank you from the beginning for the courtesy of your listening.

Now to therapy: What do the expressive or art therapies actually do? Not what do they set out to do, expect, or look for; nor how do they account for what goes on in a session. I am not now concerned with theoretical explanations of what happens in a session—explanations about fathers and mothers, about transitional objects and symbolization, about abreaction and interpretation. No. What actually goes on when a patient begins to dance, to choreograph his or her state of soul, or paint it, to speak freely aloud in a dramatic tirade or poetic elocution, or sculpt it in clay or lay it out in a collage? And I want to ask about the "it" that is being presented, expressed, shown, or formed by means of these various arts. Clearly, the "it" is emotion, an emotionally tinged state of soul. For even if it is said to be a trauma, a memory, or a present confusion and helplessness, a dream scene, or what we like to call a "problem," with a lover, an employer, a parent—the *emotion or the absence thereof* is the content that brings the person to therapy. Only when a "problem," a relationship, a memory or a dream becomes a suffering, when we are affected by the problem, does it enter us and we enter therapy.

Our theoretical models hold that rages, fears and passions are our responsibility. Somehow, somewhere, they are located inside us. Certainly we feel them there: the sadness behind our eyes, the sob in the throat, the tight chest; the grip of fear in the bowels; the fixed searching paranoid jealous state watching the beloved's face in a restaurant. Certainly, as the theories of emotion from Galen to William James have said, emotion is an interior physiological condition. Certainly, it is inside the skin, deep inside the hippocampus, the hormonal system, the personal animal body.

My contention, however, shall be, that though they be felt there, and we suffer emotions physically, this fact does not make them "mine." Rather, I believe emotions are there to make us theirs. They want to possess us, rule us, win us over completely to their vision. In short, as the English Romantic poet, William Blake, said, "Some good we may do when the man is in a passion, but no good when the passion is in the man." To have a passion in me is demonic; to be in a passion, in the world of the emotion and the way it signifies all things with a specific vision or insight, this may move the soul to a deeper and epiphanic connection with the world. Therapy, however, tends to interiorize all emotions and keep them inside, as "mine." Therapy takes uncritically and literally the feeling of affliction, of the afflicted subject; therapy literalizes the heightened sense of "me-ness" that results from emotion. Nowhere do I feel more "me" than when in the grip of an emotion; but it is *its* grip on me, not my grip on it. That an emotion gives me the feeling of "me" does not thereby make the emotion "mine."

But if imagined as inside me, they, of course, are "too much" to contain, and so become, in Blake's word "demonic," and need abreaction (exorcism). So goes our usual theory. We express emotions to get them "out." Whereas, if we follow Blake, and what emotions actually do, we begin to realize that emotions come to us from out there, invade us, and pull us into their condition. Blake also called emotions "divine influxes"...not things originating inside my skin. Rather, they are the way the gods flow into the soul, move it to a more-than-human condition of excitement and fury, of sorrow and mourning, of enchantment and ecstatic desire. So, of each emotional condition, art therapy asks this question: What does the emotion want? What are its features, its characteristics? How does *it* sound in my chest and throat—not how do I express it? How does it move through my body? What is *its* dance—not how can I dance it? How does this terrible sadness over my father's death, my love for this old man now gone, the remorse over our misunderstandings, the inexcusable and stony anger I cannot accept in my memories of him—what does all this want—not only with me, and from me—but what does it all want to do and say and show? How may I serve this divine influx so that the invisible depth in the disease is served by my movements, my colors and brushes, my words and voice?

I wake in the night and the emotions are there. I am afraid of the future, alone. I am tormented by my incapacity to meet what is expected of me. It would be easier to be just dead. Whatever I do, wherever I turn is wrong. The night thoughts assail me. They sit on the edge of my bed and fill my head with cutting criticisms and my heart with despair. I toss and turn or lie rigidly awake begging for release and sleep. Like black-winged demons, the emotions come at night for several hours. They call it insomnia; nightmares; depression. But the clinical language only masks the faces of the emotions that are visitations from another world, the underworld, reminding me of Hades. Are they asking that I pay homage, for a few hours, perhaps, to that all-important god who is invisible in the day world, whose moves are made in the dark, through the dark, who is allied with *hypnos* and *thanatos,* and who if recognized, voids life of its usual programs, offering instead the strength and fullness, and beauty, too, of the invisible background of all life?

Psychology wants to interiorize these events and make them personal. The night terrors become that, only that; they remain humanized and do not lead to figures of another world. They are *my* problem for which I see *my* therapist or take *my* sleeping pills. That the black-winged demons may also be protective angels offering familiarity with a world the day world does not allow; that they have their intentions with me other than my intentions with myself, that they are *guests* in my room and not part of me, complexes, problems, negative intuitions, rehearsals of childhood traumas, etc.

There are, of course, emotions that do not arise from the world "out there." There seems to be as well an invisible uncaused ground of emotions, emotions that suddenly come upon us—states of dark purple moods, lassitude, or stony silence.

These seem to spring from nowhere. They do not have the world as their reference; not even thought, memory, or dream has caused them. Here, a distinction first made by Aristotle between locomotion, or motion in space as between yourself and world on the one hand, and on the other, motions that are alterations. These alterations of the soul can be either qualitative—the soul going through a process of change for its own sake, or quantitative alterations, the soul decreasing or increasing its capacity. Many of the adolescent emotions that spring suddenly from nowhere as well as those of "impossible love" may be conceived as alterations in the soul increasing its capacity—"inner space" as we sometimes call it.

These alterations of the psyche initiate, accompany, and signify changes in the subjective soul. In clinical practice, we see them as autochthonous depressions, as manic increases of energy, as moods of love and despairs, rising rages. These emotions without reference are what Chinese psychology calls movements of the Heart or of Heaven. They correlate with what Jung has called the process of individuation, the soul's disclosure through time of its organic nature.

The issue for the therapist is to differentiate emotions of the first sort that come from the truck on the highway and refer to it—that fear, that outrage, that sorrow—from emotions of the second sort, so as not to reduce every emotional condition in the patient to a purely internal nonreferential alteration. For it is just this move that traps a person into a private internal life and removes emotions from the political world of the community. Nonetheless, despite this distinction between emotions connecting with the world and those that seem wholly interior, i.e., those movements of the heart or heaven, both sorts of emotions are not mine, not subjective. In both sorts, the origin lies outside of the owning person. In both sorts, the patient works with the emotion for its sake, forming it into the shape and expression that it asks for. Both sorts, in other words, recognize that an emotion is a divine influx, its gestures a mimesis of divine mythical figures. The therapist's task in both sorts is one of *epistrophé*, as the Neoplatonists called the therapeutic move: *epistrophé* or leading the human phenomenon to its divine background. For the emotions, all emotions, whatever sort, belong to the mythical world of divine figures as they break into ours. And, when you get to a certain age, and so much emotion seems to have been burned away or dissipated or dried up, we do thank the gods for the occasional rare affection that seizes the heart. If, as I say, the emotions belong to the gods, then why dance your desire, paint your fear, or let your sorrow borrow your voice to find its words?

Here we must be quite clear with our answer. Is the task of arts therapy to abreact the emotion, freeing the patient of what has gripped him or her? Or, is it to sublimate the emotion by making art of it? Or, is it to put the emotions to use: i.e., gain energy from it, become more vital, activated, filled?

What do we expect will happen a) to the patient, and b) to the emotion when we are engaged in art therapy? My answer to this question is rather simple. I believe that many aims are possible, and different therapists and schools will have different intentions. That is the simple answer: let 500 flowers bloom at once. My own personal flower among the 500, however, says that I engage in arts therapy neither directly for art, nor directly for the patient, nor directly for the emotion.

Then what else is there, besides the art product, the patient, and the emotion? What else? Imagination. For me, arts therapy takes precedence over all other therapies because it activates imagination and allows it to materialize, that is, enter the world via the emotions of the patient.

The patient is patient because he is the recipient, the channel—shall we say victim?—of the divine influxes that are never merely feeling states and affective tones, but are always as well imaginations. Imaginations of behavior, imaginations of fantasy, imaginations of movement and intention and desire. The patient is patient, in my narrow, and rather irreverently clinical, view, not because of the past, the family, the abuse, the church and education, the sexuality, the economic hardships, the afflictions of accident and disease that have brought handicaps—I do not underestimate these events, but they remain contingencies, of the second order, in my narrow view.

Primary is the disordered imagination, the incapacity of the imagination to encompass the past, and its traumas. Restrictions of imagination appear as excessive emotion. For when emotion is not held within its image, when the images have been reduced in quality, captured by collective commercialism, harnessed to exploitation, voided by rationalism, then emotion runs rampant, and we have to dose it with pharmaceuticals or exorcise it with therapies of release and expression. Instead, I am suggesting that the restoration of the imagination is the fundamental cure of disordered emotion, and especially that imagination I have touched on again and again, the imagination that welcomes and gives place to the powers once called gods.

Permit me to carry my narrow view just one step further, into the heart of therapy today. We all know that in every country and in every school the archetype of the child has come more and more to dominate the theory and practice of therapy. Abuse, victimization, empowerment, development, growth, Winnicott, Alice Miller, Melanie Klein, the reenactment in transference of the early years...these are the key words, slogans, gurus, and shibboleths of contemporary therapy. Yet we also know from Jung that the child and the childhood that so has us in its sway is not merely the actual past child or inner child. It is also the archetypal or divine child, the figure who, especially for the Romantics, was the carrier of imagination.

Therefore, when arts therapy attempts to put the patient in touch again with his or her inner child and repair the damaged child, release the true child from the false child, therapy is speaking of an imaginal figure compacted with more than personal emotions. This figure and these emotions are not the literal ones of the past only, even if wearing the clothes and moving in the rooms of the past. This figure and its emotions are the true interior of the inner child of the past. This deep interior is the imagination that has never escaped from childhood, and which now finally has its great opportunity in the expressive arts' therapy to present itself, freed from entrapment in what psychological theory insists is the child and childhood of the past.

In other words, if therapy is to move from its fascination with the child archetype it must cure itself, not by becoming more ego-heroic, or feminine, or physical, or spiritual—i.e., converting itself into another and different archetype. Rather, it must stay in and work through the symptom, i.e., the child, to its inner depth, which is the imagination. Only imagination can release us from obsession with the child. And this is precisely what arts' therapy concerns itself with. For this reason, arts therapy, to my narrow view, is the fundamental, primary, therapy, not only for the patient—to release him and her from the child of the past, but for therapy itself, to release it from its model of thought that keeps it from moving into the fullness of its imaginative possibilities.

Finally, to this claim that art therapy is the preferred mode of therapy, the therapy of choice for every patient, I would add another claim. This one about art itself and its relation with therapy.

The field of art therapy has always imagined the use of arts to be therapeutic, as we said, either for expression, or symbolization, or sublimation or communication, allowing the patient to give creative formulations to the disordered psyche.

I want to reverse this relation between art and therapy. I want now finally as last thought to suggest therapy as useful for the arts.

We would surely all agree that the arts in our Western world are in as much disarray as the patients we encounter. The arts themselves suffer from exploitation, commercialism, delusions of grandeur, low self-esteem, dried-out rationalism, careerism, galleryism, addiction to success, vulnerability to criticism, loss of direction and intention, personalism...and so on. Why enumerate! What seems lost to the arts is precisely what therapy deals with each day: soul. Through art therapy soul is returning to dance and painting, to poems and sculpture. Each gesture the patient makes attempts to place into defined form the emotional influxes that assail a human life. Each gesture is made for the sake of the gesture and not for anything external to the gesture itself. I dance my woe as fully as I can and paint my wild madness with as rich a palette as I can attain, not for reviewers of the product, not for recognition, not for the increase in size of the letters of my name. I do it for the soul's sake, and this gesture, encouraged by the art therapist in studios and clinics in city after city, town after town, may be more than a therapy of the patient. It may also be a therapy of the arts themselves, restoring to them the archetypal gestures of the soul.

19

INTRODUCTION: MOTHER AND GREAT MOTHER
FROM *THE RAG BONE SHOP OF THE HEART*

Our memories are permeated with Mother. Not only do our bodies begin in her body, but our psyches begin in hers and remain attached to hers by means of the scenes, feelings, and habits that compose our life. Memory, and therefore Mother, affects us continually. We are and always will be "stuck" in Mother because she is the ground of the experiencing soul. That umbilical cord is never bitten through, even if I put Mom right out of my mind, or pack off my actual mother to a nursing home in a pine forest. *I Remember Mama,* the title of an old Broadway play, tells it like it is because I can't forget Mama. She lives on in the memorial rooms of the soul as the happiness and fear of childhood, family, home, and the earliest desires and pain. She is like a permanent stain, a dominant chord, the warp of the carpet structuring us as we are.

C. G. Jung lists these qualities associated with the mother archetype:

> Maternal solicitude and sympathy; the magic authority of the female principle; the wisdom and spiritual exaltation that tran-scend reason; also, all that is benign, all that cherishes and sus-tains, furthers growth and fertility... On the negative side, the mother archetype may connote what devours, seduces, and poi-sons; it is terrifying and inescapable like fate. I have expressed the ambivalence of these attributes in the phrase "the loving and terrible mother."[1]

---

1. Citations from C.G. Jung, "The Psychological Aspects of the Mother Arche-type," translated by Cary F. Baynes and Ximena de Angulo, original version (1938), as published in *Spring: An Annual of Archetypal Psychology and Jungian Thought* (1943) and reprinted in *Fathers and Mothers,* edited by Patricia Berry (Dallas: Spring Publica-tions, 1990).

Essentially, Jung continues, she brings cherishing and nourishing kindness, orgiastic emotionality, and the Stygian depths of death and the underworld.

In another passage, he says of her: "Intimately known and yet strange like Nature, lovingly tender and yet cruel like fate, joyous and the untiring giver of life...Mother is mother-love, is *my* experience, my secret." She is the "carrier...of that experience that includes herself and myself and all mankind, and indeed the whole of created nature, the experience of life whose children we are."

As original ground of soul she is also final ground, burial ground in symbolisms worldwide, whether as Maria holding the dead Jesus or Kali dancing among the bones. She goes on triumphant; her sons, her heroes and warriors fall. And so we bring fear to her, and mourning. The great size of these emotions finds its equivalence in the figure of the Great Mother, such as the goddesses in myths and grandmothers, stepmothers, wise women, and witches in fairy tales, those power ladies who mother a man with care and advice all the while smothering his free spirit. Jung says, "Crudely or delicately, consciously or unconsciously, she cannot help touching in some way upon the son's masculinity." In five of the following poems, the mother's "touch" is presented quite literally as her hand.

By admitting the deep love and equally deep terror Mother inspires, the poems in this section display the range of every mother's greatness.[2] They allow Mother to enter consciousness in the guise of remembrances and mournings, and they muse the memories and sorrows into art.

According to the Greeks, memory (Mnemosyne) is the mother of all the arts, so that art—such as these poems for, to, and about Mother—is the best way "out" of the mother complex, a way of working it so that we please Mother with our art rather than sacrifice to her with our lives.

---

2. "Mother and Son" by Alden Nowlan, "My Mother Would Be a Falconress" by Robert Duncan, "The Right Meaning" by César Vallejo, "Kaddish" by David Ignatow, "Sonnet to My Mother" by George Barker, "In Memory of My Mother" by Patrick Kavanagh, "The Last Words of My English Grandmother" by William Carlos Williams, "The Goddess" by Théodore de Banville, "Old Woman Nature" by Gary Snyder, *et al.*, in *The Rag and Bone Shop of the Heart: Poems for Men*, edited by Robert Bly, James Hillman, and Michael Meade (New York: HarperCollins, 1992).

That term *mother complex*, at its deepest refers to the emotional memories distilled into our most intimate habits of feeling to which we cling as if for survival. We don't want to give up what we require in love, how we style our bodies, what we feel to be homecoming, the fears to which we have become accustomed. This is all mother memory ruling a man's life. She is the continuity of patterns we have lived with for so long that we have become them, thereby living in the ground of her body, still. She persists in these patterns until we can admit to our fascination with—now called addiction to—likes and dislikes that seem so secretly and intimately mine yet attest to my origins in her.

Psychologizing
or Seeing Through

20

FOREWORD TO *THE COCAINE PAPERS*
BY SIGMUND FREUD
(WITH A.K. DONOGHUE)

I t is curious that, for all the present concern with psychopharmacology, Freud's work in this field has been neglected. The papers that follow are not included in either the German or English editions of Freud's *Collected Works*. They are available to the German reader only after a laborious search through scattered archives. This volume therefore brings together for the first time in any language all of Freud's writings on cocaine, a study that began in 1884 and ended three years later.

The reader is advised to consult the chapter in the Jones biography of Freud, called the Cocaine Episode. Bernfeld's paper (1953) is the most thorough account of this part of Freud's work, but—perhaps owing to the death of its author before publication—it shows inaccuracies of reference and translation.[1] Because only these secondary sources have hitherto been available, and because of the current interest in psychopharmacology, it was felt that the actual writings of Freud on this subject ought not be denied the English reader. We may, therefore, be grateful to Mr. James Strachey for so generously giving his time to read through the translations, and to Mr. Ernst Freud who, in the interest of science, graciously gave his permission to print.

The neglect of Freud's work on cocaine is due partly to Freud himself. After 1887, except for occasional personal use of cocaine, he turned away altogether from following his interest in this field. But this interest was deep, as he reports in his *Autobiographical Study* so that he was not able to leave it without a certain denial. For example, Bernfeld reports

---

1. Prof. Erna Lesky, University of Vienna, has just brought to our attention Hortense Koller Becker's article "Carl Koller and Cocaine," *The Psychoanalytic Quarterly* 32 (1963), an important addition to Jones and Bernfeld.

a parapraxis attesting to repression: Freud's lecture before the meeting of psychiatrists in 1885 (Paper 3) does not appear in his own list of his writings (1897), nor could a reprint of this same publication be found among his papers.

That psychoanalysis should continue with this neglect of an influential contribution to an important topic by a major thinker is to carry on with a misapprehension stemming from Freud himself, that his work was an error and a failure. This view needs fresh evaluation.

⚜

Present-day neuropharmacological research divides drugs into two broad classes: those drugs disturbing the mental functioning of normal people, and those improving the mental functioning of abnormal people.[2] Hallucinogens belong to the first group; tranquilizers and psychic energizers to the second. It is clear from Freud's first two papers that he considered cocaine to be in the nature of an energizer, both somatic and psychic. He experienced this effect by taking cocaine himself, just as he was later to investigate the unconscious through self-analysis.

In the third paper, Freud pointed out more specifically that cocaine can raise lowered activity, thereby bringing this substance within the domain of neuropharmacology. According to McGeer, psychic energizers and monoamine oxidase inhibitors began to be introduced in 1957; tranquilizers, rauwolfia compounds and phenothiazines, in 1953; and hallucinogens, as scientific tools, in 1943. Although such hallucinogens as mescaline and peyote, etc. had been known for centuries, it was only recently that their ability to mimic aspects of mental illness and of religious experience has been studied seriously. Freud's experiments with a substance to achieve psychic energizing shows again how he was in advance of his times.

Later experiences with cocaine brought home to Freud (Paper 5) that it was a dangerous drug. Despite his hopes that cocaine would be of value in internal medicine, in psychiatry and in surgery (Paper 1), today cocaine,

---

2. [This paper, published in 1963, must be placed in historical context in that it does not reflect the current field of neuropharmacology. The core of the argument remains important and valid, but some specific assertions will receive commentary to provide the reader with some of the current thinking in the field, particularly regarding the nature of addiction.—Ed.]

as Freud used it, is generally considered medically useless. Even the one positive use that eluded Freud and contributed to his professional disappointment—local anesthesia of the eye—has been given up since the action of cocaine tends to pit the cornea. Safer, non-habit forming energizers, hallucinogens, tranquilizers, and local anesthetics have been found since the great cocaine excitement of the nineteenth century.

Therefore, the main importance of these papers is not pharmacological, except as a contribution to the history of the field. (And even here Freud's contribution is significant because Koller's discovery of the application of cocaine in eye-surgery shows the influence of Freud's experiments.) The main value of these papers for us is that they show how Freud's young mind (he was then between 28 and 31) was beginning to be fascinated with the unconscious . Here, he writes about neurasthenia, later to be the neuroses. Here, his interest is drawn to the investigation by scientific observation of his own psychic states, accentuated by a critical time in his career and marriage (1886). The reader will also find, in the first paper, Freud's characteristic thoroughness, enthusiasm for his subject, and masterly construction of argument in clear prose. In this cocaine research Freud first left the approved path of neurology for adventures into the unknown. This unknown was still concretized into a chemical substance, just as his early ideas of the libido theory assumed an organic base in the seminal fluid. Freud's failure with cocaine is a *beata culpa*. In error and defeat he turned away from a physical, organic approach to the therapy of mental difficulties that led eventually to the discovery of the unconscious and psychoanalysis.

A side effect of the cocaine episode on Freud is perhaps his subsequent embitterment with America. He had relied greatly upon American authorities to back his claim that the drug was harmless. Experience and time showed him that he had been led astray. His first encounter with America had let him down. Although the United States had been the country most receptive to psychoanalysis from the time of his and Jung's lectures at Clark University, Freud spared few occasions to find fault and pass judgement, even to the end of his life in his arguments in favor of lay analysis against American psychiatry and medicine. (He did not understand how Einstein could feel at home there, and once, in a conversation with Max Eastman, he called America an "abortion.")

Freud's experiments with cocaine belong within a tradition. Creative minds have often been drawn in this direction. Many poets, painters, and musicians took drugs, to say nothing of alcohol. Ebin and de Ropp review the literature and give examples. It is even claimed that much of the art and mysticism of the East owes its inspiration to the drug experience. And Freud's great psychological contemporary, William James, indulged in nitrous oxide inhalations. Today, orthodox psychiatry and the avant-garde seem agreed that psychopharmacology is that field offering the most promise for our troubled minds. It has been proposed that the new drugs may not only be used for treating and curing "mental illness," but that these *phantastica* may be able to revivify our civilization and its discontents by bringing us back to religious delight. This thesis has been put by Huxley, Watts, and Jane Dunlap and it has been refuted expertly by Zaehner.

Though these substances are, for the most part, new compounds, the hopes they carry are old. All periods of history and all cultures show the consumption of toxic substances for the purpose of altering perception and emotion. Alcohol in the Christian West and hashish in the Muslim East are examples. But when the substances are not native, when they come from far places and exotic peoples—as spices from Eastern islands, tobacco from the New World, rauwolfia from India, etc.—they would seem to be charged with a special significance. Coca from Peru fits this pattern.

This pattern in traditional symbolism is represented as the "healing elixir or herb of immortality," brought back from a remote land bearing an alien name, processed in a special way, distributed ritualistically, and potent even in minute quantities. Its negative effects can be toxic especially when ingested by those not right nor ripe for it. Its positive effects include healing, rejuvenation, and liberation. These ideas, carried by myth and ceremony, are so universal that we must consider the probability that we are being confronted with an archetypal phenomenon.

Not only does cocaine fulfill the pattern, but Freud's experiences with it also correspond to the tradition. The study of drug experiences tends to show that highly varied observers in different centuries and places, and with different substances, report similar phenomena. These experiences are principally euphoric. The same enthusiasm attended the discovery of tobacco and coffee as mescaline; the same magical properties were "found" in chloral hydrate and bromides as in tranquilizers; the same rituals surrounded the processing and dispensing of tea and alcohol as heroin and LSD. This similarity points to a common factor that is not in the substances, but is in the experiences.

Furthermore, as pharmacological research shows, new drugs with new names tend to be "wonder drugs," when first introduced mainly by virtue of their newness. The unknown most readily collects unconscious projections. In the case of a new drug, the unconscious factor likely to constellate is the archetype of the wonder herb bringing with it those intense emotions of hope, healing, and freedom from suffering. We are led to the conclusion that the common factor influencing Freud's experience as well as the common factor projected into the substance is of this archetypal nature, and that this same archetypal factor might also be the basis of drug craving.

Drug-craving, as we know today, is not organically determined as was once supposed. It is by far and large a psychological problem. Freud came upon this early on. Cocaine proved no threat to him but he agreed that it could lead to addiction in those already addicted to morphine. Freud did not succumb; yet his expectations from cocaine, not only colored his scientific judgment, at first, but he exhibits as well two primary signs of the drug experience of the addict. In other words, Freud was never in the grip of the drug as drug, but he seems to have been, during this period, under the spell of an archetypal factor constellated by the drug.

The archetypal factor, the "herb of immortality," is expressed psychologically by two signs. The first we may describe as the desire to rise above and beyond the daily trouble of all mortals. Seen negatively it is the escapism of the immortality drive; positively, it is spiritual ambition and the quest for liberation. The second is the belief in the properties of a substance that can achieve this aim.

In Freud's autobiographical study, he writes that he might have been famous at an early age had his studies on cocaine not been interrupted before Koller successfully applied cocaine in eye surgery, thereby winning the immortality of fame. Cocaine carried Freud's early hopes for success and recognition. Through it, he wanted to realize spiritual ambitions and scientific acclaim. The desire to rise above and beyond was channeled into science for Freud. Immediate professional recognition was the kind of liberation he sought. He did not expect Nirvana directly through taking cocaine himself and that is why he was not in danger of addiction. However, the desire of his scientific ambition was carried for three years—and perhaps much longer as the repression would indicate—by this substance.

His belief in the drug was reinforced by the freedom it brought him from his physical and psychic pain. He felt exhilarated and euphoric after using it; and he pushed cocaine on his colleagues, friends, and fiancée. We can hear echoes of this same belief in the magical properties of a new substance from those who advocate liberation through LSD-25.

The archetypal factor influencing drug craving, giving such intensity to desire and conviction to belief, never fully won Freud. Science meant too much to him. He was sobered by reason and a respect for facts. From this perspective we may now see the "Cocaine Episode" not as a youthful error to be ignored by his successors and excluded from the body of his works. Rather, it is a youthful mark of his greatness. He had the capacity to be caught up by a powerful collective pattern and yet work his way through to an individual solution. He was able to disentangle from his unconscious upon a physical substance as the carrier of the unknown, in order to turn to the unknown in itself as the unconscious. He refused the temptation of the shortcut and continued on to realize the same spiritual ambition, but on a psychological level.

Bibliography

Siegfried Bernfeld, "Freud's Studies on Cocaine, 1884–1887," *Journal of the American Psychoanalytic Association* 1, no. 4 (1953): 581–613

Robert S. De Ropp, *Drugs and the Mind* (New York: St. Martin's Press, 1957)

Jane Dunlap, *Exploring Inner Space: Personal Experiments under LSD-25* (New York: Harcourt, Brace and World, 1961)

The Drug Experience: First-Person Accounts of Addicts, Writers, Scientists, and Others, edited by David Ebin (New York: Grove Press, 1961)

Sigmund Freud, *An Autobiographical Study* (London: The Hogarth Press and The Institute of Psycho-Analysis, 1950)

James Hillman, *Emotion: A Comprehensive Phenomenology of Theories and Their Meaning for Therapy* (Northwestern University Press (1960)

Aldous Huxley, *The Doors of Perception* (London: Chatto & Windus, 1954).

Ernest Jones, *Sigmund Freud: Life and Work,* 2 vols. (London: Hogarth, 1953–55).

Marghanita Laski, *Ecstasy: A Study of Some Secular & Religious Experiences* (London: The Cresset Press, 1961)

Patrick L. McGeer, "Mind, Drugs and Behavior," *American Scientist* 50 (1962): 322–38

William Sargant, "On Chemical Tranquillizers," *British Medical Journal* 1 (1956): 939–43

Alan W. Watts, *The Joyous Cosmology: Adventures in the Chemistry of Consciousness* (New York: Pantheon Books, 1962)

R. C. Zaehner, *Mysticism, Sacred and Profane: An Inquiry into Some Varieties of Praeternatural Experience* (Oxford: Clarendon Press, 1957)

21

TOWARD THE ARCHETYPAL MODEL
FOR THE MASTURBATION INHIBITION

Just down this lake where we are gathered for our Congress, in Lausanne, a Swiss physician, inventor of the term *Nervenkrankheit* or *maladie des nerfs*, Samuel Auguste André David Tissot, professor of medicine at Lausanne and Pavia, member of the Royal Societies of London, Paris, Milan, and Stockholm, published in the year 1758, his thirtieth year, a work in Latin that in his own French translation in 1764 is called *L'Onanisme: Dissertation sur les Maladies Produites par la Masturbation* (Onanism: Dissertation on the Maladies Produced by Masturbation). This work appeared within a few years in all major European languages, and more than thirty editions were published within a century.

Tissot was a knowledgeable writer on nearly every aspect of medicine, and in the latter half of the eighteenth century enjoyed an international reputation. He has been recognized as one of the most famous physicians of his time. His word became a household authority—an eighteenth-century Dr. Spock—and his book on masturbation the standard work on the subject. Since its publication, it has been a main influence on Western attitudes and therefore still influences our psychotherapeutic work today.

✿

Before we turn to Tissot's arguments against masturbation and the theoretical model of his physiology on which those arguments are based, let us review briefly the modern and contemporary view of the "masturbation question."

Jewish and Roman Catholic traditions rigorously condemn masturbation. It is rarely mentioned, however, in writings on medicine, the *ars amatoria*, or education in Western society until the eighteenth century, i.e., the period of Tissot. Anthropological evidence from other "uncivilized" societies shows that masturbation is one of the *least* punished of sexual practices. It is generally held to be a private or family affair, not a clan or society matter. In our society, however, partly owing to the influence of Tissot, *masturbation became not only a religious sin and a social crime but a medical disease,* i.e., it was pathologized. For Kant, self-abuse was worse than suicide; Voltaire and Rousseau condemned it; Goethe and Lavater wrote of spiritual masturbation in their correspondence.

By the early nineteenth century, "masturbatory insanity" had entered psychiatry (Hare 1962). Eminent alienists—Benjamin Rush in the United States, Esquirol in France, Ellis and Yellowlees in England, Flemming and Griesinger in Germany—considered masturbation a cause of mental derangement. Clitoridectomy was practiced, mainly in England and the USA, for the relief of "masturbation-caused epilepsy" (Duffy 1963). Fantastic metal contraptions similar to medieval chastity belts were applied to prevent the act. Around 1900, in a Kansas reform school for boys, castration was performed to prevent masturbation (Hawke). One of the "general disqualifications" of a candidate to the U.S. Naval Academy (1940) was masturbation, which was considered a moral infirmity. The Boy Scout manual (before Kinsey's personal intervention), of which some ten million copies have been issued in the United States, warned against masturbation. Campbell's textbook of urology as late as the 1959 edition recommended mechanical restraints to prevent it. Although Taylor (1933) had empirically challenged the seed-conservation idea by showing a group of cases where superior athletic performances were achieved directly following masturbation, the idea that masturbation was dangerous and could drive one crazy continued to linger in our cultural attitudes.

The first reaction against the repressive, prohibitory attitudes came in 1912—a revolutionary year in psychology in many other areas as well (Hillman 1972, 164–65n.). In that year, psychoanalysts held their first symposium on *Onanie,* and the major paper in that symposium was written by Victor Tausk. For the first time, a serious attempt was made to understand masturbation and to place it within the wider context of psychosexual development. The symposium members noted and considered two psychological facts of first importance in connection with masturbation: *fantasy* and *guilt.* Furthermore, the view of the conference was more tolerant of masturbation. Freud's earlier hypothesis that masturbation, like *coitus reservatus* and *interruptus,* was a cause of anxiety and neurasthenic neurosis because it provided insufficient discharge, did not find full support (Reich 1951). (All of Freud's reflections on masturbation have been collected by Nagera 1974, 520–38.) The 1912 Symposium tended toward accepting masturbation as a usual widely practiced activity of childhood and adolescence, and hence it was normal. This led to the position of Stekel, which is, in short, that "Neurosis is a consequent of abstinence, not the result of the habit" (Stekel 1951), that is, the disturbance in sexuality is not masturbation, but the guilt feelings arising from the prohibition of masturbation in connection with oedipal conflicts and superego formation. And so the enemy is not masturbation but, rather, the prohibition and the unnecessary guilt.

In Krauss's *Anthropophyteia* (1910–12), an encyclopedia of anthropological esoterica, we can find sections on "Onanie als Heilmittel" for drying the gut in the hot period of the year, or for ridding a person of "Krankheitstoff," or as a sacrificial religious act (sacred masturbation) —all of which "evidence" lent further support to the psychoanalytic direction inaugurated mainly by Stekel.

Since 1912—and despite certain reservations expressed by the second psychoanalytic symposium in 1928 on *Onanie*—the pendulum has been swinging further and further away from Tissot, toward the unrestricted approval of masturbation so that at a modern White House Conference on Mental Hygiene the consensus fought with flying banners for adolescent masturbation (Reich 1951). The two Kinsey reports (1948, 1953) once and for all statistically whitewashed masturbation. Even the notion that masturbation could be excessive was shown as an absurdity, since the sexual impulse does not respond when sated. The only bogey left was the old-fashioned folkloric moralism—that cause of guilt, of bad conscience—traceable to Tissot.

Yet, for all this approval of masturbation, a curious disapproval remained. The disapproval was disguised, displaced. For example, "excessive" masturbation was condemned; or "masturbation fantasies" led one to "introverted schizoid withdrawal" and away from "real life and love"; or, although masturbation is normal for adolescence, it is not "mature" behavior, or it prevents, in women "vaginal orgasm."

However, the Kinsey reports note a high frequency of masturbation throughout adult life and among adults who enjoy other forms of sexual activity: "Many adults who are not immature in any realistic sense do masturbate, and there is no sense in refusing to recognize this fact." This outstanding fact—that masturbatory activity precedes runs parallel with and succeeds heterosexual activity in human life, goes on from infancy into very old age, and is in those about whom we have some reliable statistics, the Americans, after heterosexual intercourse the next most frequent form of sexual activity—raises basic questions. It can no longer be considered a substitute form of behavior but a sexual activity *sui generis*. (As such, the activity continues even in men who have been castrated for "persevering masturbation" (Bremer 1959, 86–88]. For example, eleven "schizophrenic" males, castrated between ages 23 and 49 went on masturbating, even when the penis was flaccid.) As psychologists we have a task to understand the fact of adult masturbation that the Kinsey reports note, even stress, but leave unexplained.

❀

We must first return to Tissot. In his view, masturbation was catastrophically harmful. To it he attributed a host of *maladies des nerfs*—tabes dorsalis, weak eyes, pimples, consumption, epilepsy, weakness of the intellectual faculties, sexual and genital disorders, and a full range of hypochondriacal and hysterical symptoms in what is an early description of the neurasthenic syndrome. Tissot's principal argument against masturbation was that seed loss is physiologically harmful. Tissot's ideas on "loss of seed" were confirmed by another Montpellier physician in three volumes with scores of case reports (Lallemand 1836–42).

The physiological model that Tissot uses to base his argument is so widespread and recurrent that we may with justification call it archetypal. This model of psycho-physiology appears early and forcefully in Hippocrates, whom Tissot relies upon and quotes at length. On the Hippocratic model, the nervous system is a set of very fine tubes or pipes through which circulate the *somata hormonta* or *corps excitant* (Bucher, 1958). This circulating essence is a psycho-physical vital *fluidum* described in many ways and given many names in subsequent centuries. It was linked by Galen to his theory of the four humors and their nourishment and replenishment. This "animal" or "vital spirit" has always been ambiguously psycho-physical, at times described as an actual fluid, at times as an immaterial flow (Hillman 1960, 75–77).

The hydrodynamic model of circulation goes back to the dawn of thought in China and foretells the discovery of the circulation of the blood (Boenheim 1957). Similar expressions are the "circular thrust" (*periousis*) in Plato's *Timaeus* (79–80), *prana* in Indian psycho-physiology, the notion of breath in Avicenna, the essence of which is the moist element yet which is a luminous substance like the "light" that circulates in *The Secret of the Golden Flower* (Jung and Wilhelm 1929). Freud's notion of the libido, of its damming by repression and channelling by the ego, of its special connection with the sexual instinct—even sexual fluids—is a modern restatement of the same archetypal hydrodynamic model of the psyche.

Of particular importance here is the encephalomylogenetic theory of semen held by Hippocrates, Plato, and many other authoritative figures who influenced Tissot. This theory conceived a direct anatomical line from the brain through the spine to the testicles (Lesky 1950). Similar ideas can be found in Tibetan anatomical drawings, in Kundalini yoga, and, more important for our Western ideas, in the early Greek ideas of life stuff explained by Onians (1954). This life stuff, called *aeon*, was a fluid or liquid flowing through all parts of the body, but was especially associated with sexual liquids, the brain, the spinal fluid, the water of the eyes, knees, kidneys, etc.

Tissot held semen to be an example *par excellence* of this vital fluid. Semen is both vital and visible, yet contains a semi-material invisible life principle, a sort of homunculus within, for which the visible fluid serves as a vehicle. Semen for Tissot was "the essential oil of the animal liquors." He writes: "It is true that we are ignorant whether the animal spirits and the genital liquor are the same thing; but observation teaches us...that these two fluids have a very strict analogy, and that the loss of one or the other produces the same ills" (Tissot 1772). Tissot restates in the language of his time the idea that *loss of semen is loss of soul substance,* which must circulate within the body to maintain life and not be spent.

Seed loss in masturbation was harmful because the motions of masturbation were more violent than those of coitus, resulting in excessive excitation analogous to the epileptic attack, leaving the individual exhausted, dry, and empty. Again the idea is ancient: the vital spirit, or stuff of life, is to circulate in rhythmical, moderate, harmonious flow, in keeping with Greek ideas of the soul as a harmony and the soul fibers as a chord. Passion overstimulates the flow, forcing it into wrong passages and leading to unremitting genital excitation and obsessive sexual pre-occupations, i.e., the "bad habit."

Further, the seed lost in masturbation was not replenished. For Tissot, there was an invisible torrent flowing between two people in intercourse, an exchange through the pores, a transmission of vital breath that restores vigor. Masturbation is solitary; there is no inhalation, exchange, or replenishment.

We cannot be content to reject Tissot's arguments because of their outdated physiology. As psychologists—especially as Jungian psychologists—let us look at these long-held ideas as having in themselves some archaic psychological truth, even if they be physiologically incorrect. Tissot's physiological model for the masturbation prohibition is faulty; but this model, rooted in an archetypal image, gave to Tissot's arguments their staggering collective influence. So it is not that masturbation excites and expends some quasi "nerve fluid." Rather, it is that masturbation stimulates and then releases psychic tension. We need only to translate the physiological "spending of fluid" into the psychological "leak in the circulation of psychic flow." With this rediscovery of the archetypal model in Tissot's thought, we can now approach the problem of guilt and masturbation inhibition anew.

A main conclusion of the 1912 psychoanalytic symposium on Onanism, as I have already reported was that guilt was fundamentally connected with masturbation. These guilt feelings prove unresolvable, irreducible. Fenichel (1945) writes: "In adolescence and later life, frequently not only fears and guilt feelings are still connected with masturbation, but there is even a distinct resistance on the part of the patients against enlightenment about the harmless nature of masturbation. They seem to have some unconscious interest in believing that masturbation is a dreadful thing."

In their comprehensive report on sexual offenders (Gebhard *et al.* 1965), the Kinsey researchers remark (503): "A substantial proportion of the males we interviewed had worried despite their knowledge that masturbation is well-nigh universal and despite the fact that not one of them reported being physically harmed by it. It is amazing how few persons asked themselves why a loss of semen in masturbation should be harmful while a loss of semen in coitus should have no ill effect; no one grasped the concept that if masturbation were harmful, marriage would by the same token be suicidal." Again—the archetypal model is stronger than facts and reason whether in Tissot or in these sexual offenders. It is a persuasive argument in support of our position that these men, jailed for sodomy, homosexuality, rape, incest, child molesting, and other "sexual offenses," who for the most part have great difficulty admitting guilt in relation with their offense, nonetheless experience worry, anxiety, and guilt concerning their masturbation. This statement, of course, requires a more differentiated discussion since the mechanism of denial (804–7) may work more strongly in regard to the criminal offense. But the main conclusion still stands: masturbation is accompanied by worrying guilt—"anxiety is ordinarily concomitant with the masturbation (generally ceasing when masturbation ceases)" (500)—even in those who fully act out sexuality in violation of prohibitory laws and inhibitory taboos (incest).

The *fundamental guilt* is brought out by writers on masturbation ranging from Catholic theologians (Von Gagern 1955) to D.H. Lawrence. The sin of Onan (Genesis 38:9), which has nothing explicitly to do with masturbation, nevertheless was taken up by the psyche as masturbation guilt. Anthropological data on masturbation are difficult to gather, for the act is practiced in secret, culturally disapproved, and widely ridiculed. Man is evidently uncomfortable about masturbation. Our own supposedly enlightened attitudes also express guilt; for it is usually the view in psychological literature that masturbation is either substitutive or regressive behavior, authentic only in the extenuating circumstances of *faute de mieux* or *Not-Onanie* (prisoners, sailors), or in connection with therapeutic regression to more juvenile levels.

What is the origin of this discomfort and disapproval, this widespread guilt in conscience? Can we lay it entirely to the prohibition imposed by the parental representatives of culture? Has masturbation become associated with an introjected restrictive authority, so that the two—impulse and prohibition—appear ever after together? Or has masturbation a *sui generis* inhibitor, as part of the drive itself? Prohibition or inhibition? The answer will depend in part upon how we view the psyche. If we assume the psyche to be a goal-directed, relatively closed individuating system, a basic model of which is the self as a circulating flow of psychic life within the person, then this system is also self-steering, self-guided. Conscience is the experience of the *spiritus rector* function of the self-guidance system. Guilt in conscience is inhibition of function: inhibition of function is felt as guilt in conscience. *Inhibition is self-imposed by the self-regulatory activity of the psyche.* This position appears already in Eugen Bleuler's discussion of *Onanie-Hemmung* (1913). There Bleuler recognized the signal importance of masturbation in the sexual life of the individual and its particular relation with shame, guilt, and the tendency to secrecy. Freud even went so far in a note written in 1938 (Nagera 1974, 438) as to suggest that the basis of all inhibition in the spheres of intellect and working activity seems to lie in the inhibition of childhood masturbation. The implication in both Bleuler and Freud is that masturbation and inhibition are fundamentally connected and that inhibition in its widest sense is derivative of masturbation. We cannot have the one without the other.

Jung (1958) says of conscience: "the phenomenon of conscience does not coincide with the moral code, but is anterior to it, transcends its contents." Guilt from superego formation—the masturbation prohibition coming from outside—is possible only if the psyche has the fundamental possibility already given to "feel guilty," and to find meaning in moral codes as part of its self-guiding system.

The introjected prohibition works only because it echoes the prior self-regulatory inhibition. And the lifting of the prohibition—as when Freud speaks of the "therapeutic return of masturbation"—does not remove the fundamental unease and problematics of masturbation, as psychoanalysts agree, which remain but get displaced upon such issues as "excessive," "compulsive," or "infantile-fixated" masturbation.

The hypothesis of a masturbation *inhibition* finds support in clinical findings. An adolescent patient at Burghölzli, a schizophrenic and compulsive masturbator, once told me he wanted to turn it around the other way so that it would go up into his head and make him well. (This was the impetus to the research leading to this paper.) Cases discussed in the 1928 Onanie symposium report anxiety over seed loss. Boys find masturbation without orgasm, without ejaculation and seed loss, evokes less guilt.

The anthropological fact that masturbation evokes the least punishment of all sexual activities implies a natural self-inhibition requiring little external prohibitory reinforcement. If it were a major danger to society or the species, as some have interpreted the reason for God's punishment of Onan, masturbation would be met with an even greater universal abhorrence than incest.

One further argument in favor of the inhibition hypothesis arises from attitudes toward female masturbation. Even after the ovum was discovered by Karl Ernst von Baer in 1827, thereby finally disproving the Galenic and medieval theory that the female had semen (Gerlach 1937–38) and ending the controversy over the role of the female in reproduction, female masturbation continued to be condemned with the same rigor as male masturbation. The evil was as great, the consequences as disastrous, and the measures inflicted to prevent masturbation as drastic. *Physiological fact had no effect on the archetypal idea.* In female masturbation we are not dealing with an actual vital fluid or concrete seed loss but with the archetypal meaning given to this fluid leakage by the model of the circulating flow of the psyche.

Conceding that the inhibition experienced in conscience as guilt anxiety is *sui generis* and not a cultural prohibition, perhaps its origin is biological. In other words, does guilt arise because masturbation runs counter to "natural law" by refusing procreation so that the voice of species preservation speaks through the self? This is the old idea that masturbation is a perversion of instinct. The masturbatory activity of animals, particularly primates—and in their natural habitats—shows that masturbation is a regularly occurring activity without inhibition (e.g., porcupines, too, masturbate—Wendt 1965, 297). It does not interfere with procreation but runs parallel to it. The inhibition would on this analogy with animals have to find its origin elsewhere than in "instinctual perversion" or "biologically-generated guilt." Biologically, masturbation is "natural." We can no more base the inhibition upon a biological function than we could upon introjected cultural prohibitions.

I hope that by now the difference between "prohibition" and "inhibition" has become quite clear. A prohibition is a negative command, a forbidding by authority. An inhibition is the action of hindering, restraining, checking, preventing. A prohibition requires authority, and in the history of masturbation discussion, this authority has ranged from God who smote Onan to the forbidding parental figure in Freudian superego formation. An inhibition, on the other hand, can be conceived as native to, as part of, a function itself, as a built-in check and balance necessary for self-regulation.

A prohibition is "anti-masturbation"; it is opposed to it. An inhibition hinders masturbation; it is a complication of it. Moreover, the inhibition can be conceived as *part of the masturbation function itself,* in the manner of a *partie inférieure* and *supérieure* of the same function—to use the language of Janet borrowed by Jung in his description of the archetype. Masturbation and its inhibition are aspects of the same activity. The lower end is the impulse to action, the upper end consists of fantasies and the *spiritus rector* of conscience.

The prohibition imposed by outer authority reinforces the inhibition, the upper end at the expense of the lower end, and splits instinct against itself. Then we find that familiar pattern of compulsive masturbation alternating with rigid superego restrictions, morbid guilt, and displaced erotic fantasies. The therapeutic return of masturbation means more than what Freud meant, i.e., discharge of id energies channelled by the ego now freed from intolerable superego restrictions. The therapeutic return of masturbation means the reunion of the two ends of the instinctual spectrum. It means *the return of the inhibition as well,* in the form of reawakened fantasy life, and a sense of one's own autonomy, one's own innate guiding conscience rather than an imposed superego morality.

To recapitulate briefly: our examination of masturbation guilt led to the assumption of a masturbation inhibition. We have not been able to reduce this inhibition either to cultural or to biological sources. Rather, we have followed an insight of Freud's "that something in the nature of the sexual instinct itself is unfavorable to the achievement of absolute gratification" (1912, 214). This inhibitory factor is wholly of psychological origin and is an inherent component of masturbatory activity. The model for our theory, however, goes in another direction than Freud's, for we are assuming as basis for the inhibition the archetypal idea of the self as a circulation of the psyche within a containing system, i.e., the self-containment of the psyche.

We arrive at our concluding question. What might be the meaning and purpose of the masturbation inhibition in regard to adult masturbation? As Layard (1945) has shown concerning incest, a taboo has not only a negative preventive function. The incest taboo also fosters the extension of culture. Similarly, the masturbation inhibition not only acts negatively against instinctual release; it fosters as well subjective guilt feelings, introspective worry, psychological conflict, and erotic fantasy. Without the incest taboo, biological and social culture could mainly be satisfied within the immediate family. Without the masturbation inhibition, psychological tension could be directly discharged.

We might make the claim that two psychological functions are instinctually furthered by the masturbation inhibition. These functions are conscience and imagination. About guilt, unease, secrecy, moral worry in conscience accompanying masturbation we have already spoken; about the vivid fantasy accompanying masturbation, at times even necessary for it, we need not speak since it is so well known. "Males who have never had fantasies during masturbation are relatively uncommon," says Gebhard et al. (1965, 503). Without the inhibition accompanying masturbation would there be fantasy? Is not the fantasy a part of the sexual drive itself, as the partie supérieure of the activity? Indeed, recent experimental evidence (Fisher, Gross, and Zuch 1956) supports the hypothesis that sexual excitation and fantasy are parts of the same function. Cycles of penile erection during sleep are synchronous with cycles of dreaming. Sexual fantasy that is blocked by anxiety or censorship in dream content also seems to be synchronous with loss of penile erection. Where the incest taboo through exogamy furthers extraverted development, the masturbation inhibition, through fostering intrapsychic tension, moral conscience, and mental imagery, furthers introverted development. Masturbation particularly vivifies relationships with imaginary partners (Lukianowicz 1960); it is a way of making figures of the imagination, both convincing and satisfying.

The pioneer work of Spitz on the genital play of infants also points to a relation between masturbation inhibition and introversion. He writes: "I found that genital play in infancy (or its absence) is an indicator of the nature of the child's object relations" (Spitz 1962). Infants with good object relations to mothers and their surrogates masturbate; those deprived or isolated masturbate less or not at all. Masturbatory activity of infants is directly correlated with outgoing instinctual relatedness. In infants it is not, as we usually think, compensatory autoerotic behavior activated by isolation. If we accept the view that has been put forward that all (non-autistic, "normal") babies are extraverted, that is object-oriented, the uninhibited masturbatory activity of infants belongs to extraversion.

The *partie supérieure,* the inhibition, evidently unfolds ontogenetically later. The inhibition, reinforced by Oedipal conflicts, would seem to increase with maturation and the development of subjectivity, introspection, introversion, and psychological containment. I would risk the proposition that the inhibition is reinforced more strongly around puberty than at the time of the oedipal conflicts of early childhood. On the basis of our fluid model of the soul, the appearance of genital secretions would be the determining factor. This is the critical physical experience that clicks with the archetypal model of the soul substance as a fluid, intensifying the inhibition, its conflicts and fantasies.

The words we use for masturbation—auto-erotism, solitary vice, secret vice, self-satisfaction, self-stimulation, self-abuse—draw attention to the subjectivity of the act—Bleuler's "tendency to secrecy." Because it is the only sexual activity performed alone, it has been given a negative value for biological and social culture.

The meaninglessness of masturbation for the species and for society, i.e., external culture, has long associated masturbation with suicide. However, as the only sexual activity performed alone, it may very well have another sort of meaning: *a sexual impetus to psychological or internal culture.* Its connection with fire-making and its role in creation myths point to its psychological importance (cf. *CW*5, p. 142f.; *CW*9.2, p. 207; Bachelard 1938). Of interest here is the fact that a childhood sign of the prospective Shaman among the Mohave is frequent masturbation (cf. Devereux 1936).

Although we have been showing masturbation to be "natural" (occurring throughout human life and in animals), it is at the same time an *opus contra naturam.* The *contra naturam* aspect is represented by the inhibitory concomitants of secrecy, guilt, and fantasy. Hence, its shamanistic significance. And hence the denigration of masturbation by those who hold the naturalistic and literalistic views of sexuality, i.e., that it should serve biological procreation or social relationship.

The *contra naturam* aspect of masturbation is expressed by various mythical fantasies that bring the act into connection with a monster, with an unnatural image that is both negative and creative. The monster Golem in Jewish legend is the result of sperm not entering the woman; the monster Erichthonios is the result of Hephaistos's seed falling into Gaia (rather than Athene); Pan, who was said to have invented masturbation, is himself a goat-footed monster.

As Murray Stein (1973) has suggested, Hephaistos is a god of intro-verted libido, a structure of consciousness that is both *contra naturam* and at the same time intimately connected with nature; Hephaistos activates the production of individual symbolism, forging nature into images. But it is precisely this production of individual symbolism and conscience which is opposed by orthodox religions. And it is they who have most to say about the suppression of masturbation. For instance the *Kitzur Shulhan Arukh* (§ 151), a Jewish book of laws supposedly put together originally by Rabbi Caro, explicitly compares masturbation with murder (hence God's justification for smiting Onan). Another instance is the position taken by the Roman Catholic Church under Innocent III at the Fourth Lateran Council (1215). It was at that most important meeting that the Church established vigorous modes of repression against individualistic fanta-sies (Averroism, the Albigenses); inaugurated the Inquisition and a new Crusade; circumscribed with dogma the activities of angels and defined demons as those spirits who became evil of their own accord through their own acts; and strongly reconfirmed sacerdotal celibacy, giving new impetus to the scrutiny of all sexual activities, including masturbation.

The "monstrousness" of masturbation and the fear of "excess" per-tains to the enormity of fantasy that goes beyond nature. "It is known that sexual behavior envisaged in daydreams or fantasy during masturbation will, in many cases, go far beyond any behavior the individual actually has experienced or wishes to experience in real life. This is especially true of males." (Duvall & Duvall 1961). The exorbitance of fantasy in relation with masturbation appears also in the warnings against the activity, such as those to be found in Tissot. Horrifying images of the drooling idiot boy or the febrile wasted and wanton girl presented in nineteenth-cen-tury home medical books, religious counseling, or traveling freak exhibits have their psychological source in the *contra naturam* aspect of the arche-type that presents the same idea in images of Pan and Hephaistos.

In other words, there is something profound in the old idea that "mas-turbation drives one crazy." Nydes (1950) has interpreted the craziness that one fears to be a loss of reality to magical omnipotence fantasies. The vivid tactile happening of masturbation, by giving body (concrete physical experience) to omnipotence fantasies, "fortifies the hallucinatory quality of the experience" (306). Masturbation indeed makes possible the experience of the utter reality of fantasy beyond, in excess of, and in con-tradiction to "nature."

We generally consider the capacity to contain excitation and the development of introversion as belonging to maturity rather than to youth. Perhaps now we can understand why masturbation has been condoned—and even, in some societies, encouraged—for youth, but almost universally condemned for adults.

The reasons against adult masturbation—that it is physiologically harmful, theologically evil, biologically threatening, sociologically criminal—can all be found faulty. Condemnation of adult masturbation as juvenile and regressive expresses the psychological idea that personality development requires *tapas* (internal heat), and that it is "youthful" to be unable to contain the excitation needed for this development.

Containing sexual excitation, including seed retention, for the purpose of psychological development is fundamental to sexual mysticism (*Études Carmélitaines* 1953; Evola 1968). Chinese, especially Taoist, sexual beliefs have worked out these practices in great detail. These have been authoritatively described by Maspero (1937) in the *Journal Asiatique*, and further explained in relation to tantric yoga and alchemy by Van Gulik (1961). These mystical ideas of self-nourishment through sexuality have been reduced in a Freudian way to "orality" (Weakland 1956), an approach that misses the archetypal model of self-regulatory "flow" which we are trying to put forth here.

To summarize these Oriental ideas briefly: The immortal body is not born spontaneously, nor is it given by the gods. Salvation depends on making one's own immortal body through human action. This is the basis of all gymnastics, ethics, dietetics, alchemy, etc. In all, the main work is nourishing the vital spirit, principally accomplished by "swallowing the breath", that is, by introverting the life force and developing psychic tension. The main *opus contra naturam* demands mastery of the sexual instinct. Because "a single coitus diminishes the life of the immortal body by one year" (Maspero 1937), abstinence is recommended. However, copulation is both natural and necessary. Therefore, techniques are developed for introverting or "translating" the semen through suppression of ejaculation (*coitus reservatus*), thereby forcing it, as was the fantasy in the Burghölzli patient, through those miniscule tubes (of Tissot) and making it "flow upward" to the brain. The sage has intercourse with any number of women, preferably adolescent, because of their "vital exhalations," and without violent excitation in order to nourish his vital spirits without loss, either of precious seed or through violent motion. The prescriptions correspond strikingly with Tissot's main arguments. Ackerman further expands these Taoist ideas in terms of occult masturbation instructions and a mystique of excitation, tumescence, but seed retention for internalized dispersion of the vital fluid. Preforms of this exotic practice can be found in adolescents struggling with masturbation, who allow themselves genital stimulation but not ejaculation.

Western attitudes toward sexuality are largely extraverted. We have no more been able to give full value to masturbation than we have to introversion. Their undervaluation is a corollary of the wider undervaluation of psychic life *per se*, unless it shows itself clearly in biological or social culture, that is, in extraverted forms. Therefore, we continue to find the literature on masturbation in works devoted to childhood and adolescence as if it disappears from psychological life after maturity.

Therefore, we have been blind to the anthropological and psychological evidence for the inhibition, always assuming that a prohibition is necessary—and prohibitions, coming from outer authorities, are also extraverted.

Moreover, our extraverted naturalistic prejudices have altogether cut masturbation off from significance for the soul and relation with religion. (There is no mention of "onanism" in any of these standard works bearing on religion: Frazer's *Golden Bough*, Seligman's *Encyclopedia of the Social Sciences*, Hastings's *Dictionary of the Bible*, or his *Encyclopedia of Religion and Ethics*; cf. Jeffreys 1951.) But if, as the philosopher Whitehead has said, "religion is what a person does with his own solitariness," then masturbation may have profound implications beyond a mere psychotherapy of the sexual function. Individuation itself will show its omnipotence in the fantasy world of masturbation and in the secret introspective worry accompanying the act, forcing the individual to recognize the god in the "symptom," the soul in the body, the ritual in the sexual. In the complexities inherent to masturbation, we come upon roots of the introverted aspect of the religious instinct: separation and solitariness, shame, sense of sin, individual fantasy formation, and body magic. Our individual resistance to masturbation confession and awareness of masturbation fantasies belongs, therefore, to the most profound levels of the religious instinct. These secret feelings and fantasies present patterns of our individuation.

Even the newest "free" ideas on masturbation originating with Stekel are extraverted in that they oppose the prohibition in the name of extraverted expression of psychosexuality. Extraverted prejudices appear as well in the usual discussions of masturbation and petting. Excitation that does not lead to discharge is regarded as an unhealthy practice, and—as with the early Freud on *coitus reservatus*—a source of neurosis. Whether this extraverted prejudice, supported by Western religions, has not itself had an unhealthy effect on the cultivation of eros and heightened *tapas*, I would leave for discussion.

Psychoanalysts today seem to agree with Spitz that masturbation and its inhibition belong together. Spitz (1962) writes: "From the viewpoint of our civilization, the consequences of masturbation without restriction are probably as undesirable as those of restriction without masturbation. Both lead to sterility, be it mental or reproductive." Unfortunately, the argument is based on the old model of an unchecked instinctive impulse countered by a restrictive prohibition. Spitz, and all others I have read, miss the inhibition, *the self-governing of the instinct mainly through fantasy and conscience,* which Tissot's model affords us. Whether the instinct expresses itself mainly on the lower end or the upper end would depend on whether psychic tension is to be released or held and cultivated in accordance with what is beneficial at that moment for the psychological constellation.

It is the constellation that determines the masturbation experience. If puer, then masturbation is freedom and omnipotence; if heroic, then inhibition and control become dominant; if Dionysian, then relaxation and spending take on more importance. Much of the prejudice against masturbation, including Freud's association of it with neurasthenia, can be referred to the heroic ego's stance against Dionysian weakening. Although the archetypal constellation determines the experience, the fundamental ambivalence between compulsion and inhibition is not bypassed; this ambivalence merely takes different forms by following different mythical patterns. Thus the crucial psychological value of masturbation lies precisely in the experience of ambivalence, of psychic tension, which reflects the self-inhibition of even what seems most natural, simple, and pleasure-giving.

Two dreams illustrate the importance of masturbation for introversion and the development of psychic tension. A man about forty has lived out his sexuality with women since adolescence. At the time of the dream he has projected his creative talents into a woman artist who is his mistress. His own considerable artistic gifts he neglects. He dreams that he is instructed by an older woman to masturbate into a silver cup. The dream implied to me that he should turn some sexual energy toward his own anima, contain it there, rather than all outward into the relationship.

Another man, in his late thirties, who is wrestling with his very active homosexuality—that is, whether to stay at home at night and masturbate, or go out in the street—dreams that he is in the power of a brutal hardened older homosexual. By masturbating this older man, he diminishes his power and gets free. He understood this dream to mean that masturbation was now the answer to his sexual urge, otherwise he would be under the dominion of his callous shadow. In both instances, masturbation meant the frustration of extraverted object-oriented sexuality for the sake of the subjective factor. In both cases, masturbation had been looked down upon as a childish substitute. After the dreams, masturbation could be connected to inner life and the inhibition acknowledged as the fantasy-unease function of the activity itself.

Tissot's archetypal model connecting sexual liquids with the flow of psychic energy tells us what masturbation might truly mean to the psyche. It is just what the term says: self-stimulation, a stimulus to the circulation of the psyche, at first primarily by constellating a pole for the libido opposite to the head. *Sexual energy is given to introversion.* The inhibition prevents direct discharge of the heightened excitation, thereby prolonging the circulation or rotation of the psyche. The mystery of adult masturbation may now be seen in a new light. It is an aspect of adult introversion, a primitive attempt at self-centering and self-regulation—even more, of active imagination at its fundamental level.

❀

We examined Tissot's arguments against masturbation and the theoretical model of physiology underlying these arguments giving a brief review of the modern "masturbation question" and showing the connection between masturbation, sin, crime, and disease. To Tissot, loss of semen was loss of soul substance: it could not be replenished. There seems to be an archaic psychological truth behind Tissot's physiologically incorrect arguments; his model of circulating special fluids in a self-contained circuit is rooted in an archetypal image. This rediscovered meaning of Tissot's model leads to a necessary review of the problem of guilt and of masturbatory inhibition. The unresolvable guilt feelings associated with masturbation have been acknowledged by psychoanalysts in 1912, and by many since then. Although the professional literature tends to regard masturbation as either substitutive or regressive behavior, there is collateral evidence from clinical observations and from other fields that this is by no means all. A masturbatory inhibition *sui generis,* prior to either culturally or biologically motivated prohibition, is postulated. This fits in with Jung's view of conscience as anterior to the moral code, not necessarily identical with it and transcending it, as well as with psychoanalytical findings. Clarifying the difference between prohibition and inhibition I made use of Janet's concepts of *partie inférieure* and *supérieure* of the same function. Where prohibition reinforces inhibition, instinct may get split against itself. This split may heal in analytical treatment ("the return of the repressed"), but the original inhibition returns too, manifest in such forms as a reawakened fantasy life, a sense of autonomy, and conscience. Referring to Layard's view of the positive function of the incest taboo I examined the meaning and purpose of masturbatory inhibition in relation to adult masturbation claiming that conscience and imagination are furthered by this inhibition; this fosters intrapsychic tension that may lead to increasing introverted development. Spitz discusses the relationship between masturbatory inhibition and introversion, and finds that the masturbatory activity of infants is directly correlated with satisfactory object-relationship, and is not compensatory auto-erotic behavior activated by isolation. The inhibition evidently unfolds ontogenetically later. I then ventured to submit that the inhibition is reinforced more strongly around puberty than at the time of the Oedipal conflict of earlier childhood. This would fit in with Tissot's model of the soul fluid. From the standpoint of the preservation of the species and of culture, masturbation has long been associated with suicide. It may also be viewed as the sexual impetus to the *opus contra naturam* of psychological or internal culture (cf. fire-making and creation myths).

References

Ackerman, P. "Erotic Symbolism in Chinese Literature," unpublished manuscript, Institute for Sex Research, University of Indiana

Bachelard, Gaston. *La Psychanalyse du feu* (Paris: Gallimard, 1938)

Bleuler, Eugen. "Der Sexualwiderstand," *Jahrbuch for Psychoanalytische und Psychopathologische Forschungen* 5, no. 1 (1913): 442–52

Boenheim, Felix. *Von Huang-ti bis Harvey* (Jena: Gustav Fischer Verlag, 1957)

Bremer, Johan. *Asexualization: A Follow-up Study of 244 Cases* (Oslo: Oslo University Press, 1959)

Brown, Julia S. "A Comparative Study of Deviations from Sexual Mores," *American Sociological Review* 17, no. 2 (April 1952): 135–46

Bucher, H.W. *Tissot und sein Traité des Nerfs* (Zurich: Juris-Verlag, 1958)

Devereux, Georges. "Sexual Life of the Mohave Indians: An Interpretation in Terms of Social Psychology" (diss., University of California, 1935)

Duffy, John. "Masturbation and Clitoridectomy: A Nineteenth-Century View," *JAMA* 186 (1963): 246–48

Duvall, Evelyn Ruth Millis and Sylvanus Milne Duvall, eds. *Sex Ways–In Fact and Faith: Bases for Christian Family Policy* (New York: Association Press, 1961), chap. 10 by W. B. Pomeroy

Evola, Julius. *Métaphysique du sexe* (Paris: Payot, 1968)

Fenichel, Otto. *The Psychoanalytic Theory of Neurosis* (New York: W.W. Norton, 1945)

Fisher, Charles, Joseph Gross, and Joseph Zuch. "Cycle of Penile Erection Synchronous with Dreaming (REM) Sleep," *Archives of General Psychiatry* 12, no. 1: 29–45

Freud, Sigmund (1896). "Heredity and the Aetiology of the Neuroses," *Collected Papers*, vol. 1 (London: Hogarth Press, 1924)

——. (1912), "The Most Prevalent Form of Degradation in Erotic Life," *Collected Papers*, vol. 4 (London: Hogarth Press, 1925)

Von Gagern, Friedrich. *The Problem of Onanism* (Cork: Mercier Press, 1959)

——. *Die Zeit der geschlechtlichen Reife* (Frankfurt am Main: Knecht, 1953)

Gebhard, Paul H., John H. Gagnon, Wardell B. Pomeroy, and Cornelia V. Christenson. *Sex Offenders: An Analysis of Type* (New York: Harper & Row, 1965)

Gerlach, Wolfgang. "Das Problem des 'weiblichen Samens' in der antiken und mittelalterlichen Medizin," *Sudhoffs Archiv für Geschichte der Medizin und der Naturwissenschaften* 30, no. 4/5 (February 1938): 177–93

Hare, E.H. "Masturbatory Insanity: the History of an Idea," *Journal of Mental Science* 108, no. 452 (January 1962): 1–25

Hawke, C.C. "Castration and Sex Crimes," *The Journal of the Kansas Medical Society* 51 (1950): 470–73

Hillman, James. *Emotion: A Comprehensive Phenomenology of Theories and Their Meanings for Therapy* (London: Routledge & Kegan Paul, 1960)

———. "An Essay on Pan," in *Pan and the Nightmare* (Thompson, Conn.: Spring Publications, 2020)

———. *The Myth of Analysis: Three Essays in Archetypal Psychology* (Evanston: Northwestern University Press, 1972)

Jeffreys, M.D.W. "Onanism: An Anthropological Survey," *International Journal of Sexology* 5 (1951): 61–65

Jung, C.G. *CW* 9.2: *Aion*

———. *CW* 5: *Symbols of Transformation*

———. *CW* 10: *Civilization in Transitio.*

——— and Richard Wilhelm. *The Secret of the Golden Flower: A Chinese Book of Life* (London: Routledge & Kegan Paul, 1962)

Kinsey, Alfred C., Wardell B. Pomeroy, and Clyde E. Martin. *Sexual Behavior in the Human Male* (Philadelphia: W.B. Saunders, 1948)

———, Wardell B. Pomeroy, Clyde E. Martin, and Paul H. Gebhard. *Sexual Behavior in the Human Female* (Philadelphia: W.B. Saunders, 1953)

Krauss, Friedrich S., ed. *Anthropophyteia: Jahrbücher für Folkloristische Erhebungen und Forschungen zur Entwicklunggeschichte der geschlechtlichen Moral*, vols. 7–9 (Leipzig: Ethnologischer Verlag, 1910–12)

Lallemand, M. *Des pertes seminales involontaires*, 3 vols. (Paris: Bechet Jeune, 1836)

Layard, John. "The Incest Taboo and the Virgin Archetype," *Eranos Yearbook* 12 (1945): 253–307

Lesky, Erna. *Die Zeugungs-und Vererbungslehren der Antike und ihr Nachwirken* (Wiesbaden: F. Steiner, 1951)

Lukianowicz, Narcyz. "Imaginary Sexual Partner: Visual Masturbatory Fantasies," *Archives of General Psychiatry* 3 (1960): 429–49

Maspero, Henri. "Les procédés de 'nourrir le principe vital' dans la religion taoïste ancienne," *Journal asiatique* 229 (1938): 177–252, 353–430

Nagera, Humberto, ed. *Psychoanalytische Grundbegriffe: Eine Einführung in Sigmund Freuds Terminologie und Theoriebildung*, translated by Friedhelm Herborth (Frankfurt am Main: S. Fischer, 1974)

Nydes, Jule. "The Magical Experience of the Masturbation Fantasy," *The American Journal of Psychotherapy* 4, no. 2 (1950): 303–10.

Onians, Richard Broxton. *The Origins of European Thought: About the Body, the Mind, the Soul, the World, Time and Fate* (Cambridge: Cambridge University Press, 1951)

Reich, Annie. "The Discussion of 1912 on Masturbation and Our Present-Day Views," *The Psychoanalytic Study of the Child* 6 (1951): 80–94

Spitz, René A. "Autoerotism re-examined," *The Psychoanalytic Study of the Child* 17 (1962): 283–315

Stein, Murray. "Hephaistos: A Pattern of Introversion," *Spring: An Annual of Archetypal Psychology and Jungian Thought* (1973): 35–51

Stekel, Wilhelm. *Auto-Erotism: A Psychiatric Study of Onanism and Neurosis* (London: Peter Nevill, 1951)

Taylor, W. S. *A Critique of Sublimation in Males: A Study of Forty Superior Single Men* (Worcester, Mass.: Clark University, 1933)

Tissot, Samuel Auguste André David. *An Essay on Onanism* (Dublin: James Williams, 1772)

Van Gulik, Robert Hans. *Sexual Life in Ancient China: A Preliminary Survey of Chinese Sex and Society from ca. 1500 B.C. till 1644 A.D.* (Leiden: Brill, 1961)

Various Authors. *Die Onanie: Vierzehn Beiträge zu einer Diskussion der "Wiener Psychoanalytischen Vereinigung"* (Wiesbaden: J. F. Bergmann, 1912)

Various Authors. *Mystique et Continence: Travaux scientifiques du 7ᵉ Congrès International d'Avon* (Bruges (Les Études Carmélitaines/Desclée de Brouwer, 1952)

Weakland, John H. "Orality in Chinese Conceptions of Male Genital Sexuality," *Psychiatry* 19, no. 3 (1956): 237–47

Wendt, Herbert. *The Sex Life of the Animals,* translated by Richard and Clara Winston (New York: Simon and Schuster, 1965)

Regulations Governing the Admission of Candidates into the United States Naval Academy as Midshipmen (Washington, D.C.: U.S. Government Printing Office, 1940)

22

ON PARANOIA

I shall begin with two statements from authorities of religion so as to place my topic, Paranoia, within the broader context of this *Tagung*,[1] the Hidden, and to affirm at the start that this lecture will be located at that juncture where psychology cannot be fully separated from religion— religion as relation with divinity and as relation with community—that is, where psychology is drawn to consider theology and politics.

The first of these statements is from a psychologist, William James:

> Were one asked to characterize the life of religion in the broadest and most general terms possible, one might say that it consists of the belief that there is an unseen order, and that our supreme good lies in harmoniously adjusting ourselves thereto. This belief and this adjustment are the religious attitude in the soul.[2]

The second statement is from Kittel's major theological dictionary, the entry on "Revelation."

> All religion is concerned in some way with the manifestation of deity. This consists in removing concealment. There can be no direct access to deity...deity is hidden. Even primitive man knows this. On the other hand, there could be no dealings, let alone fel-lowship, with a God who remained permanently hidden. In the broadest sense, then, all religion depends on revelation...it belongs to the nature of deity to manifest itself. What really counts is the correct method.[3]

---

1. [This lecture was given at the Eranos Conference in Ascona, Switzerland, in August 1985.—Ed.]

2. William James, *The Varieties of Religious Experience: A Study in Human Nature* (New York: Vintage Books/The Library of America, 190), 55.

3. *Theological Dictionary of the New Testament*, edited by Gerhardt Kittel, translated by Geoffrey W. Bromley, vol. 3 (Grand Rapids, Mich.: William B. Eerdmans Publishing Company, 1965), 564-65.

"What really counts is the correct method." Not revelation as such is the essential but *correct* revelation, or, in James's words, "harmoniously adjusting ourselves" to the unseen order.

The definitions of correct revelation belong to theology, while the determinations of wrong, false, or deluded revelation belong to abnormal psychology and its category of paranoia (a term I shall be using to embrace paranoid, paranoiac, etc.). Particularly, this style of behavior and this type of character is where we find sincere attempts to adjust to the unseen order, lives lived to accord with revelation that must—following from our two authoritative opening statements—be granted the description of lives lived religiously. And yet paranoia is a profound, central, often disastrous, and chronic craziness. Whereas our focus shall at first be upon the incorrect, or paranoid, method of revelation, our aim intends more; for it is the supposition here that by investigation of the incorrect, or delusion, we may gain insight into the correct, or revelation. We hope to gain even a further insight so as to understand why this language of *correct* and *incorrect* appears so crucial in the contexts of both paranoia and revelation.

Psychiatry and Paranoia

Paranoia: mental derangement, madness, *délire,* lunacy. *Para + Noia:* besides-thinking, mentation that is off, faulted, *dérouté, entgleist,* distracted. According to Aeschylus (*Thebes,* 756), it was paranoia that made Jocasta and Oedipus couple. According to Euripides (*Orestes,* 822), Clytemnestra's murder was paranoia. In Plato (*Theatetus,* 195a), that dialogue concerning right thinking, paranoia is used for a person who constantly sees, hears and thinks amiss, sorting things into wrong places. For Plotinus (*Ennead* 5.8.13: 4), *paranoeteon* refers to departure from or relaxation of strict reasoning.

Though carried forward by the Hippocratic Corpus (where paranoia appears among many similar terms—*parakruein, paraphron, paraphrosyne,* etc.), the word returns in its common sense as psychiatry elaborates itself into our present modern system, particularly through Rudolph Augustin Vogel, Johann Christian Heinroth, Wilhelm Sander, Carl Friedrich Otto Westphal, Karl Ludwig Kahlbaum, and finally Emil Kraepelin, and with them the disputes as to its structure, its origins, course and prognosis, its treatment and, especially with Karl Jaspers, its essential nature. For if the essential definition of paranoia could be established, then we would indeed be able to define true madness and minister to a mind diseased. And paranoia continues to draw important minds into its web: Jacques Lacan, whose medical dissertation is on paranoia; Elias Canetti, who concludes his great work, *Crowds and Power,* with a chapter on "Rulers and Paranoiacs."[4]

In the great pageant of clinical pictures, those disturbing images that present the history of medical psychology, paranoia stands out as the one major syndrome that has not been reduced to physiology.[5] Where mania and melancholia, the schizophrenias, and even the pathic personalities are imagined to have organic bases in biogenetics or biochemistry, paranoia remains, regardless of the school defining it, truly mental, a noetic syndrome, a disorder of *nous.*[6] Because paranoia affirms the genuine

---

4. Elias Canetti, *Crowds and Power,* translated by Carol Stewart (New York: Farrar, Strauss and Giroux, 1984).

5. Obsessions, compulsions and phobias—even if major in suffering—are generally considered minor as neuroses rather than major as psychoses; or they form part of the clinical picture of one or another of the major psychiatric disorders.

On the experience and diagnosis of paranoid states, see further: Dale Alfred Peterson, "The Literature of Madness: Autobiographical Writings by Mad People and Mental Patients in England and America from 1436 to 1975" (PhD diss., Stanford University, 1977); *The Inner World of Mental Illness,* edited by Bert Kaplan (New York: Harper & Row, 1964); Morag Coate, *Beyond All Reason* (New York: J.B. Lippincott Company, 1964); Clarence G. Schulz and Rose K. Kilgalen, *Case Studies in Schizophrenia* (New York: Basic Books, 1969); Werner Leibbrand and Annemarie Wettley, *Der Wahnsinn: Geschichte der abendländischen Psychopathologie* (Freiburg: Karl Alber, 1961); Eugen Bleuler, *Affektivität, Suggestibilität, Paranoia* (Halle a. S.: Verlag von Carl Marhold, 1906; David W. Swanson, Philip J. Bohnert and Jackson Algernon Smith, *The Paranoid* (Boston: Little, Brown, 1970); Nils Retterstøl, *Prognosis in Paranoid Psychoses* (Oslo: Universitetsforlaget, 1970).

6. By assuming the influence of larger invisible structures (*nous,* mythical or Biblical gods, or the spirit as it announces itself in our cases below), I admit my method for understanding paranoia itself reflects the paranoid style. This correlation of the method with the topic is in keeping with that principle of archetypal understanding as I have been presenting it at Eranos: *similis similibus curantur;* e.g., the understanding of erotic transference ("On Psychological Creativity," *Eranos Yearbook* 35 [1966]), of hysterical phenomena ("First Adam, then Eve: Fantasies of Female Inferiority in Changing Consciousness," *Eranos Yearbook* 38 [1969]), of developmentalism ("Abandoning the Child," *Eranos Yearbook* 40 [1971]), of dreams ("The Dream and the Underworld," *Eranos Yearbook* 42 [1973]), and of abnormal psychology in general ("On the Necessity of Abnormal Psychology," *Eranos Yearbook* 43 [1974]). The way into any

possibility for Mind to become mad, that there is *Geisteskrankheit,* paranoia affirms the autonomy and incontrovertible obduracy of *Geist,* and therefore is a topic appropriate to Eranos.

The psychiatric questions—how does it originate? what is its essential structure, characteristic course and possible remedy?—locates an inquiry not only within the medical fantasy of a disease entity but also within the topos of philosophical realism (in the medieval sense) to which we, too, shall adhere in this paper even while examining individual cases. We shall be assuming that there is a referent to the term, that the term has substantial reality, that one can analyze states of mind apart from individual minds, that the universal embraces and informs the particular.

❀

Whether defined by the French as *monomanie, folie raisonnante, délire chronique,* or by German-language psychiatry as *primäre Verrücktheit,* the determinant characteristic of paranoia is the presence of delusions (*Wahnideen*). "Delusion," writes Niel Micklem, "is the psychic essence of psychosis. Paranoia presents the delusional state most immediately and openly."[7] So, paranoia is indeed the paradigmatic *mental* disorder. The delusions may be of persecution (that I am being watched, followed, taunted); of jealousy (that my wife gives signals to men behind my back); of reference—hypochondriacal, erotic, or querulous—(that various phenomena are happening to me because of others); and, fourth, delusions of grandeur or megalomania (that I am called, high-born, or shall survive a coming doom). Regardless how peculiar the delusion and how long or tenaciously it is held, we should remember what the text books all insist, that "as a rule, the behavior, the emotions and the intellect of patients so suffering are well preserved, so that if their premises were true, their general attitude and conversation would pass for nearly normal."[8] "General demeanor, talk

---

clinical picture is to become part of the picture, and this is as valid for theoretical understanding of a syndrome as it is for the therapy of an individual case suffering the syndrome. The same method applies to theory and therapy.

7. Niel Micklem, "The Intolerable Image: The Mythic Background of Psychosis," *Spring: An Annual of Archetypal Psychology and Jungian Thought* (1979): 8.

8. David Henderson and R. D. Gillespie, *A Textbook of Psychiatry,* 7th ed. (London: Oxford University Press, 1950).

and...reactions remain unaltered."[9] "Impairment in daily functioning is rare. Intellectual and occupational functioning are usually preserved, even when the disorder is chronic."[10]

Classical psychiatry defines delusion most simply as a false belief. An ordinary false belief is incorrect, but a paranoid delusion is incorrigible; it is impervious to persuasion by feeling, to logic of reason, and to evidence of the senses.

For instance, this classical psychiatric tale. A man believes he is dead. He says to his family," I am dead." The family sends him to a specialist. At once, the man and the doctor begin to argue. The doctor appeals to his feelings about life, about his family. Then the doctor reasons with him, showing the inherent contradiction in his statement, that dead persons cannot say they are dead because that is what dead means. Finally, the doctor resorts to sensate evidence. He asks the man, "Do dead men bleed?" "Of course not," says the patient, disdainful of the slow-witted simplicity of the medical mind, "everyone knows dead men can't bleed." At that, the doctor jabs the man's thumb. Patient and doctor stare at the bubble of blood. "Well, whad'ya know, doc," says the man, "dead men do bleed!"

Incorrigible. Perceptions and reasonings support rather than contradict that he is dead. Feeling, reason, and fact contribute to explanatory, systematized defenses of the primary experience, a primary experience that is a state of knowledge, a noetic reality into which the patient is fixed and which gives meaning to all other events. "... the environment offers a world of new meanings. All thinking is a thinking about meanings...There is an immediate, intrusive knowledge of the meaning, and it is this which is itself the delusional experience."[11] Paranoia is a meaning disorder.

And now the question: Can we distinguish *delusion*—this "immediate intrusive knowledge," this "moment of fixation" so that "awareness

9. Lawrence C. Kolb, *Modern Clinical Psychiatry* (Philadelphia: W. B. Saunders, 1977), 481.

10. *Diagnostic and Statistical Manual of Mental Disorder,* 3rd ed. (DSM-III) (Washington, D.C.: American Psychiatric Association, 1980), 195.

11. Karl Jaspers, *General Psychopathology,* translated by J. Hoenig and Marian W. Hamilton (Chicago: The University of Chicago Press, 1963), 99.

313 / INHUMAN RELATIONS

of meaning, and so of reality, becomes deluded"[12] from *revelation*, as defined by Richard Niebuhr: "Revelation means this intelligible event which makes all other events intelligible."[13]

We shall now review three cases with an eye toward distinguishing delusion from revelation.

Three Cases

Our first case is that of Anton Boisen, Presbyterian minister, author of many works in psychopathology, pastoral psychology, and religion, who published in 1960 the account of his breakdown forty years previous.[14] In his foreword, Boisen writes: "I offer this as a case of valid religious experience which was at the same time madness of the most profound and unmistakable variety." At the age of forty-four, before assuming his first Church, he sequestered himself in order to examine his religious experience and formulate a Statement of Belief (78). As he was writing the Statement, he notes afterward, there occurred in the third paragraph a "transition into an abnormal state" (81). He pinpoints an exact moment: "Suddenly there came surging into my mind with tremendous power this idea" (81) "that the weak and the imperfect should be willing to give their lives, the imperfect for the perfect and the weak for the strong...that the family should consist of four and not of two, of the strong and the perfect and of the guardian angels" (80). "Along with this came a curious scheme which I copied down mechanically and kept repeating, as if learning a lesson" (81): a four-square scheme of the weak, the strong, the perfect, and imperfect (82, 88). "The impact was terrific, and I felt myself caught up, as it were, into another world" (82).

"Everything then began to whirl. It seemed the world was coming to an end. Some sort of change was due. Only a few tiny atoms we call 'men' were to be saved. I was to be one of these. I might, however, be of help to others" (83).

Three days later, Boisen was brought to the Boston Psychopathic Hospital, and he remained under medical attention for fifteen months,

---

12. Micklem, "The Intolerable Image," 7.

13. H. Richard Niebuhr, *The Meaning of Revelation* (Louisville: Westminster John Knox Press, 2006), 50.

14. Anton T. Boisen, *Out of the Depth: An Autobiographical Study of Mental Disorder and Religious Experience* (New York: Harper, 1960).

at times violent—singing and shouting and pounding on the glass (87, 94). He talked of dying that he might be born again (107); repeatedly he rammed his head into a brick wall (106) and tried to drown in the tub room where he spent many days in vigil on the floor. In the first letter he wrote together with his Statement of Belief, Boisen says, "the motive that has sustained me throughout this whole affair is the conviction that I was really acting in obedience to a divine command" (85). He remained dominated by the "idea of impending world disaster and...the family of four," which became a circulatory quaternal diagram leading to a center (88). The family of four would be a means of preventing syphilitic infection (119). During this period of intense delusional ideation, "it seemed that the world was all ears, and the words which I had spoken would bring about my undoing" (86); he "succeeded in climbing into the sun" and was persistently occupied with the moon (100), where he found himself at times and "where all interests were frankly and openly concerned with...reproduction and sex...upon one's advent in the moon the sex was likely to change and...doctors tried to determine whether you were a man or a woman." He was discovered to be neither (94), though he believed that sacrifice meant "becoming a woman" (89) and that he was the woman Magdalen and had "to go insane in order to get married" (89). He further believed that "he must descend to the lowest possible level" and often took up postures naked on the floor (120), provoking the attendants to beat him severely (100).

Boisen was continuously engaged in thinking, often of plans for defeating his enemies that required "constant watchfulness" (120). The doctors were not be trusted. "Everything had some deeper meaning. The patients...the attendants and the doctors. The different kinds of food all stood for something...and it was always difficult to know what to eat and what not to eat" (120). He was engaged in a great cosmic event, "new worlds were forming. There was music everywhere and rhythm and beauty" (89). A little lamb was being born in a room upstairs (90), and, at the same time, a terrible world disaster was taking place—"Christian civilization seems doomed" (119)—all of which produced a "titanic struggle that was still undecided" and depended at times on him alone (107). For guidance, he opened the Bible at random (53–54), concluding, in looking back forty years, that "something more than coincidence was here involved...Those passages of Scripture bore with amazing directness upon the questions uppermost in mind." (200).

Boisen recovered. His account of recovery includes, of course, insight into the disorder. By insight, here, I mean a shift or trope within a revelation so that the same idea takes on a different sense. This shift is precisely what we are in search of, for it would be nothing less than a means for distinguishing between the correct or religious and incorrect or psychopathological method of revealing. The delusions convinced Boisen that "the psychopathic ward was the meeting place between this world and the world beyond" (119), and that he had broken open a wall between medicine and religion (91, 119). He considered recovery to derive, not from reestablishing the wall that repudiates the delusions but by *"faithful carrying through of the delusion itself"* (101) because of "the curative forces of the religion which was largely responsible for the disturbed condition" (99). The contents of the delusions he lists (204–5) as ideas of rebirth, self-sacrifice, death and world disaster, mystical identification with the cosmos, and prophetic mission are authentically religious and as such are the sources of both the paranoid affliction and recovery from it. In his life, Boisen maintained the opening in the wall between medicine and religion, faithfully carrying out his delusion, which was as well his calling.

From Boisen's account we can garner three factors that made his revelation incorrect (Kittel), made inharmonious his adjustment to the hidden order (James). First, he says, "I went too far and attempted to universalize my own experience" (104–5). Second, "The fundamental fallacy was the assumption that an idea carried authority because of the way in which it came" (98). "They came surging into my mind with such a rush" (99). Third, these ideas "derived their authority from the fact that they were absolutely different from anything I had thought of or heard before" (ibid.).

In short, I gather from Boisen that revelation appears in the psychopathic ward when it has been universalized, comes with a rush of enthusiasms, and discloses itself as utterly other and novel. He attributes these fallacies to himself—the usual *mea culpa* of imperfect man.[15] But, if this is

---

15. This habit of taking the blame on oneself, so compensatory to the inflation of revelation, is one of the main delusions in Christian revelations. The spirit that speaks is highest authority, correct, and incontestable. Cf. Karl Jaspers, *Philosophical Faith and Revelation*, translated by E. B. Ashton (New York: Harper & Row, 1967): "Revelation comes from another source...no human ascertainment can say whether or what it is" (8). "We can define revelation as a direct manifestation of God by

how the revelations came, then why blame only the recipient? Could the source not as well lie in the very nature of revelation?

When paranoid delusions are religious in content and style, then religion offers shelter to paranoia. The god in the disorder both brings it and takes it away; but the god is not driven off with the disease if we are faithful, as Boisen says, to the delusion itself. Recovery means recovering the divine from within the disorder, seeing that its content is authentically religious. These delusions may, *a posteriori* upon analysis, be psychogenic; phenomenologically, nonetheless, they are theogenic, originate in a god. They are not just mental, but also *noetic*. We may attribute them not only to the unseen psychodynamics (unconscious) of the human mind, but also to the dynamics of the unseen order itself. Rilke need not lose his angels, since the psychopathic ward is also a place of epiphany; the disciplines endured there are of the spirit, the enclosure also a theology school.

The hospital as place to learn about the hidden god by means of delusions is the main theme of our next case.

This second case, that of John Perceval, is again a careful autobiography of paranoid disorder. John Perceval, born in 1803, was the son of the British Prime Minister, Spencer Perceval, assassinated in the House of Commons in 1812. Like Boisen's youth, Perceval's, too, was troubled by religious questions.

We cannot find that exact moment when Perceval's delusions commenced, inasmuch as prayer and fasting as well as visions and enthusiasms among a sect immediately preceded his incarceration, lasting three years (1831–34).[16] The criteria of paranoid insanity anyway are often

word, command, action, or event...All this happens by an objective invasion from without" (17). This allows only the frailty of the earthly vessel, the recipient's *mea culpa*, to account for the long history of "incorrect" revelations: demon possessions, hysterias, false prophets, and the paranoid delusions we are considering here. Cf. Keith Thomas, *Religion and the Decline of Magic: Studies in Popular Beliefs in Sixteenth and Seventeenth-Century England* (London: Penguin, 1991), ch. 5: "Prayer and Prophecy."

16. *Perceval's Narrative: A Patient's Account of his Psychosis, 1830–1832*, edited by Gregory Bateson (Stanford: Stanford University Press, 1961). (Originally published 1838–1840 in 2 volumes as *A Narrative of the Treatment Experienced by a Gentleman during*

social: within a sect, behaviors and experiences are less markedly bizarre and more conformist with norms of the sect than when displayed alone or in usual secular life.

Perceval does mark a specific moment, December 19, when, having been invited to dinner, he "would have it that I was to speak in an unknown tongue, and to do other marvellous feats before this family, in order to convince them" of his religious doctrines (27). "I was in a state of great excitement...urged and led to attempt utterances and singing...it is said in Scripture that the disciples should do wonders, and...it came into my head to put my hand into the fire" (28). He then awoke in the night with voices addressing him and raging conflict in his body "between Satan and Jesus." Like Boisen, he was ordered to take "a position on the floor" (29). He perceived his body to be one half white and one half scarlet (30). A physician was called. Perceval was placed in a leather straitjacket.

Perceval's account fills two volumes. The contents elaborate the pattern we saw in Boisen: inner torment; voices, violence, singing, suicide attempts; fascination with the bathing tubs; submission to degradations ("I almost ceased...to resist any temptation, and gave myself up to every low, grovelling, base, often savage feeling and thought that came upon me" (308); wanton, lewd, and lascivious scenes (151); persuasion that "the time of the end was at hand" (11), and ever-present reference to the Holy Ghost, Almighty, or the Divine; a bitter, angry hatred for the hypocrisy of his physicians whose medical measures sought to reduce the patient to "self-repudiation" (xiii); an urge to wrestle and kiss his keeper (280) and love for another man (170); and, of course, immensely cumbersome deliberations that turned on the meanings of everything and the intentions of the thoughts, the suggestions and commands to which he was perpetually subject. His narrative is descriptive of a mind working desperately, ceaselessly at understanding the "intravagance" of what he is being forced to think, witness, hear, and obey.

Perceval writes:

> I was not now aware that I was lunatic...I imagined...that I was placed here *"to be taught of the spirits,"* that is (for they all spoke in

---

a State of Mental Derangement: Designed to Explain the Causes and the Nature of Insanity and to Expose the Injudicious Conduct Pursued Towards Many Unfortunate Sufferers Under that Calamity.

different keys, tones, and measures, imitating usually the voices of relations and friends), to learn what was the nature of each spirit... whether a spirit of fun, of humour, of sincerity of honesty, of honour, of hypocrisy, of perfect obedience, or what not, and to acquire knowledge to answer to... each, as they in turn addressed me. (60)

He was, as he says, "surrounded by spiritual bodies" (285), personified spirits in the form of his asylum companions, who then were named Honesty, Simplicity, Contrition, Joviality, "according to their characters" (267). Qualities of character have a history of personification going back as far as Theophrastus. He was learning the psychology of character, how to notice individual physiognomies, differentiate his feeling perceptions by means of daily intercourse with spiritual bodies who were as well his fellow inmates and keepers. He was, in short, being taught to discern the spirits, *diakrisis.*

Boisen's experience was similar:"The patients around me were embodiments of good and bad spirits" (120). The discerning of spirits is a religious gift, a sign of Spirit (according to Paul [1 Corinthians 12:7–11]) like the gift of healing, of knowledge, of speaking in tongues, the working of miracles, and so on. The religious interpretation that both Boisen and Perceval give to their paranoid delusions implies that the entire humanistic, secular approach to therapy will be experienced by the patient as the workings of the anti-Christ, because it wilfully ignores, and attempts to subdue, the noetic, spiritual quality of the revelations. We can draw the lesson for our own times and our own work that attempts at humanizing patients through group therapy and feeling encounters will miss the mark so long as these measures do not at the same time recognize what the delusions themselves state: people are not merely people, humans not merely humans; bodies are also embodiments, disclosing in their characteristics and looks archetypal presentations of spirit. An individual human person is also always the bearer of eternal verities that nonsecular, nonagnostic psychology perceives as *daimones* or spirits.

It is, however, to his notion of cure that I want to draw your special attention. Remember Boisen, when reviewing his cure, stated: "I went too far and attempted to universalize my own experience." Boisen also noticed within a few months of the initial onset that "things are working out more literally than I had anticipated. It makes life a very stern and exacting affair" (111). Perceval makes much of both these points: universalism and literalism. He writes:

> I suspect that many of the delusions which ... insane persons labour under consist in their mistaking a figurative or a poetic form of speech for a literal one ... the spirit speaks poetically, but the man understands it literally. Thus you will hear one lunatic declare that he is made of iron, and that nothing can break him ... The meaning of the spirit is, that this man is strong as iron ... but the lunatic takes the literal sense ... his imagination not being under his own control ... it does not follow that things seen in the spirit are to be practised in the flesh. (270–71, 307)

Again, he writes :

> Thus, lunacy is also the mistaking of a command that is spiritual for that which is literal—command which is mental for one that is physical, and so I conceive when I was commanded to kiss and wrestle with Herminet Herbert, the intention was to cultivate such and such dispositions to him, not practically to put the words in execution. (279)

Perceval here opens a way to understand that paranoid reaction called homosexual panic, perhaps psychotic panic in general. It goes hand-in-hand with psychotic concretism. Panic implies a single-minded, only-natural perception, what Perceval calls "physical." As when you panic you literalize, so when you literalize you are susceptible to the panic of putting "words in execution," a premetaphorical reaction: the Arcadian fundamentalism of Pan.[17] An unreflected primordial response, the "all-or none" reaction is always immediate to the mind embedded in the only-natural. Pan, the great god of natural reactions, desired above all others Silene, the moon of reflected light and measured rhythm. So lunacy, by virtue of its intense mentation, sophisticates, distilling in the constrictions and regulations of the asylum the panicky compulsions of primary materiality into the cultivation of "dispositions."

17. See my "An Essay on Pan," in James Hillman, *Pan and the Nightmare* (Thompson Conn.: Spring Publications, 2020), on "Panic."

Perceval's education into psychic reality, into the distinction between spirit and letter—and their confusion, which, in modern terms, becomes "acting-out"—took him beyond that naive understanding of Christian psychology that identifies mind and action: "everyone who looketh on a woman to lust after hath committed adultery with her already" (Matthew 5:28).

In fact, when "the express image of a female of great beauty, married to one of my friends, appeared" to Perceval while "lying on the grassy bank in my wretched prison-yard," unites with him and fills him with comfort (308), Perceval receives this image and those of other naked females "in actions of refined voluptuousness" (306) as subtle body. They are taken as imaginal figures, images that heal.

The noetic distinctions of imagination become finally what cures him. Reflecting upon his three years, he presents at the end of his narrative his theory of lunacy.

> I conceive therefore that lunacy is also a state of confusion of understanding, by which the mind mistakes the commands of a spirit of humour, or of irony, or of drollery; that many minds are in this state; that, perhaps, this is the state of every human mind...I mean that in the operations of the human intellect, the Deity...often intimates his will by thus jesting, if I may be allowed to call it so...that in the misapprehending or perverting of this form of address may consist original sin; or that such misapprehension...is the first consequence of original sin (if such there be)...making false every future deliberation, and conception, and action. Hence, I imagine, it is, that those who profess religion are often so hypocritical. (281)

He then explains his own agonizing ambivalence of wanting and not wanting at the same time, an ambivalence that tortured him all through his delusional states. He continues:

> Hence, I imagine, also, arises the great mystery spoken of by St. Paul, "That which I would, I do not—that which I do, I allow not" ...because the mind of man, fallen from a state of grace, thinks in a spirit of humour, as if that spirit were a spirit of truth. (281)

> For this, again, is...lunacy, to mistake a spirit of humour...for a spirit of sincerity, or, as the French say, to take it *"au pied de la lettre."* (275)

Quite a revelation! Fallen man is sincere man is insane man; for, having lost the spirit of humor, which is the state of grace, he takes the levity of God's spirit for the gravity of truth. From levity to gravity: this is the Fall.

❀

Perceval—without of course saying so directly—arrives here at the ety-mology of delusion: *de-ludere*, to play with, to mock, taunt, as if the spirit speaks playfully, ludicrously, allusively. The spirit speaks delusionally, let us say, or paranoetically: the Word is elliptical, parabolic, jesting, playing with our defining minds. The spirit's speech becomes psychiatrically delu-sional when heard as truth, command, mission, prophesy. The Almighty thinks in the spirit of humor, a trickster god; God, a child playing games (Heraclitus, ed. Diels-Kranz, fr. 52); God playing with Satan over Job. God, darkened with Mercurius, as Jung would say. Perceval writes that he "obeyed the spirit of humor, which made me try to deceive my spirits" (113). (As for the grace of humor, I would remind you of David Miller's lecture on comedy here ten years ago:[18] the return of Eranos to the same eternal themes.)

Perceval concludes: "The Almighty condescended to heal by the imagination that which, by tricks on the imagination, he had wounded, broken and destroyed" (308). He was learning not to repudiate the delu-sions, to drive them out, but, as Boisen said: "The cure has lain in the faithful carrying through of the delusion itself"—as *de-fusion*, however, in a playful mode, learning to elude the delusions, to trick the trickster, using imagination to cure imagination.

He even declares:

> When I grew older in my afflictions, I found that no patient could escape from his confinement in a truly sound state of mind with-out...admitting...that deception and duplicity are consistent with a sound conscience I could not seek health by sane conduct. I could not recover sanity, but by ways which can alone be justi-fied by insanity. (125)

So, Perceval, when summing up his cure, suddenly uses an extended metaphorical conceit of Mercurius and the two serpents of his wand as the

---

18. David L. Miller, "Images of Happy Ending," *Eranos Yearbook* 44 (1975): 61–89.

male and female constituents of two-sided human nature. "The weaker or more feminine" brings "humour, mirth, and merrymaking [which] are necessary to the mind's pliability" (311). He lived into his seventies and, like Boisen, married after his release, maintaining, like Boisen, into old age an active concern with lunacy laws (viii) and the plight of lunatics. This is social interest: *Gemeinschaftsgefühl.*

At the end of *Perceval's Narrative,* we find that our author still sees visions and hears voices. Persons speak in his dreams. Cure does not consist in their eradication. He relates these phenomena with imagination: "I did not heed them more than I would my own thoughts, or than I would dreams, or the ideas of others" (329). He refuses to literalize even his own hard-won understanding of psychic reality: "Neither do I pretend to determine what was the nature of the influences by which I was misguided. Others may expect, that as I profess to be of sound mind, I ought to be able to express a decided opinion; but I consider...that I should not be of sound mind if I did not hesitate...I leave it to others to determine... [those influences]" (326). Above all, he has learned to doubt, and is of sound mind since it was to his inability or lack of doubt that he attributed the root cause of his insanity. "I perished from an habitual error of mind, common to many believers...that *of fearing to doubt*" (37).

At the very end, he says, he was tempted in view of his long suffering to play an *imitatio Christi,* "but I resolutely refused...with all the defects, as well as all the sincerity of a natural man—a plain and very weak Englishman" (329). So concludes *Perceval's Narrative.*

❀

Our last case of three, the most famous self-description in the literature, is that of *Senatspräsident* Daniel Paul Schreber, born in Leipzig in 1842. His *Denkwürdigkeiten eines Nervenkranken,* published in 1903, recounts nine years in clinics, 1893–1902.[19]

---

19. Daniel Paul Schreber, *Memoirs of My Nervous Illness,* translated by Ida MacAlpine and Richard A. Hunter (London: Dawson, 1955). (Pagination follows the original German edition as indicated in the Dawson edition). Further on Schreber: Roberto Calasso, *L'impuro folle* (Milano: Adelphi, 1974); Morton Schatzman, *Soul Murder: Persecution in the Family* (New York: Random House, 1973); C. Barry Chabot, *Freud on Schreber: Psychoanalytic Theory and the Critical Act* (Amherst: University of Massachusetts Press, 1982).

Schreber writes toward the beginning of his five-hundred page
volume:

> The voices which talk to me have daily stressed ever since the
> beginning of my contact with God (mid-March 1894) [notice
> again the attempt to fix an exact date of onset]:[20] the fact that the
> crisis that broke upon the realms of God was caused by somebody
> having committed soul murder. (23)

Soul murder has since become the title of a book explaining Schreber's
case in terms of his childhood when his soul was supposedly murdered by a
cruelly repressive father (remembered pleasantly for having invented
the *Schrebergarten*), who promulgated an *Erziehungslehre* with mechanical
restraints—his *Pangymnastikon* was an early Nautilus machine fitness program—the aim of which was *"direktes Niederkämpfen"* of desire in childhood.

Instead, we turn to Schreber's adulthood, to his most passionate and
sustained achievement, his memoirs, the content of the psychosis, in accordance with Jung's method, attempting both to envisage what the patient
experiences and to account for these experiences as the patient accounts
for them. If we listen to a patient's contents, why not also the patient's
carefully constructed thoughts about the contents? These, too, are contents. To stick with the images, to be phenomenological, means also to
listen to the delusions explaining the delusions. Essential to paranoia is
the patient's meaning of it, his thought about it. And this thought cannot
be separated from the delusions. "[T]he thought of revelation rests upon
the revelation itself."[21] "Revelation...is the premise of all reasoning."[22]
The delusions invite their own theoretical account, which, because of the
religious content of the delusions, is nothing else than a theology. "The
understanding of original revelation is what we call theology."[23] Religious megalomania brings a megalomanic theology. Theology becomes

---

20. The attempts to date onset, that is, to fix precisely the fixating moment, that
we have seen in the three cases and in many others attested to in the literature, raises
the thought that historical dating may be a paranoid gesture. What are we doing,
psychologically, when we fixate the flow of events and their many conditions into a
precise moment of origin? Perhaps we need to look again and with a psychiatric eye
at the fantasies of *Quellenforschung, fons et origo,* and *Urtext.*

21. Jaspers, *Philosophical Faith and Revelation,* 22.

22. Ibid., 27.

23. Ibid., 21.

the container, the keeper, of the paranoid experience. Boisen said he was acting"in obedience to a divine command."[24] Schreber writes that it was his "holy time": "Owing to my illness I entered into peculiar relations with God." Schreber was engaged during those nine years in a monumental task: "I had to solve one of the most intricate problems ever set for man and that I had to fight a sacred battle for the greatest good of mankind" (146). This battle was to understand the conflict in the realm of God and the "Order of the World." The crisis in the order was due to the fact that God was ignorant of living human beings: "He was accustomed to dealing only with corpses or at best human beings lying asleep (dreaming). Thus arose the almost monstrous demand that I should behave continually as if I myself were a corpse" (141). God "saw living human beings *only from without.*" "His omnipresence and omniscience did not extend within *living* man" (30). He was, in our terms, not psychological, not existential, not phenomenological. This was a huge fault in the Order of the World, and Schreber was called to solve this problem within God—nothing less than re-ordering the cosmos that, again in our terms, means making God conscious of His failings. Communication with the forecourts of Heaven, with the upper and lower gods (Ahriman and Ormuzd), and the little people (*flüchtig hingemachte Männer*) occurred by means of nerve rays, nerve language, *Grundsprache,* and *das Aufschreibesystem* (126) that eventually became the *Memoirs*—but all this had essentially a theological task. The thorough re-ordering of God and the World thoroughly disordered Schreber even while "testing" his soul (14).

These basic religious ideas allowed Schreber to survive his torment. "I can only see," he writes near the end of his book, "a real purpose in my life if I succeed in putting forward the truth of my so-called delusions so that...mankind gain a truer insight into the nature of God" (p. 352).

The torment follows the pattern we have already seen in Boisen and Perceval: violence and suicide attempts; bellowing and singing; preoccupation with meanings while ambivalent in actions; painful though miraculous operations upon the organs of the body; sleepless vigils; degradations; solar fascination and *Mondscheinseligkeit;* thoughts of world catastrophe and visions of beauty; faith in his individual importance—"my person has become the center of divine miracles" (252)—fierce hatred and

24. Boisen, *Out of the Depth,* 85.

distrust focused upon physicians; learning to communicate with spirits—and all the while a ceaseless, intense, perplexing concentration upon
God's meaning, the agony of theologizing, amid the long monotony of
outward life. "The reason for my immobility . . . that I considered absolute
passivity almost a religious duty" (141).

Erotic sexuality permeates Schreber's delusions. He calls it voluptuousness and its aim, *Entmannung*. This component is also present in both Boisen's and Perceval's accounts. Bleuler has written that uncertain sexual
identity (gender ambiguity, neutrality, or androgyny) is present in nearly
all cases of paranoid schizophrenia. But already here, before we return
to this theme, let us be careful to distinguish between unmanning and
voluptuous effeminization on the one hand, and homosexual desire on
the other.

Schreber's process of *Entmannung* began even before the idea of soul
murder, before the breakdown in November and the special contact with
God. Schreber reports this dreamlike experience:

> One morning while still in bed . . . I had a feeling which . . . struck
> me as highly peculiar. It was the idea that it really must be rather
> pleasant to be a woman succumbing to intercourse. This idea was
> so foreign to my whole nature that . . . I would have rejected it with
> indignation, if fully awake. (36)

"This idea was so foreign to my whole nature" recalls Schreber, saying his ideas were so absolutely different from anything he had thought
before. The otherness of the idea, not mine, not made up by me, striking
as a force without anticipation; an annunciation of the *totaliter aliter* as
an intelligible event that makes all other events intelligible (Niebuhr's
definition of revelation). This sudden disclosure of otherness in a full-
formed idea that I experience as external to me, gives supreme spiritual
authority to the idea. It's ground—alien to my feeling, to tradition, to
reason—is wholly other, *the* wholly other, the incorrigible and numinous
ground of God.[25]

---

25. Karl Barth describes revelation as: "The 'instant' is and remains something
unique in comparison to what preceded and what followed it, it is different, strange,
does not extend itself in what follows, nor does it have its roots in what went before.
It stands in no temporal, causal or logical relation, it is always and everywhere the
absolutely new, always the being, the having and doing of God." *Der Römerbrief,*
quoted from H. Martin Rumscheidt, *Revelation and Theology: An Analysis of the Barth-
Harnack Correspondence of 1923* (Cambridge: Cambridge University Press, 1972),

Of course, delusions do not suffer correction any more than do revelations. "Every historic example shows that revelation is established only by itself, not by anything else."[26] Of course, I must ask what claim has this idea on me, who am I that this has come to me, what is my signal role? And so begins from that fixating moment (Micklem), that *Schlüsselerlebnis* (Kretschmer) in mid-March, or October 6 or December 19, the recognizable features of megalomania: epiphanic onset, prophetic anxiety of cosmic reordering, fundamentalist incorrigibility, grandeur of my singled-out person and singleness of vision or *monomanie*, and the passionate theologizing, that is, systematized explanations of the primary revelation or *primäre Verrücktheit.*

In Schreber's case, necessary to the cosmic reordering and concomitant with it through the nine years in hospital and even after was the process, at first agonizing, then evermore pleasurable, of *Entmannung,* unmanning, which means not emasculation in the narrowest sense but removal from the category of men (51). Schreber experienced retraction of the male member, rudimentary female genitalia, swelling of the breasts, quickening of the embryo. Voices called him Miss Schreber. His stature diminished, taking on the appearance of the female form and, after release, he continued to cultivate "femaleness" by wearing ribbons and jewelry, by sewing, dusting and making beds, and by contemplating pictures of naked women.

Unmanning did not intend the love of men, homoeros in the literal, homosexual sense. Its intention was not effeminization so much as anima, soul, and it proceeded by voluptuousness, an ever developing *voluptas;* Voluptas, the child in the belly of pregnant Psyche in Apuleius's tale. Voluptuousness "is the soul's form of existence within the Order of the World" (332). "This state of Blessedness is mainly a state of voluptuous enjoyment (*Wollust*), which...needs the fantasy of either being or wishing to be a female being" (337). "Manly contempt of death,

---

153–54. The possible confusion of revelation and delusion was put to Barth by Adolf von Harnack in "Frage 3" of his fifteen questions. Barth replied that the faith awakened by God is "practically indistinguishable from uncontrolled fanaticism. But why could it not be a...confused symptom of and testimony to the awakening of faith?" (ibid., 32).

26. Jaspers, *Philosophical Faith and Revelation,* 28.

as expected of men...such as soldiers and especially officers in war-time, is not in the soul's nature" (333).

> There are periods everyday, when I float in voluptuousness...an indescribable feeling of well-being corresponding to feminine feelings...It is by no means always necessary to let my imagination play on sexual matters; on other occasions, too, like reading a particularly moving part of a poem, playing a piece of music on the piano which particularly pleases me aesthetically, or enjoying nature...soul-voluptuousness creates...a kind of foretaste of Blessedness. (336)

As you may know, Schreber returned to wife and home in 1902 (at age 60). He functioned as a lawyer for some five years; published his book. Two weeks after his wife died in 1907, he was readmitted to a mental hospital, where he died forty months later at age 68.

Schreber was not cured; Perceval was. From Perceval we can begin to understand why Schreber wasn't. Both men's accounts are *récits*, at least partly in Corbin's sense,[27] that is, written witnesses to imaginal experiences of revelation, yet the two accounts differ. Perceval says that the spirit speaks poetically and the lunatic takes the literal sense. For Perceval, lunacy is literalism, literalism is lunacy. But Schreber writes that he often observed souls or rays appearing as diminutive little men: "One must assume therefore that the capacity to be transformed into human shape...is an innate potentiality of divine rays. An entirely new light is thus shed on the Bible; 'He created man in His image'...this passage from the Bible has to be understood *literally*, which no human being has so far dared to do" (256).

Furthermore, where Perceval overcame his fear to doubt, Schreber confesses (29) that he was a doubter "until divine revelation taught me better." At the end of his account, Perceval speaks of himself as a "plain and very weak Englishman." Schreber, at the end of his account, offers "*my person as object of scientific observation for the judgment of experts,*" including the "*dissection of my body,*" which will provide stringent proof" (358). As literalism is lunacy, so is mission. Perceval modified mission into concern for

---

27. Henry Corbin, *Avicenna and the Visionary Recital,* translated by Willard R. Trask (Princeton, N.J.: Princeton University Press, 1990), 42–44; *Creative Imagination in the Sūfism of Ibn 'Arabī*, translated by Ralph Manheim (Princeton, N.J.: Princeton University Press, 1981), 21–22.

lunatics. Schreber literalized mission into substantiating evidence for his private claim.

Schreber—after nine years—does recognize mockery and jesting in the delusions, saying, "a kind of practical joke is played with the things I most commonly use" (352). This jesting ambiguity appears significantly in what Schreber calls "the system of not-finishing-a-sentence," "unfinished ideas, or only fragments of ideas," which "became more and more prevalent in the course of years" (217).

Perceval was similarly afflicted in language: "...in the midst of my sentence...words have been suggested contradictory of those that went before; and I have been deserted, gaping, speechless, or stuttering in great confusion" (269). "One word is put for another, and one letter transposed with another, and as the mind by a positive law always thinks in contraries at the same time...the word made use of by mistake is the contrary to that intended. The universal for the particular—the affirmative for the negative, and the like" (290). "He who rules the imagination has the power to...cover written or printed words with other words or letters that are not there...and it generally happens in little words that will derange the whole sense of a sentence; such as *no*, for *yes*...*unlike*, for *like*; or in words similar, *humour,* for *honour*; *quack,* for *quick*; and *sample,* for *simple*" (310).

Self-contrary, punning, aphoristic, incomplete fragments would make literalism impossible right at its roots, in the words and letters themselves. The symptom proposes the cure of the syndrome. Philosophy is still trying to establish what Heraclitus's fragments literally mean, even though Heraclitus himself is reported to have said (ed. Diels-Kranz, fr. 93) that speech that originates in spirit is neither hidden nor revealed, but hinted. Neither hiddenness nor revelation. These opposites confound. Instead: hint, suggestion, allusion.

This "broken speech...the vein of poetry that would run through his discourse"[28] is being offered to Schreber in the "system-of-not-finishing-a-sentence," presenting as well the linguistic style of continuous creation, the Word as open-ended, incomplete, the statement not finished. Schreber, however, says it was "left to my nerves to complete the fragments in a manner satisfactory to a thinking mind" (217). By writing his *Memoirs* into sentences, turning the *Aufschreibesystem* into a publishable book—at first

---

28. *Perceval's Narrative,* 219.

conceived only as a private account for his wife—Judge Schreber fixes beliefs into the completed statements of his madness. His book turns him into "The Schreber Case." While writing his Statement of Belief, Boisen first went insane. Revelation written into rational statements may become theology, and it also may become insanity.

Freud and Jung

Because Daniel Paul Schreber has been named "the most famous patient in psychiatry,"[29] and because Sigmund Freud has been the most frequently quoted psychoanalyst in medical psychology, tradition obliges us to look at what that analyst said about that patient.

Freud's analysis of Schreber's memoirs and Freud's subsequent papers on paranoia interpret the four major configurations of paranoid delusions as modes of denying homoerotic desire. Freud does not include in his schema *Abstammungswahn, sensitiver Beziehungswahn,* hypochondriacal delusions, litigious querulousness, or other delusions named for their main contents or styles. These, however, could be subsumed within one or another of the classical four (outlined below) of which we have been engaged with these three: delusions of grandeur or megalomania; of erotic reference ("everything that happens is in reference to me," said Schreber); and of persecution whether by enemies, physicians, family, spirits or God.

Of the four, megalomania seems to be the more encompassing and even of another order in that the delusions of reference and persecution, in all three of our cases followed necessarily from the primary religious grandiosity. Their other torments and mentations derived directly from their special relation with God. Were we to conform with Freud's method of reducing all paranoia to a single etiology (denial of homoerotic desire), we would rather assert that etiology to be an attempt to live harmoniously with hidden meaning, and paranoia would be defined as the demonstration of a noetic revelation lived literally.

Freud's interpretative system published in his 1911 study of the Schreber case asserts "that the familiar principal forms of paranoia can all be represented as contradictions of a single proposition: *'I* (a man) *love him* (a

---

29. Schreber, *Memoirs of My Nervous Illness,* 8.

man),' and indeed that they exhaust all the possible ways in which such contradictions could be formulated."[30]

The proposition, "*I love him*" can first be contradicted by delusions of persecution, which state: "I do not *love* him—I *hate* him." This internal perception of feeling cannot be admitted by paranoid consciousness and must therefore be experienced in projection, that is, "I do not *love* him— I *hate* him, because *he persecutes me.*"

The second form of contradiction produces delusions of erotic reference. These assert, "I do not love *him*, I love *her.*" And in obedience to the same need for projection, the proposition is transformed into: "I notice that *she* loves me." These delusions, Freud says, "invariably begin not with any internal perception of loving, but with an external perception of being loved." ("Everything that happens is in reference to me.") One feels oneself singled out, chosen, called, the object of another's desire.

"The third way in which the original proposition [I love him] can be contradicted leads us to delusions of jealousy." "It is not *I* who love the man— she loves him, and a man suspects the woman in relation to all the men whom he himself is tempted to love."[31] The fourth contradiction "rejects

---

30. Sigmund Freud, "Psycho-Analytical Notes upon an Autobiographical Account of a Case of Paranoia (Dementia Paranoides)," in *CP3*; and "A Case of Paranoia Running Counter to the Psycho-Analytical Theory of the Disease," in *CP2*.

31. I have omitted delusions of infidelity or morbid jealousy for several reasons: a) our three cases were spared this suffering; b) morbid jealousy is the least severe form prognostically and therefore less essential to paranoia; c) it is often an accompaniment of organic factors such as alcoholism, and therefore may lie partly outside a wholly psychological account such as ours. My fourth reason takes some explaining. Infidelity delusions seem to present a defense against the divine. The divine aspect of Eros is displaced to the human, from faith in divine Eros to human erotic faithfulness that divinizes a wife, husband, lover—and especially the invisible imagined third party—in place of Eros, the god. It is this divinization that makes the fantasy of infidelity archetypally loaded, hence unbearable, and personally concrete at the same moment. The fundamental infidelity—deserting and being deserted by the god—that infidelity, which is a source of humanism, becomes an agonizing personal experience, so that jealousy, like any other morbid psychological symptom, is a compromise. The symptom attempts to recover the god by divinizing the other person without whose erotic faithfulness I cannot live. To see it this way implies that morbid jealousy, too, is a religious delusion, even if secularized beyond recognition as such, a secularization that is its very ground. For what the erotic fantasies of

the proposition as a whole." As I suggested above, it is of another order, total, megalomanic in its form. This contradiction states: "*I do not love at all—I do not love anyone.*" Yet, says Freud, "libido must go somewhere, [thus] this proposition seems to be the psychological equivalent of the proposition: 'I love only myself.' So that this kind of contradiction would give us megalomania" (*CP*3: 451).

I do not intend to dispute Freud but, rather, to enlist the contents of his interpretative system in what I shall be subsequently presenting. Freud's two essential contents are: first, that the material cause is homoerotic desire, the desire of sames, of like for like; and second, that the formal cause of paranoid delusions is noetic. The desire is converted, or subverted, by logic, using the transcendent laws of thought (principle of contradiction, assertion by proposition, subject/object grammar). It is the noetic organization of desire that yields paranoia, not homoeroticism as such, which as Freud says contributes "to friendship and comradeship, to *esprit de corps* and to the love of mankind" (*CP*3: 447). Paranoia is indeed its very name: paranoetic, mental, cognitive, a disorder of meaning. As Perceval says, "my mind was constantly occupied" (53). This mental activity shows the formal cause at work, converting the libidinal, erotic relation to the world into a semantic, hermeneutic relation to the world. The world of *Gemeinschaftsgefühl* becomes a world of meanings. Instead of desire, meaning.

When we look very closely into Freud's theory, we discover that it is neither the material desire nor the formal denial of desire that gives rise to the disorder, but their *double literalization.* When desire is literal, then the defeat of that desire is also literal. Instances of this double literalization occur in religious practices, where concupiscence is countered by an asceticism equally literal, and in philosophy, where utilitarian materialism is countered by metaphysical idealism, which, despite its abstractions, remains nonetheless literal.

---

jealousy reveal is the supreme autonomy of whatever is divinized. The attempt to own the god, to bind its movements and locate its boundaries to this or that relationship is proven impossible by the tormenting fantasies. The invisible Other has invaded the personal pair.

Cf. Ronald Rae Mowat, *Morbid Jealousy and Murder: A Psychiatric Study of Morbidly Jealous Murderers at Broadmoor* (London: Tavistock, 1966); Gabriel Langfeldt, "The Erotic Jealousy Syndrom: A Clinical Study," *Acta Psychiatrica et Neurologica Scandinavica* (1961), suppl. 151.

In the tandem, material and formal, when either is literalized, the other follows. When fellow feeling becomes homosexuality (even if only in theory and not in concrete behavior), then the countermovement becomes equally fundamentalist, the noetic aspect literalized in Statements of Belief (Boisen), writing-down systems (Schreber), hallucinatory voices, words as shibboleths. Denial of desire as theology. Perceval's cure is illustrative of the way out. He had to distinguish the poetic intentions from the literal commands, the spirits from the bodies of his companions. Freedom from both the materialism of desire and the formalism of denial requires that middle ground of the poetic, metaphorical, humorous, deceptive, imaginal, incomplete, that moon (Boisen) where there is no gender, where consciousness is neither this nor that.

From this middle ground, Freud's explanatory scheme itself looks like a noetic formula for eluding the actual theological material in Schreber's delusions. And now we can see why Freud's theory has proved so successfully resistant to change, having been held by orthodox psychoanalysis without major objection or deviation for seventy years.[32] For it is not to be taken literally. Facts have nothing to do with it.

Although our three cases each showed homoerotic contents and confused gender identity (i.e., deliteralized gender fixation), the manifest expression of these contents was not the ground of cure. Homoeroticism and paranoia are not convertible, as if homosexuals could not be paranoid and paranoids could not also be homosexual. Both behaviors can occur without conflict in the same person (Kolb). Furthermore, only a minor percent of diagnosed paranoids present homosexual material.[33] Psychoanalytic theory, however, is not concerned with these "facts," since theory maintains that actual homosexual behavior does not eliminate the latent repressed homoeroticism in the unconscious, which remains the ground of paranoia.

---

32. For a wide review of the literature, see the annotated bibliography in Yehuda Fried and Joseph Agassi, *Paranoia: A Study in Diagnosis* (Dordrecht and Boston: D. Reidel Publishing Company, 1976); for reviews within the Freudian school, including deviations, see W. W. Meissner, "Schreber and the Paranoid Process," The Annual of Psychoanalysis 4 (1976): 3–40; Philip M. Kitay, "Symposium on 'Reinterpretation of the Schreber Case,'" *International Journal of Psychoanalysis* 44 (1963): 191–94.

33. William G. Niederland, *The Schreber Case: Psychoanalytic Profile of a Paranoid Personality* (New York: Quadrangle, 1974), 160.

Because "hard" facts are not pertinent to the Freudian schema, the enduring brilliance of its logic can transcend concrete cases. It persists because of a tight noetic structure, the root metaphor of fourfoldedness, that metaphysical fundament used by Aristotle, Schopenhauer, and Jung for a complete explanation.[34] The absolute universality of form requires an equally universal and intractable material—sexuality; as if to say, the literalized idea of homoeroticism is the necessary counterpart of the logical schema. Double literalization. We must keep in mind that occasions of paranoia are not sufficiently accounted for by actual concrete homosexuality, its presence or its absence. What the psychoanalytic account does require, or has invented, is a latent, unconscious, nonphenomenal homoeroticism—a metaphysical idea taken literally. In other words, the idea of latent homosexuality has been necessitated by the theory of paranoia. It may even be a paranoid idea.

Freud's view that Schreber's theologizing avoids sexuality converts to my view that Freud's sexualizing avoids theology. Freud's sexual explanation serves precisely the same defensive function of denial that, according

---

34. Aristotle's four causes (*Metaphysics* A), Schopenhauer's fourfold root of the principle of sufficient reason, and Jung's fourfold explanatory structures (typology, synchronicity, theology, etc.) are only three examples of a model to be found as well in the holy *tetraktys* of the Pythagoreans, the humors of Hippocratic medicine, the *quattuor coaequeva* of Augustine's theology, Eruigena's ontological division of nature, Heidegger's four principles of being, and, axiomatically, in the four directions, elements, seasons, phases of the moon, letters in the name of God, and the four-footed mythical beast on whom the world rests. Freud's account of paranoia invokes this noetic structure. And we are immovably convinced, not by empirical demonstration, but by the persuasive power of the system's internal logic, or psycho-logic, which, as Freud says, "exhaust[s] all the possible ways" ("We cannot name any beyond these," as Aristotle says, *Metaphysics* A.10). The rhetoric of an archetype convinces that there is no further question. "Whenever a fourfold root is used to circumscribe phenomena it seems to be self-evident and to include its own demonstration. Or, to push the point further, this model is used to account for the undemonstrable...the four causes of Aristotle provide explanation as the minimum requirements for total comprehension, because they are a form of the symbol of the fourfold root. This is a symbol of completion and fulfilment, the undemonstrable ground of being itself. As such it is what Jung calls a symbol of the Self. It represents a psyche which no longer asks 'why.' The question...is answered—or rather, has disappeared." James Hillman, *Emotion: A Comprehensive Phenomenology of Theories and Their Meanings for Therapy* (London: Routledge and Kegan Paul, 1960), 247–48.

to Freud, theologizing serves in Schreber: Freud's theory functions as a theology. What is specifically denied in the Freudian account is the actual subject of the memoirs: Schreber's relation with God, Schreber's manifest theology.

Caution is behovely: explanations of paranoia tend to entrap us in the very meanings we find to account for it. Paranoia seems contagious. Yet we must plunge on, danger or not, because the question with which we began—how characterize the difference between delusion and revelation —still lies before us, unanswered.

❀

Unlike Freud, Jung wrote very little directly about paranoia. Schizophrenia was his main psychiatric focus. Indirectly, however, Jung's writings offer profound instruction regarding paranoia. The instructive texts are less his early psychiatric works than his late—shall we say theological—works: *Aion: Researches into the Phenomenology of the Self* (CW9.2), "The Undiscovered Self" (CW10), "Flying Saucers: A Modern Myth of Things Seen in the Skies" (CW10), *Mysterium Coniunctionis* (CW14), "On Synchronicity" (CW8), his biography with Aniela Jaffé,[35] and especially "Answer to Job" (CW11).

Jung, too, was continually occupied with the feminization of masculine one-sidedness, whether in his enthusiasm over the Assumption of Maria, his emphasis upon Sophia, Regina, or Luna in alchemy, his many elaborations of the anima archetype, or his choice of the *Rosarium*, with its fantastical and explicitly sexual hermaphroditism for depicting the structure of psychologically fruitful relationships.

Jung also drew quaternion diagrams and laid down his own "family-of-four." And, like Schreber's division of God into Ahriman and Ormuzd, Jung, too, imagined a critical self-division within the God image, and speculated about the "inner instability of Yahweh" (CW11: 686).

Like the others we have described, Jung also experienced his thoughts and figures as autonomous. His memoirs tell how he learned "that there are things in the psyche which I do not produce, but which produce themselves and have their own life..." "In my fantasies I held conversations

---

35. C.G. Jung, *Memories, Dreams, Reflections* (MDR), edited by Aniela Jaffé; translated by Richard and Clara Winston (New York: Vintage Books, 1989).

with him, and he said things which I had not consciously thought. For I observed clearly that it was he who spoke, not I" (*MDR*, 183). "I have realized," he writes, regarding his own visions, "that one must accept the thoughts that go on within oneself of their own accord as part of one's reality…The presence of thoughts is more important than our subjective judgement of them" (*MDR*, 298).

Jung, too, used mantic rites, like Boisen opening the Bible at random; Jung, too, invented a rich, at times archaic, terminology and acknowledged the "alchemystical" and personified nature of his concepts. The *kobold*, the complex, the *daimon*, and the spirit were also his familiars.

So, let us listen now to Jung with paranoia in mind and with an ear to discerning differences between the first three cases and this fourth. First, the prophetic voice with its mission: "We are living in…the right moment—for a 'metamorphosis of the gods'…Coming generations will have to take account of this momentous transformation if humanity is not to destroy itself" (*CW*10: 585). He felt called to warn of doom: "It is not presumption that drives me," he writes in the essay on flying saucers, "but my conscience as a psychiatrist that bids me fulfil my duty and prepare those few who will hear me for coming events which are in accord with the end of an era" (*CW*10: 589).

In defense of his *Answer to Job*, Jung writes:

> Things are comparatively easy as long as God wants nothing but the fulfilment of his laws, but what if he wants you to break them…To be God's voice is not a social function anymore…what did I get for my serious struggle over *Job*…? I am regarded as blasphemous, contemptible, a fiend, whose name is mud. It fell to my lot to collect the victims of the Summum Bonum and use my own poor means to help them. (*CW*11: 1637)

While on a walk before discharge from the asylum, Perceval obeyed the instruction to "lift up my head and open my voice." To his shock he uttered horrible oaths, blasphemies and obscenities toward heaven (284). Schreber uses similar blasphemous, and coarse language; in fact, blasphemy occurs frequently in paranoid megalomania. From Jung we learn that this is an effect of the divine, as if the one called by heaven must also curse heaven. Jung says in a letter about his Job book:

> …"coarse" is mild in comparison to what you feel when God dislocates your hip or when he slays the first-born…That is *one*

side of my experiences with what is called "God." "Coarse" is too weak a word for it. "Crude," "violent," "cruel," "bloody," "hellish," "demonic" would be better.[36]

Jung, too, was convinced that the destiny of the human race and the aim of the Christian message depended upon the single individual, "that infinitesimal unit on whom the world depends" (*CW* 10: 588) and he speaks of himself as one such "individual." "*If the whole is to change, the individual must change himself*" (*CW* 10: 1378), which is precisely what Boisen and Schreber believed and were engaged in. Jung writes that "the alpha and omega of religion is the subjective individual experience" (the very justification to which Schreber ever and again appeals). "The will of God can be terrible," Jung goes on, "and can isolate you from your family and your friends and, if you are courageous or foolish enough, you may end up in the lunatic asylum. And yet how can there be religion without experience of the divine will?" (*CW* 11: 1637). And it is Jung, who in *Answer to Job* propounds an idea—blasphemous to theology and megalomanic to psychiatry—that "*the idea of the higher man* by whom Yahweh is morally defeated" (*CW* 11: 665). The individual man is supremely important because of God's egoism according to Schreber (359) or God's blindness (*CW* 11: 585–91) according to Jung.[37] And Jung, too, speaks from inner certainty against the hypocrisy of false religion, almost as if true religion were the sect of psychology. "I have a real communion only with those who have the same or similar religious experience, but not with believers in the Word...they use the Word to protect themselves against the will of God."

Let us turn to the idea of meaning to carry further the parallels between our first three cases and that of Jung. Following Karl Jaspers, paranoia is a meaning disorder: "All thinking is a thinking about meanings...*the experiences of primary delusion are analogous to this seeing of meaning.*"[38] The seeing of

---

36. C. G. Jung, *Letters,* edited by Gerhard Adler and Aniela Jaffé, 2 vols. (Princeton, N.J.: Princeton University Press, 1973), 2: 156.

37. "*Thus the ordinary man became a source of the Holy Spirit...*This fact signifies the continued and progressive divine incarnation. Thus man...seems destined to play a decisive part in it; that is why he must receive the Holy Spirit. I look upon the receiving of the Holy Spirit as a highly revolutionary fact which cannot take place until the ambivalent nature of the Father is recognized" (*CW* 11: 1551).

38. Jaspers, *General Psychopathology,* 99.

meaning was Jung's main endeavor: his was *The Myth of Meaning*, as Aniela Jaffé titled one of her books on Jung.[39] Jung extended the very idea of meaning in two directions: by his hypothesis of synchronicity that raised meaning to equal significance with space time, causality, and energy, and by claiming the autonomy of meaning, independent of human consciousness: "an *objective meaning* which is not just a psychic product" *CW* 8: 915).

The archetype of meaning in Jung's system is the Self. It follows then that paranoia as a meaning disorder is a Self disorder, and that the phenomenology of paranoia presents the pathologizings of the Self. Self phenomena have been evident all through our cases: preoccupation with God, fourfoldness, hermaphroditism, cosmic grandeur, transcendence, etc. The Self, which is the most important archetype in Jung's scale, becomes the vessel for our most important mental disorder. We turn to our individual Self symbols and experiences not only for revelations but also for elucidating our paranoia.

As one can fall into love and be possessed by eros, or fall into soul, bewitched by anima, so one can fall into meaning and be deluded by Self as witnessed in the certainties, exaltations, and conjuncted sexualities we saw in these cases, and by their contents, like Boisen's "family-of-four" diagrams or Schreber's ability to look into the sun, "*punctum solis*" (*CW* 11: 1638).

What Jung means with meaning means more than meaning usually means. Meaning transcends the explanations of meaning. He equates it with the reality of the spirit (*CW* 11: 554). Meaning is more than semantic, contextual, or even hermeneutic; it is cosmological, so that the soul's struggle with meaning, whether in Job or in each patient, is ultimately a struggle with God, the spirit, the cosmos. This extension of meaning to utmost fundaments brings to the fore precisely those contents that customarily appear in the tormented religious delusions of paranoia. Hence, the soul's quest for meaning, or, to paraphrase William James, its harmonious adjustment with the divine, requires working on one's paranoia. Psychological endeavors are always partially paranoid because, as Jung says, the psyche offers no outside objective standpoint. We are always caught in our own vision of things. Moreover, our professional

---

39. Aniela Jaffé, *The Myth of Meaning in the Work of C. G. Jung*, translated by R. F. C. Hull (Zurich: Daimon Verlag, 1985).

calling depends on the paranoid ability to detect, suspect, and interpret to make strange connections among events. We must "see through" the screens of appearances into their meanings, and listen with a third ear. We must perceive in the other what he denies exists and rely on a theory of "the unconscious"—by definition, the invisible workings of an invisible mind—to account for this behavior licensed as professional psychology.

Each time we open a meaning we invite in the paranoid potential. Psychology walks the borderline between meaning and paranoia: psychologists, too, are borderline cases. Jung himself, with the irony of Perceval, remarks on this: "...meaning is something mental or spiritual. Call it a fiction if you like" (CW 11: 494). That is the mercurial twinkle in Jung, deconstructing the very fulcrum of his theorizing: meaning as fiction or fiction as meaning. Paranoid ideas manifesting Self, Self manifesting paranoid ideas. Where does delusion stop and revelation begin? Hermes walks the borders. And Hermes, Jung says, in a lecture delivered at Eranos,[40] is the "god of revelation" (CW 13: 256). So we must expect in revelation what Perceval learned—the jest, the twist, the hint. And, since Hermes is the God of revelation, revelations are to be heard only with a hermetic, a mercurial ear, their meanings as fictions, transposing the spirit's word into a poetic image, a move poor Schreber could not make because of Soul Murder, because he was deprived of the intermediary psychic echo, leaving literal the message. So Schreber had to transpose his actual gender, become a transvestite, to find the mercurial duplicity, while Perceval and Jung could imagine Mercurius as analogies, as images.

Yet the revelatory import, the thematic contents and divine imposed suffering in our three cases, and in Jung, remain alike.

Revelation and Delusion

Where then lies the difference between the case of Schreber and the case of Jung, between an incorrect and a correct method of revelation? We have seen it does not lie in the *contents* revealed. Bizarre, illogical, cosmogonic, blasphemous material appears as well in texts of the sane and the insane. Nor does it lie in the mission and prophecy urged by these contents. Consider Ezekiel and Jeremiah, Swedenborg and Blake. Consider Jung. Vocation, forewarning, vision of catastrophe, prospect of

---

40. "Der Geist Mercurius," *Eranos Yearbook* 9 (1942).

regeneration, androgyny—these, as Boisen said, are authentic religious themes, appearing as well in sane and insane. If Boisen's mistake was universalizing his experience, is that "mistake" not one that religious revelation requires? Is that not precisely what mission and prophecy demand? Nor does the criterion of paranoia lie in *societal acceptance.* It is still taught in psychiatry that if enough people, a very few even, share a vision, it can hardly be clinically called paranoid. If you can gather a few to accompany you up the mountain to sit the night through in chiliastic expectation for the end of the world tomorrow, then by virtue of your companions you belong to a sect and not to a diagnosis. "Where two or three are gathered together in my name" (Matthew 18:20). Yet at Jonestown, Guyana, some nine-hundred were gathered in a pathetic suicidal delusion, to say nothing of the collective delusions we shared during the nineteen-thirties and are probably sharing unawares right now. Delusion cannot be determined by societal criteria.

Perhaps the criterion is *context.* Are the contents alien to the carrier of them? Schreber's ideas, indeed, had little to do with the life history and mind of the *Senatspräsident* and his milieu, but Boisen's, in general, and Jung's ideas fit well within the context of their interests and *niveau.* Boisen said he was deluded partly because some of the ideas were utterly alien to anything he had ever thought or heard of, altogether out of context. But what of Hosea, or the naive Saint? Does their supreme value not lie precisely in the spontaneous novelty of their experience, completely out of context? Is it not the aim of miracles, glossolalia, and other descents of the spirit to break, defy, and annul the context? Revelation must *briser l'histoire* because it is revelation of *totaliter aliter,* the wholly, holy other.

Harmfulness—another distinguishing mark psychiatry sometimes offers. Is the idea harmful or dangerous to self or others? But what religious ideas are not dangerous? As Jung said "man's true relation to God must include both love and fear to make it complete" (*CW* 18:1630). Look at Job, and Abraham who drew the knife on his son, and look at what happened to the people who followed Moses's vision: all expired in the desert. And, have the ideas of Jesus about love or Mohammed about fraternity been only benign? What has been more dangerous to self and others than the revelations of Christianity and Islam—martyrdom of self and massacres of unbelievers, primitives, pagans, natives, animals, trees...No; harmfulness will not stand up as a criterion.

Then the difference must lie in the *person*. Surely, there is a glaring distinction between the persons of Schreber and Jung. Yet Schreber was a rather conventionally rational, even bureaucratic, man—and insane; Jung, a rather idiosyncratic man—and sane. Besides, how much does judgment of the person affect our judgment of the revelations? Suppose Biblical archeology were to dig up that shard that could demonstrate that the historical Ezekiel had been an asylum inmate, finger-painting his wheels in the art room. Would his visions be disqualified as revelations? That Jung had conversations with the phantoms, Philemon and Elijah, during what Ellenberger[41] calls Jung's "creative illness" does not devalue those visions or the revelation received concerning the mandala, the autonomy of psychic figures and voices, or the discipline of active imagination.

We can keep distinct paranoid texts and paranoid individuals. A syndrome exists not only inside a personality style; it can display itself as well in a textual style—illogical, defensive, apodictic, fantastical. Many of us exhibit paranoid personality characteristics; we are rigid, suspicious, hypervigilant, mirthless, and self important, yet we have been spared delusions and revelations. Syndromes and persons may overlap, but must not coincide. As the eminent German psychiatrist Kurt Schneider wrote: "Delusion formation has nothing to do with traits of personality...Delusion cannot be explained away in terms of a particular personality, its development and inner conflicts."[42] The personality psycho-dynamics of repressed homoeroticism, even actual persecution and betrayal, do not cause delusions or revelations of persecution or jealousy, nor are such actual experiences necessary conditions for them. That we trace revelations to personality factors is always *a posteriori*, as is much of psychiatric reasoning. The diagnosis of paranoid personality does not at all predict that we shall enter into a peculiar relationship with God—or that God shall enter into a relationship with us.[43] Hysterics, manics, epileptics, schizoids

---

41. Henri F. Ellenberger, *The Discovery of the Unconscious: The History and Evolution of Dynamic Psychiatry* (New York: Basic Books, 1970), 672.

42. Quoted in Theodore Millon, *Disorders of Personality: DSM-IV™ and Beyond* (New York: Wiley-Interscience, 1981), 377.

43. Cf. Emil Brunner, *The Divine-Human Encounter* (Philadelphia: Westminster Press, 1943), 51: "The revelation of God to men is the decisive element in what God does for them...God is the God who approaches man just because, and in so far as He

may be called too. "The spirit bloweth where it listeth and thou hearest the voice thereof, but knowest not whence it cometh" (John 3: 8). We have not found the signal difference between revelation and delusion. We have not answered the question.

Since I have set this impossible question, I feel obliged to give it my impossible reply. I question the question: it is a false one, rising from the assumption, both theological and psychiatric, that there is a clear distinction between revelation and delusion, between correct and incorrect method of manifestation of the hidden. Hence, "incorrigibility" has always been the stigma distinguishing true paranoia. "Well, whad'ya know, doc," says the man, "dead men do bleed!" Incorrigible.

Suppose, however, we start with another assumption: there is no, and can be no, clear distinction. Revelation always comes as incorrigible, always comes in delusional form. As "*delusion proper* is incorrigible,"[44] so, too, is revelation. It comes from the Highest Authority, the very voice of Truth with all the certainty of the transcendent *nous*. What possibly could be corrected, and from what but an inferior, fallible, and only-human perspective could such correction come?

Rather than searching to establish the context and criteria of correct revelation, thereby inviting systematic theology and systematic paranoia, I would correct that notion of revelation and delusion that separates them, and I would assume instead that all delusion is revelatory, all revelation, delusional. I would hold that Niebuhr's definition pertains equally to both: an "intelligible event which makes all other events intelligible."[45] As long as it is insisted, as those key passages in James and Kittel insist, that Deity is hidden and relation to the hidden is the essence of religion, then revelation becomes necessary to religion, and delusion as well. Paranoia is given with our theological *Weltbild*. Consequently, psychiatry cannot reach the endemic paranoia, the delusional potential, in individuals without addressing its source in the collective: that doctrinal need for a hidden God to reveal himself and whose revelations cannot be clearly distinguished from delusions.

---

reveals Himself...the event which is the relation between God and man hence is always an act of revelation."

44. Jaspers, *General Psychopathology*, 105.

45. Niebuhr, *The Meaning of Revelation*, 50.

It becomes clearer now why we have had to enter theology in order to pursue our topic to its psychological roots—as did Freud in *The Future of an Illusion,*[46] and Jung in his theological writings and his controversies with theologians. Psychology and theology need their inherent link, else theology loses soul and psychology forgets the gods. This interpenetration *is* the Eranos tradition since its inception with C.G. Jung and Rudolf Otto, continued by Gershom Scholem, Henry Corbin, and Ernst Benz, and now by Ulrich Mann, David L. Miller, and Wolfgang Giegerich. We may not divide psychology from theology any more than we may divide soul from spirit.

When Jacques Lacan warned, as it is said, that psychoanalysis is over and done with should religion triumph, I understand him to mean psychology is impossible wherever literal meanings triumph,[47] wherever theologizing breaks its connecting thread with psychologizing. Yet that menace is ever-present. As long as the culture requires revelation for its religion, there will be religious madness endemic in that culture; as long as revelation is necessary to the essence of religion, we must have dogmatic theology, and a Church, and a psychiatric establishment to guarantee the correctness of revelations, and we must expect as quite usual those contents we saw in our three cases, and which we see as well in our present-day apocalyptic crisis, our fundamentalist sectarianism, and our politically paranoid world.

Perceval said his madness was literalism: "The spirit speaks poetically" but "the lunatic takes the literal sense." Yet this lunatic literalism results directly from revelation that excites and ensures literalisms of every sort by announcing itself as the voice of the hidden, speaking truth. We cannot suppress the fact that the God of our culture's theology is a divinity

46. Sigmund Freud, *The Future of an Illusion,* translated by W.B. Roleson-Scott, revised and edited by James Strachey (New York: Doubleday and Co., 1983).

47. "Religion exists whenever a group of human beings fastens upon a meaning, be it divine or human...the question of meaning remained crucial...[Lacan] launched an attack on the very idea of meaning: his was an anticlerical campaign...The struggle against the domination of the notion of 'meaning' was thus for Lacan a way of defending...psychoanalysis...'It is not frivolous to say that the stability of religion is due to the fact that meaning is always religious,' Lacan said when he dissolved his school." Catherine Clément, *The Lives and Legends of Jacques Lacan,* translated by Arthur Goldhammer (New York: Columbia University Press, 1983), 183–84.

who must reveal to be divine, reveal in words, words that are literal, that this theological God is himself a literalist who, if pursued to the end, is therefore "lunatic," or paranoid; not because this God is admittedly an avengingly jealous God or because of the monomanic self reference—all things refer to and signify him, or because he is by dogma hypervigilant and without weakness, that is, omniscient and omnipotent, but because he is a theological God, a God of scripture, the holiness of Writ, who identifies himself with his word. Was Schreber really so wrong, or Jung, to announce a terrible conflict in the realm of God? Was Jung so wrong to connect the horrors of the Revelation of John with the Gospel of John, which opens: "In the beginning was the word and the word was with God and the word was God."

So, no, John Perceval. The spirit speaks not poetically, but noetically; or as William James says, with a *noetic quality*—"illuminations, revelations, full of significance and importance;" and these, he says, are "states of knowledge."[48] The spirit speaks literally with utterly literal instructions and prophesies and with intensely sensate miracles of flesh and things. Dead men do bleed, the lame shall walk, Lazarus shall rise—all shall rise from the dead, born again also in flesh. And this physically literal Resurrection requires a literally physical Apocalypse, an actual end of this actual world.

Jung's insistence on Mercurius—*extra Mercurius nulla salus,* might be his motto—is superbly pragmatic, an insistence that is therapeutic, even salvational. His invocation of Mercurius is not merely an alchemistical quirk, to provide an opposite compensation to the image of Christ, or to fulfill the formula of the mandala, *his* "family-of-four." *Anima mercurialis* gives the ear that tricks the mind out of hearing "true" meaning. Without Hermes the Messenger, divine hints and gestures become literal commands, and the religious instinct becomes disordered,paranoid.

Jung equates Mercurius with the collective unconscious (*CW* 13: 284). The very idea of the unconscious, unlike that of homoeroticism, becomes crucially therapeutic regarding paranoia because, as Jung defines the unconscious, it is a *negativer Grenzbegriff.* As such, it saves itself from literalization; it cannot be identified with any actual state of mind or behavior (unlike homosexuality). The unconscious can have no phenomenology

---

48. James, *The Varieties of Religious Experience,* 343.

proper to it and statements about it cannot be verified (CW8: 417). Elusive and mercurial, the unconscious is not a place, not a state but a dark ironic brother, an echoing sister, reminding.

This pragmatic, functional sense of the unconscious serves as a prophylactic against anything and everything that might delusionally be assumed to reveal the hidden. As Jung observes, revelation cannot be distinguished from an "autonomous functioning of the unconscious" (CW11: 237). The idea of the unconscious shadows the theology of revelation with the psychology of delusion, saving the soul from blinding certainty and theology, founded upon revelation, from its inherent insanity. *Deus absconditus* cannot become manifest apart from the images that present the manifestation. Revelation cannot be parted from imagination. Between the hidden and the perception of the hidden lies the third, the soul's imagining power, the bearer of the messages, *anima mercurialis*. By virtue of the mercurial idea of the unconscious, Jung's theological statements, so much like those of the first three cases, remain psychological rather than paranoid. Hermes the thief, tricky Mercurius, an impish prankster, is the soul guide to the hidden, saving us from literalism, and paranoia. "Deception and duplicity," said Perceval, save from delusion, for delusion as false belief appears only with true belief, only with revelation.

So there is a way through, and Perceval may still be a guide. As his cure progressed, he "obeyed the spirit of humour" because "the Deity...often intimates his will by jesting." We may let revelations, epiphanies, prophesies descend without believing, or disbelieving, them. *Serio ludere,* said the Renaissance maxim. We let them not provoke a belief response, instead keeping them tinged with Mercury. Believing *in* places oneself *within* the text. Boisen, you recall, broke down while writing his "Statement of Belief", suddenly captured by his text as he entered into its third paragraph. Perceval, you remember, learned to doubt, whereas Schreber overcame doubt and never recovered. For it is a psychological function of doubt—not merely to chasten or try belief—but to prevent the belief-response inherent to which is the lunacy of literalism. Original sin, said Perceval, is nothing other than taking the commands of a spirit of humor and perverting it into truth, illumination, a state of knowledge.

The last laugh, however, is on John Perceval himself who, at the end of his memoirs, was deluded about his cure. His final incurable delusion—of course by him unrecognized, for essential to delusion is that we cannot ourselves see it as such—is encased in Perceval's theology: God speaks poetically, and the lunatic takes the literal sense. But "[r]evelation exists in affirmation and commandment,"[49] and it was John Perceval who learned to hear literal commands with a metaphorical ear. Only as he becomes doubting, deceiving, ironic and imaginative does he become a sane man. We should not miss this point: when Perceval declares Original Sin consists in a Fall from the poetic and humorous, because Deity manifests his will by jesting, we would be taking him literally should we read this to mean that the gods speak jokes, or the one true God is Mercurius because he is not true. Rather, we read Perceval to be *attributing divinity to the poetic and humorous,* imagining that, before the Fall and the tearful narratives of exile Eden was full of humor, and our nostalgia for the Garden is a longing for laughter. The move into humor represents also, on the one hand, a transit of genres from Perceval's dark autumn of tragedy through bitter irony to comedy, his release from confinement, and marriage, Spring; on the other hand, an alchemical process from primary chaos through the nigredo into silver and the albedo.[50]

What is implied by Perceval's experience of the poetic as therapeutic? Paranoia overcome by poetry? Of course, not literal poems, poetry, poets. They are not mentioned. Rather, much as we study myths to gain a mythic sense and not to match ourselves with mythical typologies— I am living the Oedipal myth, you are an Artemis woman or an Aphroditic type (which is altogether a literal and not mythical understanding of myth)—so we may turn to poetic texts to educate the poetic sense. The poetic perplexes meaning as humor transposes it, preventing captivity in the revelatory text. Its declarative sentences provide a security structure of meaning. At the end of his book, Perceval no longer tries to declare the meaning of events. He is freed from revelation, and so, free of delusion.

---

49. Jaspers, *Philosophical Faith and Revelation,* 22.

50. On the "humors" of Eden, see David L. Miller, "Achelous and the Butterfly: Toward an Archetypal Psychology of Humor," *Spring: An Annual of Archetypal Psychology and Jungian Thought* (1973): 1–23. On the passage through the genres to comedy and Spring, see Northrop Frye, *Anatomy of Criticism: Four Essays* (Princeton, N.J.: Princeton University Press, 1957), "The Mythos of Spring: Comedy." On the alchemical process, see James Hillman, "Silver and the White Earth, I and II," *Spring: An Annual of Archetypal Psychology and Jungian Thought* (1980): 21–48 and (1981): 21–66.

The poetic would defeat paranoia, a meaning disorder, because "A poem should be equal to/Not true...A poem should not mean/But be."[51]

When inside the text, the person is inside the syndrome, feeling himself filled with its significance, one's person signified by the grandeur of God, oneself the monomanic referent, signifier of all things, or what psychiatry calls delusions of self-reference and grandeur. Yet psychiatry promulgates the same self-referent grandeur in the pedestrian disguise of its ego theory, ego as center of consciousness, giver of meaning, and to which all events must be related for signification.

Revelation and the Hidden

The very first word that desperately needs our de-literalizing therapy is "revelation" itself. Instead of literal revelation—from concealment to disclosure, from a dark and enigmatic mirror to illumination and a state of knowledge (William James)—there would be ongoing shiftings within any presentation; "revealed" and "concealed," little else than an interplay of foreground and background, surface and depth; "revealed" and "concealed," happy transpositions within any metaphor, modes of jesting, allusion. Then apocalypse becomes unnecessary, the veils delusional, no veil to lift or part or rend.

The veil, let us say, becomes no more than that suggestive hint, an *aidos* (a shame or shyness) that resides in disclosure, in the startle and shock of all direct presence, an Artemisian *aidos* inherent to all newness, all nudeness; the veil, a feeling in the soul that keeps us, in Hilary Armstrong's word, "diffident," reserved in regard, holds us back from pronouncement even in the midst of meaning. The veil does not cloak the body suddenly come upon but is the emotion appropriate to encounter, the response to full presence that would keep it partly absent, hidden.

Revelatory visions and voices and truths, synchronistic moments, too, then are recognized to be no more fundamental, no more superordinate—regardless that they come with a rush of splendor—than the immediate presence of aesthetic display. By this I refer to Adolf Portmann's *Selbstdarstellung* as revelation, here on earth everyday, the radiance shining in each thing as a *phainoumenon*, the affordance given by each

---

51. "Ars Poetica," in Archibald MacLeish, *Poems, 1924–1933* (Boston: Houghton Mifflin, 1933).

event.[52] Each event intelligible by its own affordance of intelligibility, the world as inherently intelligible in its aesthetic presentation, requiring no revelation for its divinity, no *sousterrain* or hiddenness for its meaning, no *Schlüsselerlebnis*. Exegesis then becomes not a disclosing of hidden meaning but, rather, a *poiesis*—a poetic working of the given in the enjoyment of ongoing imagining.

Then, too, the so-called "hidden" can be recognized as having been a necessary literalization *a posteriori* of insight; as if the animal delight we take in insight, in discovery or in explanatory accounts required for its arousal the fantasy of something actually hidden. Insight is primary and the idea of hiddenness its correlate—not the other way around. Hiddenness might then be recognized as a hypostasis or literalism of inwardness, which, again following Portmann, is manifested in the aesthetic display of animated phenomena.

Revelation, then, is always going on in display. It requires no literal witness, no special prophetic gift, only exegetical intelligence, that ability to read display, to sense beauty. No testimony, only a careful noticing, a considerate appreciation of "eachness" (William James), each thing in its image, each word in its echo. To say it again: hiddenness is not an absence that becomes presence through revelation, the unintelligible made now intelligible, the invisible now visible. Rather, let us say, hiddenness is a category of existence which, if "revealed" becomes literalized as the "concealed," whereas as a category of existence, hiddenness affords depth, secrecy, inwardness, pregnancy, chambering, resonance, potential, and death in any phenomenon, promoting attention to it, a studious care, a rewarding watchfulness and an evaluation of any phenomenon as never what it seems plainly and sheerly to be.

This careful noticing of an awakened *aisthesis* is nothing other than "paranoid hypervigilance" returned to sanity. For that watchful sensitivity which notices the extraordinary otherness of the usual world is the paranoid ground of psychological consciousness. It is also the paranoid ground of scientific consciousness, empirically respectful of the given,

---

52. I have tried to elaborate upon Portmann's idea of self-presentation as well as James J. Gibson's idea of affordance—direct perception by organisms of what is afforded in the display of their environment—in my two earlier Eranos lectures, "The Thought of the Heart," *Eranos Yearbook* 48 (1979), and "The Animal Kingdom in the Human Dream," *Eranos Yearbook* 51 (1982).

observing the object minutely. And this sensitivity is the observant consciousness of religion, religion not dependent upon the revelation of meaning but religion as Jung defines it in "The Undiscovered Self": "Religion means dependence on and submission to the irrational facts of experience" (CW 10: 505). "I make my patients understand that all things which happen to them against their will are a superior force...God is nothing more than that superior force in our life. You can experience God everyday."[53]

❀

The irrational facts of experience are here, there, everywhere. Otherness abounds; aliens everywhere, so we can never be alienated unless we become wholly other to these irrational facts, estranged in our subjectivism, projecting our alienation upon the gods and declaring them to be the Wholly Other. Once we can abandon the primary delusion of subjective rational superiority—the supposedly normal perspective of normal ego psychology—and its addiction to meaning as relation to subjectivity, we begin to find ourselves living familiarly, daily, in the mercurial, unwilled, irrational of otherness; the whole world religious, revelation so continuous and hiddenness so present that these terms become redundant.

The Politics of Paranoia

Nearing now the end of time—our time for this lecture—I want briefly to review what we have been doing, and then look once more at the content of paranoid delusions, especially Schreber's.

Our first move was to recognize the essentiality of paranoia in mental disorders because it demonstrates a paradigmatic parade of incorrigible delusions. We concluded that the incorrigible certainty of these delusions attests to an impersonal, noetic factor in paranoia, thereby locating this disorder of mind in a prior disorder of spirit. We then connected delusion with revelation and the hidden spirit or God, attempting to see through or deconstruct the theological background that, we suggested, actually necessitates paranoia. On the one hand, we refused to differentiate definitively between revelation and delusion, insisting both have their ground

---

53. C.G. Jung Speaking: Interviews and Encounters, edited by William McGuire and R.F.C. Hull (Princeton, N.J.: Princeton University Press, 1977), 250.

in the noetic beyond the personal mind, maintaining that where delusion is there is revelation and where revelation is there is also delusion. On the other hand, we did indicate in the example of Jung a sane relation to the noetic, owing to the intervention of the idea of the unconscious and the phenomena of the *anima mercurialis,* as the poetic, metaphorical, and humorous sense described by Perceval in contrast with the "soul murder" and literalism described by Schreber. Additionally, we questioned the base of paranoia in a literalized idea of homoeroticism and its cure in literalized attempts at *Entmannung.*

In the short remaining time, we shall take a second look at paranoia, now with a political rather than theological eye.

I am aware that the forum of Eranos is apolitical and has been so since its inception in the 1930s. That Eranos arose within that political background, as if in courageous defiance of it, is already deeply political. The very freedom to speak here indicates the politics of freedom of speech and assembly; the encouragement to pursue one's discipline wherever it leads, the respect for individual differences, the international congregation, and that we are on Swiss soil—these are fundamental to Eranos and fundamentally political. Political, as I understand it, does not imply political party but political piety; it suggests that we not allow political implications of ideas to become grossly unconscious, that we admit the political part of the psyche and take political part.

Besides these more evidently political aspects of Eranos, there is also an archetypally political claim upon us. I find it best expressed by Hellmut Wilhelm almost twenty years ago. Here, in 1967, he gave one of his subtle, extraordinary lectures on the *I Ching.* He showed that the *I Ching,* especially in its older layers, used political facts with "astonishingly pitiless realism," transforming the facts so that "they were seen as images." Wilhelm said that these political realities like the patterns in history, in myths and art, "emerge from basic archetypal situations."[54] The patterns or "primordial images," he said, "are offered by Heaven...heaven dangles them down. Earth offers forms or shapes or even institutions (*fa*)."[55]

Political institutions receive and form the great images; government, too, has an archetypal necessity. By not admitting the *polis,* the city, as a

54. Hellmut Wilhelm, "The Interplay of Image and Concept in the Book of Changes," *Eranos Yearbook* 36 (1967): 52–53.

55. Ibid., 36–37.

primordial psychic phenomenon, as symbolic expression of the Self in Jung's language, we are simply maintaining that eighteenth-century literalism called secularism. Secularism divides God from Caesar, excludes divinity from state, thereby risking the return of the excluded into the *polis* in those literal and soulless ways of materialist bureaucracy and fundamentalist theocracy: the boring city of matter and the fanatic city of spirit, neither a city of soul.

The mythic imagination that governs psychic life and is the depth of depth psychology is anchored, let us remember, in a *polis* and not only in texts. An archetypal psychology that would follow the gods to Olympus also will find them where they dangle down in the institutions of society, in the city streets that are also habitations of mythical figures. *Eusébia* was the Greek term. The tragedies by Aeschylus and Sophocles whose mythical configurations still describe our behavior are plays about political Athens, not only literature or psychology. Socrates's witness to soul in the *Phaedo* takes place in a jail cell. The prophets, the apostles in their acts and letters, and Jesus's revolution concern the order of the community, even if now we read their transcriptions in a carrel or a pew remote from the agora. And the Renaissance masters of myth and soul, including Dante, Petrarch, and Ficino, could not escape *polis*.

As myth is only half itself when severed from cult, so psyche is only half realized when not enacted in *polis*. Plato's *Republic* provides the root metaphor for this relation of psyche and *polis*, soul and city, that analogy between the state of the soul and the soul of the state. If, as we have been describing, there be a paranoid state of soul, today called "the paranoid personality style," so we may expect to find an analogous paranoid psychology in the state. We may therefore read the conventional descriptions of the paranoid soul (which I have extracted mainly from the standard *Diagnostic Manual* used by practitioners in the United States[56]) as also descriptions of the soul of the paranoid state.

"Pervasive and unwarranted suspiciousness and mistrust." "Individuals are hypervigilant and take precautions against perceived threat." "Perceive an unusually wide range of stimuli." "Tend to avoid blame even

---

56. *DSM-III* (see note 10 above) and also from David Shapiro, *Neurotic Styles* (New York: Basic Books, 1965); Fredrick C. Redlich and Daniel X. Freedman, *The Theory and Practice of Psychiatry* (New York: Basic Books, 1966); Kolb, *Modern Clinical Psychiatry*; and Millon, *Disorders of Personality*, ch. 13.

when it is warranted." "Avoidance of depression." "Question the loyalty of others." "Insist on secrecy." "Severe and critical with others." "Tendency to counterattack." "Unwilling to compromise." "Intense but suppressed anger." "Driving, ambitious, aggressive, and unusually hostile and destructive." "Generate uneasiness and fear in others." "Often interested in mechanical devices, electronics, and automation." "Avoid group activities unless in a dominant position." "Avoid surprise by virtually anticipating it." "Dread...passive surrender." "Friends are constantly tested until they withdraw or actually become antagonistic." "Inordinate fear of losing power to shape events in accordance with their own wishes." "Transformation of internal tension into external tension." "Continuous state of total mobilization." "Giving into external domination and giving into internal pressure involve a threat." "Fear of being tricked into surrendering some element of self-determination." "Generally uninterested in art or aesthetics." "Rarely laugh." "Lack of a true sense of humor." "What looks like comfortable familiarity...seems like an imitation...It is not friendly; it is only designed to look friendly." "Keenly aware...of who is superior or inferior." "They disdain people seen as weak, soft, sickly, or defective."

To hear these descriptions as pertaining to the soul of the Soviet or the American state[57] literalizes "political" into party politics, *parteiisch*, grasping only a part. Instead, we need to hear these descriptions as pertaining to politics and government as such so as to recognize the inherent paranoia in the soul of the state as such. The deepest problem of statecraft is how to govern the inherent paranoia of government so that its symptoms not exacerbate into corrupt tyranny and byzantine paralysis, symptoms such as secret police, loyalty oaths, lie detection, electronic surveillance, fear of weakness, systematized defenses and predictions (domino theory), and the absence of those soul qualities, humor, aesthetics, and softness replaced by grand eschatological ideals: order, peace, humanity, fraternity, rights, and God.

---

57. Cf. Richard Hofstadter, *The Paranoid Style in American Politics* (New York: Alfred A. Knopf, 1965), for specifically American political paranoia, although the author "would like to emphasize again that the paranoid style is an international phenomenon." He draws upon Norman Cohn's *The Pursuit of the Millennium* (London: Oxford University Press, 1957), 38–39, to show "a persistent psychological complex" in Mediaeval Europe. Military-political metaphors (enemy, mastery, defense, mobilization, battle, two fronts, etc.) mark the description of Shapiro's "The Paranoid Style."

Given this inherent unconscious paranoia, there will be a need for a projected fantasized enemy and fantastical defenses against the fantasized enemy. Situations will always be evaluated by constructs of strength and weakness, winning and losing. Demand for unconditional surrender and the fear of it will be paramount. Treaties based on compromise will be all but impossible to negotiate. A nation in league with others will be forced—whenever it becomes unable to dominate the group—to veto or withdraw. The potential for open hostility is ever-present and will be denied. Official denial will be essential to maintaining a government "above suspicion" and true to its idealizations. There will be little interest in art or aesthetics, and when government should intervene then the aesthetic tends to be suborned as state art in service of national resolve. Even the most solicitously conducted foreign relations will tend to generate uneasiness and fear in others. Defense against depression will motivate ever-increasing defenses. The disdain for the weak, sickly, and defective will bring to the fore that contemporary, though ever-recurring, conflict between security and compassion (guns vs. butter, swords vs. plowshares), between the burden of armaments for defense and the burden of welfare for the failing. Owing to the fear of dependency, self sufficiency will be idealized into an isolation called "splendid."

Above all else will be mistrust and expectations of deceit between the governed and their government, requiring watchdog committees, bureaus of investigation, advocacies of every sort of reform, since paranoid suspicion is inherent to the very soul of state. Not only will the state mistrust the foreign (xenophobia), but within its borders also the alien, the subculture, and the minority—unless it be "strong," thereby necessitating minority pressure groups and division of the body politic into rivalrous single-issue or monomanic constituencies. The more rigidly demanding government is of the governed, and vice versa, the more suspicions of corruption abound, particularly suspicions regarding "security," and the more information-gathering and -storing be comes prized and litigation the mode of decision. For, the negative relation with Mercurius results in that basic proposition of all paranoia: whatever is hidden is harmful (hence revelation equals security), requiring continuous scanning, hypervigilance toward the food we eat, the reports we hear, the contracts we sign. Expose and cover-up become the *modus operandi*—our theological paradigm of revelation and concealment in the political sphere.

Despite the promulgation of the nation-state by the nation-state, its inherent paranoia fosters mistrust in the very institutions that are its pillars including the validity of the city and the calling of politics. The welfare of the citizens and the institutions that serve the common good become secondary, owing to the primary confusion of welfare with security, the common good with national strength, or "military needs." (It should be evident that I am referring not only to the contemporary world but to the nation-states from Assyria through Rome, and others analyzed by Toynbee.) When the noble institutions of political life, such as political rhetoric, the providential role of leadership, public office and public service, fall prey to paranoid systematization, then the great images of justice, prudence, equity, community, and the like, dangle down from heaven unreceived, the containing shapes for the archetypal powers in disarray. All the while, obsessed by its delusional need for security, the paranoid state takes recourse in defense mechanisms of projection and reaction formation, that is, increased scanning for enemies, terrorists and defectors (defectives), with policies sponsored not by initiative that is paralyzed by ambivalence (immobility combined with bellowing) but that are rationalized as "purely" defensive reactions to threat.

Threat belongs to what Jung calls the end of the *aeon* (CW 9.2: p. ix); The Book of Revelations announces apocalyptic catastrophe. We live in a *Zeitgeist* of threat, in a soul-state, and political state of paranoia. This has been scripturely revealed and is being confirmed politically in the Soviet state of mind (ever-homaging the twenty million who died defending against the last Western invasion) and the American (ever-defending against penetration into the body politic by emissaries of the Evil Empire—colored pinko, terrorists and spies). Threat of catastrophe justifies the measures taken against threat, thereby making the menace ever more literal: "the fear of catastrophe is most likely to elicit the syndrome of paranoid rhetoric"[58] Worse: the syndrome requires catastrophe to fulfil its own prophecy. The vicious circle of paranoid psychology is the present political reality.

If our Platonic analogy between soul of state and state of soul holds, then we should be able to find remedy for the paranoia of the state in the remedies proposed by our patients for their paranoid souls. I refer to

---

58. Hofstadter, *The Paranoid Style in American Politics*, 39.

two particular remedies—Perceval's poetic sense and Schreber's *Entmannung*—and one general: Jung's idea of the unconscious.

This idea appeared in less secular and rational societies as the gods, Fate or Fortuna. The state acknowledged the limits of its ruling consciousness, propitiating the interventions of Mercurius by turning to oracles, augurs, seers, and prophets, as the individual turns to dreams, doubts and echoes. Suspicion ritualized as superstition. Of course, ancient states were no less paranoid despite these consultations because they, too, read signs literally, as dreams may still be read today, or as economic forecasts about depression and inflation may be read in the public sphere. Nonetheless, the idea of an unconscious shifts attention to the others beyond human control and away from fixation upon the enemy's hidden intentions (e.g., Kremlin-watching). That fixated attention is precisely pathognomonic of paranoia according to Freud's observation: "His abnormality really reduced itself to this, that he watched his wife's unconscious mind... by becoming conscious of hers and magnifying it enormously he succeeds in keeping unconscious his own" (CP2: 235–36). The idea of an unconscious enables enemies to recognize that they are seeing not the other's concealed intentions, but a screen on which they may read their own. Every statement about the other would be self-reflexive, and the threat could come home.

In the penultimate paragraph of Freud's study of Schreber, Freud writes: "It remains for the future to decide whether there is more delusion in my theory... or whether there is more truth in Schreber's delusion" (CP3: 456–66). This extraordinarily psychological twist not only relativizes Freud and Schreber, but also truth and delusion, opening the way to reading Schreber as truth-teller, as prophet. All century long we have ignored this comment by Freud, successfully suppressing Schreber's revelations with Freud's analysis of them. Yet both men transmit the same message—whether it be truth or delusion: as *Entmannung* is for the sake of the soul's redemption, so homoeros is for the sake of social sanity, and both *Entmannung* and homoeros as amity, social interest (*Gemeinschafts-gefühl*), fellow feeling give indications for a new world order, that major content of paranoid delusions.[59]

---

59. To paraphrase William James ("What we now need to discover in the social realm is the moral equivalent of war," *The Varieties of Religious Experience*, 332–33),

Freud, we must remember, considered the end of analysis, the cure, comes only when the "repudiation of femininity," also called "the struggle against passivity," comes to an end when a person can submit without defeat, when phallic ego-consciousness,[60] penis envy, the masculine protest is overcome in both a man and a woman.[61] "Man[liness]...as expected of...soldiers...in wartime, is not in the soul's nature," said Schreber (333). Instead, the passivity that is voluptuousness.

Weakness, submission, perimeters violated; trust in what one cannot read; learning the art of surrender by surrendering first to art,[62] humor, and the voices of the other; doubt, even fear, of one's own certainty, rather than suspicion of the other—all this, and what we brought to this podium in 1969 on psychological femininity,[63] is *Entmannung* when heard in the metaphorical manner of Perceval. A dedication to the pleasure of soul instead of standing tall, erected multi-headed, deep-penetrating missiles, early warning systems, protective shields, tridents, titans, mega thrust.

Remember: the prodromal symptom in Schreber's case was "succumbing" as a woman; the primary delusion (*Schlüsselerlebnis*) in Boisen's

---

Schreber and Freud indicate an *erotic* equivalent of war. But homoeros is not sufficient, since the emotion that bonds sames together in fellow feeling still casts shadow on the different. In the love of likes there is shadow collusion against the unlike; the need for an enemy remains. This shows in the fiercely loyal bonding of buddies in war against a common enemy. And both sides in war engage in the larger collusion of war itself in which need for an enemy and homoerotic bonding are coterminous. The common project (war) requires a common projection (enemy). For an erotic equivalent of war to be successful, it would have to imagine an even more delusional enemy, beyond the biosphere altogether—principalities, powers, forces, aliens—so that the globe itself and all values of it be bonded by the feeling of sames.

60. Sigmund Freud, *CP* 5: 354–56.

61. The spectrum of psychology, from phenomenology and psychoanalysis through behaviorism and brain physiology, defines consciousness with phallic metaphors: awake, active, intentional, one-sided, overt behavior, object responsive, spontaneous firing, (cortical) arousal. These definitions all desert the inherent sense of the word: knowing with, together knowing.

62. On art as surrender, see Kurt H. Wolff, *Surrender and Catch: Experience and Inquiry Today* (Dordrecht and Boston: D. Reidel Publishing Company, 1976).

63. James Hillman, "First Adam, then Eve: Fantasies of Female Inferiority in Changing Consciousness," *Eranos Yearbook* 38 (1969), and as Part III of *The Myth of Analysis* (New York: Harper & Row, 1978).

case was expressed in the language of strength and weakness, the weak to be sacrificed for the strong. Yet all three cases showed that survival depended upon surrender. This because, as Jung said, the human connection is not through superiority, which isolates, but through weakness: the human need for community, *Gemeinschaftsgefühl*. If theological delusion is literalism and sanity is doubt and jesting, political delusion is superiority and sanity, the trust in weakness.

As theology has explored the importance of doubt, so politics may explore weakness in its varieties, as humbling, bending, yielding, giving, resigning, surrendering, losing and loss. It is a psychological exploration beyond negotiation, compromise, or conflict resolution, for it starts in the psychic reality of defeat. "Take a position on the floor" (Perceval); "Descend to the lowest possible level" (Boisen). What is the psyche's *telos* in defeat? How can it be imagined beyond the paranoid literalisms in which it is fixed?

When I suggest reading Schreber's delusions as prophetic, it is not only because the same loss of soul or anima murder, the same conflict in the realm of God and order of the world were wrestled with by Jung, the Jung who said what Schreber could have: "My problem is to wrestle with the big monster of the historical past, the great snake of the centuries, the burden of the human mind, the problem of Christianity" (*CW* 18: 279).

By reading Schreber as prophet, I also mean something more: Schreber as prophetic experimenter who, in his body, experienced the incarnation of the Assumption of Maria while doing time in that psychic laboratory or monastery of the nineteenth century called the madhouse where the wall opens between medicine and religion, and where surrender to degradations, dissolution in tubs, supine postures, beatings, vigils, and silence were the literal introduction to his new theology of the soul's bliss through unmanning. In much, Schreber's delusions prophesized our current literalisms: the feminist movement; the Gaia hypothesis that the globe is an organic female being; the psycho-religions of matriarchy and the goddesses; fundamentalism of literalized beliefs; the intellectual obsession with linguistic signification; bisexual androgyny as recommended behavior; *flüchtig hingemachte Männer*; the invasion of the human world by alien others; diet determinism and the ambivalent bewitchment of food. Truth or Delusion—or both? Where two or three are gathered, ideas and movements are only questionably paranoid. Let John Perceval be your guide: listen with a poetic mercurial ear.

For Schreber, unmanning was integral to a new cosmology in which there would be no more Soul Murder, a cosmology in which psyche would return to life, *esse in anima,* being in a pleasurable soul. If we have elected to hear this prophet, by venturing into far-out places in theology and politics, and by surrendering to a mission of our own, this has been to unfix theology from its revelational delusion and politics, from its paranoid state, so as to recall them both to the service of soul.

23

THE WILDMAN IN THE CAGE:
COMMENT

There are many kinds of strength. The strength of experience (Humphrey Bogart), of endurance (Sylvester Stallone), of moral rectitude (Spencer Tracy) and idealism (Jimmy Stewart), of the martial arts and of the street and the woods. When the word strength comes up in analysis, we have to get to the image. the figure of it. I always try to qualify generalized nouns by working with the patient on imagining what act or what person he is seeing as "strong." There is a great difference between Lorne Greene and James Dean.

Strength of penis, throat (words, expression, talking), nose (common sense, direction), legs—these four "bodies" frequently appear as dream images and symptom locations in the men I see in practice. Some men haven't found their legs, and they dream of growing legs or they feel paralyzed in the legs. This sort of strength bears on the ability to work (and not only to stand up): legwork, pound the pavement, move on. Others have blockages in the nasal-throat passages. They have to "clear their heads" of coagulated gook, the young sap that clogs their breath. They require operations (in their dreams) to open the throat. I take this not only as opening downward the connection so that the lower "breath" can rise up and be "expressed," but also that they begin to tongue words, taste events allow connections within their own heads between what they hear and what they say, what they take in and what they swallow. Developing strength of throat is a work on what the Kundalini yoga refers to as the *Visuddha* chakra, that center of consciousness, where the power of words becomes more and more real.

So much has been said about the penis in the last one hundred years of psychology that I don't want to gild the lily. Still, we all know the strength of confidence that seems to stem from it. Gaining confidence from it seems to require giving it confidence—confiding in it, letting it confide in you.

What do you want from it? Use it for? Expect? What does it want from you? Men need to notice its inherent requirements, and whether they really originate in the penis or derive from propaganda about what it should be feeling and doing. Men begin to discover its inherent freedom, one's own Statue of Liberty (hence license and licentiousness and libido). Many men feel that they get their penis confidence back only from a woman. This is so overwhelming for them that they can leave wife and children, risk livelihood and life just for its sake. This "strength" seems what they have waited for all their lives. I respect these happenings in the patients even while ironically reflecting them against their archetypal nature: foolishness of the Trickster, antisocial Don-Juanism, psychopathic. The penis body has the great virtue of putting a man in touch with his psychopathy—and this is the wild man, too, and needs to be recognized, else it becomes utterly inhuman.

Before taking up the fourth body, the nose, I want to say something about anger. The hairy man in the cage has been here a very long time. He is angry. We are all sons of Jacob, not Esau, his hairy brother. Civilization looks back to Gilgamesh, the hero, not to Enkidu, his hairy companion who dies. As Bly says, the wildman is the repressed, and always threatening, and threatening in therapy as anger. What can we do with him?

First of all, we have to watch out that our professional style doesn't keep him out: the modulated voice, the quizzical gaze, the understanding manner. He does not want to be "understood," because understanding, he feels, always tends to undermine his wants. Mirroring is not enough. To engage him, we have to raise our voices, grunt, and growl. As a therapist I have to allow Esau and Enkidu into the armchair. If I repress, what the patient learns in the hour from my role-modeling is my style of repression. If I avoid the wild man, how can the patient be expected to let him in?

Anger. As a son of Mars I easily become angry and the wildman comes into my therapy sessions directly. Handling this anger in front of the patient, our handling it together, letting it walk in, walk by, walk out—and not explaining it or apologizing for it—this is a "martial art." It serves to depotentiate the fear in the patient of his own wild man. It shows him that rage and outrage belong and have a place in human intercourse. I don't mean simply his sitting with me through an outburst of *Heilige Zorn* (the holy rage fathers were proud to indulge in the German family). Nor do I mean putting him through trial by ordeal. Rather, I mean recognizing anger as an impersonal factor in nature, recognizing that it brings with it not only scorn or senseless tempestuousness but a strength and warmth, something mineral like iron, like flint. It contributes something proud and noble, and not only mean-spirited viciousness. Much of my rage in analysis has to do with stupidity and shallowness; rage at the patient's weak, unfelt, self-indulgent reactions. His being "personal" rather than "intelligent." My anger seems to put a claim on the patient for "more" or "better."

For a long time I was ashamed at this anger over the other's inferiority: Should I not be giving that inferiority shelter? Does my angry superiority not polarize us so I become wildman and he scared victim? S/M? But I have since found that even after I recognized the anger that rises from my own anxiety over inferiority, my own anxiety over therapy being so ineffective, I also recognized in this anger, and even in this anxiety, a certain ambition that we get somewhere and that what we are doing together, and life too, really matters. Sometimes the anger emerges from the teacher banging down his ruler, sometimes maybe Captain Bligh, sometimes from my retarded frustrated adolescent whose feelings appear in an unsorted lump—anger simply as intensity. But sometimes, too, it is the wildman inside the cage of therapy who cannot bear its politeness and its routines. He seems to explode whenever things get too set and taken for granted. By envisioning my anger at his attack—not on the patient but on the therapeutic vessel—I keep the wildman therapy-minded. He gives it huge value just because of his anger with it. Of course, my anger gets caught up on moralisms, in personal opinions, in peeves. A certain distortion or perversion comes with it, just as distortions and perversions come with sexuality, eating, or making art. This is the amusing part. From iron to irony. And, of course, the personal part of my anger is destructive, that is, attacking the other person personally or taking an attack only personally—egocentric anger. When you are attacked personally, you identify with the fault under attack (defense identification), and this is hardly therapeutic!

I have found that my anger is a kind of love; it appears over social injustice, at insults the patient has not noticed, as an expression of concern (and not only frustration or envy). If we didn't get angry, we would never sense what was "wrong."

Part of developing anger is extending its expression—cursing rather than bitching, sharpening the emotion's point rather than a general hostile mood, active rather than passive aggression, holding with it (like Jacob wrestling the angel) rather than letting it all fly away. So long as the anger stays focused on the parents or on the system or on me, the therapist, it has nothing much to do. It stays stuck and is chained with guilt. By extending the horizon of anger, the patient does begin to wake up to the world. It is a way into *Gemeinschaftsgefühl* (Alfred Adler's social feeling).

I've found that this wildman also comes as an ethnic ancestor. That is, the wildman is not only savage and hairy, or threateningly remote from the soft male. He may be your own grandfather. He often brings with him an Irish or Swedish or Russian memory. Not necessarily a personal memory of your own grandfather or great uncle (whom you may never have actually known), but a memorial image or family legend of a Great Strong Ancestor. By recounting (or inventing) tales of this ancestor, place is made for a giver of strength. The strength of the ancestor, by the way, is usually not macho; the strength is tempered with folly. The ancestor from Cork and how he got to be a policeman because of his huge hands; the Russian Jew and what he did when he landed in Hoboken; the mistakes of the Swede on the wrong train. Machoism hasn't the humor and can't take being ridiculous. But in fairy tales, the giant, fearful as he is, is also a character you laugh at, uneasily maybe, but there is a laugh there.

As soon as possible and wherever possible in therapy, I try to circumvent discussion of the parents for discussion of the ancestors. I want to reconstruct the Family Tree. What strength there! Jung refers to the ancestor as the 2,000-year-old man. We each carry him within our instinctual reactions, our natural wisdom. And to reach him, the key is under the mother's pillow, as Robert Bly's tale says.[1] Where the mother's cushion is, is where the key lies hidden.

Now this is not merely the longing to be back in bed with Mother— really, for most men that is a revolting idea and not a repressed wish at all. No, it is rather that mother's strength—the archetypal fairy-tale mother—rests comfortably pillowed on the ancestors. She derives her

---

1. Robert Bly, *The Pillow & the Key: Commentary on the Fairy Tale Iron John* (Saint Paul, Minn.: Ally Press, 1987).

strength from the great forces beneath her that dream onward in her mind. Jungian psychology and mythology speak of the "phallic mother." Where does she get her strength from? From her ancestors. So one goes back to that mother's pillow, feels beneath the sleepiness and passive regression, gets below it, under it, where resides the secret of the mother's strength: her ambition, her drive, her fantasies for her sons, her forebodings and hopes, fantasies from ancestral roots, their ancient claims on life arising again into life through her dreaming head on the pillow.

The wildman as ancestor shifts the prejudice that he is merely a grunt with a club. The waking ego defends itself with prejudices, assuming the wildman is just a big cock, or has no language, or has dumb simple perceptions, unschooled. Our notions of instinct are loaded with notions of this sort. Actually, animals are terribly refined in their perceptions, receptivity, social relations, and forms of expression. Just look at their tails. The hairy part of us partakes in this animal refinement. This idea, that it is the animal that is refined, produces a wonderful realization, freeing a patient tangled up in the civilized prejudices about the wild.

Ancestral strength brings forms with it. Bly and I have talked about this just this past summer in Maine where my wife and I were honored to take part in his seminars. I was saying there that we fear the wildman, perhaps, not so much because he will be spontaneous and uncontrolled, but because he is conservative and formal. Instinct is formal, form giving and form fulfilling. The wildman is the radical in us, the radical takes strength from the roots (radix = root), and the roots are embedded in solid old forms. So a man fears his Russian-Jewish shtetl, another his Sicilian peasantry because of the restrictive ritualistic formalisms. The wildman brings the beauty of the old ways. I think he ushers in a life that is more aesthetic because it is more animal. But we may not experience this until we first strike a deal with him, as Bly says. And the first exchange in the deal is to bring to him your softness. You have to admit your fear and weakness, your lostness, your pseudo-strength. Admit your love of cushions. That gives him an opening to be more comprehensive and compassionate than your prejudice about him as only savage.

All of which take me back to the nose. The soft male has a soft nose. He has lost his direction. As Bly says about these men, "They could not say what they wanted and stick by it. They could not lift the sword."[2] Some core of intention has been enucleated. The leprosy of the nuclear age has eaten away at the nose. Or at least the soft male blames the nuclear age: Any moment we will all be blown up. So life is led as if after the catastrophe, a blown-away life: blown-up subjectivism in self-important inflations and depressions, blown about by this or that novelty, experience, woman.

I tend to see blaming the nuclear blow-up in these men not as a literal prediction but as a catatonic dissociation from their own explosive vital-ity. However, to say to these men, "What do you want? What do you think? What do you feel?" only backs them further into lostness. Nose to the wind, introspective meditation, sniffing all sorts of possibilities, but no true scent and sticking to its track. These questions only force them into a psychology of will: "making up their minds," "decisions." But willpower is powerless without its animal vehicle; and, without a nose, the will doesn't know where to go. Besides, Bly's soft males have anyway asked themselves what they want a thousand times over and have been asked by their parents and their women a thousand times over.

In fairy tales, the witch has a long nose and so do the animals that come to help. The giants have a keen sense of scent too. The hero often has to get his nose on straight, that is, find his sense of direction. It's these soft males who go to the "ironmasters," the gurus of the will, like Werner Erhard and Don Juan and the Orient. They have no orientation and so they are suckers for spiritual directors.

Once there was no question for a young man about his direction in life. You did what your forefathers did and were lucky to be apprenticed. Caste and tradition. We are glad to be free of that confinement today; but if you take the idea of caste less literally it means that we are born with a congenital sense of direction that is given with our ancestors and/or our animal totem of the clan. Hence my insistence on the wildman as ances-tor. In the emotions rising from him comes a sense of direction.

I feel strongly about this "nose body," having been a 97-lb weakling myself for many years. I had a nose for the wind and followed hunches

---

2. Keith Thompson, "What Men Really Want: An Interview wit Robert Bly," *New Men, New Minds: Breaking Male Tradition,* edited by Franklin Abbot (Freedom, Calif.: The Crossing Press, 1987), 168.

and gambles and felt in touch with the Great Invisibles that soft males pick up on in our Great Spirit quests (meditations, introspections, and confessional poems). But what the soft male needs is closeness with the softness, first of all. Under the mother's pillow is a mole; also, if you look closely enough, a rabbit, a furry creature who has a nose that is not Magical and Marvelous but concrete, shortsighted, and particular. A nose that not so much desires ("What do you want, really? What's your goal in life?") as it does more surely keep you awake and on track. Without the nose, you have to plan a direction and force yourself to stick with it—psychology of willpower. With a nose you don't need those awful American moralisms about commitment and responsibility and choice. Did you ever see a responsible rabbit or a committed mole? But are they ever determined! The nose is not an instrument of will but of keening knowledge, pursuit, and survival. As Jimmy Durante used to say: "Only the nose knows."

24

"HOW DO WE STAY PSYCHOLOGICAL?"

Introduction

I feel some constraint talking with you today. What can justify my borrowing your attention? For after all, you all know as much about the trade and traffic of psychotherapy as I do—probably a lot more, since you are out there, tending the store facing the clients hearing the complaints, while I am in the back room, thinking and writing. I stopped actual practice with actual persons. In fact, I won't touch it. I am too out-of-touch. I no longer do hands-on tinkering. I practice now with ideas, their unconsciousness, their relationships, their dysfunctions and pathologies. I still try to get inside people's minds, much as I suppose you do, for that is where the ideas I tinker with have their habitat and do their damage.

Having come out of the closet of private practice, I am nowadays more in public practice. I practice my kind of psychology in arenas like this—with architects and business managers, philosophers and theater people, university students and art critics, attempting the same aims I suppose we all share—helping the psyche from the oppression of its unthought ideas, helping it remember archetypally. For the ideas we have that we do not know we have, have us. So, like you, I am engaged in lifting repression or raising consciousness, attending to pathologies, and revivifying significant emotions and the imagination.

I regard this step from private to public practice not idiosyncratic to my career and fate, enabled by earning money outside the consulting room; I consider this step from private to public to be necessary to the therapeutic profession as a whole. *Today, the world of therapy is therapy of world.* And this internet, this web of world and therapy is some of what I want to address today, for I think therapy and therapists have a much larger part to play in the world.

According to most psychological theory, the world out there beyond the consulting room is definitely not a psychological scene. Let's make that quite clear. Psychology still practices under the inner-outer, subject-object roof brilliantly designed by René Descartes: soul, mind, thought, experience, feeling are all inside the person's skin; outside is the extended world of nonliving objective matter. Nothing out there has any consciousness; nothing in here has any extension (and so how can it be measured?).

So for most psychotherapy, the world of institutions, marches, elections, strikes, prisons, hospitals, toxic waste and corporate profit, traffic and schools and taxes is utterly unpsychological. Psychology uses a special set of terms for the public sphere, its buildings and its institutions. Mere "persona," "other-directed," social conformity, the "collective," a place of "acting out," of sociopathy, belonging to the "power principle" or the "reality principle," but not the principle of eros.

Moreover, we are rather convinced that activism in the world of government, business, administration, or even our training institutes becomes "unpsychological." We lose the psychological angle, touch, flair, attitude, capability. So the question becomes: is there some way of staying psychological in the midst of the world. Can one keep psychological and yet be worldly, engaged, activized? That is the plainest way of stating the question that I shall be addressing—addressing if not perhaps satisfactorily answering: *How can we stay psychological?*

✵

The absence of soul from world, Descartes's soulless world, seems a peculiarly accurate description today when millennial ideas flood the mind. The close of the millennia. The new millennium coming. The unveiling (apocalypse) of a new age. The world and the soul are going through a radical transition according to the calendar myth (Y2K) we live by. Those messes we call dysfunctions are where the transitions of myth appear most personally and vividly. The messes are myths in action; the myths are the messes. (And that by the way is one method of staying psychological: see the mess as a myth.)

Of course, a major world myth going on today is the millennium, an apocalyptic moment when the veils are lifted. Revelation. In the Christian Bible's last book, its final chapter called Revelations; we can read a description in myth of radical millennial transition. It's a huge catastrophic mess. The four horsemen arrive, one white, one red, one black, and the last one, the pale rider of death and Hades, of famine and pestilence.

Let's imagine that the four horsemen are among us, since the millennium is both a literal and mythical event. The millennial apocalyptic myth is literalized into the calendar; the literal date, 2000, mythologized beyond all calendars.

John Keats's dictum that the world is the place of soul-making is so difficult to hold to because, let us remember, the world long before Descartes was already condemned by New Testament doctrines declaring it to belong to Caesar and not God, aligning it with the flesh and the devil. Thus, we are not merely under pressure from managed care administrators or licensing regulators or from fear of losing practice to competitors and cultists. Behind these practical problems are age-old mythical realities. And the world is where we engage these myths.

Let me then go on unveiling the apocalypse taking place right now in our situations.

According to the final chapter of the New Testament, the transition to the new time period means the appearance of the Four Horsemen of the Apocalypse. Let's say, you can't have one without the other, no millennial change without them. If we are now at the cusp of 2000, they are already among us. And it is these Four Riders who are the mythical figures in the issues that threaten the soul of psychology and make it so immensely difficult to stay psychological. Psyche, psychology, is engaged in a struggle of cosmic proportions.

The first of the four is the white horse of spiritualism. Tradition takes this white rider with a sword to be Jesus and his conquering mission. But the white rider is the force within all fanatic fundamentalism that wants to abolish all psychological insight, a force that infiltrates our practices with every variety of spiritual mishmash: *satori* and Zen and Buddhism; promise keepers and new warriors; Vedanta and born-again in Christ and miracles, Wilbur and Williamson, orthodoxies, channeling, spirit guides, shamanism...every possible mode of conquering the soul in the name of the white, pure, better, truer, cleaner, less messy spirit.

To consider the Red Rider simply as War is too narrow, unless we expand the idea to Thomas Hobbes's vision of society as a "war of all against all." This red rider is more likely the spirit of competition, today backed by the revival of Darwinism. You find it in Dawkin's "selfish gene" and Dennet's elimination of consciousness and experience in favor of atomistic, materialist, blindly competitive, and manipulative genetics that pushes all things for predatory survival. Of course this idea could have been cooked up on Wall Street or in Hollywood as well as at MIT, for new geneticism suits marvelously with the predatory capitalism happily called the free-enterprise system.

The third horseman is black. He comes with a scale in his hands and he weighs things in terms of coins, says the text. You are not dealing only with HMOs and insurance companies. Behind them is the black rider of the apocalypse, a mythical invisible demon who is out to destroy the world and its soul by means of economics.

The fourth rider on the pale horse is much harder to see than white spiritualism, red competitive geneticism, and the black plague of economics. Perhaps, that is why this rider is called "pale" and conjoined with Hades who is always invisible. This horse says the text brings *death, famine,* and *pestilence.* We do not see the prevalence of these ugly facts. We don't see, don't want to see, are denying. How? By practical adaptation, co-operating, adjusting, making things work, the good enough; hey, no problem: *the pale rider of denial.*

Keep serene says AA; don't let the world out there upset you. I call it Gumpism—a special American brand of innocence of the horror, ignorance of the complexity. Have a nice day. Have another chocolate. Hey, no problem. Stupid is as stupid does. Are you comfortable with that? "Serenity" is the name most registered for private boats in the USA. Serenity rather than famine and pestilence; serenity is famine and pestilence! Practical adaptation starves the soul, rids it of its odd individuality. Each of us a pale rider of serene denial.

So the question becomes: how do we stay psychological? How can we, who are dedicated to psychology, keep on track, soul-focused, soul-making? Oh, we will succumb to those riders of the Apocalypse for they do run the historical show, but we each can find ways to subvert, to resist, to deviate, and above all we can at least remember that it is a *mythical* power in competitive economics, in genetic reductionism, in white transcendent spiritualism and in the practical adaptations that wear the pallor of niceness. To beat the myth you would have to step out of the entire millennial, new age, Christian, hope-depraved, future-driven bag.

We probably each have our own methods, our own private rituals that keep faith with the psyche despite the millennial pressures. I want today merely to offer three words that may help your private endeavors and may guide your attention. And, I'll elaborate a little on each of the three. So you know where I'm heading, my ideas are encapsulated in these three words: Image, Depth, Destiny.

Image

There is a motto I use that has become a motto or slogan of Archetypal Psychology. It originates with C.G. Jung—"Stick to the Image." By this we mean, relax your interpretations, your knowing, your ideas about what's going on in a symptom, a problem, a dream, a transference knot, a body habit or gesture, and stick to what is actually presented by the psyche as it shows itself. For, as Jung said, "psyche is image." The psyche is primarily an image-maker, a fantasy producer, an inventor of thought, a transmitter of feeling.

The psyche displays its productions in dreams, in behaviors, and in the forms of culture, as well as in everything we do and say and sing, everything we build and wish for. Its fantasy-making activity can't be stopped (except perhaps by the pharmaceutical industry). Even locked in a cell, or paraplegic, or enslaved to routine, still the psyche imagines, dreams, envisions, projects. The psyche as such we cannot define, but we know it first by its image-making acts. Primary among these images, the world over, are animal forms—and here I should say I have a new book out called *Dream Animals*, precisely relevant to this theme of staying psychological by focusing on images.[1]

When I say "stick with the images," I am also saying, "be phenomenological." Study what's there, not what should have been there, how it can be improved upon, where it came from, why it got there now, where it's heading. Try not to reach for meaning, finding associations in memory, or symbolic ramifications. Take an image as a painting or a poem: let it

---

1. James Hillman and Margot McLean, *Dream Animals* (San Francisco: Chronicle Books, 1997).

strike you. Then, by this focus on the phenomenon, the image as is—say, a growling dog in a dream; say, a constant, quasi-compulsive brushing back of the hair from the forehead, or clearing the throat, or a repetitive phrase "well, maybe it's just my luck," or "I don't know, I've always been this way"—then the habit, the figure, takes on its own life. It becomes static, it stands still, like an icon; simply there, a kind of eternity. You watch it, see it, hear it for its own sake. It becomes strange, odd, funny even, and very much alive.

You are treating it ritually, even devotionally, with all this careful attention. You are allowing it its own imaginative life.

By sticking to the image I have left my doctrinal learning and my training in clinical skills. The two of us—or the group, the couple, the family—in therapy have joined together as naturalists of the phenomenon. We wait to see what happens, what the image is doing, what it will do rather than what I or the patient will do.

Images are living things with their own intentions, their own kind of consciousness. We need to back off to give them a chance to show us what they can do.

Thus, the image keeps us psychological in the following ways:

1. It keeps us wondering, curious, open. We become more and more impressed by it, drawn into it. It is therefore ego-limiting, even ego-defeating, disempowering, as potential shifts to it, to its otherness.

2. An image has cultural resonances. Gestures recall paintings and movies; there is an archetypal echo in body parts, in animals, in language, in places of geography and the landscapes of nature. Images take a person away from the personal into history and culture. They come with their own memories.

3. Not only beyond the personal. Beyond the human, to the eternalities that are always archetypally affecting human life.

Depth

We call our field *depth* psychology. This idea of deep and surface layers of the psyche comes mainly from eighteenth-century German thinking, going back to Moses Mendelssohn and Immanuel Kant. They separated out a section of the psyche called Feeling (*Gemüth*), and this was placed below and deeper than the other two areas, the Will and the Reason. So, to go deep, we believe still, we must go to Feeling.

Vertical layering has been and remains a mainstay bias in depth psychology, even cognitive and behavioral psychology that focus more on Reason/Cognition reframing your mind set and its language, or on Will, restructuring your patterns of action. Some often argue that cognitive reframing or behavioral change in symptoms leaves deeper structures untouched.

Feeling as "deep" is further complicated by a Christian bias, as everything in our culture is flavored by 2,000 years of the Christian twist, which insists that the deepest area of soul is that of love. Again, therapy is devoted to this combination of ideas: feeling is deep and the deepest feeling is love.

But you don't have to follow this way of thinking about depth. In a polytheistic, or pagan, less-Christianized psyche—and the psyche, a Greek word after all, existed before Jesus came on the scene—the soul is in service to many gods. We would not regard any single emotional complexity like Love to be deeper by definition than any other. Fear can be deep indeed. So, too, Grief, Anger, Pity, Revenge, Devotion, and Shame. Each has its occasion, each does its duty. Love, as Bruno Bettelheim said, is not enough.

But to go even further, I object to the identification of depth with feeling. Of course there are deep feelings, but there are also deep thoughts, deep ideas, deep insights; powerfully motivating ideals, visions; deep memories, deep acts of courage, of generosity; there are deep and lasting impressions that can change the course of a life and guide it. There are also deep seas, deep forests, deep pockets, and deep sleep.

So depth is not simply love and not simply feeling. What, then, is depth, that depth to which we adhere to stay psychological?

Let me offer my description of depth. Depth evokes and makes present those inevitable eternalities that nourish and destroy every one of our lives. They bring the inhuman dimension to human lives. These are the eternalities that compose the substance of Greek tragedies, of Bible stories, of myths and classic unvarnished fairy tales. Deep refers to the archetypal necessities and inhuman persons that form the imagination of great art and music and writings. Deep refers to the bottomless, the always opening downward, darkening and enlightening both. Deep shows up in the works of Dostoevsky, Beethoven, and Rembrandt, but not in the college texts we are assigned to become psychologists. Deep goes beyond the personal and feeds the personal. Deep means beauty, tragedy, sorrow, pondering, pity. It means obsessive devotion, vivid imaginings, rich humor. It means extraordinary insight and radical implication. It absorbs like silence.

To stay deeply psychological then would mean to have an eye and an ear for the eternalities that plague each life—family knots, mothers, sisters, sons, fathers, whether in the suburbs or in Sophocles; the confusions of sexuality; the prospect of dying and the mystery of death; the burden of pain; the struggle with the necessities of food and shelter; the circumstances of place, its geography, its culture, its spirits; the inadequacies of the human body; the perpetual recurrence of the word, "God"; the absurdities of change; the subjective, even delusional, pull of emotions; the desperate need for beauty. Each is bottomless, unfathomable, beyond human reach.

These are eternal issues. *Eternals*: not externals and not internals. For the true depths of external trivialities are eternals; and the true depths of subjective personal internals are eternals.

Practice of depth would mean imagining the immediate issues, complaints, troubles, as reflections of these deeps that do not ever go away and cannot ever be "solved." Psychology gives eternal value, an eternal background to externals and internals.

Freud aimed for this with the universals of the Oedipus myth. Jung also insisted on the eternals with his theory of archetypes and the collective unconscious. So did Adler with his universal strivings and inferiorities and communal feeling. They each made their therapies deep by remembering that the psyche is basically embroiled in eternals who are more than human. That is why our field is neither humanistic psychology, nor social psychology nor analytical psychology but depth psychology—and our therapy embodies these inhuman, implacable deeps.

Destiny

We come finally to the third mode of staying psychological, and we come directly to the printed title for this time slot on your program. *The Soul's Code*—Character, Calling, Fate.

Because the four horsemen are so prevalent, so seductive, and so strong, I wanted with my book *The Soul's Code* to tell a very different story.[2] A story that since has found resonance in readers, a story that seemed to them so utterly new, startlingly so, revelatory even, although this story is older than Plato and is told in many parts of the globe—West Africa, Native America, Kabbalah, India, ancient Mediterranean, Central Asia.

In brief, our civilization's version of the story appears most famously in Plato, at the end of his Republic. It's called the Myth of Er—Er being a mighty warrior who fell in battle and who reported what he witnessed about the soul beyond this world. I condensed Plato's long tale in my book: "The soul of each of us is given a unique daimon before we are born, and it has selected an image or pattern that we live on earth. This soul companion, the daimon, guides us here; in the process of arrival, however, we forget all that took place in choosing our lot and believe we come empty into the world. The daimon remembers what is in your image and belongs to your pattern, and therefore your daimon is the carrier of your destiny."[3]

The greatest of later Platonists, Plotinus some six hundred years after Plato made it even clearer. He said our soul elected the parents, the body, the circumstances, and the place that suited the soul, and that belongs to its necessity. The myth suggests that the whole bag we occupy ourselves with in therapy—the circumstances, including my body and my parents whom I may curse—are actually my soul's own choice. I don't understand this because I have forgotten it, and no longer remember even that I have a daimon, a soul companion, or even a soul.

Now this is a myth, not an argument. It is not told in metaphysical language of a religious doctrine to believe in. Nor is this myth a scientific hypothesis to be verified or falsified. It allows for genetics, for bodily inheritance; it allows for the influences of parents and geography and economic circumstances—these are somehow needed by the soul and chosen by it. The soul incorporates or colonizes these alien unpleasantnesses. The story does what stories do: they tell your questions into a tale, a tale,

---

2. James Hillman, *The Soul's Code: In Search of Character and Calling* (New York: Random House, 1996).

3. Ibid., 8.

in this case, which says, yes, there are the four horsemen, but there is also a fifth factor something even closer to you than the mathematics of your gene code, closer than the parenting you received or didn't receive, more significant than the four apocalyptic riders: that is, beyond being driven by white spiritual mission, red competition, black economic reductivism, or invisible denial and practical adaptation. And this other factor is your daimon and your destiny—that particular unique you, the character that is you that wants you to be here and calls you to some destiny. You are not merely the result of accidental combinations of genes, of parental mistakes, economic pressures, or bad decisions and good luck. You are not a result, not a victim.

Nor are you essentially self-made by ego strength in freedom of choice. Nor do you become who you are by following a spiritual practice. Your paradigm already imagines who you are and your daimon uses every sort of ruse to keep you close to your soul.

This worldwide story of character and calling presumes a cosmology. The personal soul is placed within a wider soul, the world soul, the *anima mundi*. But we practice psychology in America in the absence of a cosmology. In absence of any creation myth, which tells you why you get up in the morning and go to work, what you serve, how you belong to the whole big complex conundrum. We get up for economic reasons: to earn a living, or fear of falling behind. Or, we have only science's myth of origins: I am here because of a big bang so far away and long ago that my mind cannot grasp it (any more than I can grasp the unknowable transcendent God of the major American religions). And, I will vanish into nothing, cosmic dust. At core I am an accident.

The myths within which we operate our therapy need reflection, else we only increase unconsciousness as we work at the personal, individual consciousness of our patients. Now, a myth doesn't ground in truth, it opens. It opens the heart, giving it a second chance at imagining your life, opening your eye to seeing your memories differently, finding some connection between the foibles, idiosyncrasies, and obsessions of your character with your needed place in the world. The truth it brings is the ring of truth, that it accords with subjective experience, and is buttressed by anecdote and experience. Myth claims no more than that, and no less. As a "creation myth," Plato's story of the soul works creatively by re-creating your life, and the lives you encounter in your practice.

The basic component of this myth that is useful for psychological practice is the idea that each of us is meant to be here. Something remembers your destiny, and therapy attempts to reconnect you with the voice that guides your soul, your paradigm, your pattern, what belongs to your image. It affirms that you have a calling and that your character is always trying to hold you to your necessity. And often it is pathology that is the instrument of this stubborn invisible daimon.

Staying psychological then comes to mean something more than staying analytical, reflective, insightful, related, empathetic, benignly attentive. It means more likely hearing the daimon's promptings. It means more likely a nonhuman relation with the daimon who may also appear outside in the world, in things, without Cartesian restriction; for the daimon as the soul's guide and essential memory is, of course, the primary, perhaps the only, therapist of the soul. So, we must look to the images and see them deeply. Lo and behold the images, be beholden to them for they hold you and keep you, keepers of depth.

End

May I add a final word about staying psychological? Uniqueness. I offer the unique rather than the unified, the unity of personality, or wholeness, that so dominates humanistic language. I take my cue here from William James, father of American psychology, a tough-minded sufferer, no Forrest Gump he, who argued for what he called "eachness" against the then-fashionable, as now, prevalence of holism and wholeness.

Each image is unique, each destiny unique. Let's not lose the unique in symbolic interpretations or other systematic reductions.

Hear what Miguel de Unamuno, the Spanish philosopher wrote in his *The Tragic Sense of Life*:

> Each man is unique and irreplaceable; there cannot be any other I; each one of us—our soul, that is, not our life—is worth the whole Universe.[4]

Then he tells us how to live in terms of one's calling:

> All of us, each one of us, can and ought to determine to give as much of himself as he possibly can—nay, to give more than he can,

---

4. Miguel de Unamuno, *The Tragic Sense of Life in Men and in Peoples*, translated by J. E. Crawford Flitch (London: Macmillan and Co., 1921), 269.

to exceed himself, to go beyond himself, to make himself irreplace-
able...And each one in his own civil calling or office...ought
not so much to try to seek that particular calling which we think
most fitting and suitable for ourselves, as to make a calling of that
employment in which...Providence...has placed us...to endeavor
to make the occupation in which we find ourselves our vocation."[5]

That "civil calling" is the world as civilization into which we must
throw ourselves fully aware of the horsemen. "In the destructive element
Immerse!" said Joseph Conrad.[6] "Call the world the vale of Soul-making,"
said John Keats.[7] And Unamuno adds: "Act in such a way as to make our
annihilation an injustice, in such a way as to make our brothers, our sons,
and our brothers' sons, and their sons' sons, feel that we ought not to
have died."[8] This is destiny lived; this is being your image and standing
in depth. Of course you are not thereby saved, or creative, integrated, or
wise, nor even good. But at least you are you.

<hr />

5. Ibid., 269–71.

6. Joseph Conrad, Lord Jim: A Romance (New York: McClure, Phillips & Co., 1905), 313.

7. Letter from John Keats to his brother George, 21 April 1819.

8. De Unamuno, The Tragic Sense of Life, 269.

SOURCE NOTES

"Training and the C.G. Jung Institute, Zurich." First published in *Journal of Analytical Psychology* 7, no. 1 (1962).

"Jung's Contribution to "Feelings and Emotions: Synopsis and Implication." First published in *Feelings and Emotions: The Loyola Symposium*, ed. Magda B. Arnold (New York and London: Academic Press, 1970).

"Some Early Background to Jung's Ideas: Notes on *C.G. Jung's Medium* by Stefanie Zumstein-Preiswerk" First published in *Spring: An Annual of Archetypal Psychology and Jungian Thought* (1976).

"Friends and Enemies." Presented at the Annual Conference of the Analytical Psychology Club, London, 1961.

"Schism as Differing Visions." Presented at Guild of Pastoral Psychology, London, 1972. First published in James Hillman, *Loose Ends: Primary Papers in Archetypal Psychology* (Dallas: Spring Publications, 1978).

"Extending the Family (From Entrapment to Embrace)." Presented at the Symposium on Myth and Imagination at Swarthmore College, Swarthmore, Penn., 1984. First published in *The Texas Humanist* 7, no. 4 (1985).

"Loving the Community and Work." First published in *The Rag and Bone Shop of the Heart: Poems for Men*, edited by Robert Bly, James Hillman, and Michael Meade (New York: HarperCollins, 1992).

"Marriage, Intimacy, Freedom." Presented at the Dallas Institute of Humanities and Culture, Dallas, 1993. First published in *Spring: A Journal of Archetype and Culture* 60 (1996).

"A Note on Story." First published in *Children's Literature* 3 (1974).

"Sex Talk: Imagining a New Male Sexuality." First published in *Utne Reader* 29 (1988).

"Foreword." First published in John Allan, *Inscapes of the Child's World* (Dallas: Spring Publications, 1988).

"The Courage to Risk Failure." Delivered as the Graduation Address at the American International School, Zurich, 1965.

"Life and Death in Analysis." Paper delivered at the International Conference on Suicide, San Francisco State University, San Francisco, 1967.

"Commentary." First published in Gopi Krishna, *Kundalini: The Evolutionary Energy in Man* (Berkeley: Shambala, 1971).

"Three Ways of Failure and Analysis." First published in *Journal of Analytical Psychology* 17, no. 1 (1972).

"A Psychology of Transgression Drawn from an Incest Dream: Imagining the Case." First published in *Spring: An Annual of Archetypal Psychology and Jungian Thought* (1987).

"The Bad Mother: An Archetypal Approach." First published in *Spring: An Annual of Archetypal Psychology and Jungian Thought* (1983).

"Your Emotions Are Not Yours: Arts Therapy and the Disabled." Delivered as the Keynote Address for the conference "La Sapienza" at the University of Rome, Italy, 1990.

"Introduction: Mother and Great Mother." First published in *The Rag and Bone Shop of the Heart: Poems for Men*, op. cit.

"Foreword" (with A.K. Donoghue). First published in Sigmund Freud, *The Cocaine Papers* (Vienna and Zurich: Dunquin Press and Spring Publications, 1963).

"Toward the Archetypal Model for the Masturbation Inhibition." First published in *Journal of Analytical Psychology* 11, no. 1 (1966).

"On Paranoia." Presented at the Eranos Conference in Ascona, Switzerland, 1985. First published in *Eranos Yearbook* 54 (1985).

"The Wildman in the Cage: Comment." First published in *Voices: Journal of the American Academy of Psychotherapists* (1984).

"How Do We Stay Psychological?" Presented at 105th Annual Convention of the American Psychology Association, Chicago, 1997.

www.ingramcontent.com/pod-product-compliance
Lightning Source LLC
Chambersburg PA
CBHW031423270326
41930CB00007B/548

* 9 7 8 0 8 8 2 1 4 9 4 2 4 *